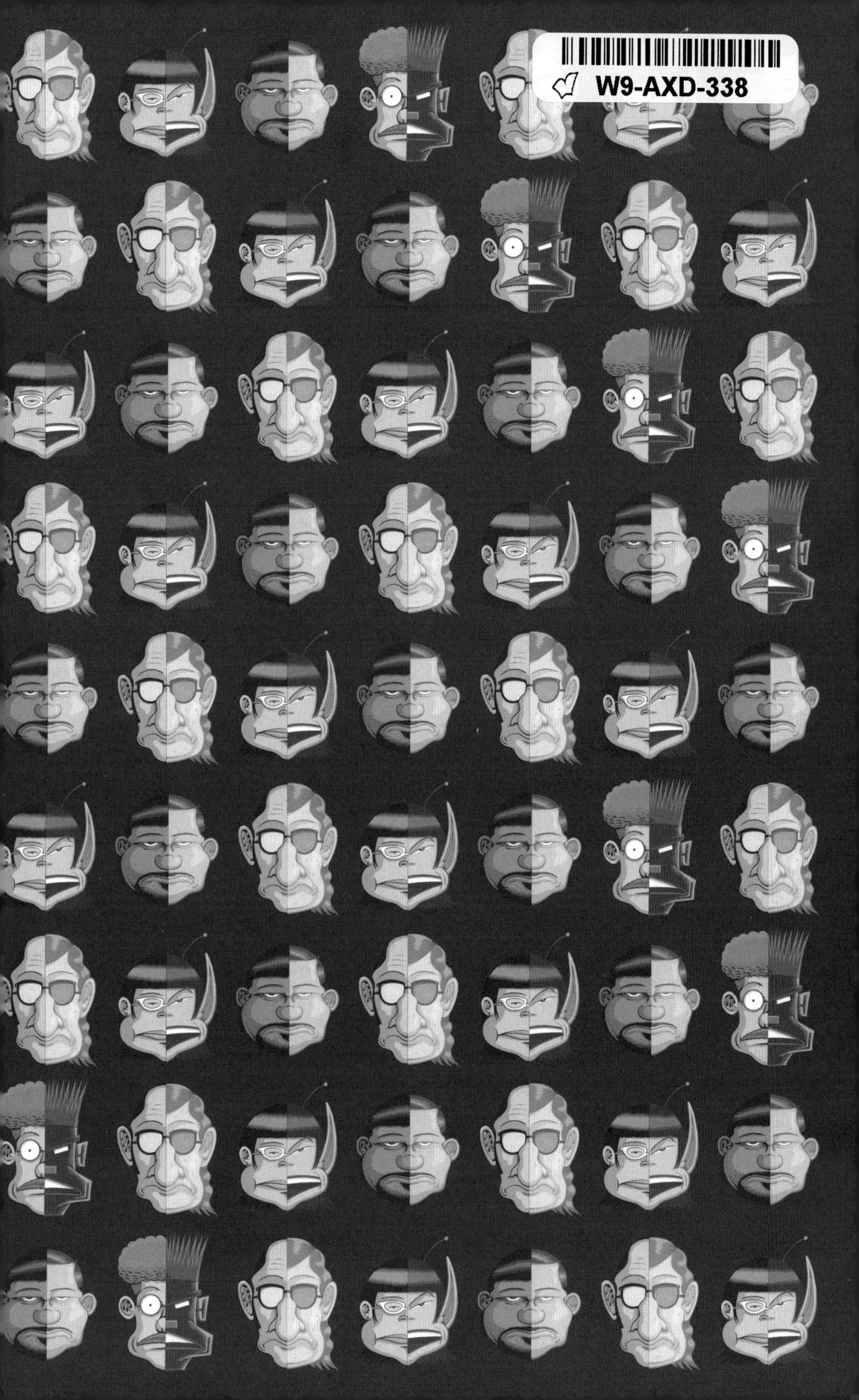

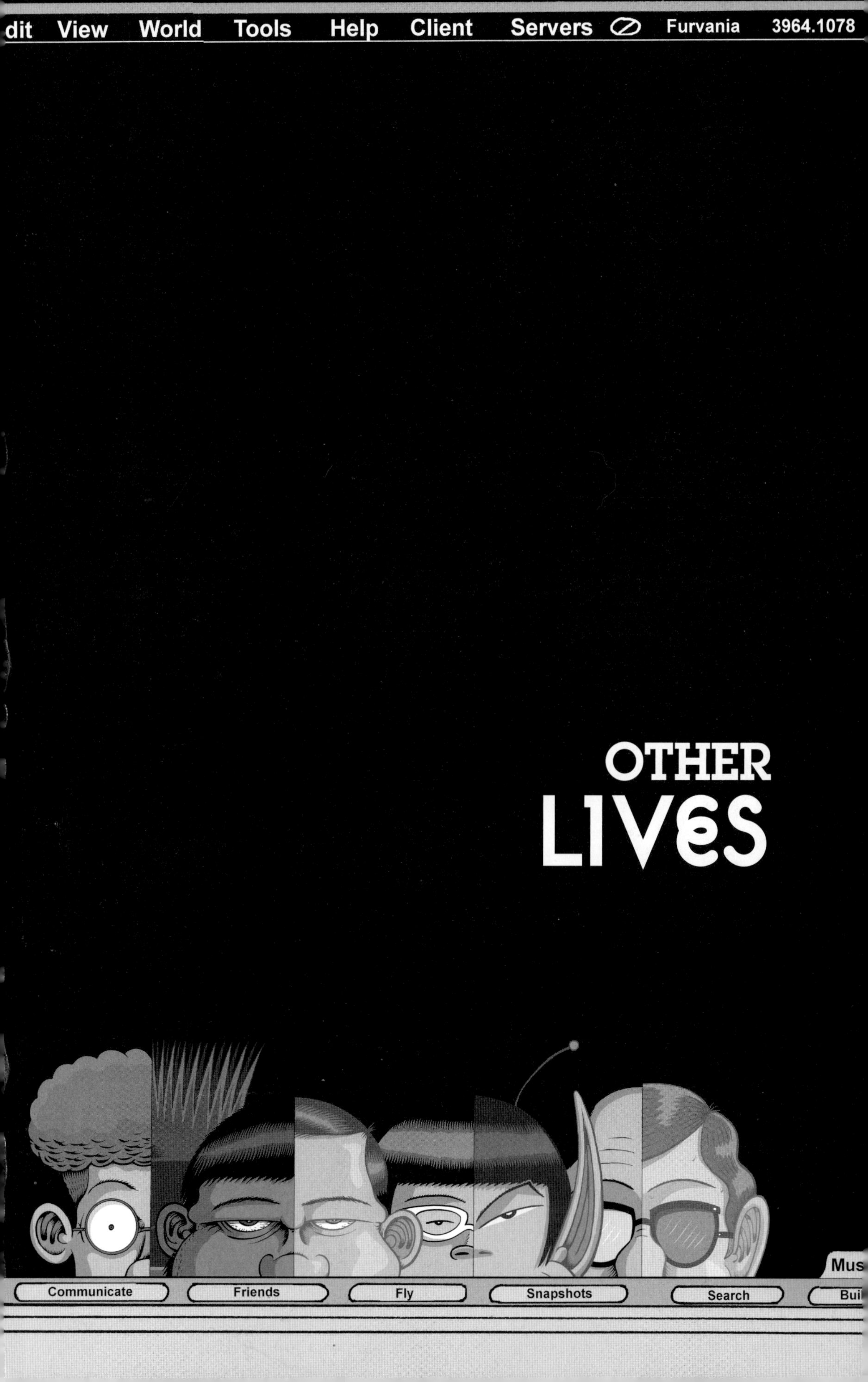
dit View World Tools Help Client Servers Furvania 3964.1078
OTHER
LIVES
Mus
Communicate
Friends
Fly
Snapshots
Search
Bui

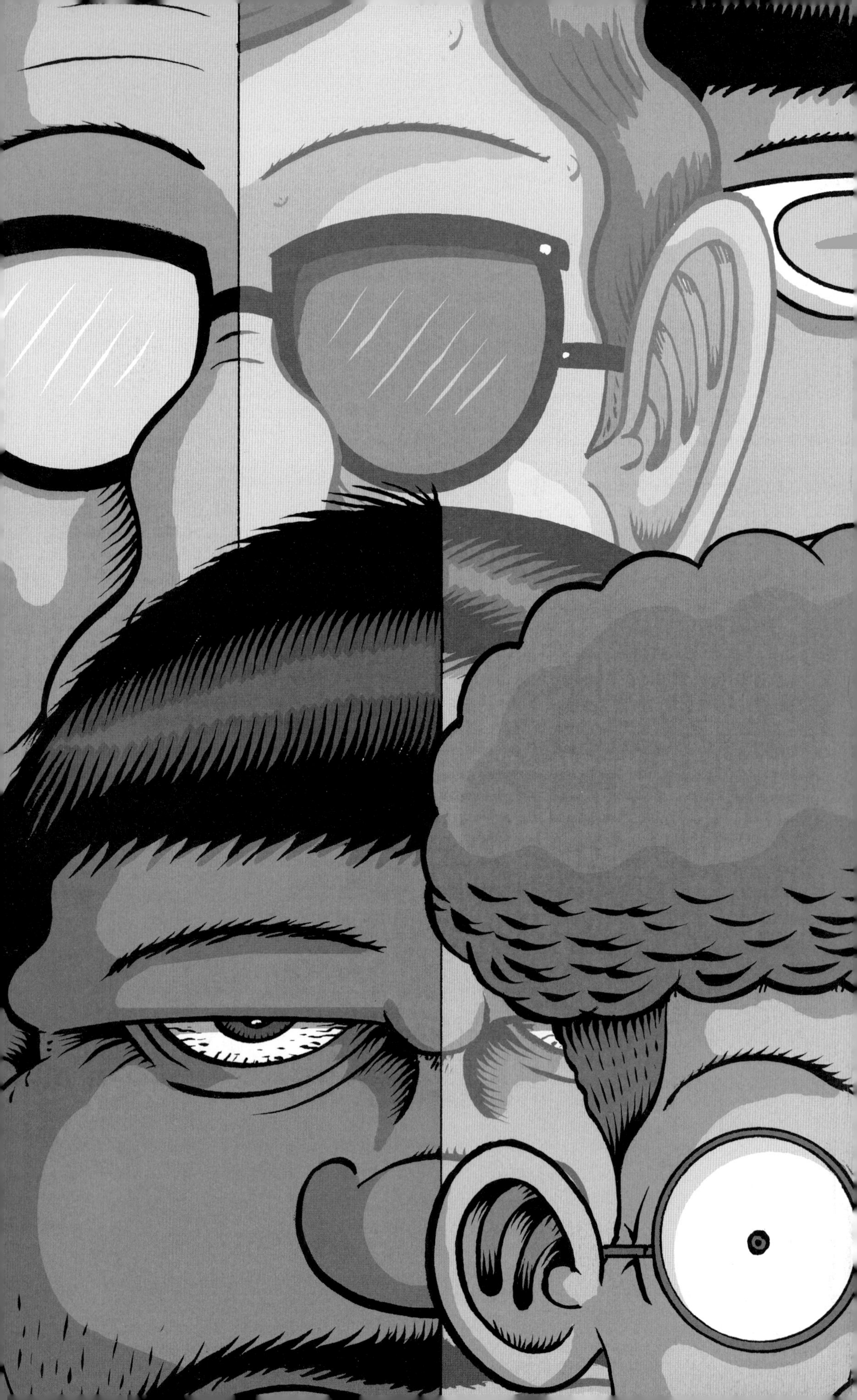

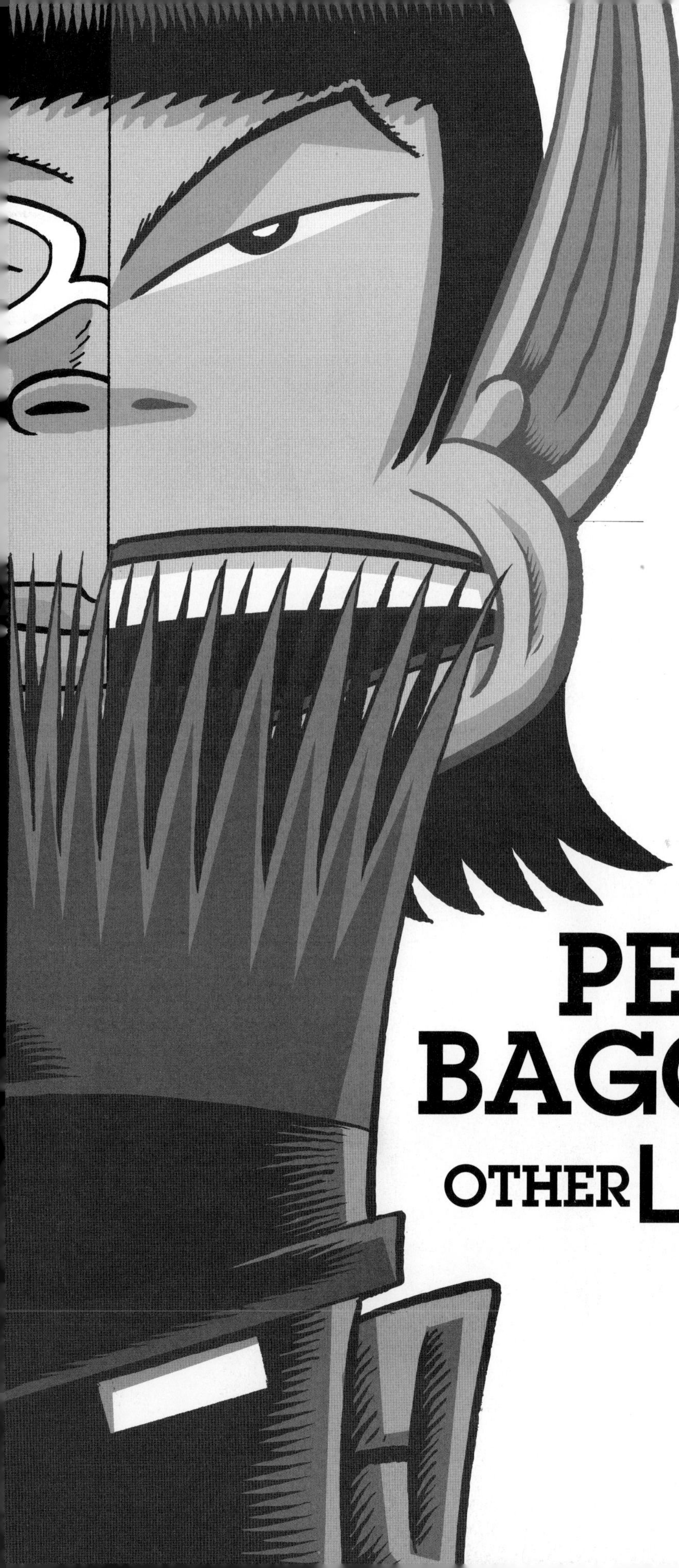

PETER BAGGE'S OTHER LIVES

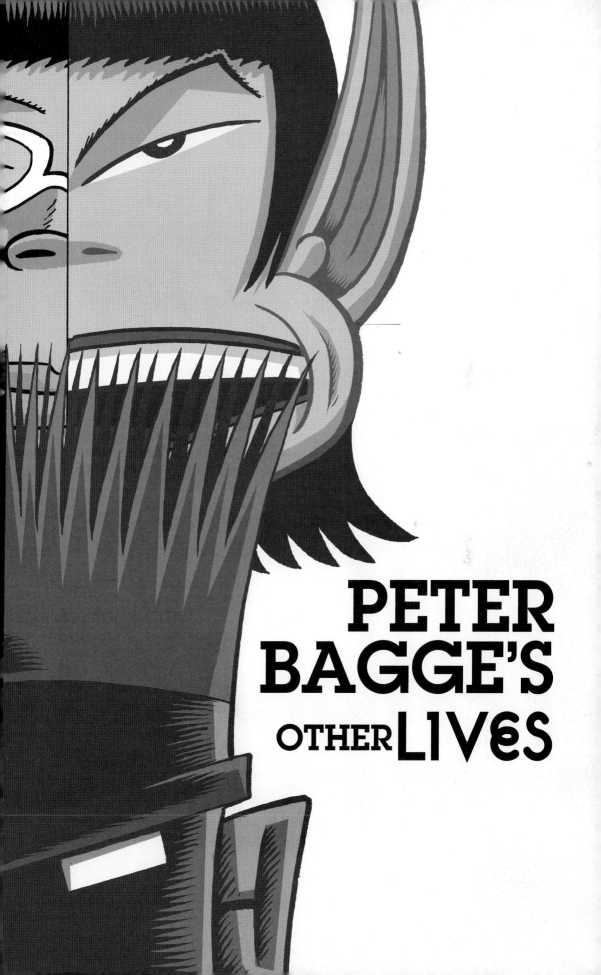

dit View World Tools Help Client Servers Furvania 3964.10

Communicate

Karen Berger SVP – Executive Editor
Bob Schreck & Shelly Bond Editors
Brandon Montclare Assistant Editor
Robbin Brosterman Design Director – Books
Louis Prandi Art Director

DC COMICS
Paul Levitz President & Publisher
Richard Bruning SVP – Creative Director
Patrick Caldon EVP – Finance & Operations
Amy Genkins SVP – Business & Legal Affairs
Jim Lee Editorial Director – WildStorm
Gregory Noveck SVP – Creative Affairs
Steve Rotterdam SVP – Sales & Marketing
Cheryl Rubin SVP – Brand Management

 HC ISBN: 978-1-4012-1902-4. SC ISBN: 978-1-4012-2557-5. Printed in the USA. First Printing. DC Comics, a Warner Bros. Entertainment Company.

SUSTAINABLE FORESTRY INITIATIVE
Certified Chain of Custody
Promoting Sustainable Forest Management
www.sfiprogram.org

Fiber used in this product line meets the sourcing requirements of the SFI program. www.sfiprogram.org NFS-SPIC0C-C0001801

Send

Electra Music

Communicate Friends Fly Snapshots Search

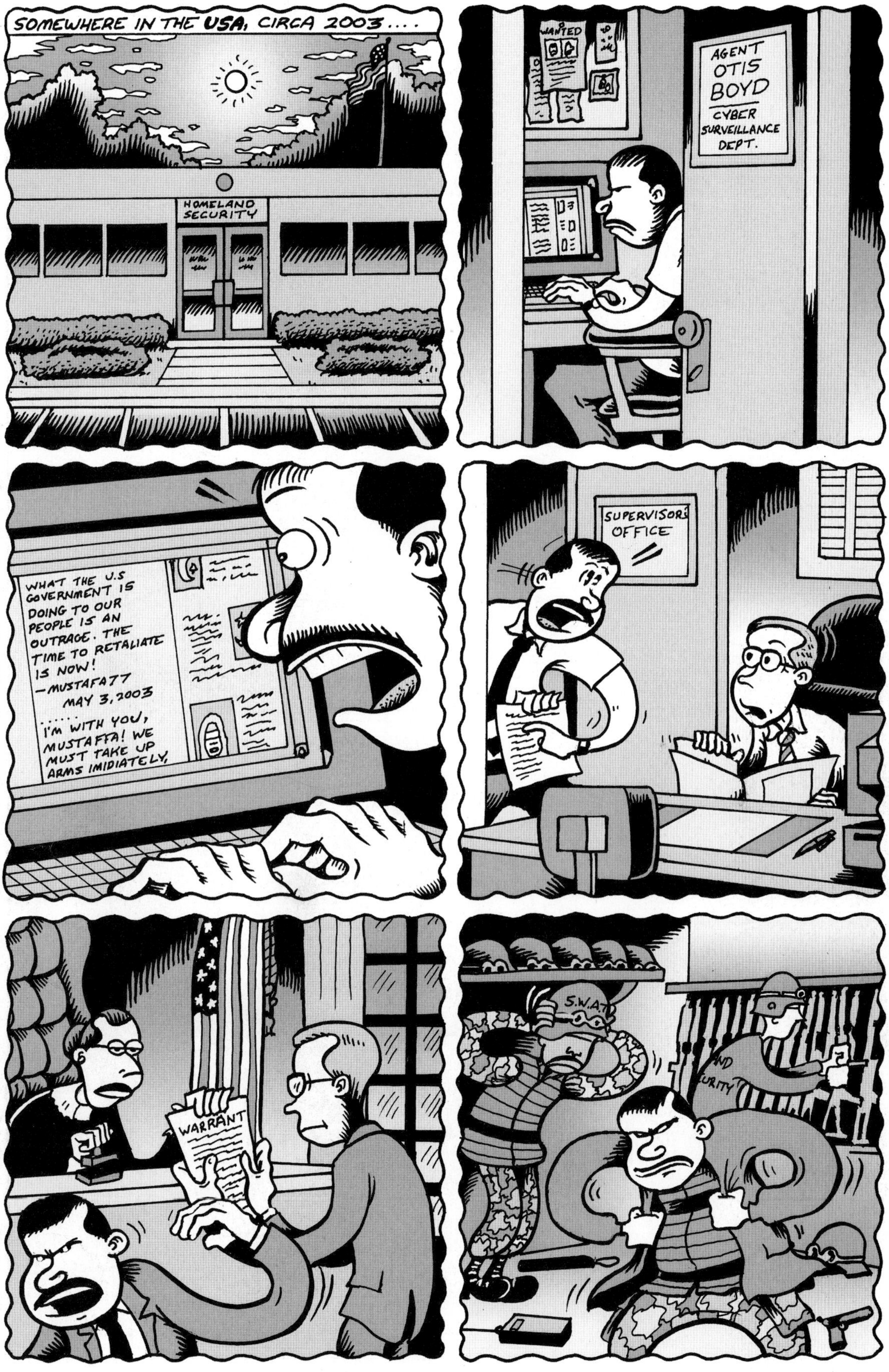
SOMEWHERE IN THE USA, CIRCA 2003....
HOMELAND SECURITY
WANTED
AGENT OTIS BOYD
CYBER SURVEILLANCE DEPT.
WHAT THE U.S GOVERNMENT IS DOING TO OUR PEOPLE IS AN OUTRAGE. THE TIME TO RETALIATE IS NOW! —MUSTAFA77 MAY 3, 2003
I'M WITH YOU, MUSTAFFA! WE MUST TAKE UP ARMS IMIDIATELY,
SUPERVISOR'S OFFICE
WARRANT
S.W.A.T.

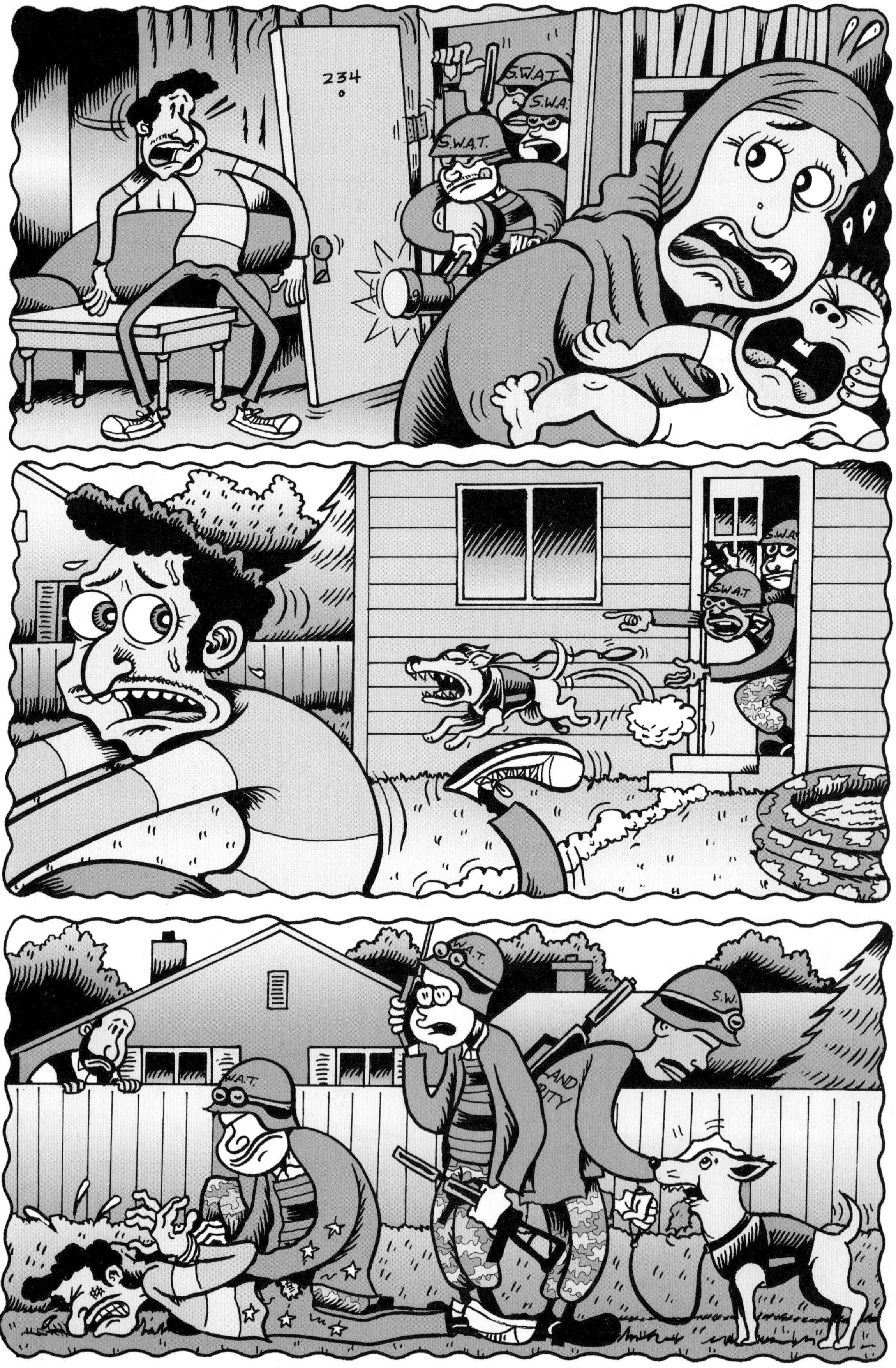
234
S.W.A.T.
S.W.A.T
S.W.A.T.
S.W.A.T

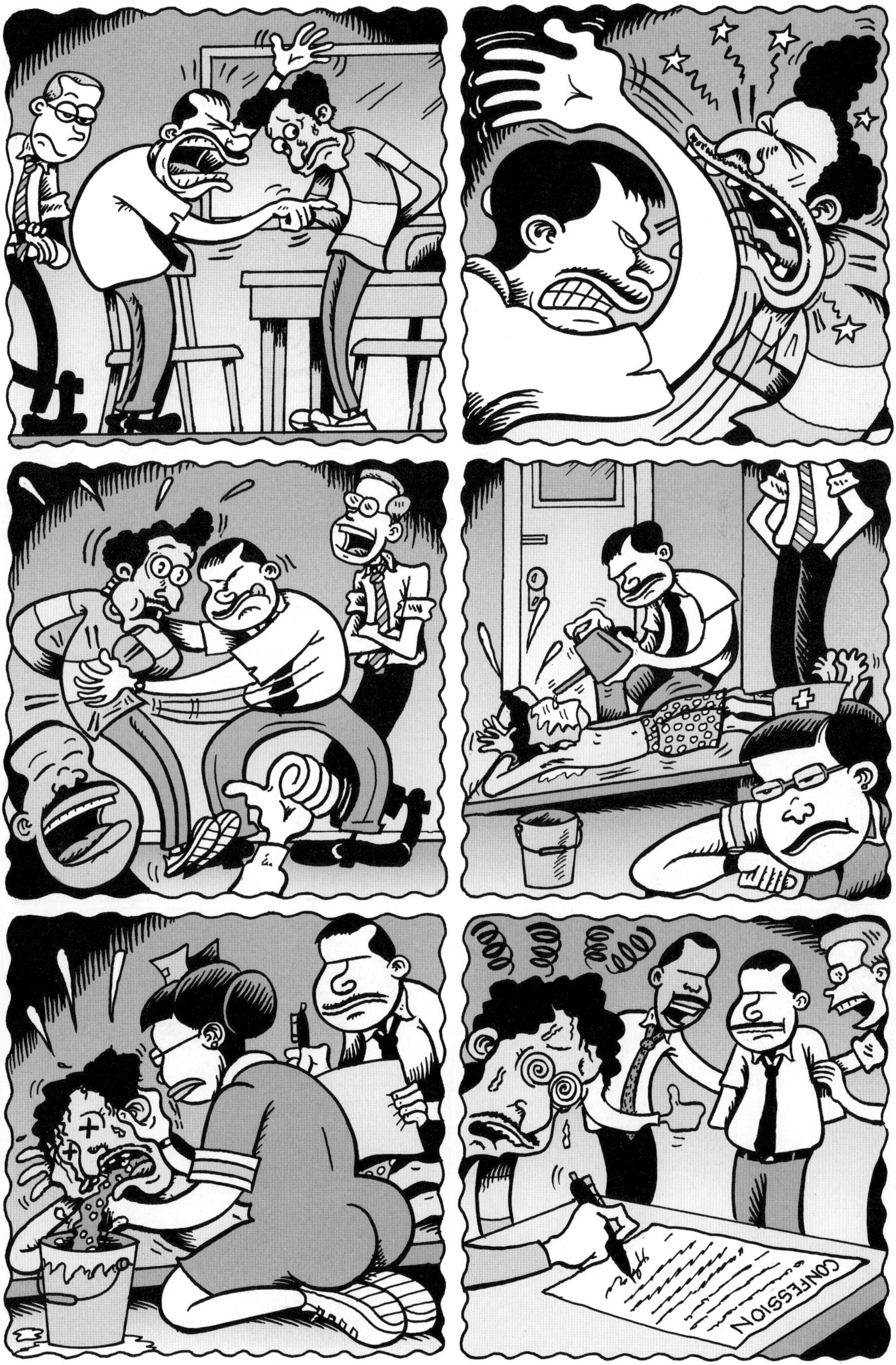
CONFESSION

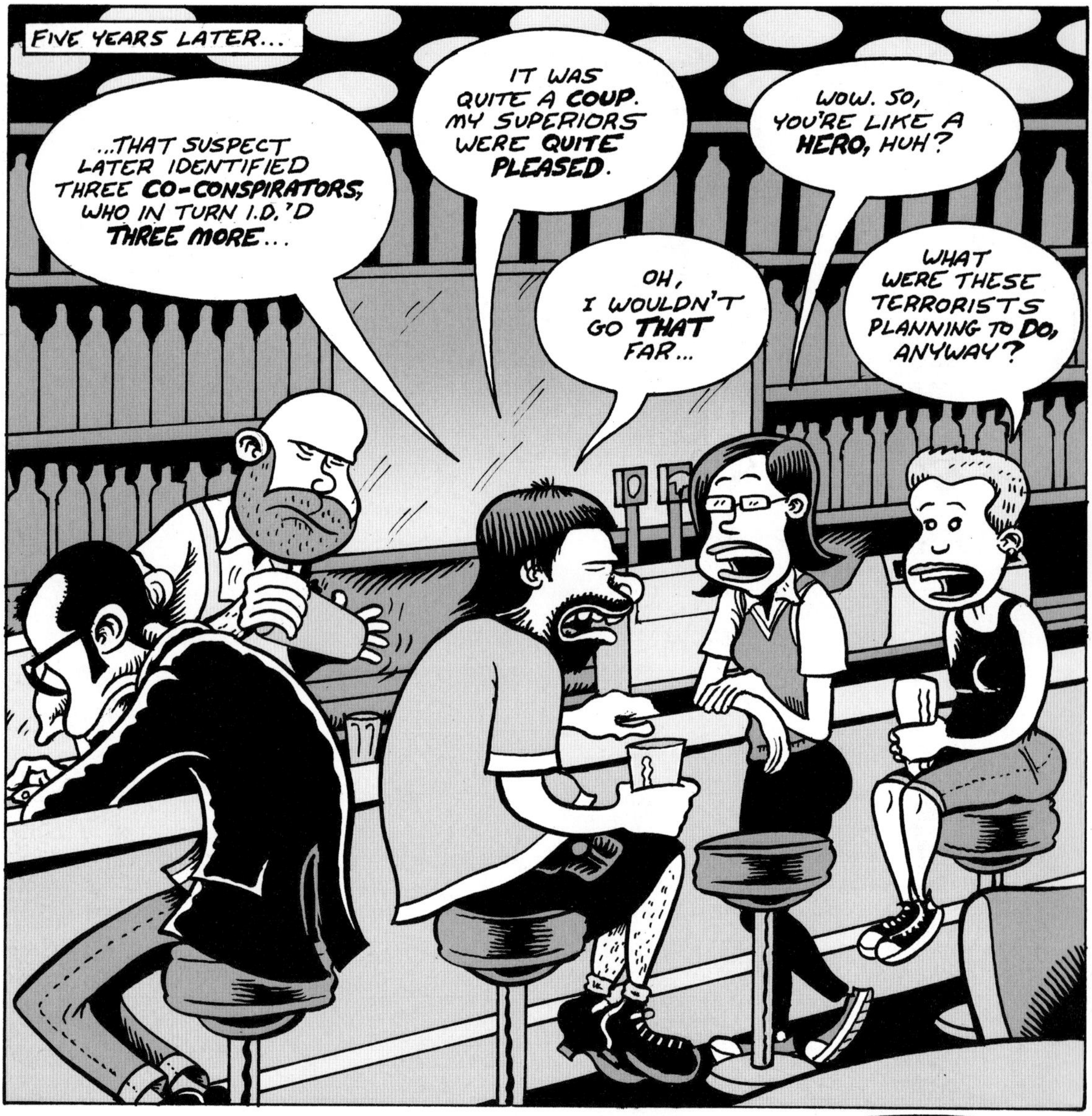
FIVE YEARS LATER...
...THAT SUSPECT LATER IDENTIFIED THREE CO-CONSPIRATORS, WHO IN TURN I.D.'D THREE MORE...
IT WAS QUITE A COUP. MY SUPERIORS WERE QUITE PLEASED.
OH, I WOULDN'T GO THAT FAR...
WOW. SO, YOU'RE LIKE A HERO, HUH?
WHAT WERE THESE TERRORISTS PLANNING TO DO, ANYWAY?

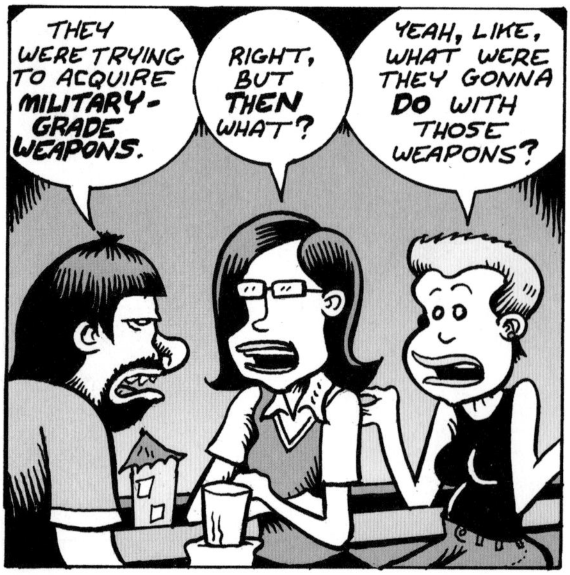
THEY WERE TRYING TO ACQUIRE MILITARY-GRADE WEAPONS.
RIGHT, BUT THEN WHAT?
YEAH, LIKE, WHAT WERE THEY GONNA DO WITH THOSE WEAPONS?

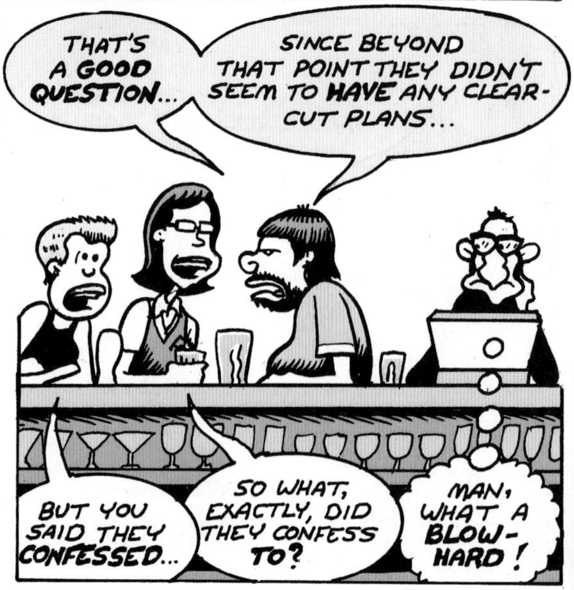
THAT'S A GOOD QUESTION...
SINCE BEYOND THAT POINT THEY DIDN'T SEEM TO HAVE ANY CLEAR-CUT PLANS...
BUT YOU SAID THEY CONFESSED...
SO WHAT, EXACTLY, DID THEY CONFESS TO?
MAN, WHAT A BLOW-HARD!

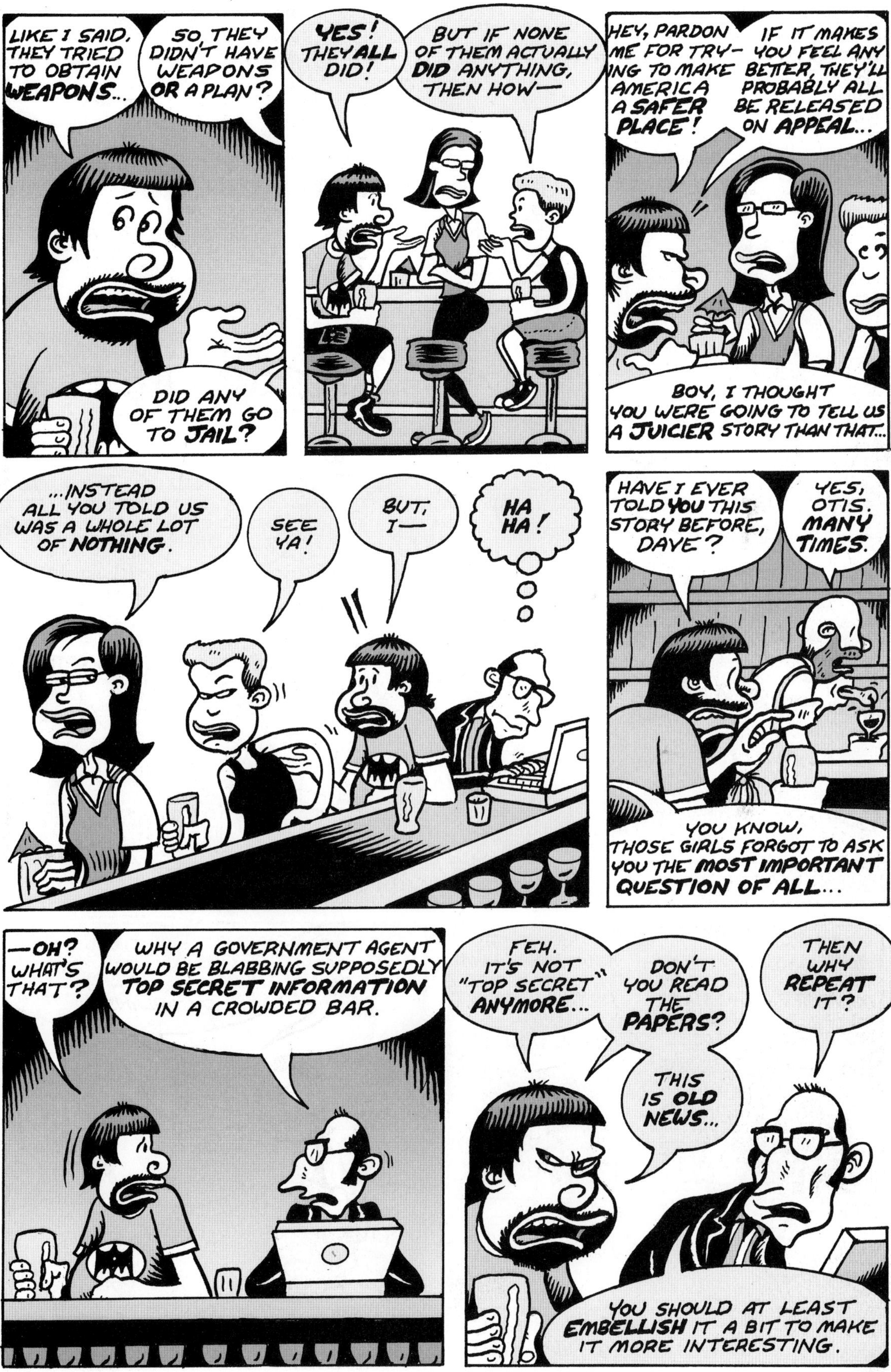
LIKE I SAID, THEY TRIED TO OBTAIN WEAPONS...
SO, THEY DIDN'T HAVE WEAPONS OR A PLAN?
DID ANY OF THEM GO TO JAIL?
YES! THEY ALL DID!
BUT IF NONE OF THEM ACTUALLY DID ANYTHING, THEN HOW—
HEY, PARDON ME FOR TRYING TO MAKE AMERICA A SAFER PLACE!
IF IT MAKES YOU FEEL ANY BETTER, THEY'LL PROBABLY ALL BE RELEASED ON APPEAL...
BOY, I THOUGHT YOU WERE GOING TO TELL US A JUICIER STORY THAN THAT...
...INSTEAD ALL YOU TOLD US WAS A WHOLE LOT OF NOTHING.
SEE YA!
BUT, I—
HA HA!
HAVE I EVER TOLD YOU THIS STORY BEFORE, DAVE?
YES, OTIS. MANY TIMES.
YOU KNOW, THOSE GIRLS FORGOT TO ASK YOU THE MOST IMPORTANT QUESTION OF ALL...
—OH? WHAT'S THAT?
WHY A GOVERNMENT AGENT WOULD BE BLABBING SUPPOSEDLY TOP SECRET INFORMATION IN A CROWDED BAR.
FEH. IT'S NOT "TOP SECRET" ANYMORE...
DON'T YOU READ THE PAPERS?
THIS IS OLD NEWS...
THEN WHY REPEAT IT?
YOU SHOULD AT LEAST EMBELLISH IT A BIT TO MAKE IT MORE INTERESTING.

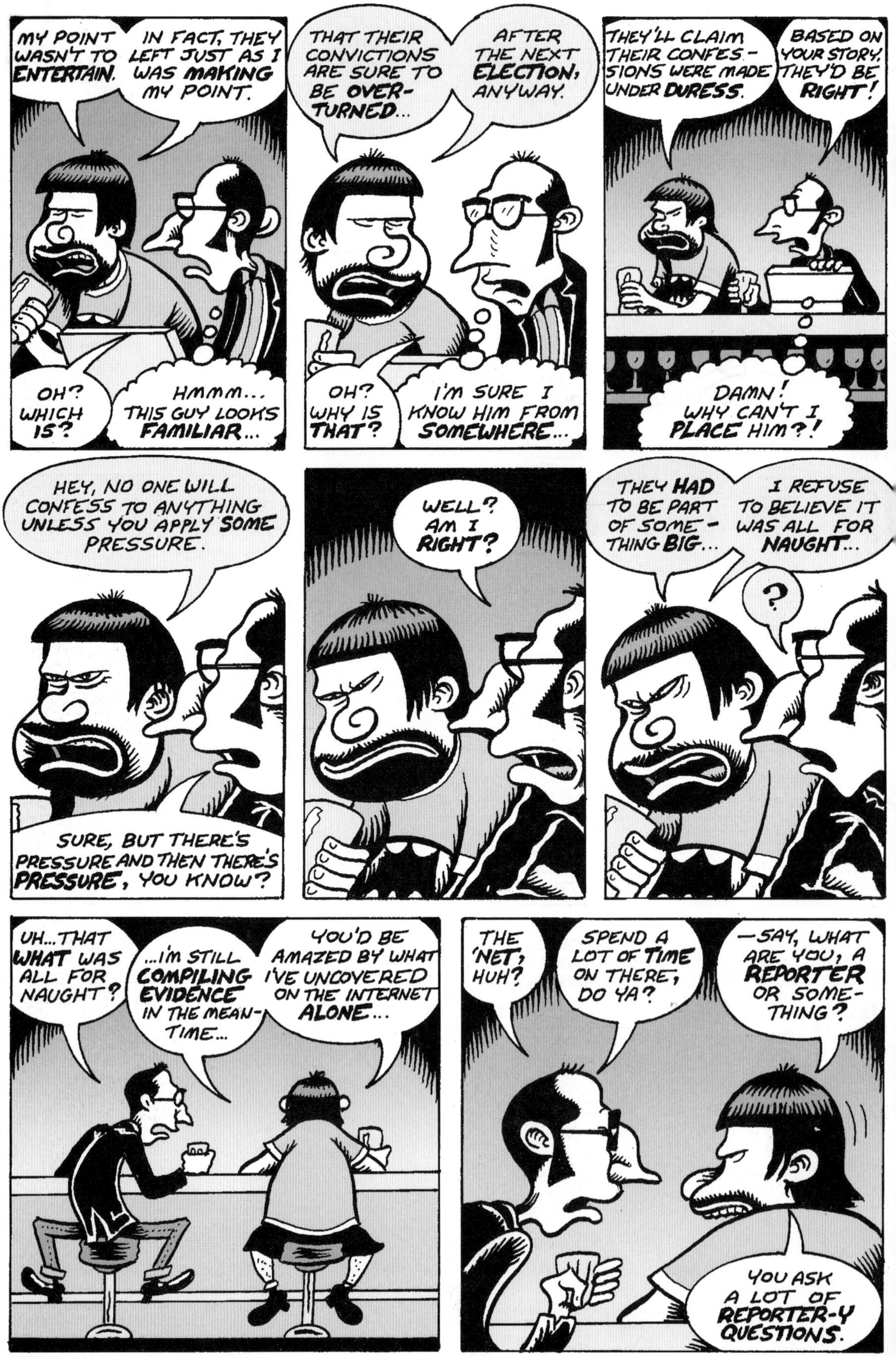
MY POINT WASN'T TO ENTERTAIN.
IN FACT, THEY LEFT JUST AS I WAS MAKING MY POINT.
OH? WHICH IS?
HMMM... THIS GUY LOOKS FAMILIAR...
THAT THEIR CONVICTIONS ARE SURE TO BE OVER-TURNED...
AFTER THE NEXT ELECTION, ANYWAY.
OH? WHY IS THAT?
I'M SURE I KNOW HIM FROM SOMEWHERE...
THEY'LL CLAIM THEIR CONFES-SIONS WERE MADE UNDER DURESS.
BASED ON YOUR STORY, THEY'D BE RIGHT!
DAMN! WHY CAN'T I PLACE HIM?!
HEY, NO ONE WILL CONFESS TO ANYTHING UNLESS YOU APPLY SOME PRESSURE.
SURE, BUT THERE'S PRESSURE AND THEN THERE'S PRESSURE, YOU KNOW?
WELL? AM I RIGHT?
THEY HAD TO BE PART OF SOME-THING BIG...
I REFUSE TO BELIEVE IT WAS ALL FOR NAUGHT...
?
UH...THAT WHAT WAS ALL FOR NAUGHT?
...I'M STILL COMPILING EVIDENCE IN THE MEAN-TIME...
YOU'D BE AMAZED BY WHAT I'VE UNCOVERED ON THE INTERNET ALONE...
THE 'NET, HUH?
SPEND A LOT OF TIME ON THERE, DO YA?
—SAY, WHAT ARE YOU, A REPORTER OR SOME-THING?
YOU ASK A LOT OF REPORTER-Y QUESTIONS.

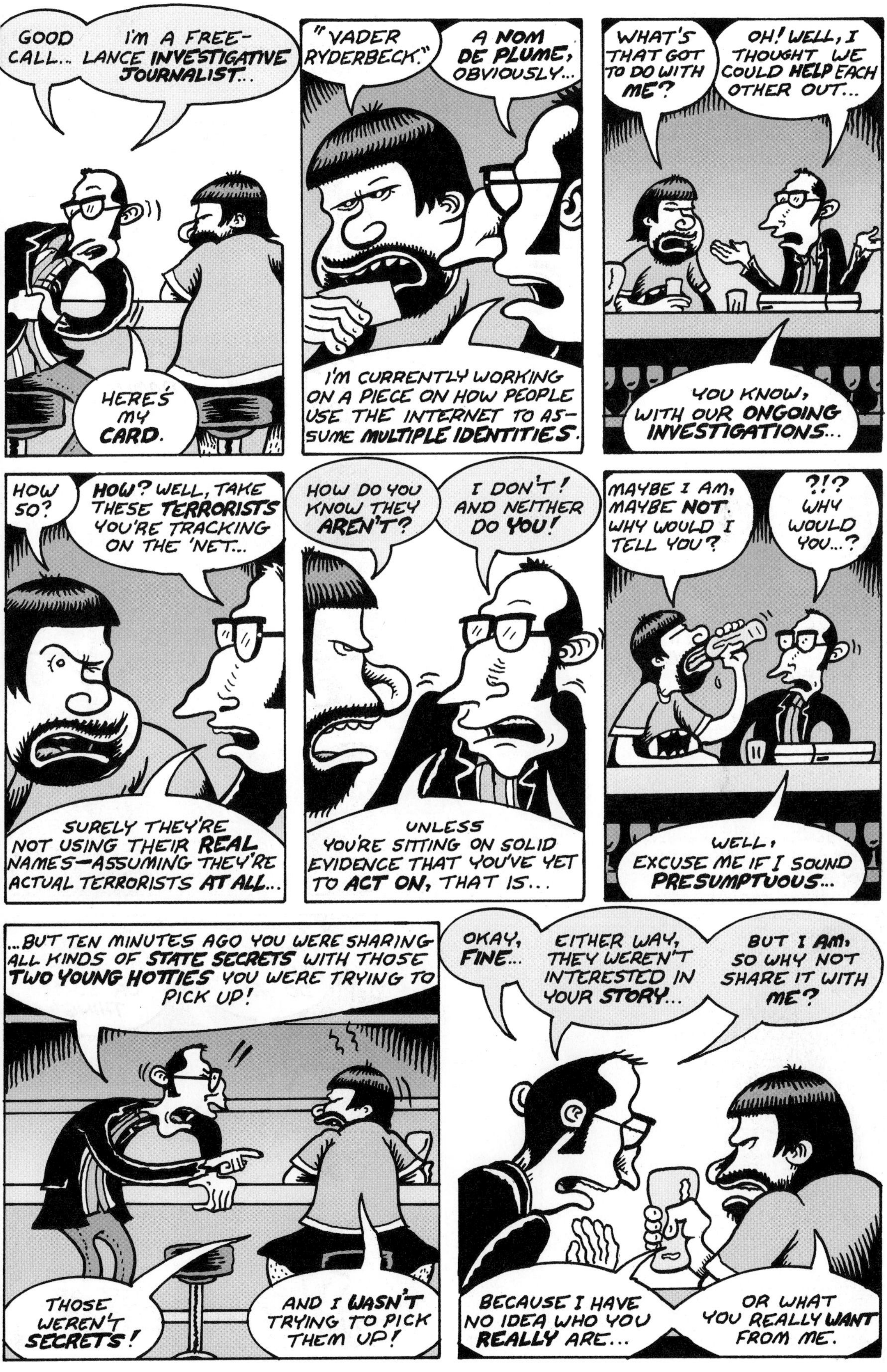
GOOD CALL...
I'M A FREE-LANCE INVESTIGATIVE JOURNALIST...
HERE'S MY CARD.
"VADER RYDERBECK."
A NOM DE PLUME, OBVIOUSLY...
I'M CURRENTLY WORKING ON A PIECE ON HOW PEOPLE USE THE INTERNET TO AS-SUME MULTIPLE IDENTITIES.
WHAT'S THAT GOT TO DO WITH ME?
OH! WELL, I THOUGHT WE COULD HELP EACH OTHER OUT...
YOU KNOW, WITH OUR ONGOING INVESTIGATIONS...
HOW SO?
HOW? WELL, TAKE THESE TERRORISTS YOU'RE TRACKING ON THE 'NET...
SURELY THEY'RE NOT USING THEIR REAL NAMES—ASSUMING THEY'RE ACTUAL TERRORISTS AT ALL...
HOW DO YOU KNOW THEY AREN'T?
I DON'T! AND NEITHER DO YOU!
UNLESS YOU'RE SITTING ON SOLID EVIDENCE THAT YOU'VE YET TO ACT ON, THAT IS...
MAYBE I AM, MAYBE NOT. WHY WOULD I TELL YOU?
?!? WHY WOULD YOU...?
WELL, EXCUSE ME IF I SOUND PRESUMPTUOUS...
...BUT TEN MINUTES AGO YOU WERE SHARING ALL KINDS OF STATE SECRETS WITH THOSE TWO YOUNG HOTTIES YOU WERE TRYING TO PICK UP!
THOSE WEREN'T SECRETS!
AND I WASN'T TRYING TO PICK THEM UP!
OKAY, FINE...
EITHER WAY, THEY WEREN'T INTERESTED IN YOUR STORY...
BUT I AM, SO WHY NOT SHARE IT WITH ME?
BECAUSE I HAVE NO IDEA WHO YOU REALLY ARE...
OR WHAT YOU REALLY WANT FROM ME.

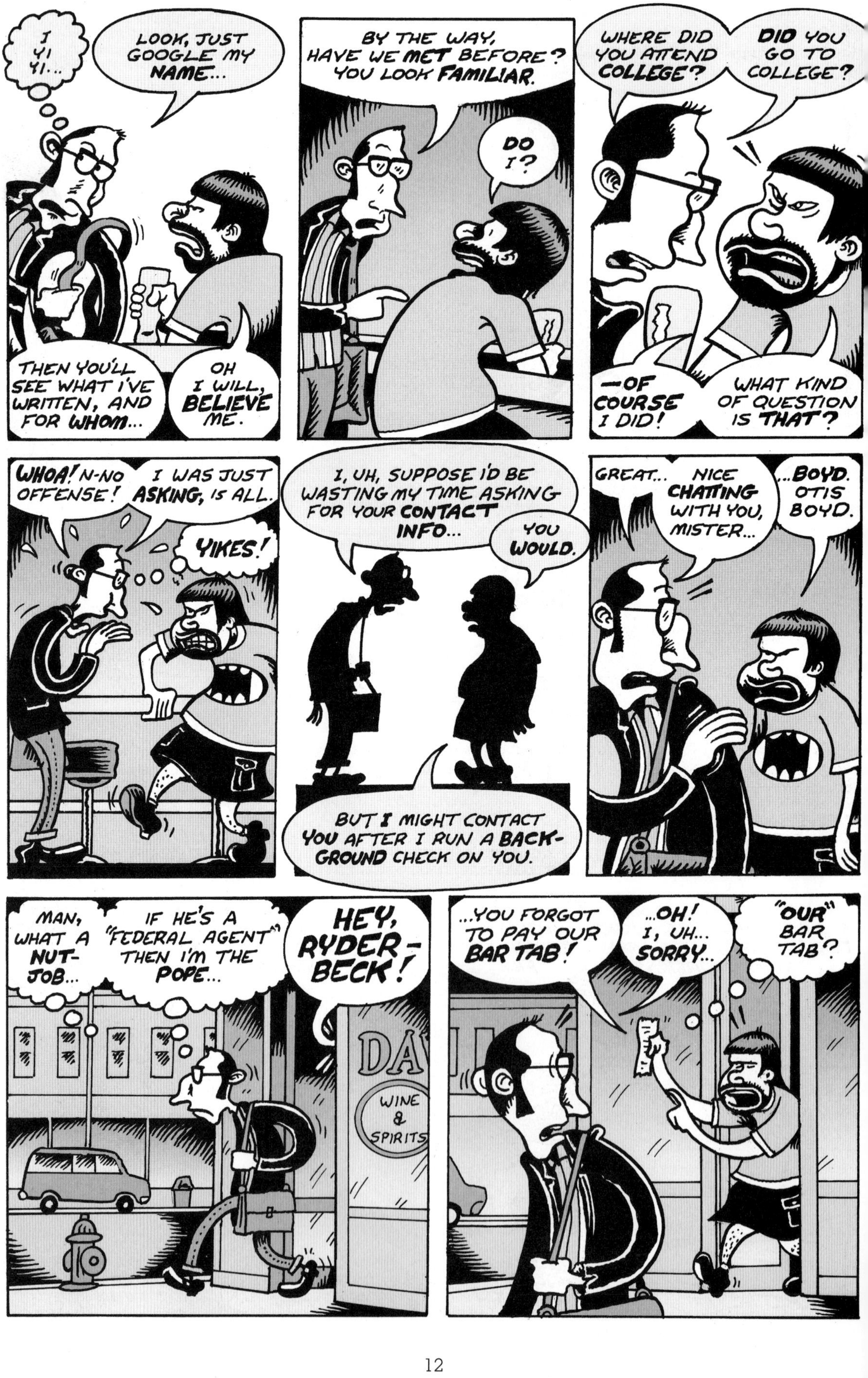

I YI YI...
LOOK, JUST GOOGLE MY NAME...
THEN YOU'LL SEE WHAT I'VE WRITTEN, AND FOR WHOM...
OH I WILL, BELIEVE ME.
BY THE WAY, HAVE WE MET BEFORE? YOU LOOK FAMILIAR.
DO I?
WHERE DID YOU ATTEND COLLEGE?
DID YOU GO TO COLLEGE?
—OF COURSE I DID!
WHAT KIND OF QUESTION IS THAT?
WHOA! N-NO OFFENSE!
I WAS JUST ASKING, IS ALL.
YIKES!
I, UH, SUPPOSE I'D BE WASTING MY TIME ASKING FOR YOUR CONTACT INFO...
YOU WOULD.
BUT I MIGHT CONTACT YOU AFTER I RUN A BACK-GROUND CHECK ON YOU.
GREAT...
NICE CHATTING WITH YOU, MISTER...
...BOYD. OTIS BOYD.
MAN, WHAT A NUT-JOB...
IF HE'S A "FEDERAL AGENT" THEN I'M THE POPE...
HEY, RYDER-BECK!
DA
WINE & SPIRITS
...YOU FORGOT TO PAY OUR BAR TAB!
...OH! I, UH... SORRY...
"OUR" BAR TAB?

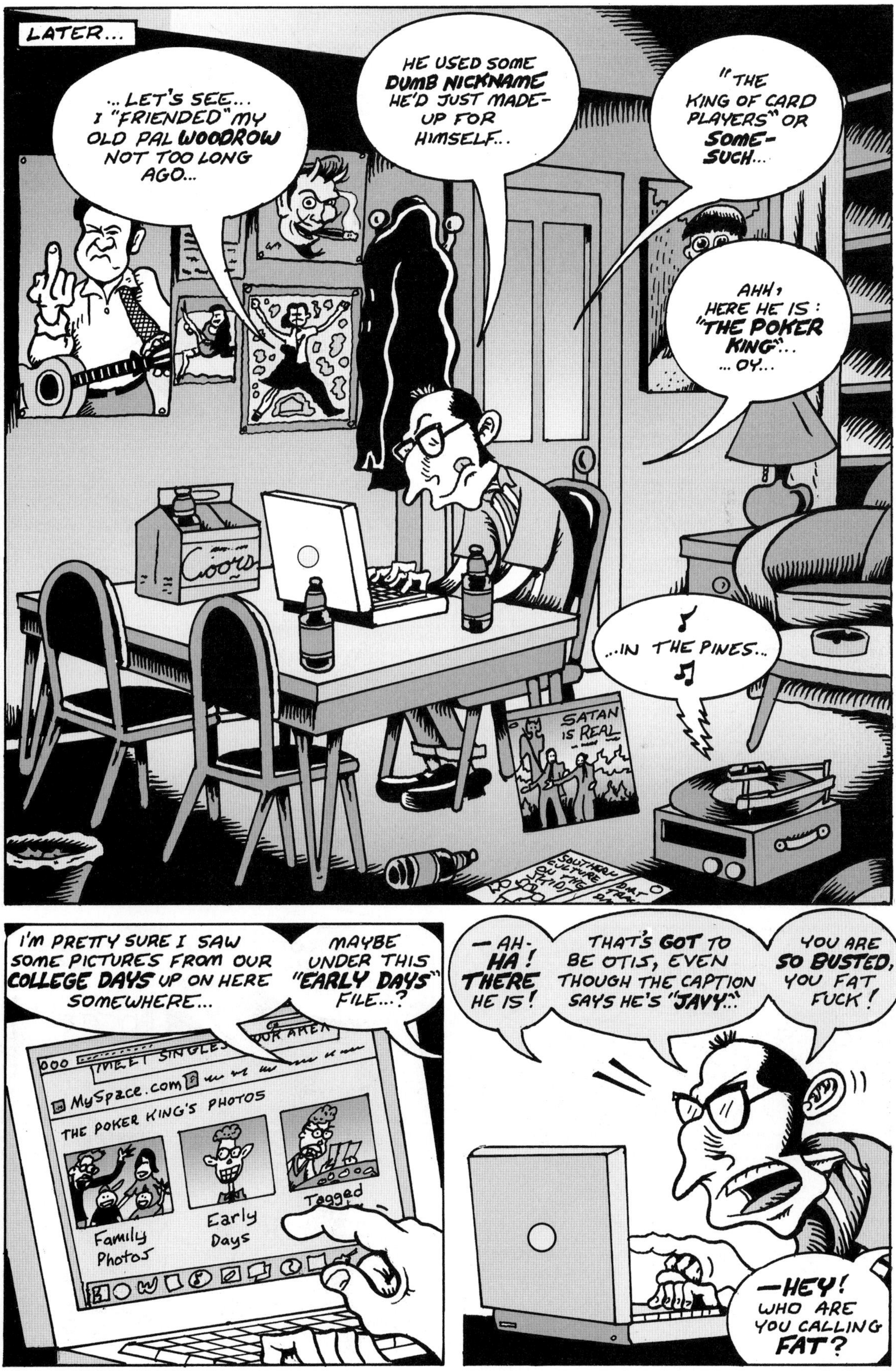
LATER...
...LET'S SEE... I "FRIENDED" MY OLD PAL WOODROW NOT TOO LONG AGO...
HE USED SOME DUMB NICKNAME HE'D JUST MADE-UP FOR HIMSELF...
"THE KING OF CARD PLAYERS" OR SOME-SUCH...
AHH, HERE HE IS: "THE POKER KING"... ...OY...
Coors
...IN THE PINES...
SATAN IS REAL
I'M PRETTY SURE I SAW SOME PICTURES FROM OUR COLLEGE DAYS UP ON HERE SOMEWHERE...
MAYBE UNDER THIS "EARLY DAYS" FILE...?
MySpace.com
THE POKER KING'S PHOTOS
Family Photos
Early Days
Tagged
—AH-HA! THERE HE IS!
THAT'S GOT TO BE OTIS, EVEN THOUGH THE CAPTION SAYS HE'S "JAVY"...
YOU ARE SO BUSTED, YOU FAT FUCK!
—HEY! WHO ARE YOU CALLING FAT?

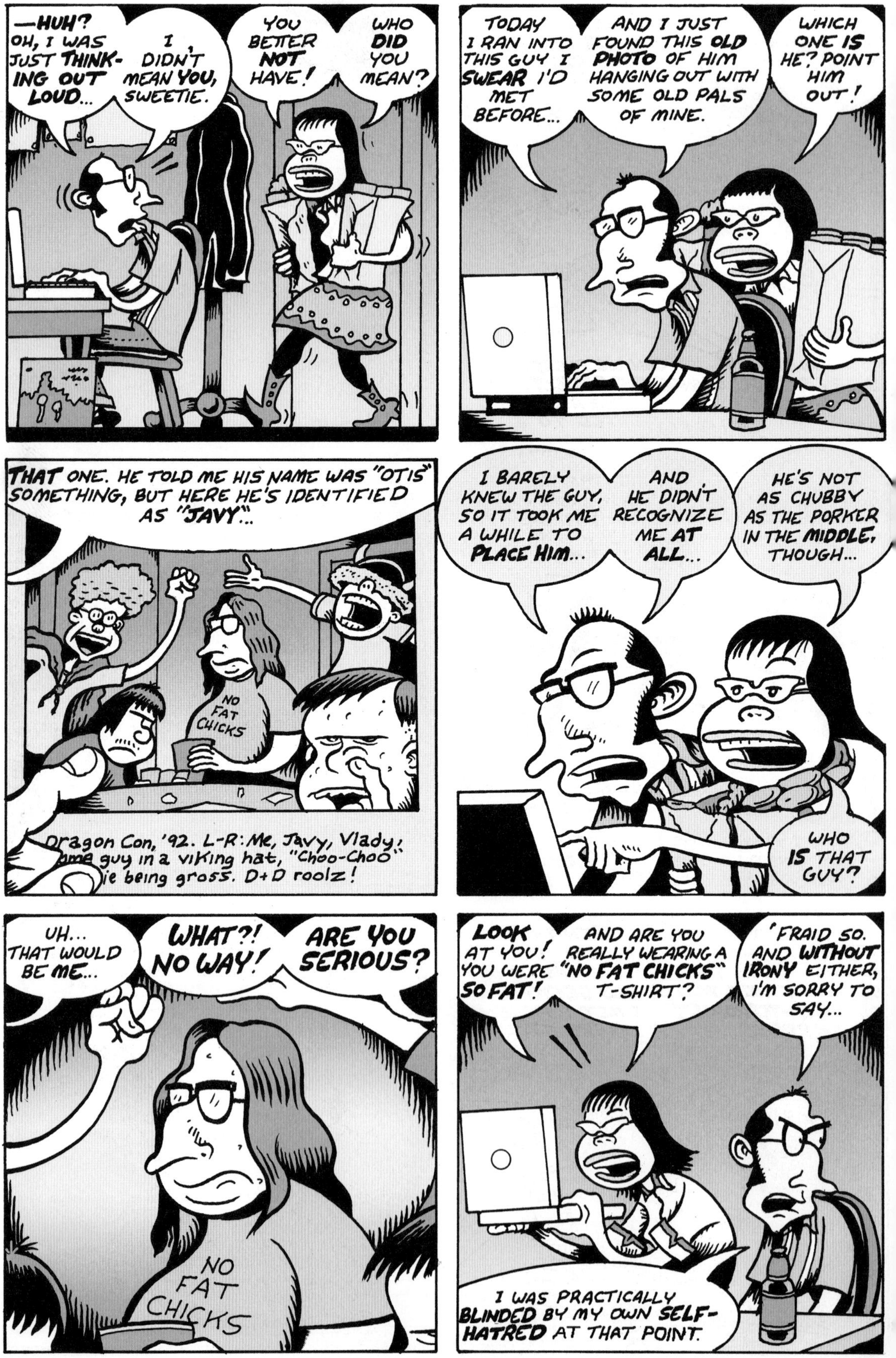
—HUH? OH, I WAS JUST THINKING OUT LOUD...
I DIDN'T MEAN YOU, SWEETIE.
YOU BETTER NOT HAVE!
WHO DID YOU MEAN?
TODAY I RAN INTO THIS GUY I SWEAR I'D MET BEFORE...
AND I JUST FOUND THIS OLD PHOTO OF HIM HANGING OUT WITH SOME OLD PALS OF MINE.
WHICH ONE IS HE? POINT HIM OUT!
THAT ONE. HE TOLD ME HIS NAME WAS "OTIS" SOMETHING, BUT HERE HE'S IDENTIFIED AS "JAVY"...
NO FAT CHICKS
Dragon Con, '92. L-R: Me, Javy, Vlady,
ome guy in a viking hat, "Choo-Choo"
ie being gross. D+D roolz!
I BARELY KNEW THE GUY, SO IT TOOK ME A WHILE TO PLACE HIM...
AND HE DIDN'T RECOGNIZE ME AT ALL...
HE'S NOT AS CHUBBY AS THE PORKER IN THE MIDDLE, THOUGH...
WHO IS THAT GUY?
UH... THAT WOULD BE ME...
WHAT?! NO WAY!
ARE YOU SERIOUS?
NO FAT CHICKS
LOOK AT YOU! YOU WERE SO FAT!
AND ARE YOU REALLY WEARING A "NO FAT CHICKS" T-SHIRT?
'FRAID SO. AND WITHOUT IRONY EITHER, I'M SORRY TO SAY...
I WAS PRACTICALLY BLINDED BY MY OWN SELF-HATRED AT THAT POINT.

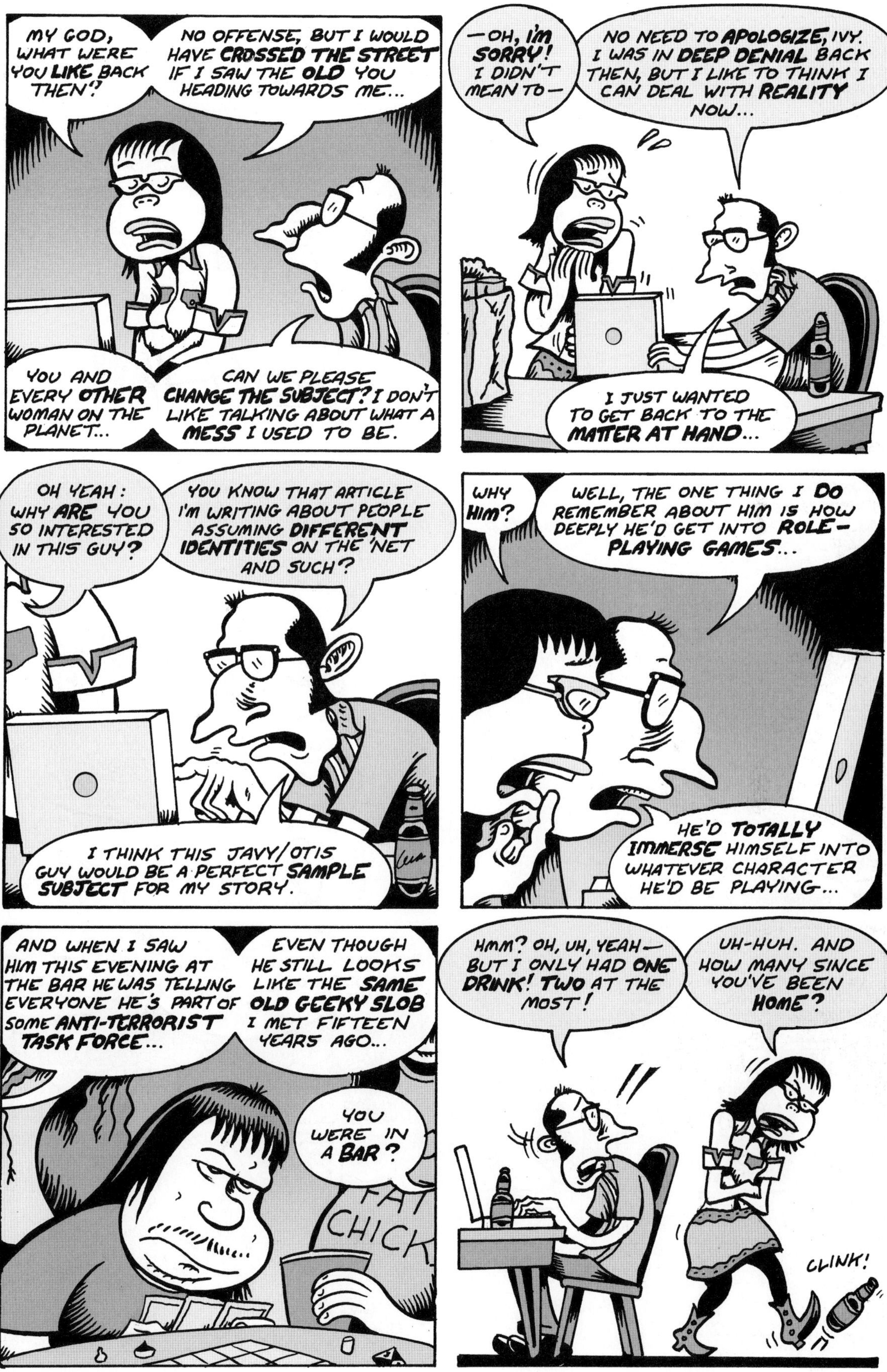
MY GOD, WHAT WERE YOU LIKE BACK THEN?
NO OFFENSE, BUT I WOULD HAVE CROSSED THE STREET IF I SAW THE OLD YOU HEADING TOWARDS ME...
YOU AND EVERY OTHER WOMAN ON THE PLANET...
CAN WE PLEASE CHANGE THE SUBJECT? I DON'T LIKE TALKING ABOUT WHAT A MESS I USED TO BE.
—OH, I'M SORRY! I DIDN'T MEAN TO—
NO NEED TO APOLOGIZE, IVY. I WAS IN DEEP DENIAL BACK THEN, BUT I LIKE TO THINK I CAN DEAL WITH REALITY NOW...
I JUST WANTED TO GET BACK TO THE MATTER AT HAND...
OH YEAH: WHY ARE YOU SO INTERESTED IN THIS GUY?
YOU KNOW THAT ARTICLE I'M WRITING ABOUT PEOPLE ASSUMING DIFFERENT IDENTITIES ON THE 'NET AND SUCH?
I THINK THIS JAVY/OTIS GUY WOULD BE A PERFECT SAMPLE SUBJECT FOR MY STORY.
WHY HIM?
WELL, THE ONE THING I DO REMEMBER ABOUT HIM IS HOW DEEPLY HE'D GET INTO ROLE-PLAYING GAMES...
HE'D TOTALLY IMMERSE HIMSELF INTO WHATEVER CHARACTER HE'D BE PLAYING...
AND WHEN I SAW HIM THIS EVENING AT THE BAR HE WAS TELLING EVERYONE HE'S PART OF SOME ANTI-TERRORIST TASK FORCE...
EVEN THOUGH HE STILL LOOKS LIKE THE SAME OLD GEEKY SLOB I MET FIFTEEN YEARS AGO...
YOU WERE IN A BAR?
FAT CHICK
HMM? OH, UH, YEAH— BUT I ONLY HAD ONE DRINK! TWO AT THE MOST!
UH-HUH. AND HOW MANY SINCE YOU'VE BEEN HOME?
CLINK!

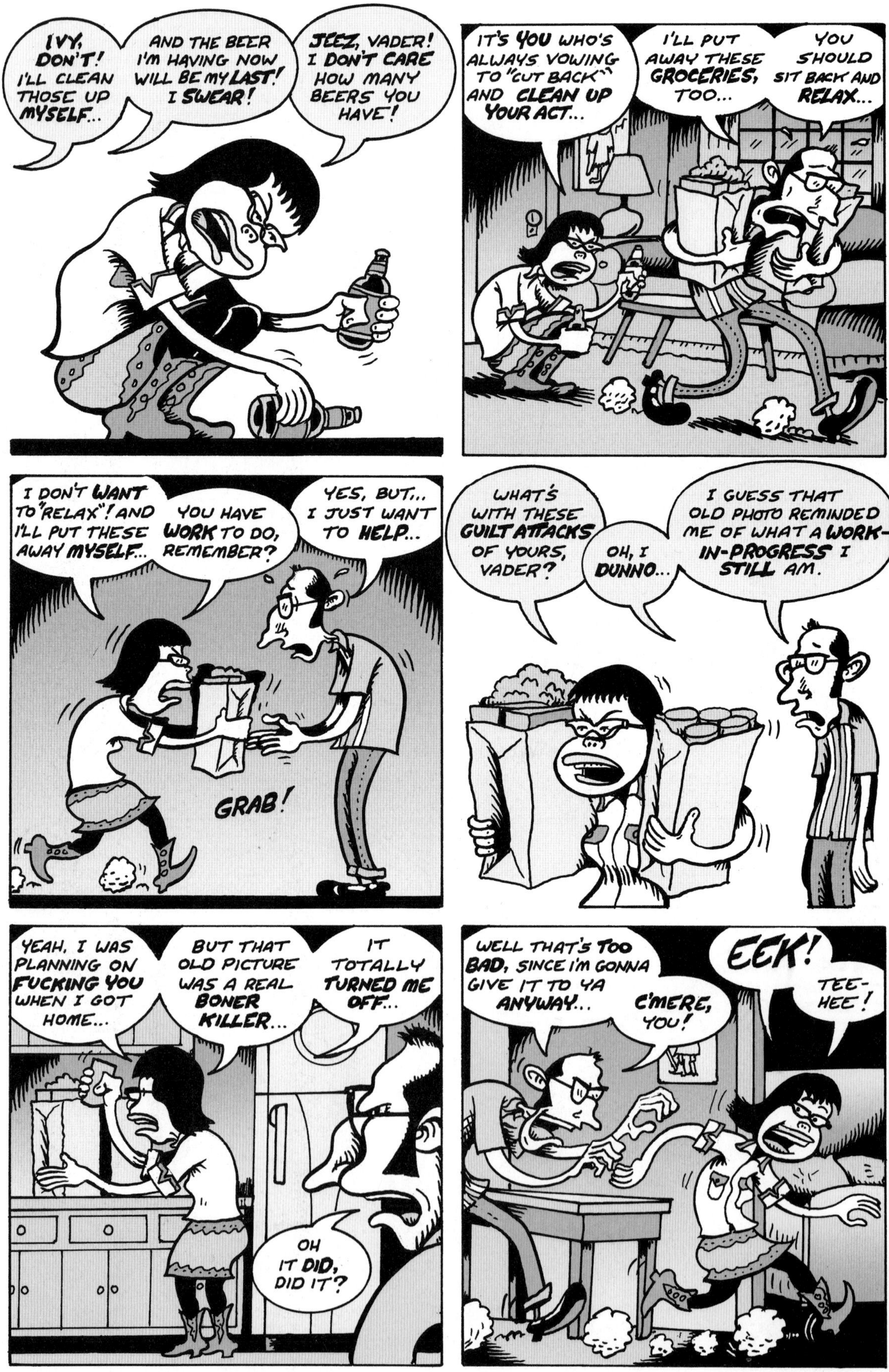
IVY, DON'T! I'LL CLEAN THOSE UP MYSELF...
AND THE BEER I'M HAVING NOW WILL BE MY LAST! I SWEAR!
JEEZ, VADER! I DON'T CARE HOW MANY BEERS YOU HAVE!
IT'S YOU WHO'S ALWAYS VOWING TO "CUT BACK" AND CLEAN UP YOUR ACT...
I'LL PUT AWAY THESE GROCERIES, TOO...
YOU SHOULD SIT BACK AND RELAX...
I DON'T WANT TO "RELAX"! AND I'LL PUT THESE AWAY MYSELF...
YOU HAVE WORK TO DO, REMEMBER?
YES, BUT... I JUST WANT TO HELP...
GRAB!
WHAT'S WITH THESE GUILT ATTACKS OF YOURS, VADER?
OH, I DUNNO...
I GUESS THAT OLD PHOTO REMINDED ME OF WHAT A WORK-IN-PROGRESS I STILL AM.
YEAH, I WAS PLANNING ON FUCKING YOU WHEN I GOT HOME...
BUT THAT OLD PICTURE WAS A REAL BONER KILLER...
IT TOTALLY TURNED ME OFF...
OH IT DID, DID IT?
WELL THAT'S TOO BAD, SINCE I'M GONNA GIVE IT TO YA ANYWAY...
C'MERE, YOU!
EEK!
TEE-HEE!

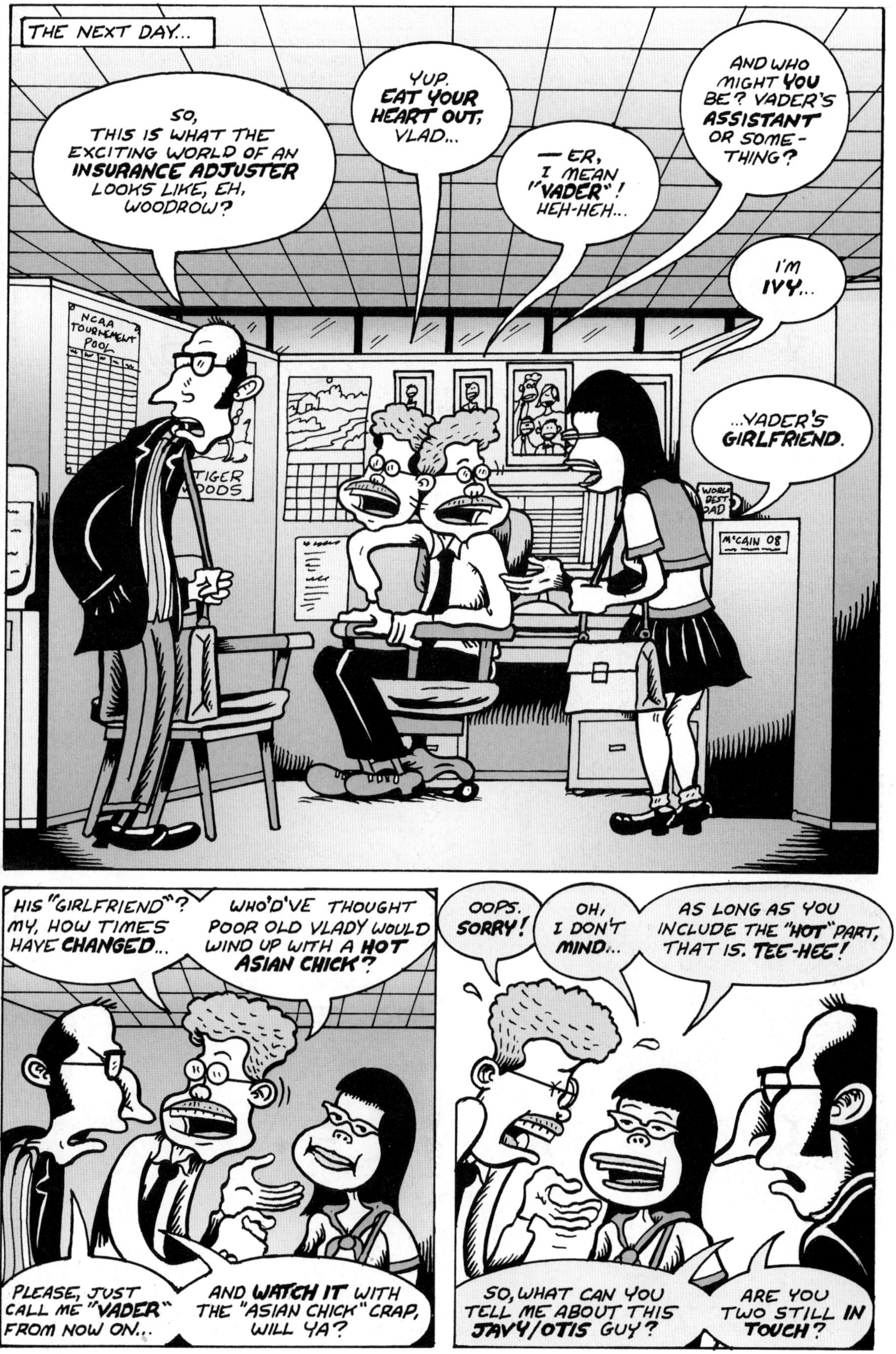

THE NEXT DAY...
SO, THIS IS WHAT THE EXCITING WORLD OF AN INSURANCE ADJUSTER LOOKS LIKE, EH, WOODROW?
YUP. EAT YOUR HEART OUT, VLAD...
—ER, I MEAN "VADER"! HEH-HEH...
AND WHO MIGHT YOU BE? VADER'S ASSISTANT OR SOME-THING?
I'M IVY...
...VADER'S GIRLFRIEND.
NCAA TOURNEMENT POOL
TIGER WOODS
WORLD BEST DAD
McCAIN 08
HIS "GIRLFRIEND"? MY, HOW TIMES HAVE CHANGED...
WHO'D'VE THOUGHT POOR OLD VLADY WOULD WIND UP WITH A HOT ASIAN CHICK?
PLEASE, JUST CALL ME "VADER" FROM NOW ON...
AND WATCH IT WITH THE "ASIAN CHICK" CRAP, WILL YA?
OOPS. SORRY!
OH, I DON'T MIND...
AS LONG AS YOU INCLUDE THE "HOT" PART, THAT IS. TEE-HEE!
SO, WHAT CAN YOU TELL ME ABOUT THIS JAVY/OTIS GUY?
ARE YOU TWO STILL IN TOUCH?

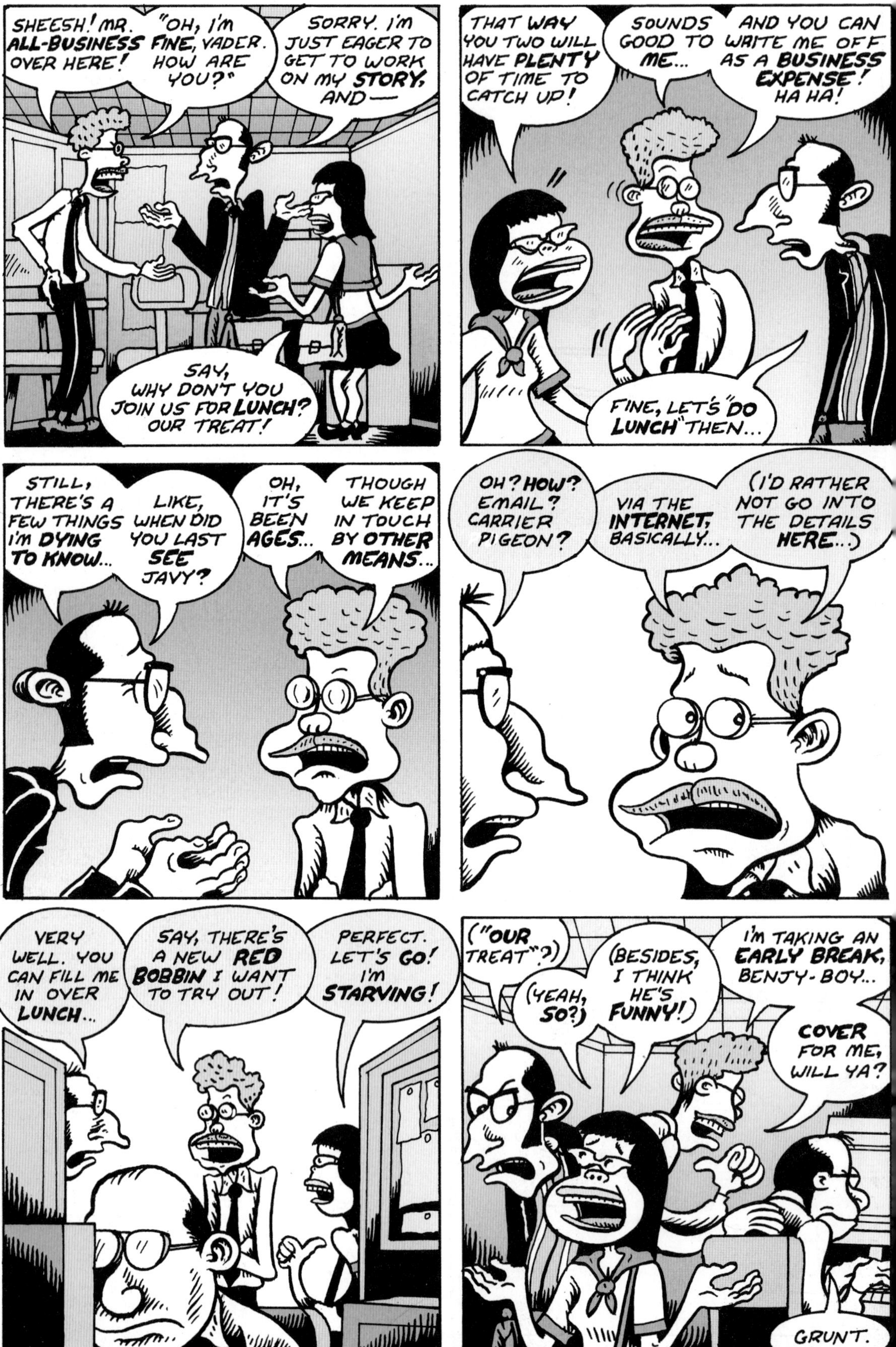
SHEESH! MR. ALL-BUSINESS OVER HERE!
"OH, I'M FINE, VADER. HOW ARE YOU?"
SORRY. I'M JUST EAGER TO GET TO WORK ON MY STORY, AND—
SAY, WHY DON'T YOU JOIN US FOR LUNCH? OUR TREAT!
THAT WAY YOU TWO WILL HAVE PLENTY OF TIME TO CATCH UP!
SOUNDS GOOD TO ME...
AND YOU CAN WRITE ME OFF AS A BUSINESS EXPENSE! HA HA!
FINE, LET'S "DO LUNCH" THEN...
STILL, THERE'S A FEW THINGS I'M DYING TO KNOW...
LIKE, WHEN DID YOU LAST SEE JAVY?
OH, IT'S BEEN AGES...
THOUGH WE KEEP IN TOUCH BY OTHER MEANS...
OH? HOW? EMAIL? CARRIER PIGEON?
VIA THE INTERNET, BASICALLY...
(I'D RATHER NOT GO INTO THE DETAILS HERE...)
VERY WELL. YOU CAN FILL ME IN OVER LUNCH...
SAY, THERE'S A NEW RED BOBBIN I WANT TO TRY OUT!
PERFECT. LET'S GO! I'M STARVING!
("OUR TREAT"?)
(YEAH, SO?)
(BESIDES, I THINK HE'S FUNNY!)
I'M TAKING AN EARLY BREAK, BENJY-BOY...
COVER FOR ME, WILL YA?
GRUNT.

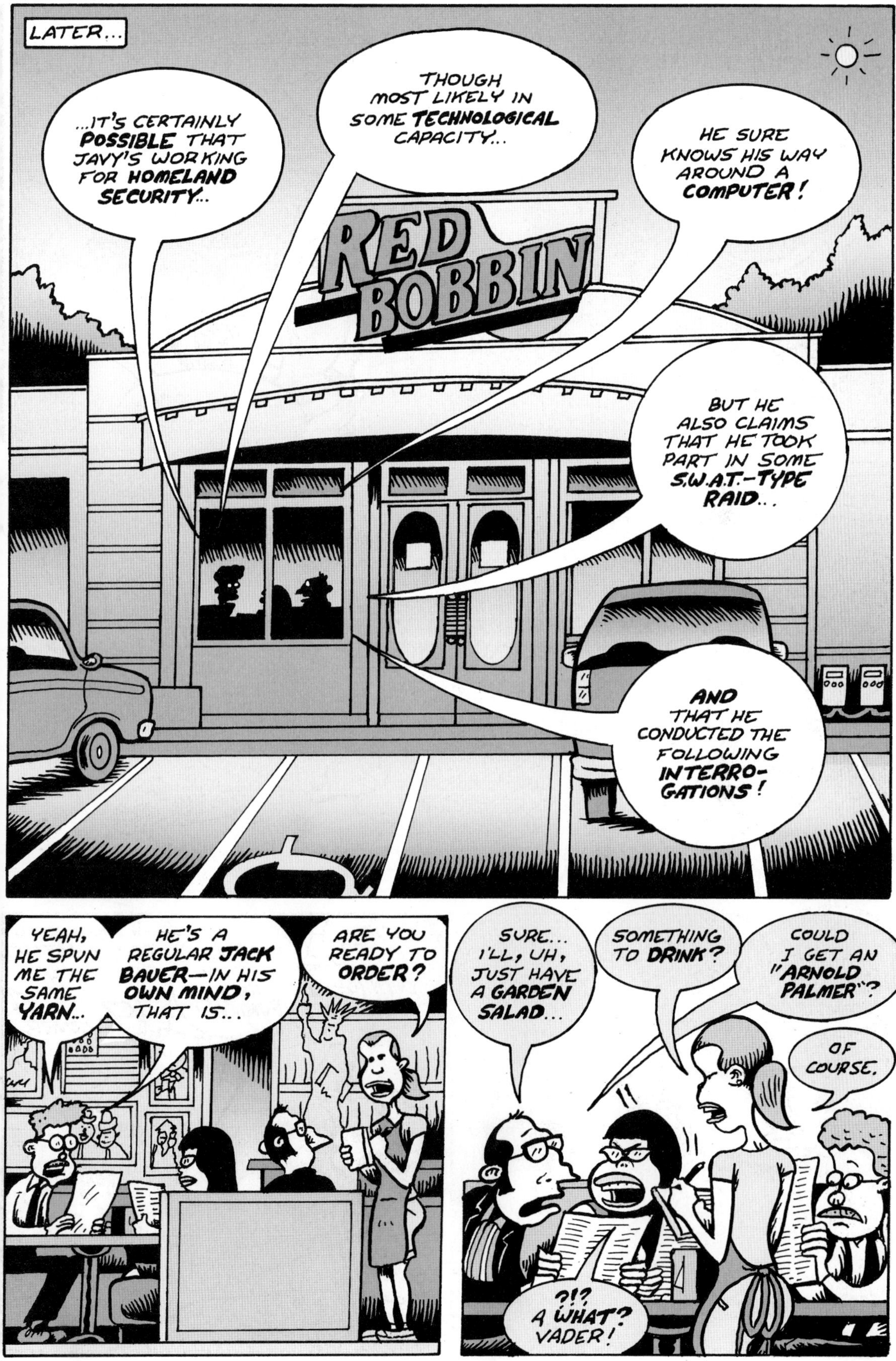
LATER...
...IT'S CERTAINLY POSSIBLE THAT JAVY'S WORKING FOR HOMELAND SECURITY...
THOUGH MOST LIKELY IN SOME TECHNOLOGICAL CAPACITY...
HE SURE KNOWS HIS WAY AROUND A COMPUTER!
RED BOBBIN
BUT HE ALSO CLAIMS THAT HE TOOK PART IN SOME S.W.A.T.-TYPE RAID...
AND THAT HE CONDUCTED THE FOLLOWING INTERRO-GATIONS!
YEAH, HE SPUN ME THE SAME YARN...
HE'S A REGULAR JACK BAUER—IN HIS OWN MIND, THAT IS...
ARE YOU READY TO ORDER?
SURE... I'LL, UH, JUST HAVE A GARDEN SALAD...
SOMETHING TO DRINK?
COULD I GET AN "ARNOLD PALMER"?
OF COURSE.
?!? A WHAT? VADER!

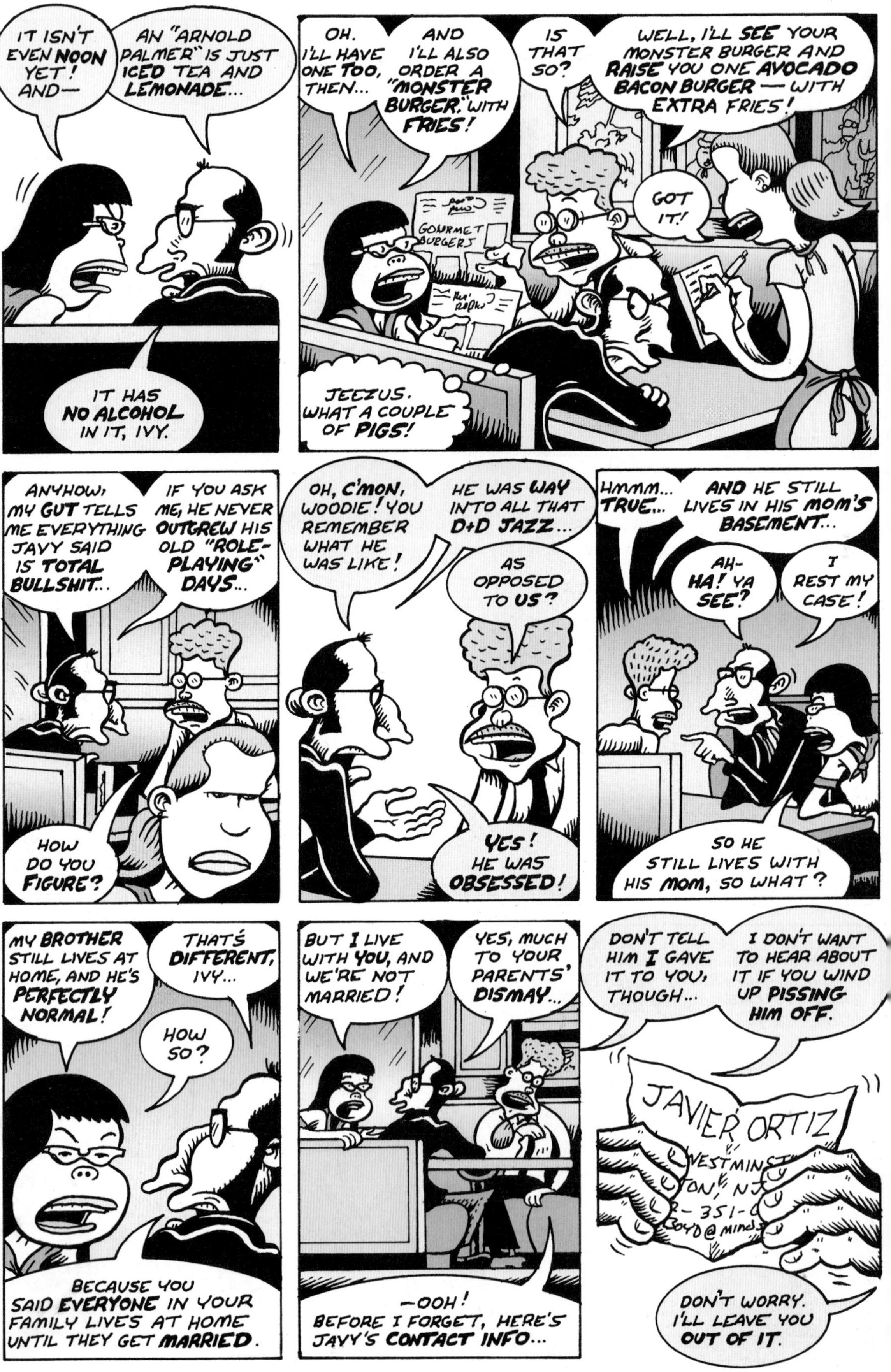
IT ISN'T EVEN NOON YET! AND—
AN "ARNOLD PALMER" IS JUST ICED TEA AND LEMONADE...
IT HAS NO ALCOHOL IN IT, IVY.
OH. I'LL HAVE ONE TOO, THEN...
AND I'LL ALSO ORDER A "MONSTER BURGER" WITH FRIES!
IS THAT SO?
WELL, I'LL SEE YOUR MONSTER BURGER AND RAISE YOU ONE AVOCADO BACON BURGER — WITH EXTRA FRIES!
GOT IT!
GOURMET BURGERS
JEEZUS. WHAT A COUPLE OF PIGS!
ANYHOW, MY GUT TELLS ME EVERYTHING JAVY SAID IS TOTAL BULLSHIT...
IF YOU ASK ME, HE NEVER OUTGREW HIS OLD "ROLE-PLAYING" DAYS...
HOW DO YOU FIGURE?
OH, C'MON, WOODIE! YOU REMEMBER WHAT HE WAS LIKE!
HE WAS WAY INTO ALL THAT D+D JAZZ...
AS OPPOSED TO US?
YES! HE WAS OBSESSED!
HMMM... TRUE...
AND HE STILL LIVES IN HIS MOM'S BASEMENT...
AH-HA! YA SEE?
I REST MY CASE!
SO HE STILL LIVES WITH HIS MOM, SO WHAT?
MY BROTHER STILL LIVES AT HOME, AND HE'S PERFECTLY NORMAL!
THAT'S DIFFERENT, IVY...
HOW SO?
BECAUSE YOU SAID EVERYONE IN YOUR FAMILY LIVES AT HOME UNTIL THEY GET MARRIED.
BUT I LIVE WITH YOU, AND WE'RE NOT MARRIED!
YES, MUCH TO YOUR PARENTS' DISMAY...
—OOH! BEFORE I FORGET, HERE'S JAVY'S CONTACT INFO...
DON'T TELL HIM I GAVE IT TO YOU, THOUGH...
I DON'T WANT TO HEAR ABOUT IT IF YOU WIND UP PISSING HIM OFF.
JAVIER ORTIZ
DON'T WORRY. I'LL LEAVE YOU OUT OF IT.

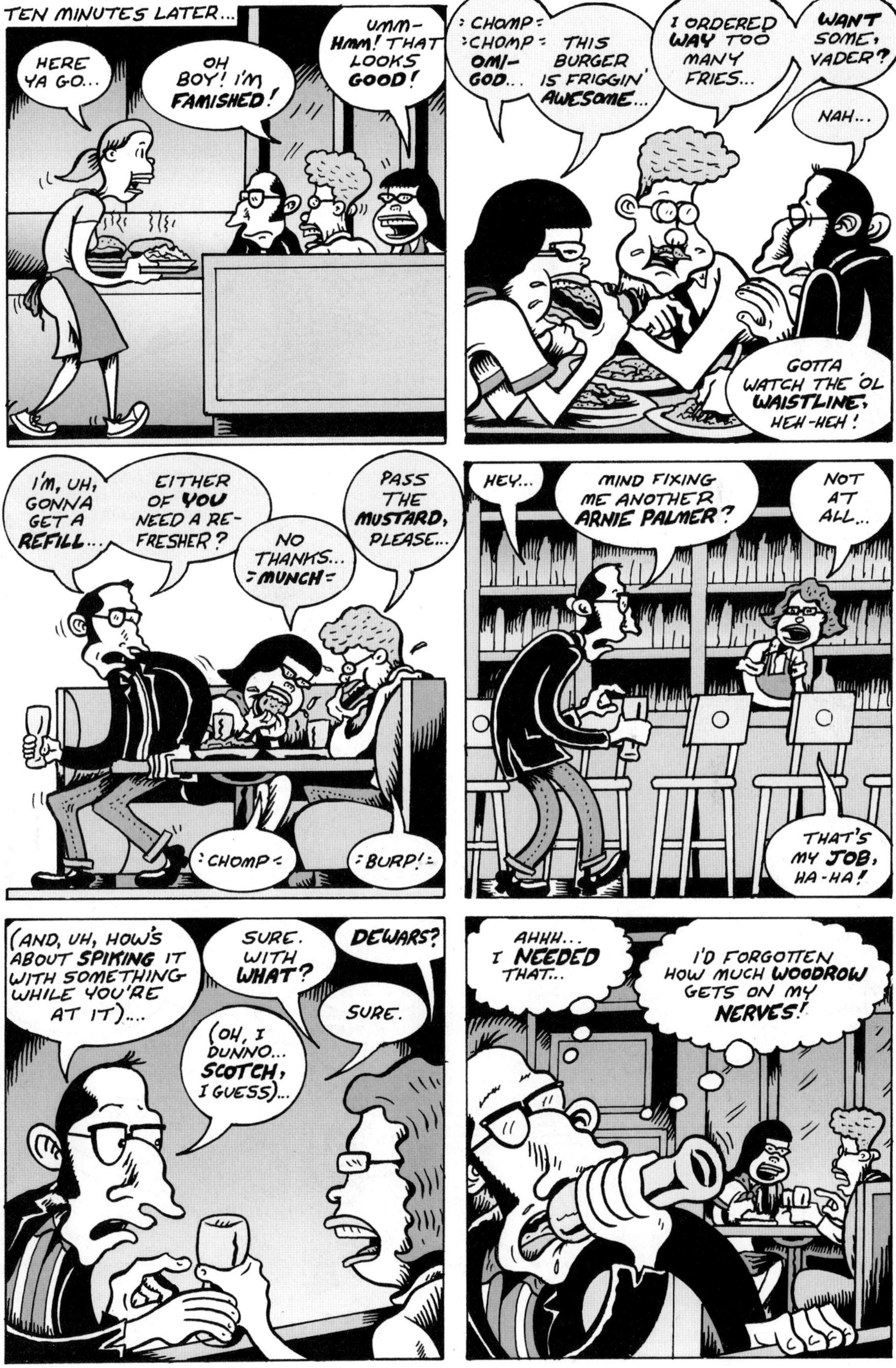
TEN MINUTES LATER...
HERE YA GO...
OH BOY! I'M FAMISHED!
UMM-HMM! THAT LOOKS GOOD!
:CHOMP: :CHOMP: OMI-GOD...
THIS BURGER IS FRIGGIN' AWESOME...
I ORDERED WAY TOO MANY FRIES...
WANT SOME, VADER?
NAH...
GOTTA WATCH THE 'OL WAISTLINE, HEH-HEH!
I'M, UH, GONNA GET A REFILL...
EITHER OF YOU NEED A RE-FRESHER?
NO THANKS... :MUNCH:
PASS THE MUSTARD, PLEASE...
:CHOMP:
:BURP!:
HEY...
MIND FIXING ME ANOTHER ARNIE PALMER?
NOT AT ALL...
THAT'S MY JOB, HA-HA!
(AND, UH, HOW'S ABOUT SPIKING IT WITH SOMETHING WHILE YOU'RE AT IT)....
SURE. WITH WHAT?
(OH, I DUNNO... SCOTCH, I GUESS)...
DEWARS?
SURE.
AHHH... I NEEDED THAT...
I'D FORGOTTEN HOW MUCH WOODROW GETS ON MY NERVES!

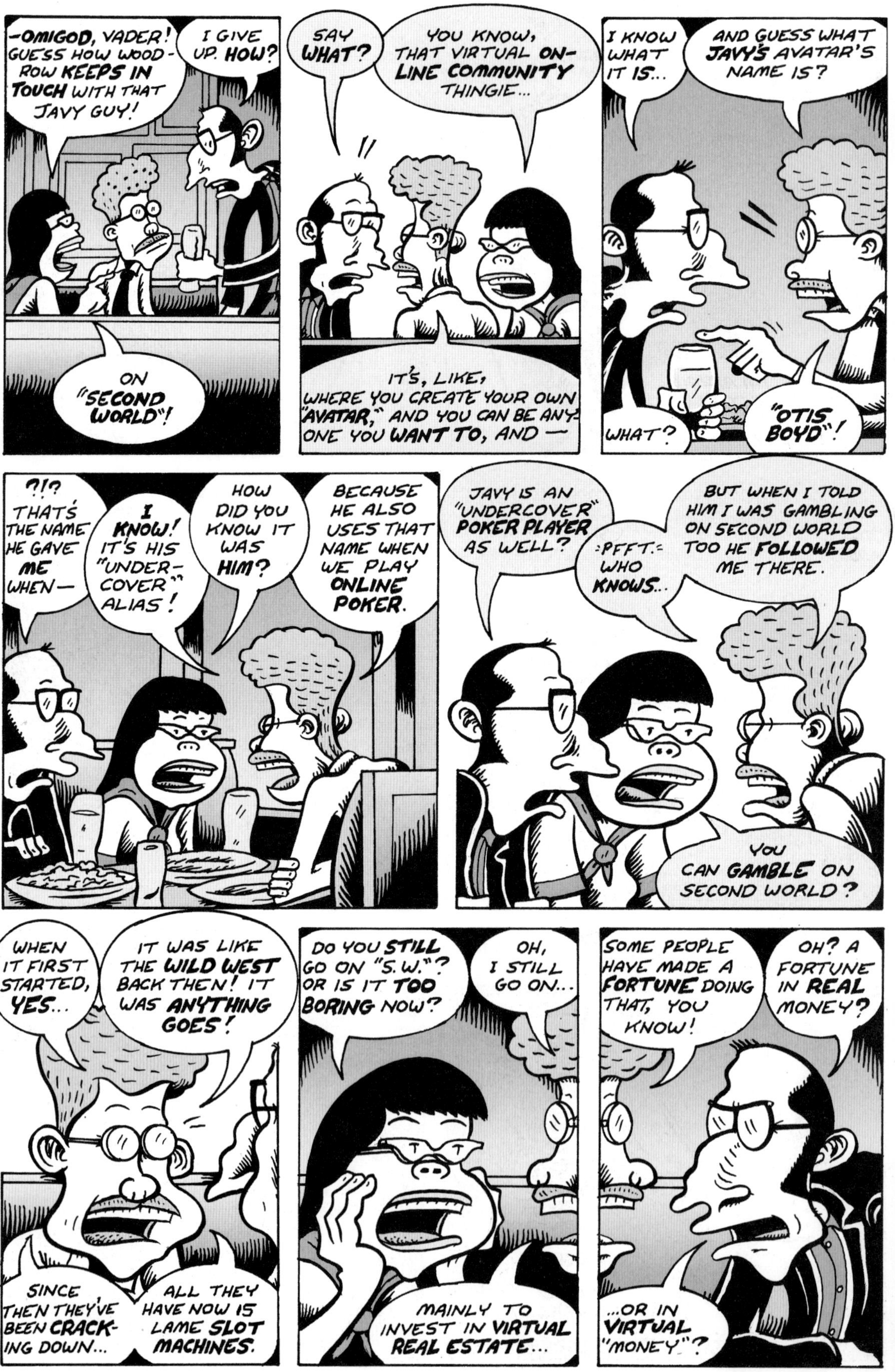

–OMIGOD, VADER! GUESS HOW WOOD-ROW KEEPS IN TOUCH WITH THAT JAVY GUY!
I GIVE UP. HOW?
ON "SECOND WORLD"!
SAY WHAT?
YOU KNOW, THAT VIRTUAL ON-LINE COMMUNITY THINGIE...
IT'S, LIKE, WHERE YOU CREATE YOUR OWN "AVATAR," AND YOU CAN BE ANY-ONE YOU WANT TO, AND —
I KNOW WHAT IT IS...
AND GUESS WHAT JAVY'S AVATAR'S NAME IS?
WHAT?
"OTIS BOYD"!
?!? THAT'S THE NAME HE GAVE ME WHEN—
I KNOW! IT'S HIS "UNDER-COVER" ALIAS!
HOW DID YOU KNOW IT WAS HIM?
BECAUSE HE ALSO USES THAT NAME WHEN WE PLAY ONLINE POKER.
JAVY IS AN "UNDERCOVER" POKER PLAYER AS WELL?
:PFFT.: WHO KNOWS...
BUT WHEN I TOLD HIM I WAS GAMBLING ON SECOND WORLD TOO HE FOLLOWED ME THERE.
YOU CAN GAMBLE ON SECOND WORLD?
WHEN IT FIRST STARTED, YES...
IT WAS LIKE THE WILD WEST BACK THEN! IT WAS ANYTHING GOES!
SINCE THEN THEY'VE BEEN CRACK-ING DOWN...
ALL THEY HAVE NOW IS LAME SLOT MACHINES.
DO YOU STILL GO ON "S.W."? OR IS IT TOO BORING NOW?
OH, I STILL GO ON...
MAINLY TO INVEST IN VIRTUAL REAL ESTATE...
SOME PEOPLE HAVE MADE A FORTUNE DOING THAT, YOU KNOW!
OH? A FORTUNE IN REAL MONEY?
...OR IN VIRTUAL "MONEY"?

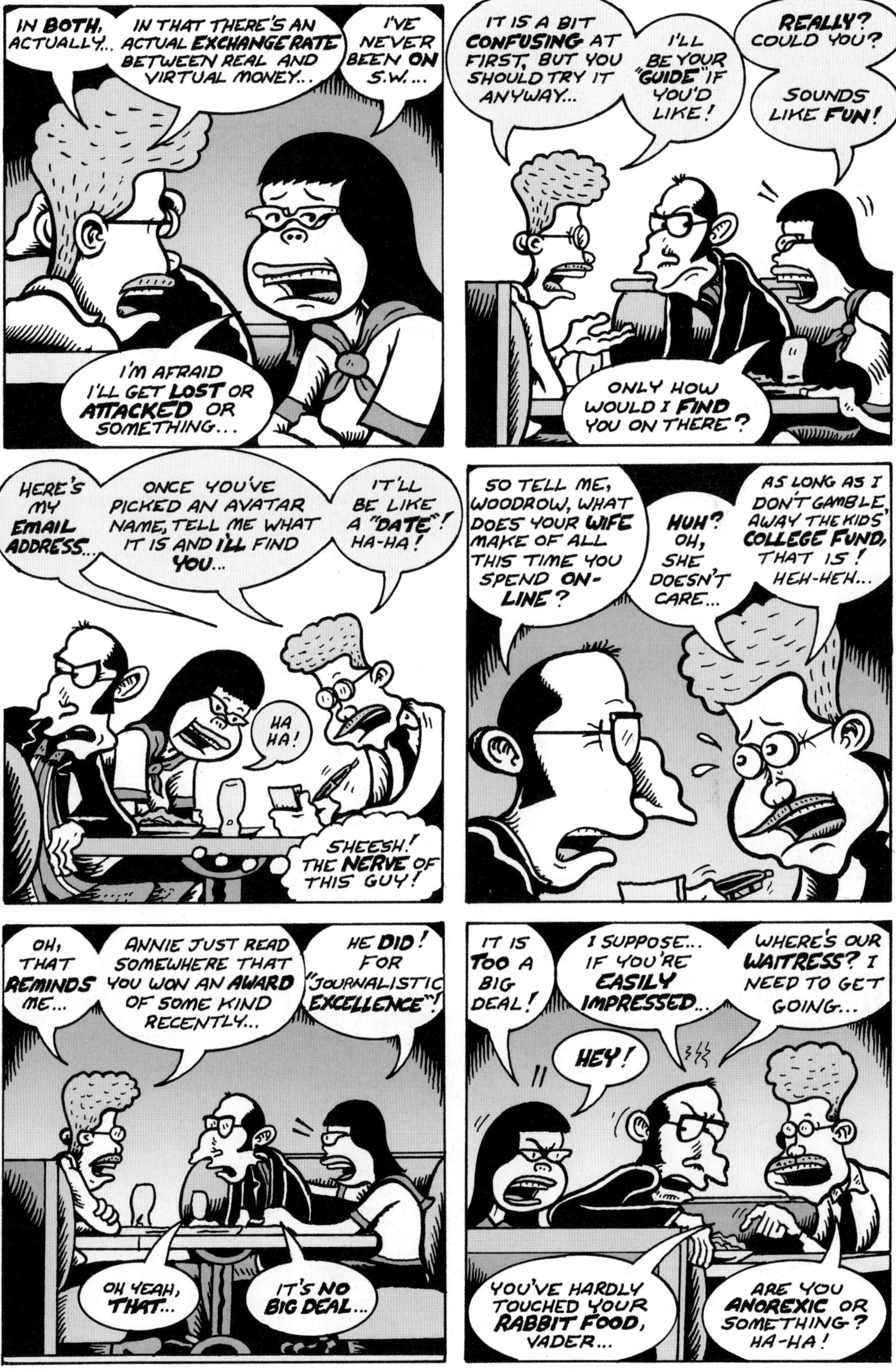

IN BOTH, ACTUALLY...
IN THAT THERE'S AN ACTUAL EXCHANGE RATE BETWEEN REAL AND VIRTUAL MONEY...
I'VE NEVER BEEN ON S.W. ...
I'M AFRAID I'LL GET LOST OR ATTACKED OR SOMETHING...
IT IS A BIT CONFUSING AT FIRST, BUT YOU SHOULD TRY IT ANYWAY...
I'LL BE YOUR "GUIDE" IF YOU'D LIKE!
REALLY? COULD YOU?
SOUNDS LIKE FUN!
ONLY HOW WOULD I FIND YOU ON THERE?
HERE'S MY EMAIL ADDRESS...
ONCE YOU'VE PICKED AN AVATAR NAME, TELL ME WHAT IT IS AND I'LL FIND YOU...
IT'LL BE LIKE A "DATE"! HA-HA!
HA HA!
SHEESH! THE NERVE OF THIS GUY!
SO TELL ME, WOODROW, WHAT DOES YOUR WIFE MAKE OF ALL THIS TIME YOU SPEND ON-LINE?
HUH? OH, SHE DOESN'T CARE...
AS LONG AS I DON'T GAMBLE AWAY THE KIDS' COLLEGE FUND, THAT IS! HEH-HEH...
OH, THAT REMINDS ME...
ANNIE JUST READ SOMEWHERE THAT YOU WON AN AWARD OF SOME KIND RECENTLY...
HE DID! FOR "JOURNALISTIC EXCELLENCE"!
OH YEAH, THAT...
IT'S NO BIG DEAL...
IT IS TOO A BIG DEAL!
I SUPPOSE... IF YOU'RE EASILY IMPRESSED...
WHERE'S OUR WAITRESS? I NEED TO GET GOING...
HEY!
YOU'VE HARDLY TOUCHED YOUR RABBIT FOOD, VADER...
ARE YOU ANOREXIC OR SOMETHING? HA-HA!

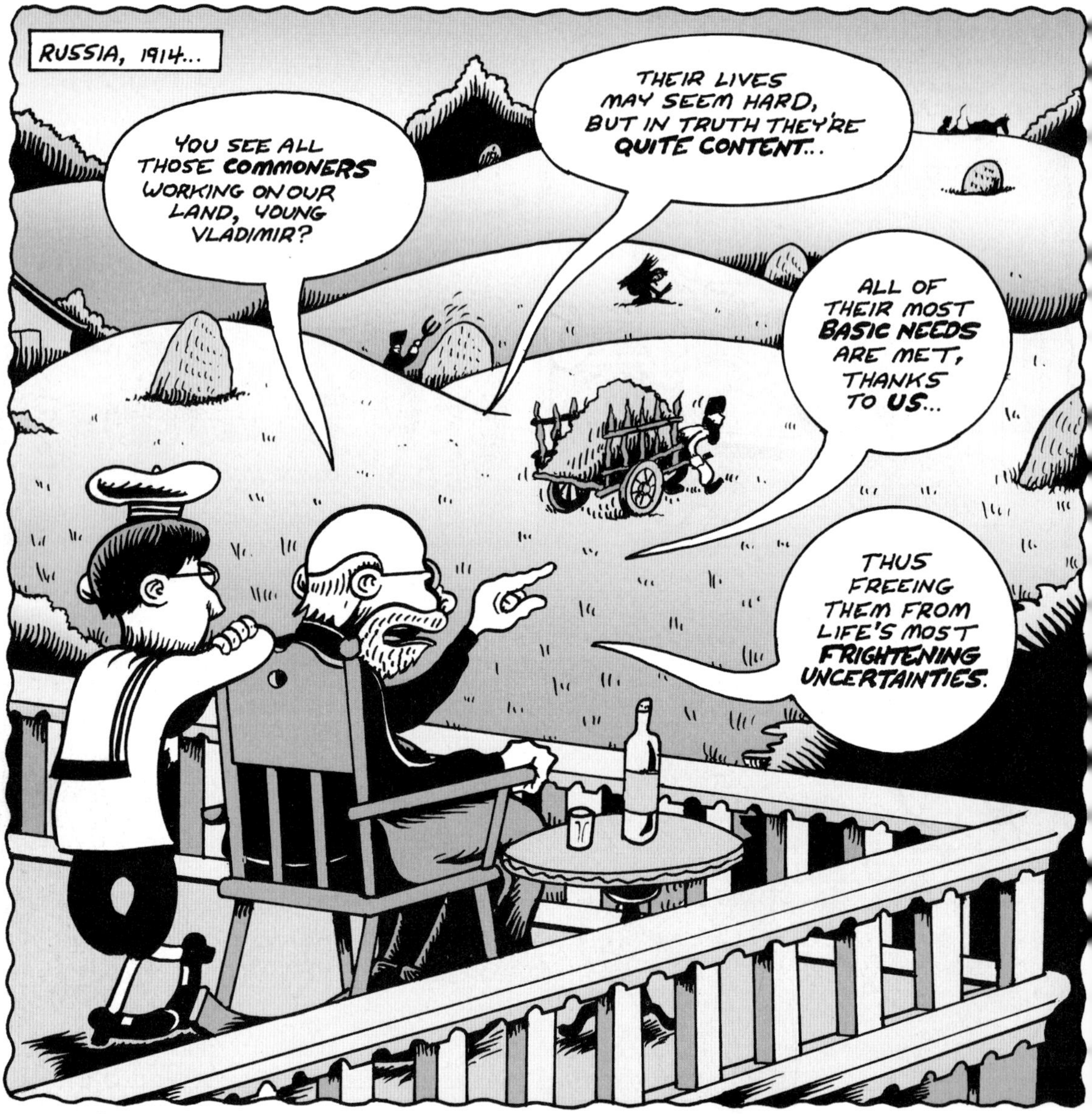
RUSSIA, 1914...
YOU SEE ALL THOSE COMMONERS WORKING ON OUR LAND, YOUNG VLADIMIR?
THEIR LIVES MAY SEEM HARD, BUT IN TRUTH THEY'RE QUITE CONTENT...
ALL OF THEIR MOST BASIC NEEDS ARE MET, THANKS TO US...
THUS FREEING THEM FROM LIFE'S MOST FRIGHTENING UNCERTAINTIES.

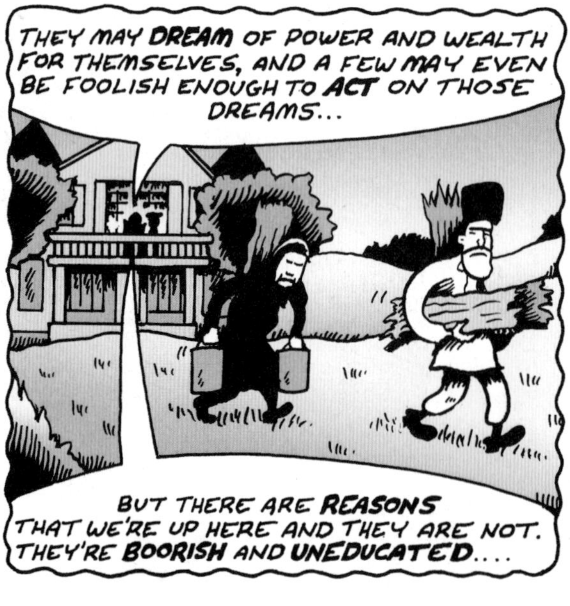
THEY MAY DREAM OF POWER AND WEALTH FOR THEMSELVES, AND A FEW MAY EVEN BE FOOLISH ENOUGH TO ACT ON THOSE DREAMS...
BUT THERE ARE REASONS THAT WE'RE UP HERE AND THEY ARE NOT. THEY'RE BOORISH AND UNEDUCATED....

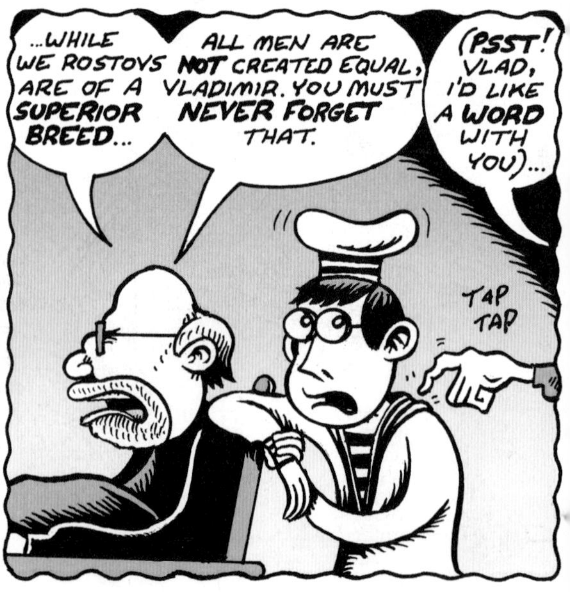
...WHILE WE ROSTOVS ARE OF A SUPERIOR BREED...
ALL MEN ARE NOT CREATED EQUAL, VLADIMIR. YOU MUST NEVER FORGET THAT.
(PSST! VLAD, I'D LIKE A WORD WITH YOU)...
TAP TAP

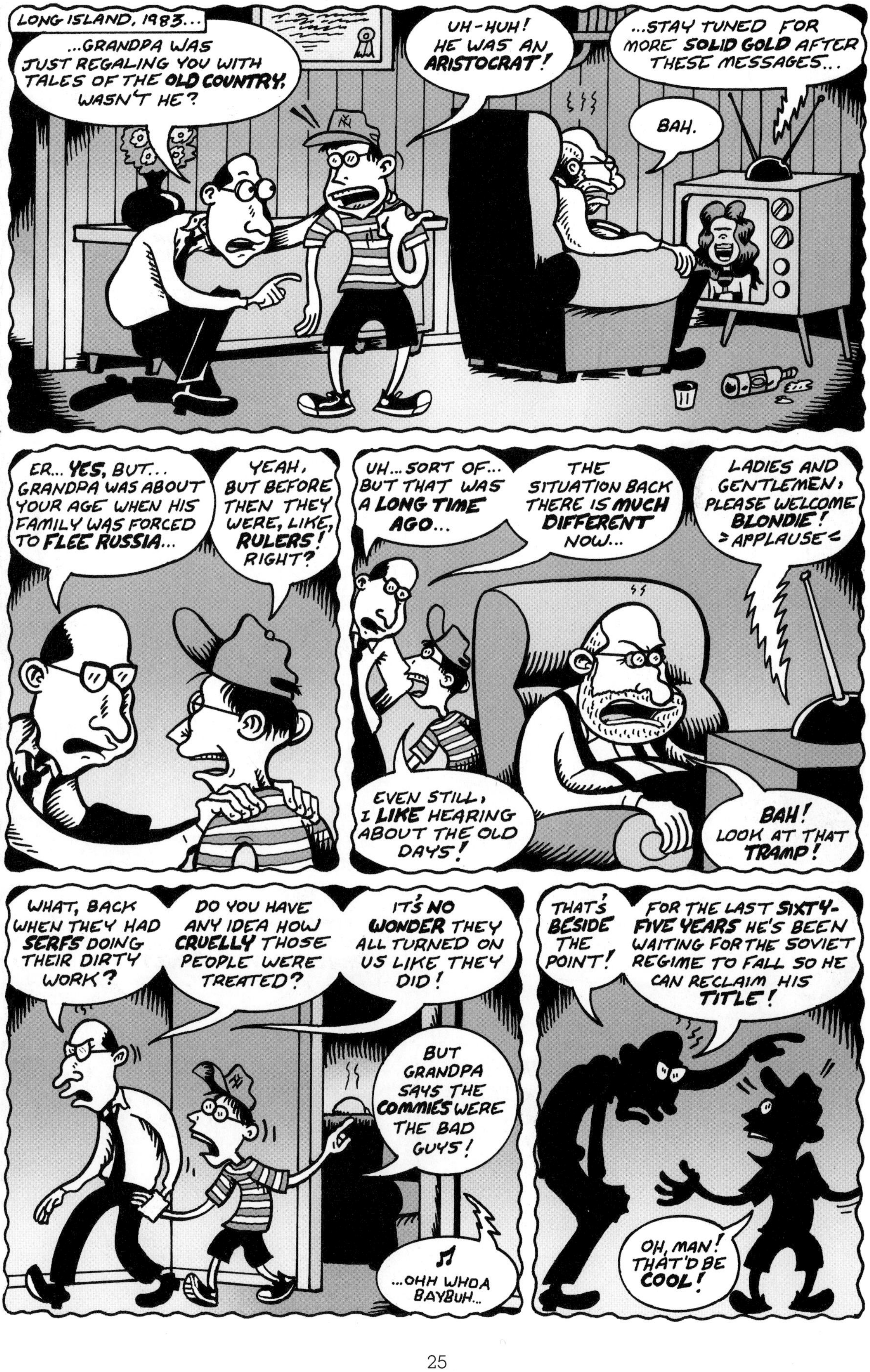

LONG ISLAND, 1983...
...GRANDPA WAS JUST REGALING YOU WITH TALES OF THE OLD COUNTRY, WASN'T HE?
UH-HUH! HE WAS AN ARISTOCRAT!
...STAY TUNED FOR MORE SOLID GOLD AFTER THESE MESSAGES...
BAH.
ER... YES, BUT... GRANDPA WAS ABOUT YOUR AGE WHEN HIS FAMILY WAS FORCED TO FLEE RUSSIA...
YEAH, BUT BEFORE THEN THEY WERE, LIKE, RULERS! RIGHT?
UH... SORT OF... BUT THAT WAS A LONG TIME AGO...
THE SITUATION BACK THERE IS MUCH DIFFERENT NOW...
LADIES AND GENTLEMEN, PLEASE WELCOME BLONDIE! >APPLAUSE<
EVEN STILL, I LIKE HEARING ABOUT THE OLD DAYS!
BAH! LOOK AT THAT TRAMP!
WHAT, BACK WHEN THEY HAD SERFS DOING THEIR DIRTY WORK?
DO YOU HAVE ANY IDEA HOW CRUELLY THOSE PEOPLE WERE TREATED?
IT'S NO WONDER THEY ALL TURNED ON US LIKE THEY DID!
BUT GRANDPA SAYS THE COMMIES WERE THE BAD GUYS!
♪ ...OHH WHOA BAYBUH...
THAT'S BESIDE THE POINT!
FOR THE LAST SIXTY-FIVE YEARS HE'S BEEN WAITING FOR THE SOVIET REGIME TO FALL SO HE CAN RECLAIM HIS TITLE!
OH, MAN! THAT'D BE COOL!

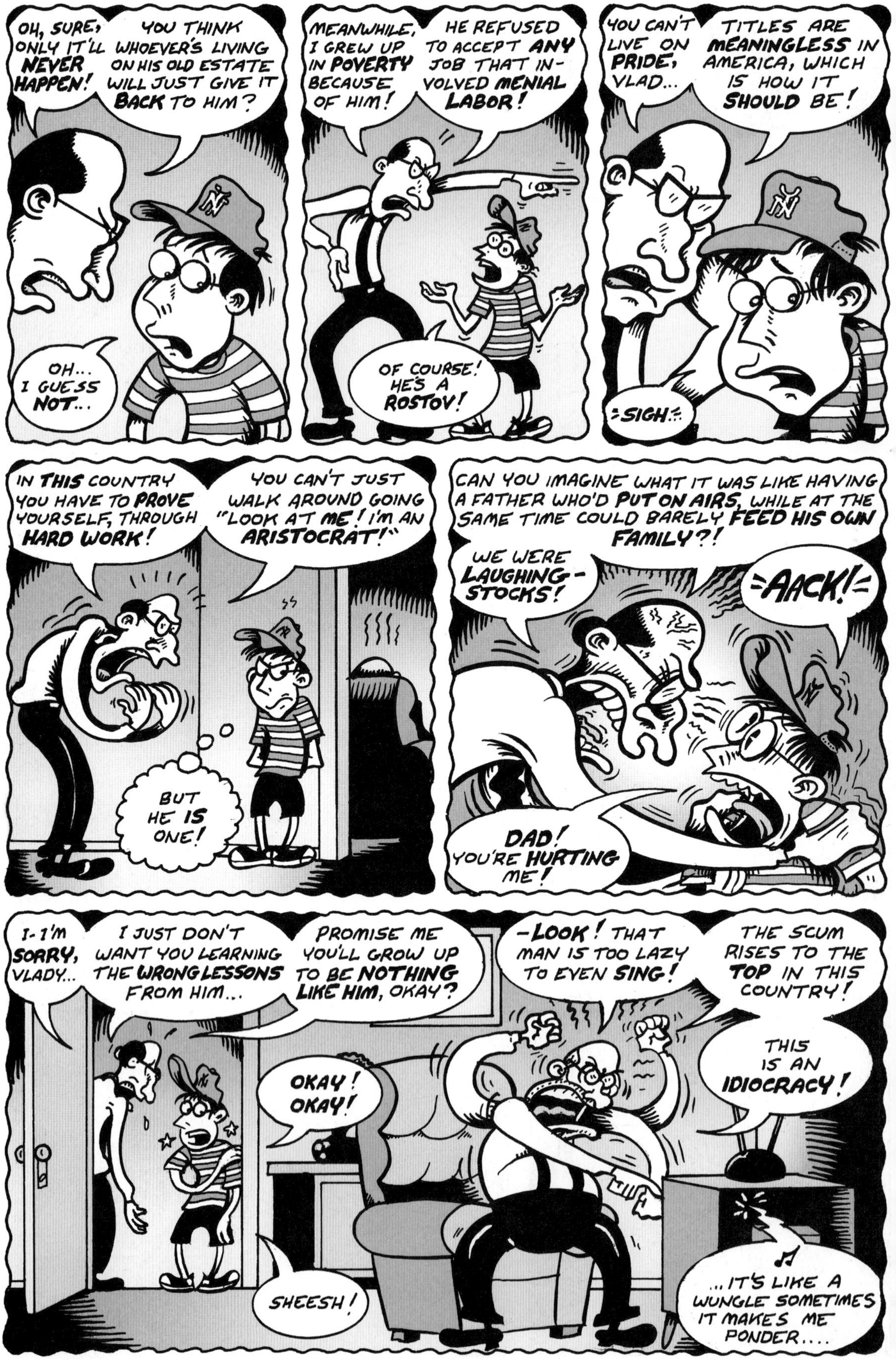
OH, SURE, ONLY IT'LL NEVER HAPPEN!
YOU THINK WHOEVER'S LIVING ON HIS OLD ESTATE WILL JUST GIVE IT BACK TO HIM?
OH... I GUESS NOT...
MEANWHILE, I GREW UP IN POVERTY BECAUSE OF HIM!
HE REFUSED TO ACCEPT ANY JOB THAT INVOLVED MENIAL LABOR!
OF COURSE! HE'S A ROSTOV!
YOU CAN'T LIVE ON PRIDE, VLAD...
TITLES ARE MEANINGLESS IN AMERICA, WHICH IS HOW IT SHOULD BE!
SIGH
IN THIS COUNTRY YOU HAVE TO PROVE YOURSELF, THROUGH HARD WORK!
YOU CAN'T JUST WALK AROUND GOING "LOOK AT ME! I'M AN ARISTOCRAT!"
BUT HE IS ONE!
CAN YOU IMAGINE WHAT IT WAS LIKE HAVING A FATHER WHO'D PUT ON AIRS, WHILE AT THE SAME TIME COULD BARELY FEED HIS OWN FAMILY?!
WE WERE LAUGHING-STOCKS!
AACK!
DAD! YOU'RE HURTING ME!
I-I'M SORRY, VLADY...
I JUST DON'T WANT YOU LEARNING THE WRONG LESSONS FROM HIM...
PROMISE ME YOU'LL GROW UP TO BE NOTHING LIKE HIM, OKAY?
OKAY! OKAY!
SHEESH!
-LOOK! THAT MAN IS TOO LAZY TO EVEN SING!
THE SCUM RISES TO THE TOP IN THIS COUNTRY!
THIS IS AN IDIOCRACY!
...IT'S LIKE A WUNGLE SOMETIMES IT MAKES ME PONDER....

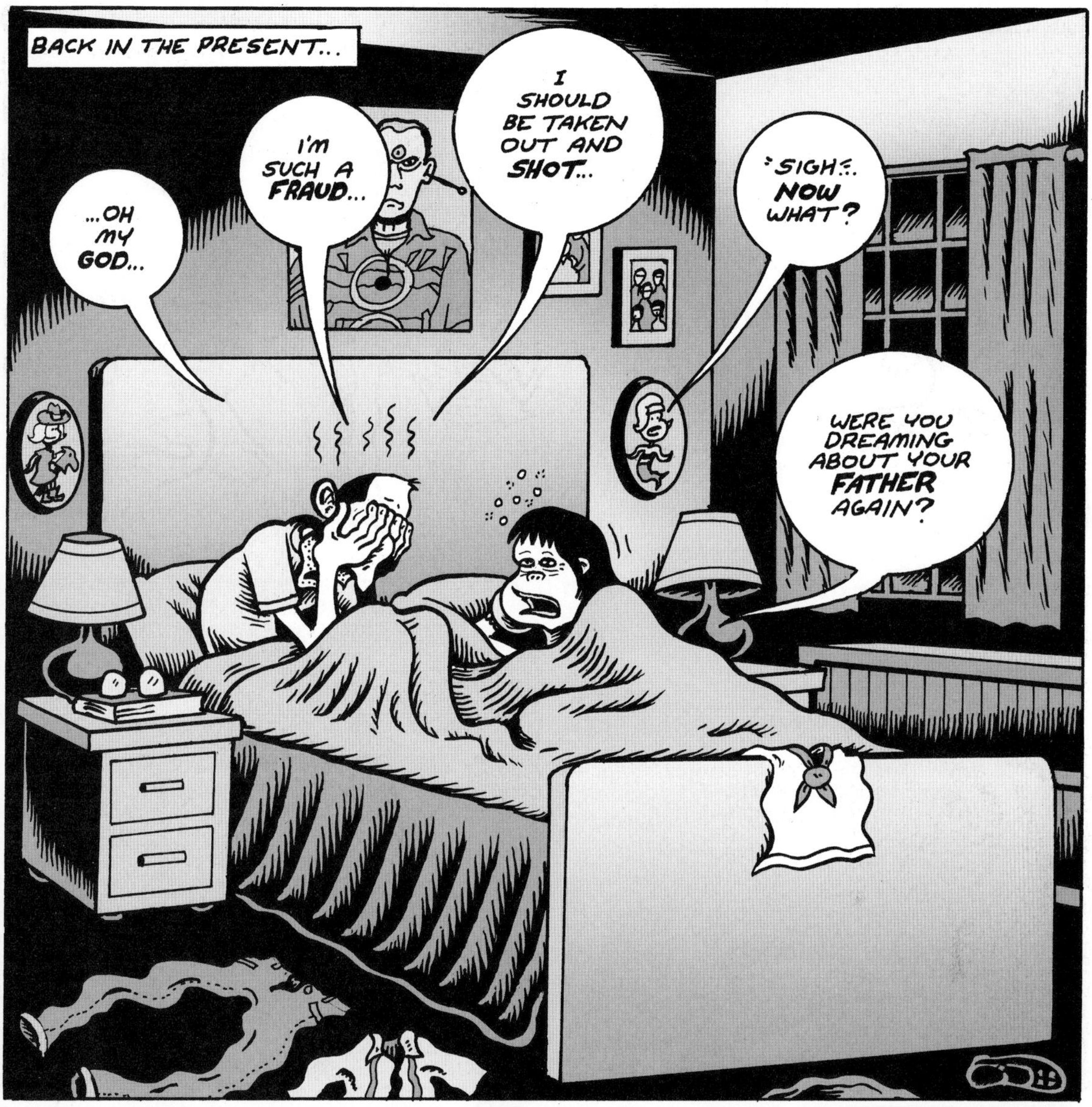
BACK IN THE PRESENT...
...OH MY GOD...
I'M SUCH A FRAUD...
I SHOULD BE TAKEN OUT AND SHOT...
SIGH... NOW WHAT?
WERE YOU DREAMING ABOUT YOUR FATHER AGAIN?

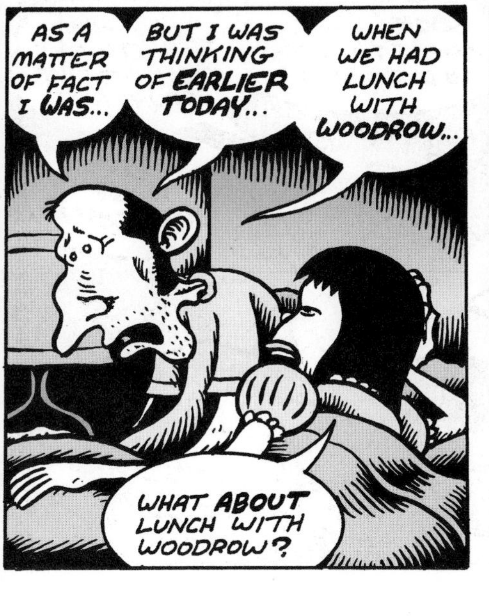
AS A MATTER OF FACT I WAS...
BUT I WAS THINKING OF EARLIER TODAY...
WHEN WE HAD LUNCH WITH WOODROW...
WHAT ABOUT LUNCH WITH WOODROW?

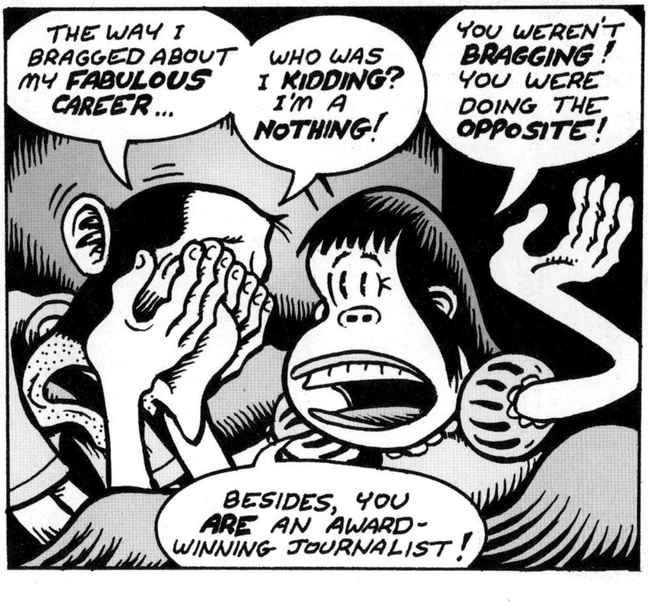
THE WAY I BRAGGED ABOUT MY FABULOUS CAREER...
WHO WAS I KIDDING? I'M A NOTHING!
YOU WEREN'T BRAGGING! YOU WERE DOING THE OPPOSITE!
BESIDES, YOU ARE AN AWARD-WINNING JOURNALIST!

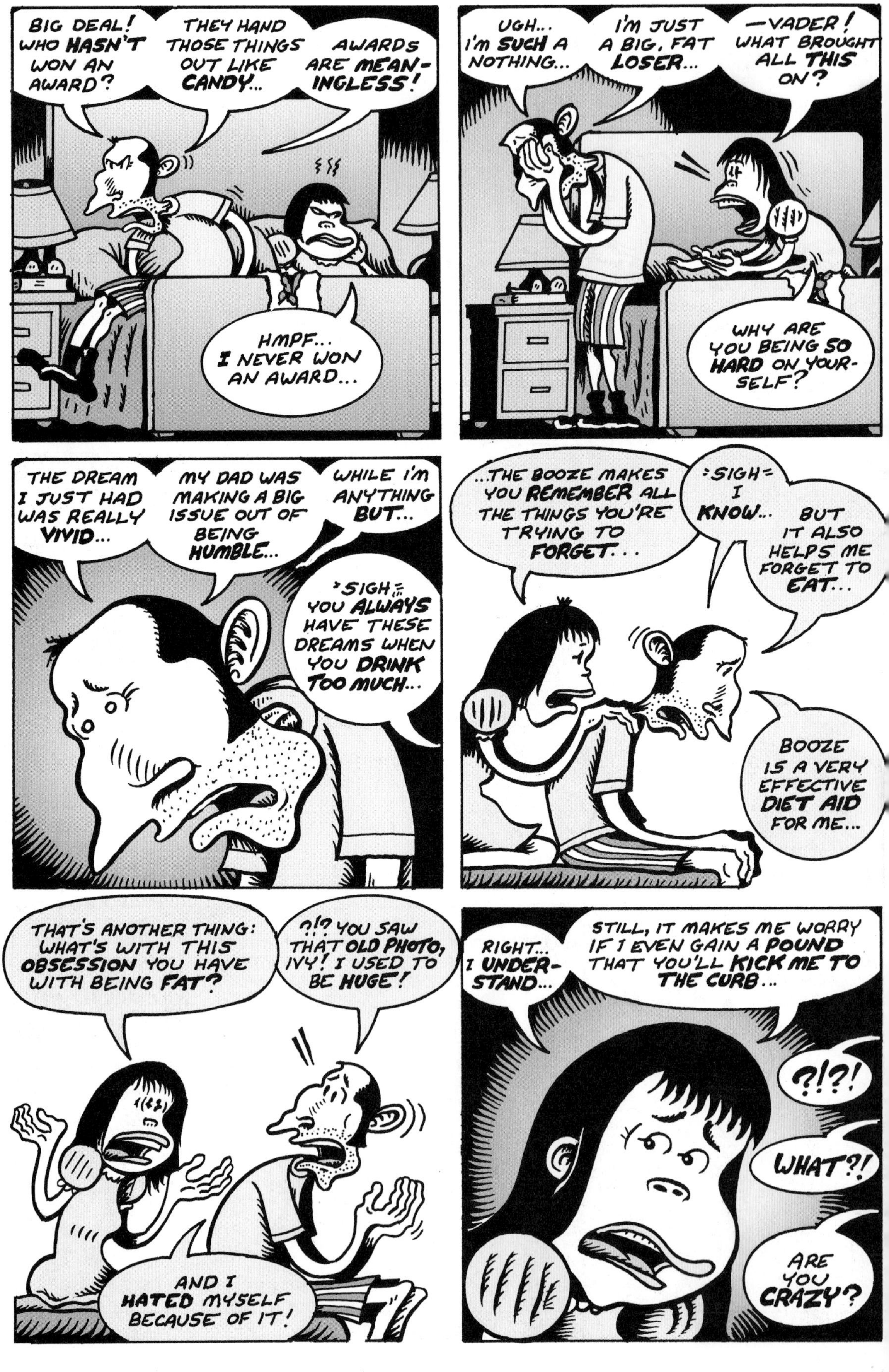
BIG DEAL! WHO HASN'T WON AN AWARD?
THEY HAND THOSE THINGS OUT LIKE CANDY...
AWARDS ARE MEANINGLESS!
HMPF... I NEVER WON AN AWARD...
UGH... I'M SUCH A NOTHING...
I'M JUST A BIG, FAT LOSER...
—VADER! WHAT BROUGHT ALL THIS ON?
WHY ARE YOU BEING SO HARD ON YOURSELF?
THE DREAM I JUST HAD WAS REALLY VIVID...
MY DAD WAS MAKING A BIG ISSUE OUT OF BEING HUMBLE...
WHILE I'M ANYTHING BUT...
SIGH YOU ALWAYS HAVE THESE DREAMS WHEN YOU DRINK TOO MUCH...
...THE BOOZE MAKES YOU REMEMBER ALL THE THINGS YOU'RE TRYING TO FORGET...
SIGH I KNOW...
BUT IT ALSO HELPS ME FORGET TO EAT...
BOOZE IS A VERY EFFECTIVE DIET AID FOR ME...
THAT'S ANOTHER THING: WHAT'S WITH THIS OBSESSION YOU HAVE WITH BEING FAT?
?!? YOU SAW THAT OLD PHOTO, IVY! I USED TO BE HUGE!
AND I HATED MYSELF BECAUSE OF IT!
RIGHT... I UNDERSTAND...
STILL, IT MAKES ME WORRY IF I EVEN GAIN A POUND THAT YOU'LL KICK ME TO THE CURB...
?!?!
WHAT?!
ARE YOU CRAZY?

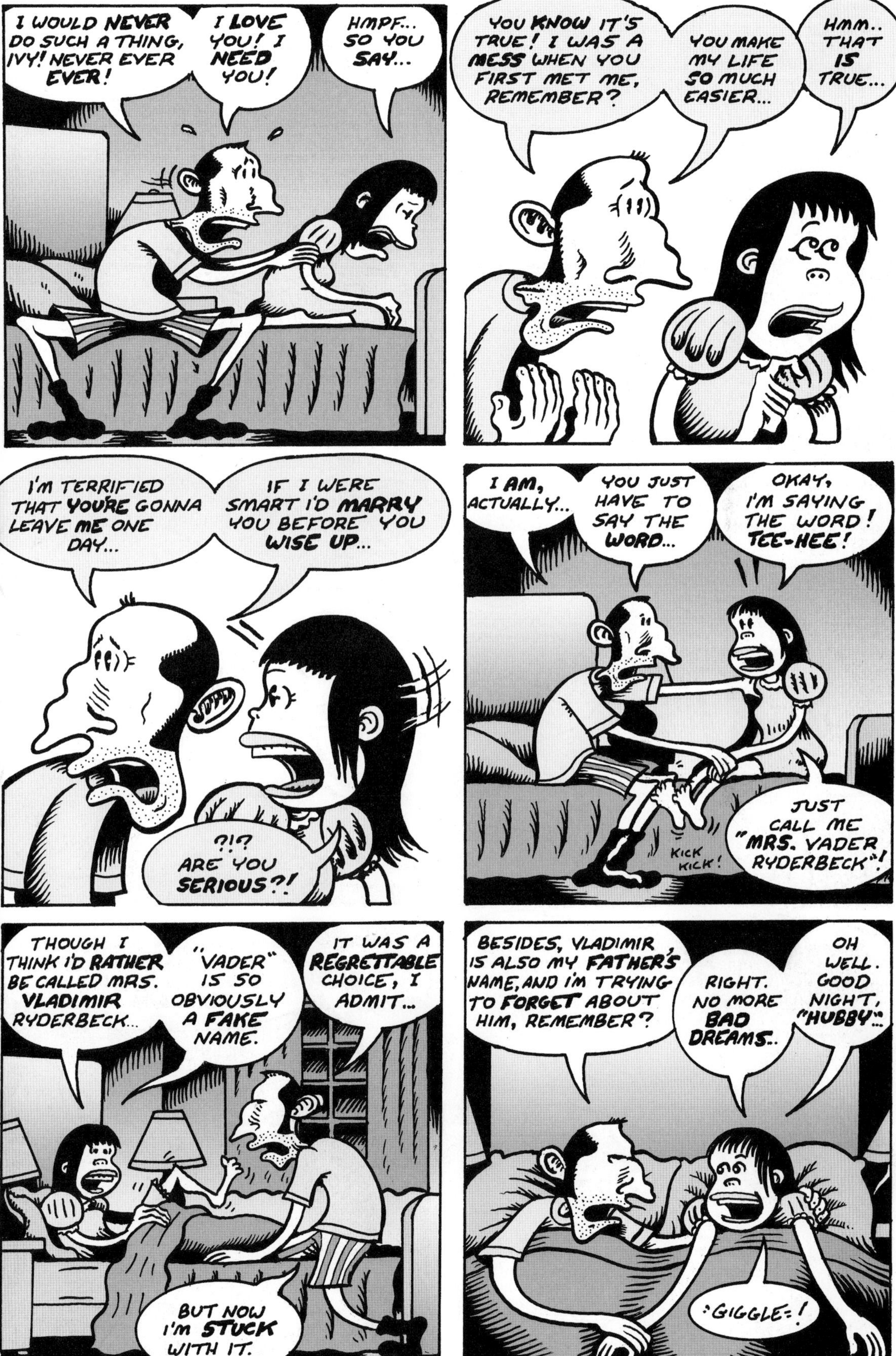
I WOULD NEVER DO SUCH A THING, IVY! NEVER EVER EVER!
I LOVE YOU! I NEED YOU!
HMPF... SO YOU SAY...
YOU KNOW IT'S TRUE! I WAS A MESS WHEN YOU FIRST MET ME, REMEMBER?
YOU MAKE MY LIFE SO MUCH EASIER...
HMM.. THAT IS TRUE...
I'M TERRIFIED THAT YOU'RE GONNA LEAVE ME ONE DAY...
IF I WERE SMART I'D MARRY YOU BEFORE YOU WISE UP...
?!? ARE YOU SERIOUS?!
I AM, ACTUALLY...
YOU JUST HAVE TO SAY THE WORD...
OKAY, I'M SAYING THE WORD! TEE-HEE!
JUST CALL ME "MRS. VADER RYDERBECK"!
KICK KICK!
THOUGH I THINK I'D RATHER BE CALLED MRS. VLADIMIR RYDERBECK...
"VADER" IS SO OBVIOUSLY A FAKE NAME.
IT WAS A REGRETTABLE CHOICE, I ADMIT...
BUT NOW I'M STUCK WITH IT.
BESIDES, VLADIMIR IS ALSO MY FATHER'S NAME, AND I'M TRYING TO FORGET ABOUT HIM, REMEMBER?
RIGHT. NO MORE BAD DREAMS..
OH WELL. GOOD NIGHT, "HUBBY"...
:GIGGLE:!

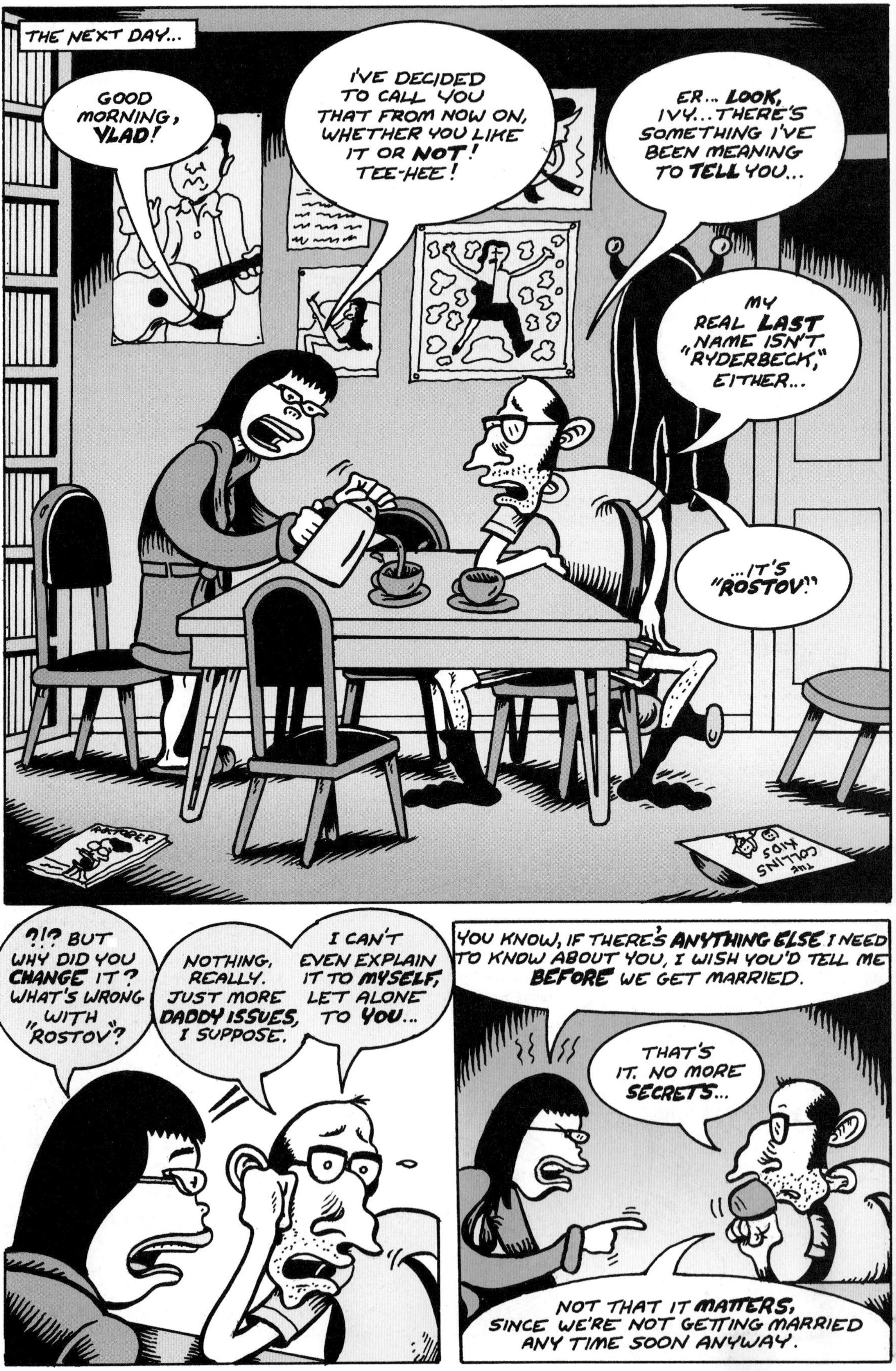
THE NEXT DAY...
GOOD MORNING, VLAD!
I'VE DECIDED TO CALL YOU THAT FROM NOW ON, WHETHER YOU LIKE IT OR NOT! TEE-HEE!
ER... LOOK, IVY... THERE'S SOMETHING I'VE BEEN MEANING TO TELL YOU...
MY REAL LAST NAME ISN'T "RYDERBECK," EITHER...
..."IT'S "ROSTOV."
THE COLLINS KIDS
?!? BUT WHY DID YOU CHANGE IT? WHAT'S WRONG WITH "ROSTOV"?
NOTHING, REALLY. JUST MORE DADDY ISSUES, I SUPPOSE.
I CAN'T EVEN EXPLAIN IT TO MYSELF, LET ALONE TO YOU...
YOU KNOW, IF THERE'S ANYTHING ELSE I NEED TO KNOW ABOUT YOU, I WISH YOU'D TELL ME BEFORE WE GET MARRIED.
THAT'S IT. NO MORE SECRETS...
NOT THAT IT MATTERS, SINCE WE'RE NOT GETTING MARRIED ANY TIME SOON ANYWAY.

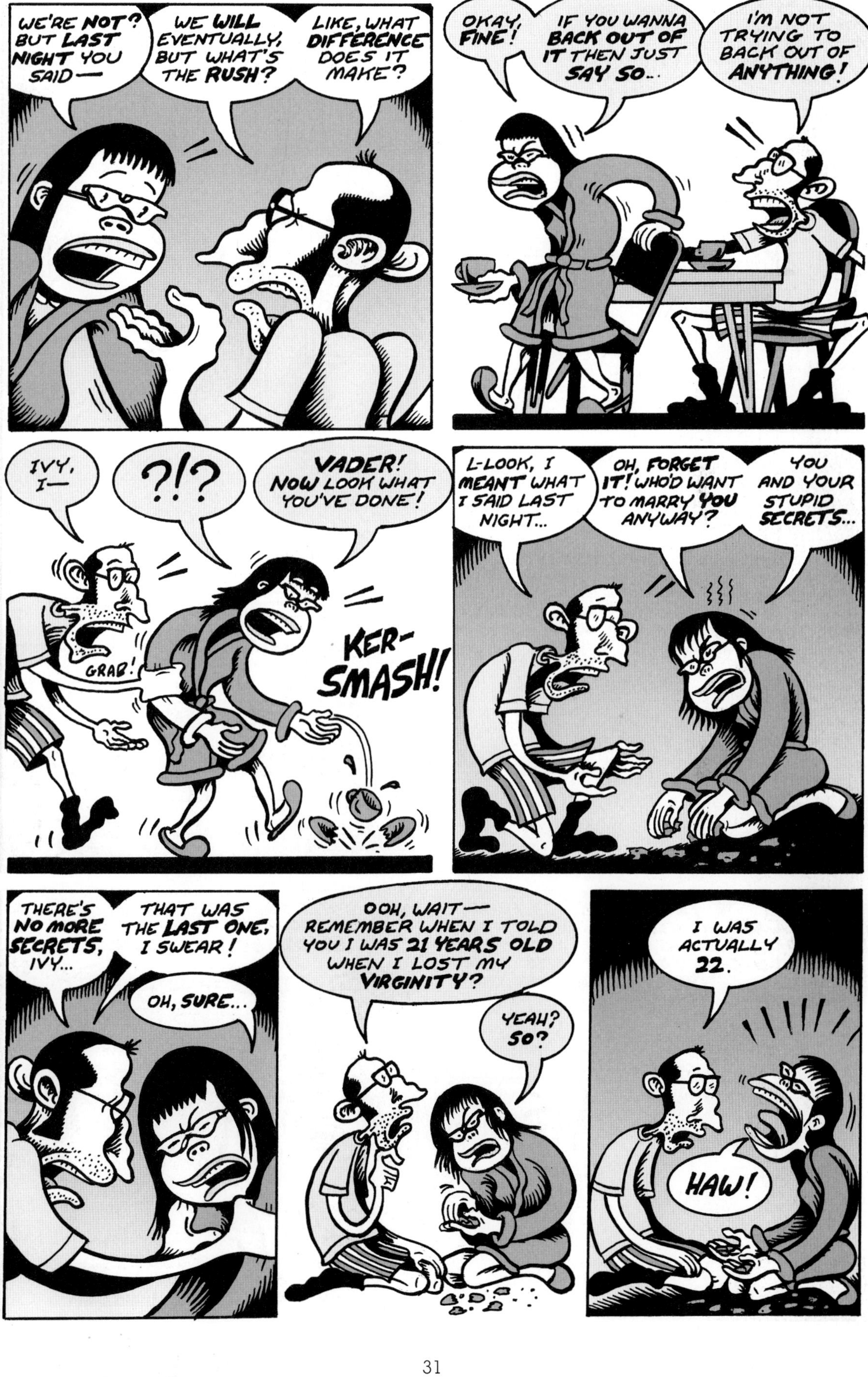
WE'RE NOT? BUT LAST NIGHT YOU SAID—
WE WILL EVENTUALLY, BUT WHAT'S THE RUSH?
LIKE, WHAT DIFFERENCE DOES IT MAKE?
OKAY, FINE!
IF YOU WANNA BACK OUT OF IT THEN JUST SAY SO...
I'M NOT TRYING TO BACK OUT OF ANYTHING!
IVY, I—
?!?
VADER! NOW LOOK WHAT YOU'VE DONE!
GRAB!
KER-SMASH!
L-LOOK, I MEANT WHAT I SAID LAST NIGHT...
OH, FORGET IT! WHO'D WANT TO MARRY YOU ANYWAY?
YOU AND YOUR STUPID SECRETS...
THERE'S NO MORE SECRETS, IVY...
THAT WAS THE LAST ONE, I SWEAR!
OH, SURE...
OOH, WAIT— REMEMBER WHEN I TOLD YOU I WAS 21 YEARS OLD WHEN I LOST MY VIRGINITY?
YEAH? SO?
I WAS ACTUALLY 22.
HAW!

HOW ABOUT *YOU?* SURELY THERE'S SOMETHING YOU'RE HOLDING BACK FROM ME...

PFFT. YEAH, *RIGHT...*

I *WISH* I HAD SOME *DEEP, DARK SECRETS* TO SHARE...

BUT SO FAR MY LIFE HAS BEEN PRETTY *UNEVENTFUL...*

BUT AREN'T YOU CONSIDERED THE *"REBELLIOUS"* ONE IN YOUR FAMILY?

SURE, *RELATIVELY* SPEAKING...

THEY THINK I'M *"WILD"* BECAUSE I LIVE WITH A *WHITE BOY.*

HEH-HEH...

WELL, IT *COULD* BE WORSE...

WHEN I FIRST MET YOUR *MA* ALL SHE SAID WAS *"AT LEAST YOU'RE NOT KOREAN."*

EVEN MY FAMILY'S *NAME* IS BORING: *"CHIN"...*

AS IN *"HE'S GOT MORE CHINS THAN A CHINESE PHONEBOOK."*

HAW! MAYBE *YOU* SHOULD'VE CHANGED YOUR NAME, TOO!

THAT'S *WHY* I WAS ATTRACTED TO A NUT LIKE YOU...

I NEEDED A LITTLE *YIN* TO GO WITH MY FAMILY'S *YANG.*

I SEE... SO I *AM* A FORM OF REBELLION FOR YOU.'

STILL, I *RELATE* TO YOU MORE THAN YOU REALIZE.

OH? HOW SO?

HERE, LET *ME* DO THAT...

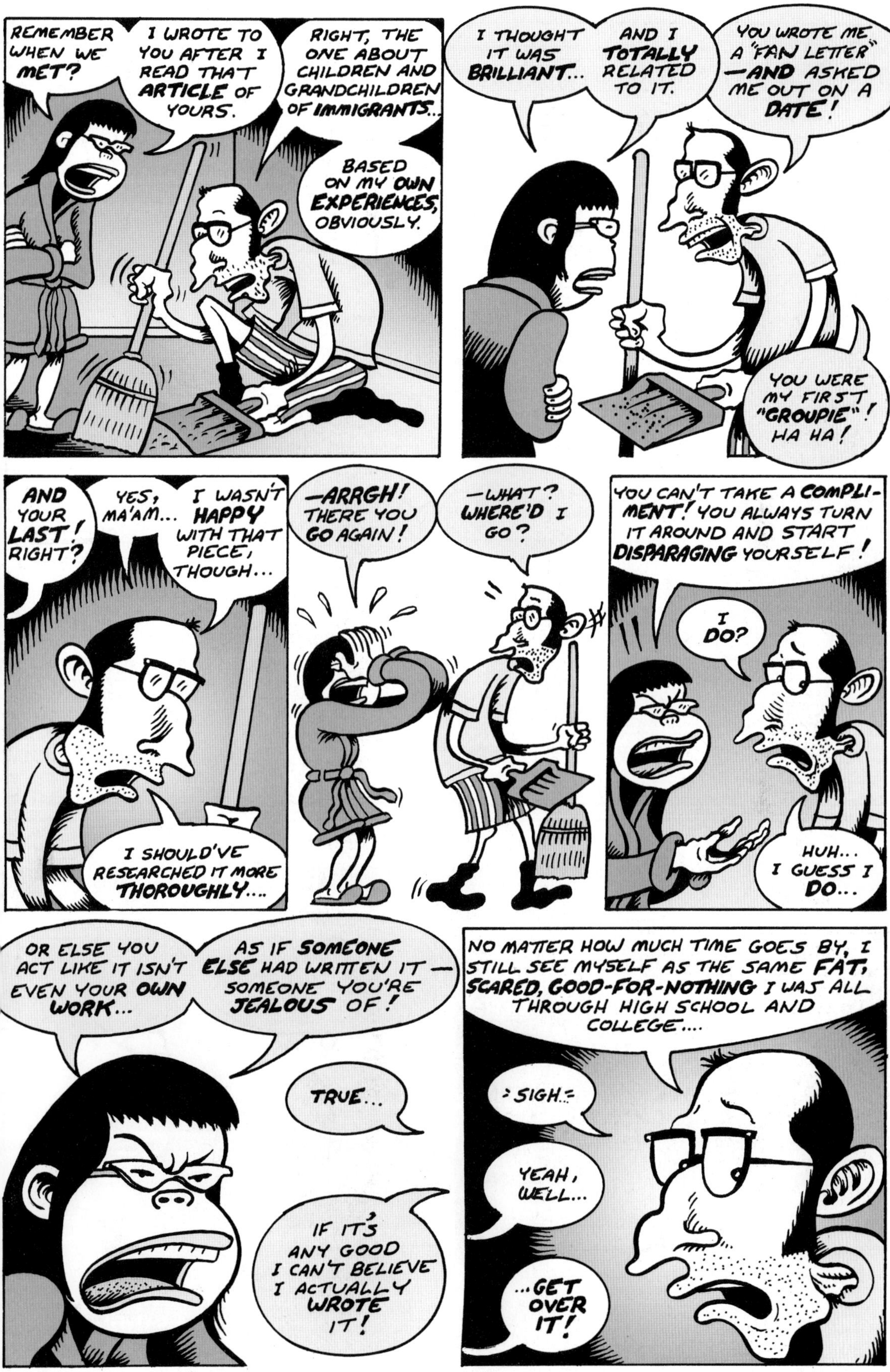
REMEMBER WHEN WE MET?
I WROTE TO YOU AFTER I READ THAT ARTICLE OF YOURS.
RIGHT, THE ONE ABOUT CHILDREN AND GRANDCHILDREN OF IMMIGRANTS...
BASED ON MY OWN EXPERIENCES, OBVIOUSLY.
I THOUGHT IT WAS BRILLIANT...
AND I TOTALLY RELATED TO IT.
YOU WROTE ME A "FAN LETTER" —AND ASKED ME OUT ON A DATE!
YOU WERE MY FIRST "GROUPIE"! HA HA!
AND YOUR LAST! RIGHT?
YES, MA'AM...
I WASN'T HAPPY WITH THAT PIECE, THOUGH...
I SHOULD'VE RESEARCHED IT MORE THOROUGHLY....
—ARRGH! THERE YOU GO AGAIN!
—WHAT? WHERE'D I GO?
YOU CAN'T TAKE A COMPLIMENT! YOU ALWAYS TURN IT AROUND AND START DISPARAGING YOURSELF!
I DO?
HUH... I GUESS I DO...
OR ELSE YOU ACT LIKE IT ISN'T EVEN YOUR OWN WORK...
AS IF SOMEONE ELSE HAD WRITTEN IT — SOMEONE YOU'RE JEALOUS OF!
TRUE...
IF IT'S ANY GOOD I CAN'T BELIEVE I ACTUALLY WROTE IT!
NO MATTER HOW MUCH TIME GOES BY, I STILL SEE MYSELF AS THE SAME FAT, SCARED, GOOD-FOR-NOTHING I WAS ALL THROUGH HIGH SCHOOL AND COLLEGE....
=SIGH=
YEAH, WELL...
...GET OVER IT!

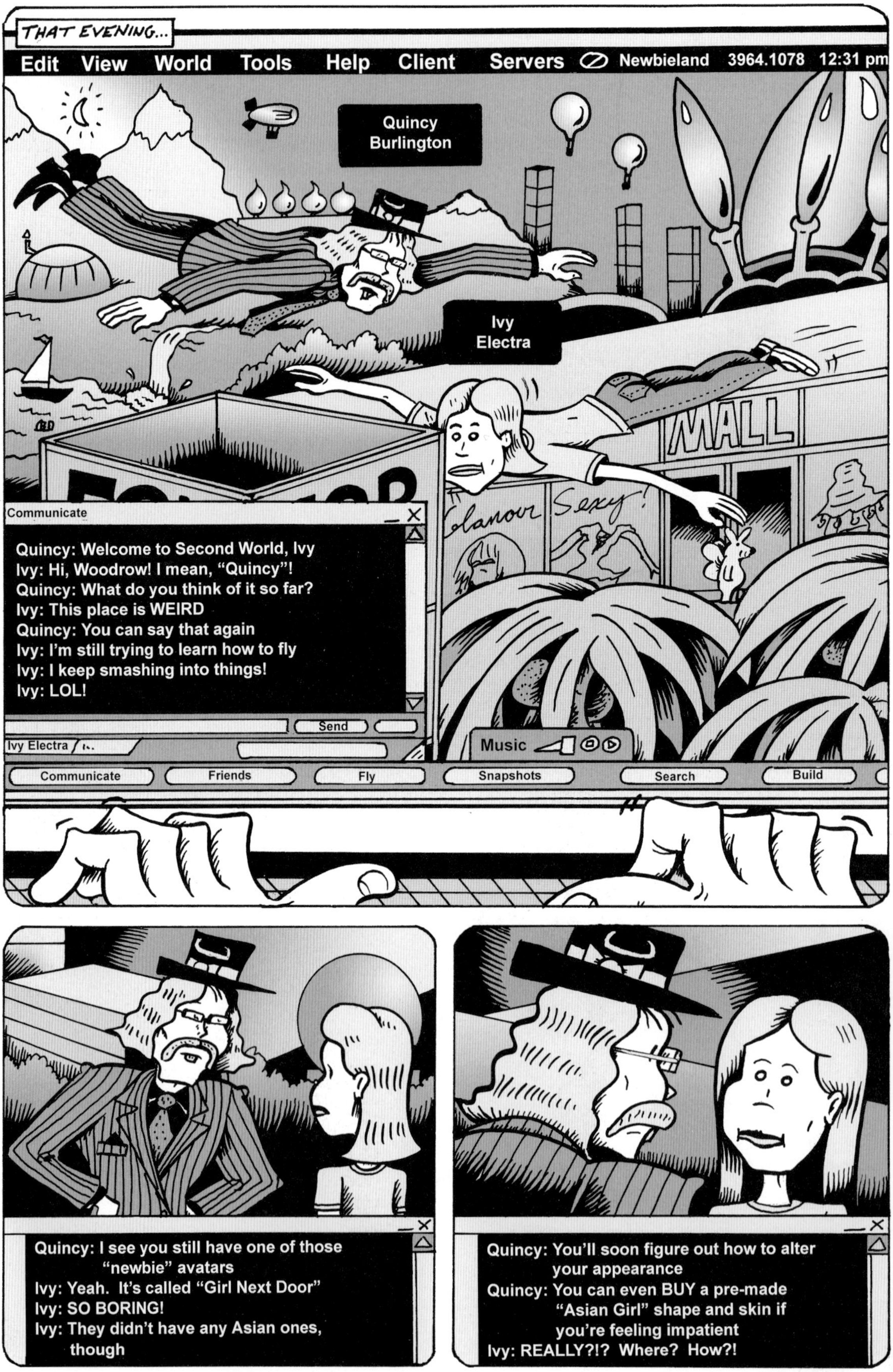
THAT EVENING...
Edit View World Tools Help Client Servers Newbieland 3964.1078 12:31 pm
Quincy Burlington
Ivy Electra
MALL
Sexy!
Communicate
Quincy: Welcome to Second World, Ivy
Ivy: Hi, Woodrow! I mean, "Quincy"!
Quincy: What do you think of it so far?
Ivy: This place is WEIRD
Quincy: You can say that again
Ivy: I'm still trying to learn how to fly
Ivy: I keep smashing into things!
Ivy: LOL!
Send
Ivy Electra
Music
Communicate
Friends
Fly
Snapshots
Search
Build
Quincy: I see you still have one of those "newbie" avatars
Ivy: Yeah. It's called "Girl Next Door"
Ivy: SO BORING!
Ivy: They didn't have any Asian ones, though
Quincy: You'll soon figure out how to alter your appearance
Quincy: You can even BUY a pre-made "Asian Girl" shape and skin if you're feeling impatient
Ivy: REALLY?!? Where? How?!

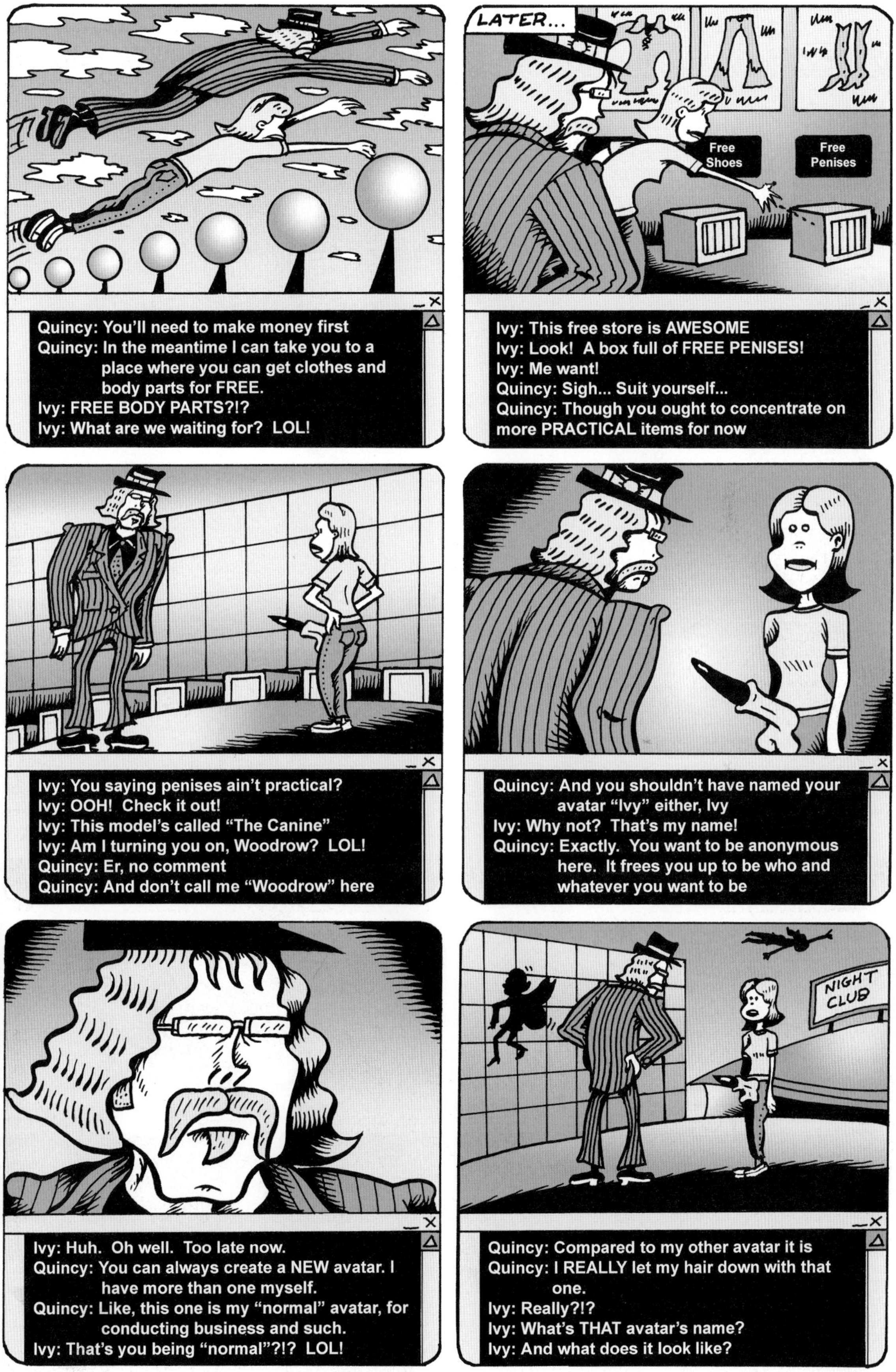
Quincy: You'll need to make money first
Quincy: In the meantime I can take you to a place where you can get clothes and body parts for FREE.
Ivy: FREE BODY PARTS?!?
Ivy: What are we waiting for? LOL!
LATER...
Free Shoes
Free Penises
Ivy: This free store is AWESOME
Ivy: Look! A box full of FREE PENISES!
Ivy: Me want!
Quincy: Sigh... Suit yourself...
Quincy: Though you ought to concentrate on more PRACTICAL items for now
Ivy: You saying penises ain't practical?
Ivy: OOH! Check it out!
Ivy: This model's called "The Canine"
Ivy: Am I turning you on, Woodrow? LOL!
Quincy: Er, no comment
Quincy: And don't call me "Woodrow" here
Quincy: And you shouldn't have named your avatar "Ivy" either, Ivy
Ivy: Why not? That's my name!
Quincy: Exactly. You want to be anonymous here. It frees you up to be who and whatever you want to be
Ivy: Huh. Oh well. Too late now.
Quincy: You can always create a NEW avatar. I have more than one myself.
Quincy: Like, this one is my "normal" avatar, for conducting business and such.
Ivy: That's you being "normal"?!? LOL!
NIGHT CLUB
Quincy: Compared to my other avatar it is
Quincy: I REALLY let my hair down with that one.
Ivy: Really?!?
Ivy: What's THAT avatar's name?
Ivy: And what does it look like?

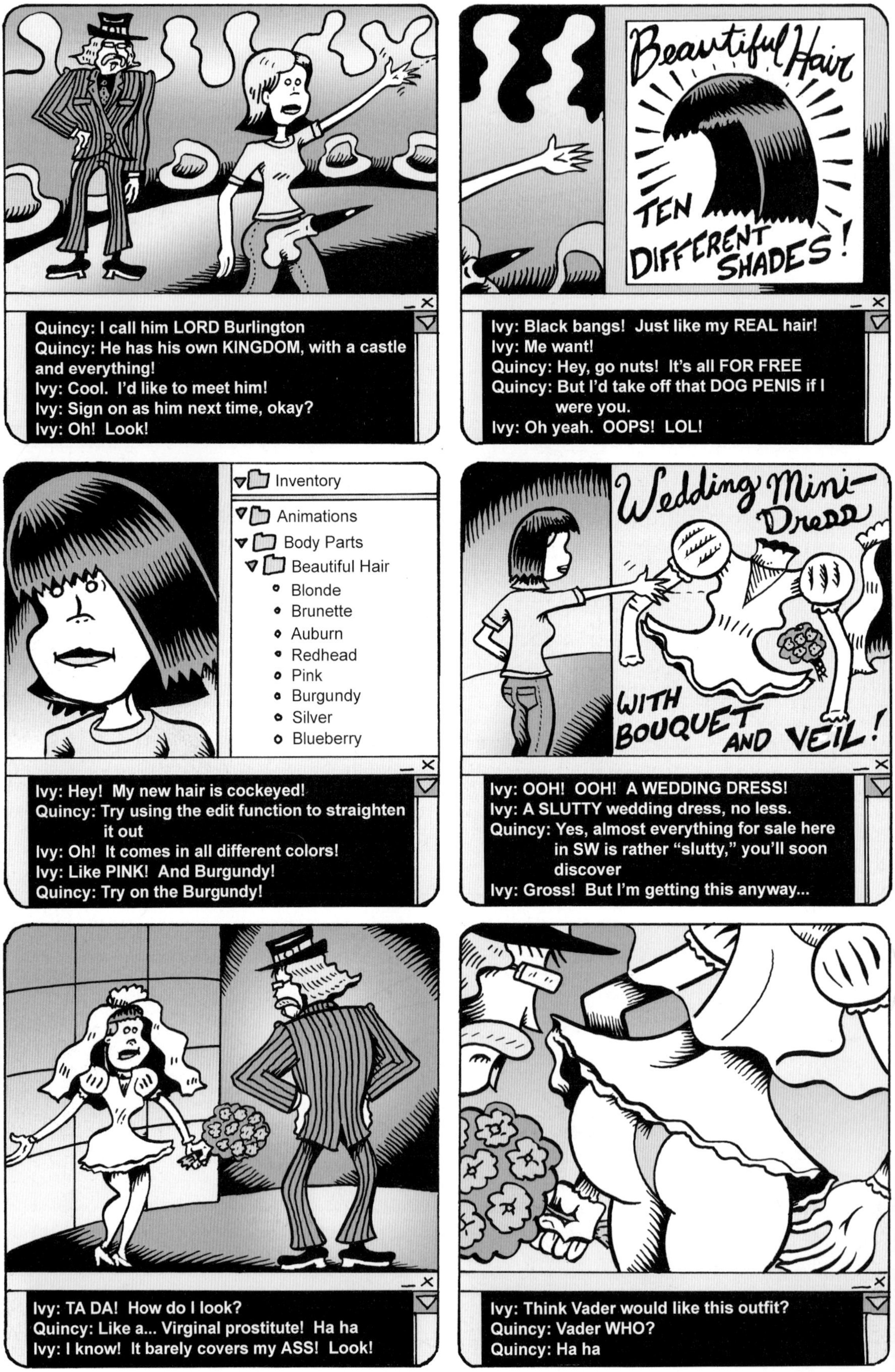
Quincy: I call him LORD Burlington
Quincy: He has his own KINGDOM, with a castle and everything!
Ivy: Cool. I'd like to meet him!
Ivy: Sign on as him next time, okay?
Ivy: Oh! Look!
Beautiful Hair
TEN DIFFERENT SHADES!
Ivy: Black bangs! Just like my REAL hair!
Ivy: Me want!
Quincy: Hey, go nuts! It's all FOR FREE
Quincy: But I'd take off that DOG PENIS if I were you.
Ivy: Oh yeah. OOPS! LOL!
Inventory
Animations
Body Parts
Beautiful Hair
Blonde
Brunette
Auburn
Redhead
Pink
Burgundy
Silver
Blueberry
Ivy: Hey! My new hair is cockeyed!
Quincy: Try using the edit function to straighten it out
Ivy: Oh! It comes in all different colors!
Ivy: Like PINK! And Burgundy!
Quincy: Try on the Burgundy!
Wedding Mini-Dress
WITH BOUQUET AND VEIL!
Ivy: OOH! OOH! A WEDDING DRESS!
Ivy: A SLUTTY wedding dress, no less.
Quincy: Yes, almost everything for sale here in SW is rather "slutty," you'll soon discover
Ivy: Gross! But I'm getting this anyway...
Ivy: TA DA! How do I look?
Quincy: Like a... Virginal prostitute! Ha ha
Ivy: I know! It barely covers my ASS! Look!
Ivy: Think Vader would like this outfit?
Quincy: Vader WHO?
Quincy: Ha ha

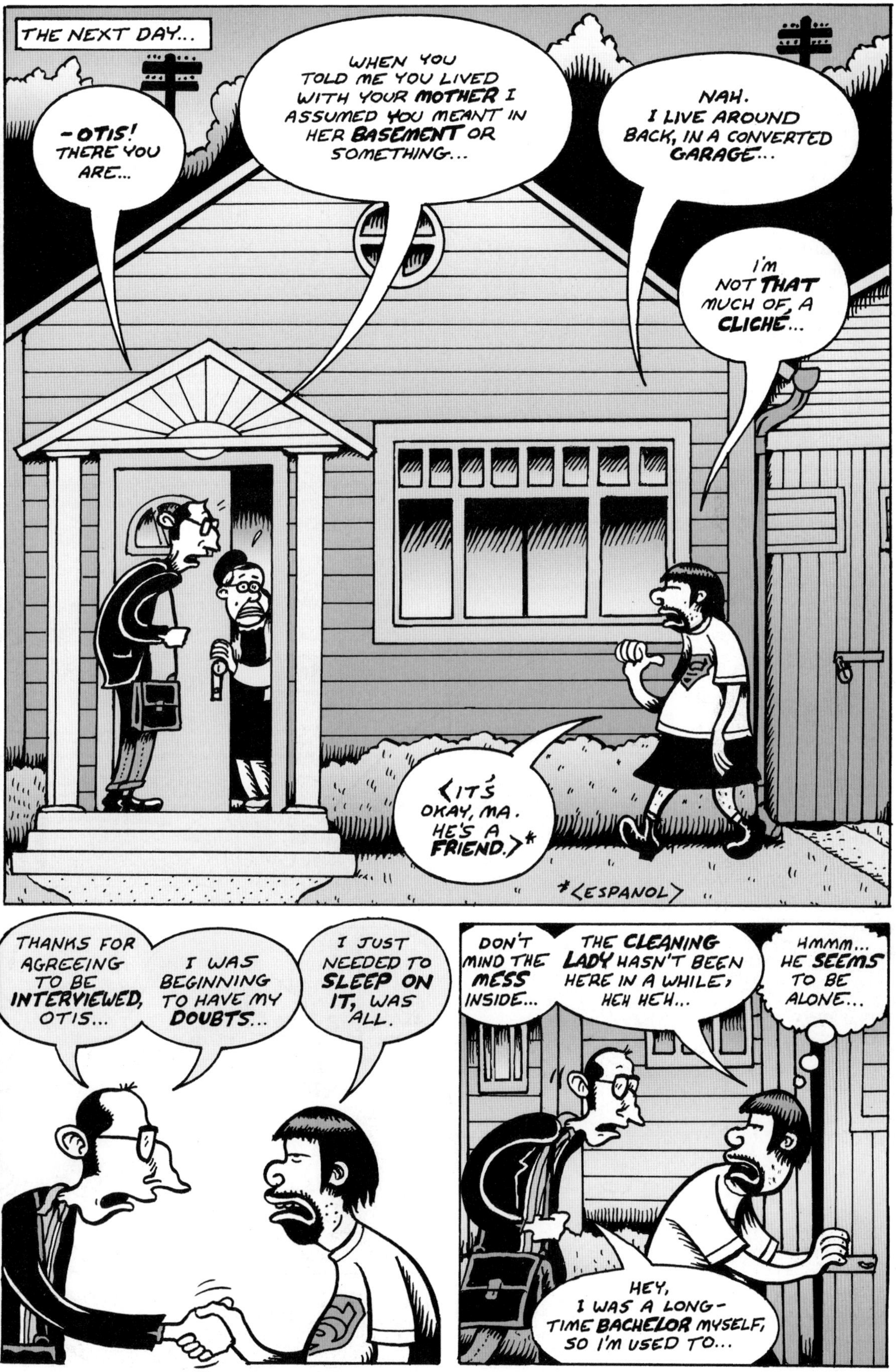
THE NEXT DAY...
-OTIS! THERE YOU ARE...
WHEN YOU TOLD ME YOU LIVED WITH YOUR MOTHER I ASSUMED YOU MEANT IN HER BASEMENT OR SOMETHING...
NAH. I LIVE AROUND BACK, IN A CONVERTED GARAGE...
I'M NOT THAT MUCH OF A CLICHÉ...
<IT'S OKAY, MA. HE'S A FRIEND.>*
*<ESPANOL>
THANKS FOR AGREEING TO BE INTERVIEWED, OTIS...
I WAS BEGINNING TO HAVE MY DOUBTS...
I JUST NEEDED TO SLEEP ON IT, WAS ALL.
DON'T MIND THE MESS INSIDE...
THE CLEANING LADY HASN'T BEEN HERE IN A WHILE, HEH HEH...
HMMM... HE SEEMS TO BE ALONE...
HEY, I WAS A LONG-TIME BACHELOR MYSELF, SO I'M USED TO...

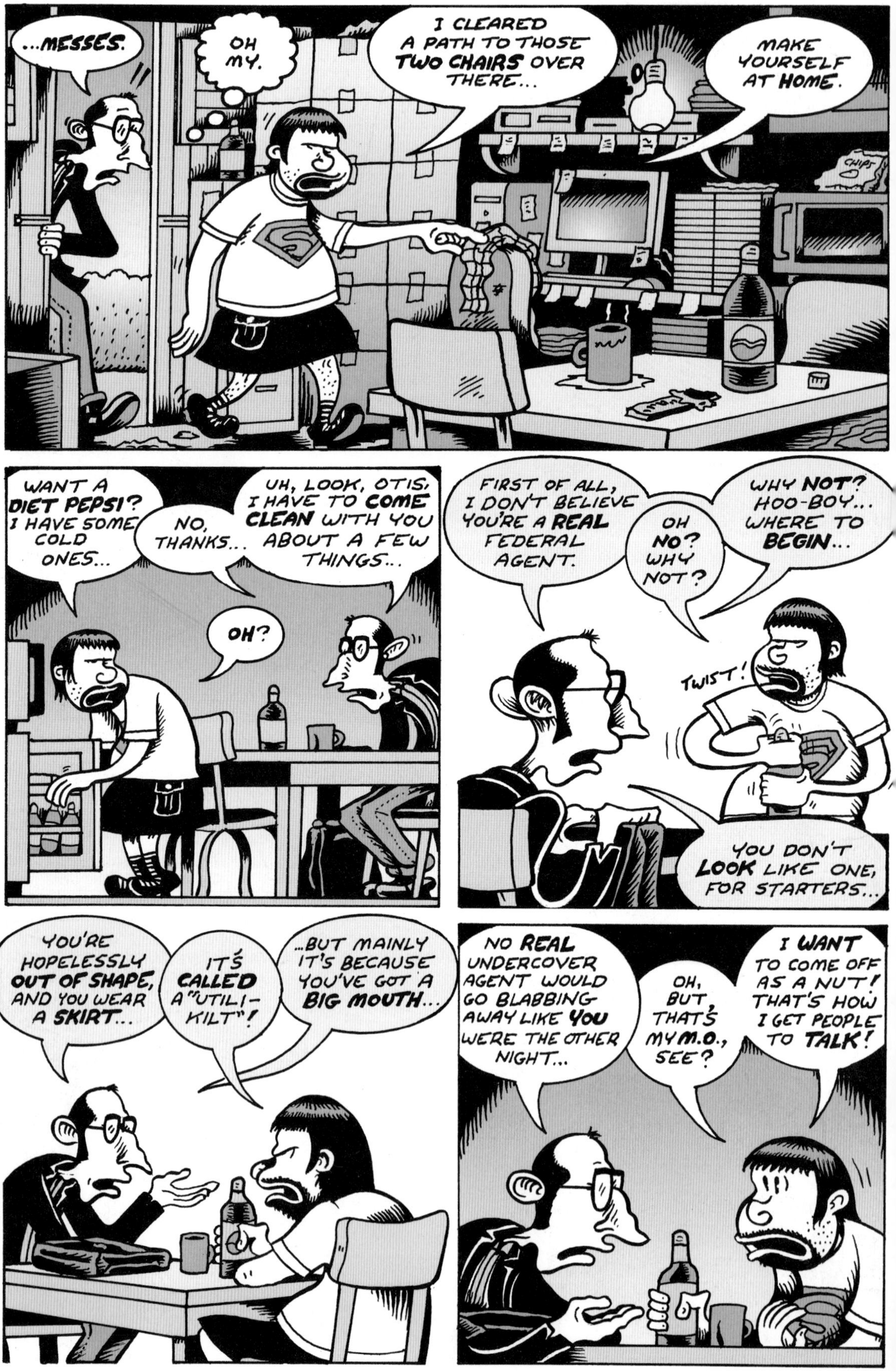
...MESSES.
OH MY.
I CLEARED A PATH TO THOSE TWO CHAIRS OVER THERE...
MAKE YOURSELF AT HOME.
CHIPS
WANT A DIET PEPSI? I HAVE SOME COLD ONES...
NO, THANKS...
UH, LOOK, OTIS, I HAVE TO COME CLEAN WITH YOU ABOUT A FEW THINGS...
OH?
FIRST OF ALL, I DON'T BELIEVE YOU'RE A REAL FEDERAL AGENT.
OH NO? WHY NOT?
WHY NOT? HOO-BOY... WHERE TO BEGIN...
TWIST!
YOU DON'T LOOK LIKE ONE, FOR STARTERS...
YOU'RE HOPELESSLY OUT OF SHAPE, AND YOU WEAR A SKIRT...
IT'S CALLED A "UTILI-KILT"!
...BUT MAINLY IT'S BECAUSE YOU'VE GOT A BIG MOUTH...
NO REAL UNDERCOVER AGENT WOULD GO BLABBING AWAY LIKE YOU WERE THE OTHER NIGHT...
OH, BUT, THAT'S MY M.O., SEE?
I WANT TO COME OFF AS A NUT! THAT'S HOW I GET PEOPLE TO TALK!

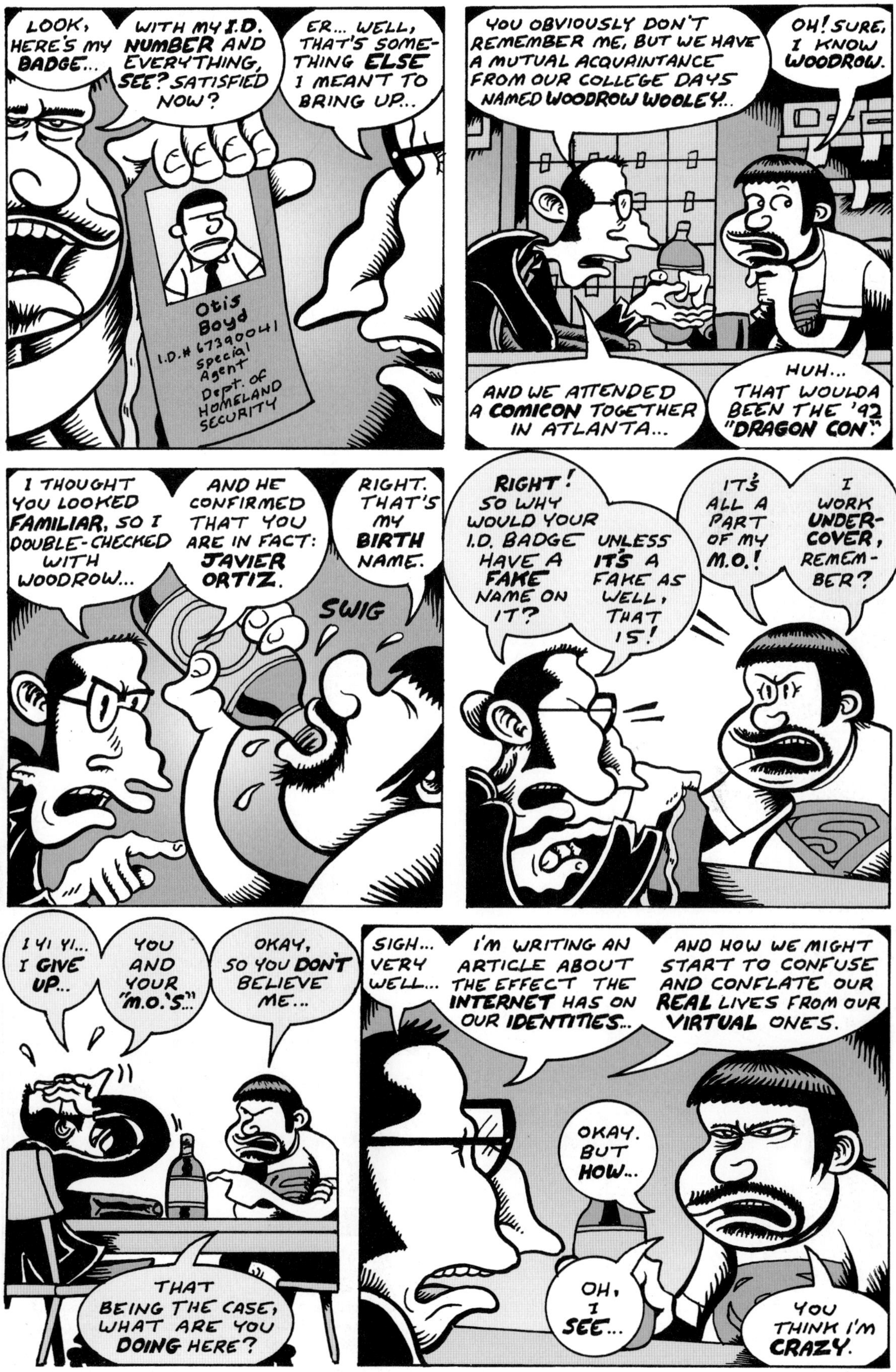
LOOK, HERE'S MY BADGE...
WITH MY I.D. NUMBER AND EVERYTHING, SEE? SATISFIED NOW?
Otis Boyd
I.D.# 67390041
Special Agent
Dept. of HOMELAND SECURITY
ER... WELL, THAT'S SOMETHING ELSE I MEANT TO BRING UP...
YOU OBVIOUSLY DON'T REMEMBER ME, BUT WE HAVE A MUTUAL ACQUAINTANCE FROM OUR COLLEGE DAYS NAMED WOODROW WOOLEY...
OH! SURE, I KNOW WOODROW.
AND WE ATTENDED A COMICON TOGETHER IN ATLANTA...
HUH... THAT WOULDA BEEN THE '92 "DRAGON CON".
I THOUGHT YOU LOOKED FAMILIAR, SO I DOUBLE-CHECKED WITH WOODROW...
AND HE CONFIRMED THAT YOU ARE IN FACT: JAVIER ORTIZ.
RIGHT. THAT'S MY BIRTH NAME.
SWIG
RIGHT! SO WHY WOULD YOUR I.D. BADGE HAVE A FAKE NAME ON IT?
UNLESS IT'S A FAKE AS WELL, THAT IS!
IT'S ALL A PART OF MY M.O.!
I WORK UNDERCOVER, REMEMBER?
I YI YI... I GIVE UP...
YOU AND YOUR "M.O.'S"...
OKAY, SO YOU DON'T BELIEVE ME...
THAT BEING THE CASE, WHAT ARE YOU DOING HERE?
SIGH... VERY WELL...
I'M WRITING AN ARTICLE ABOUT THE EFFECT THE INTERNET HAS ON OUR IDENTITIES...
AND HOW WE MIGHT START TO CONFUSE AND CONFLATE OUR REAL LIVES FROM OUR VIRTUAL ONES.
OKAY. BUT HOW...
OH, I SEE...
YOU THINK I'M CRAZY.

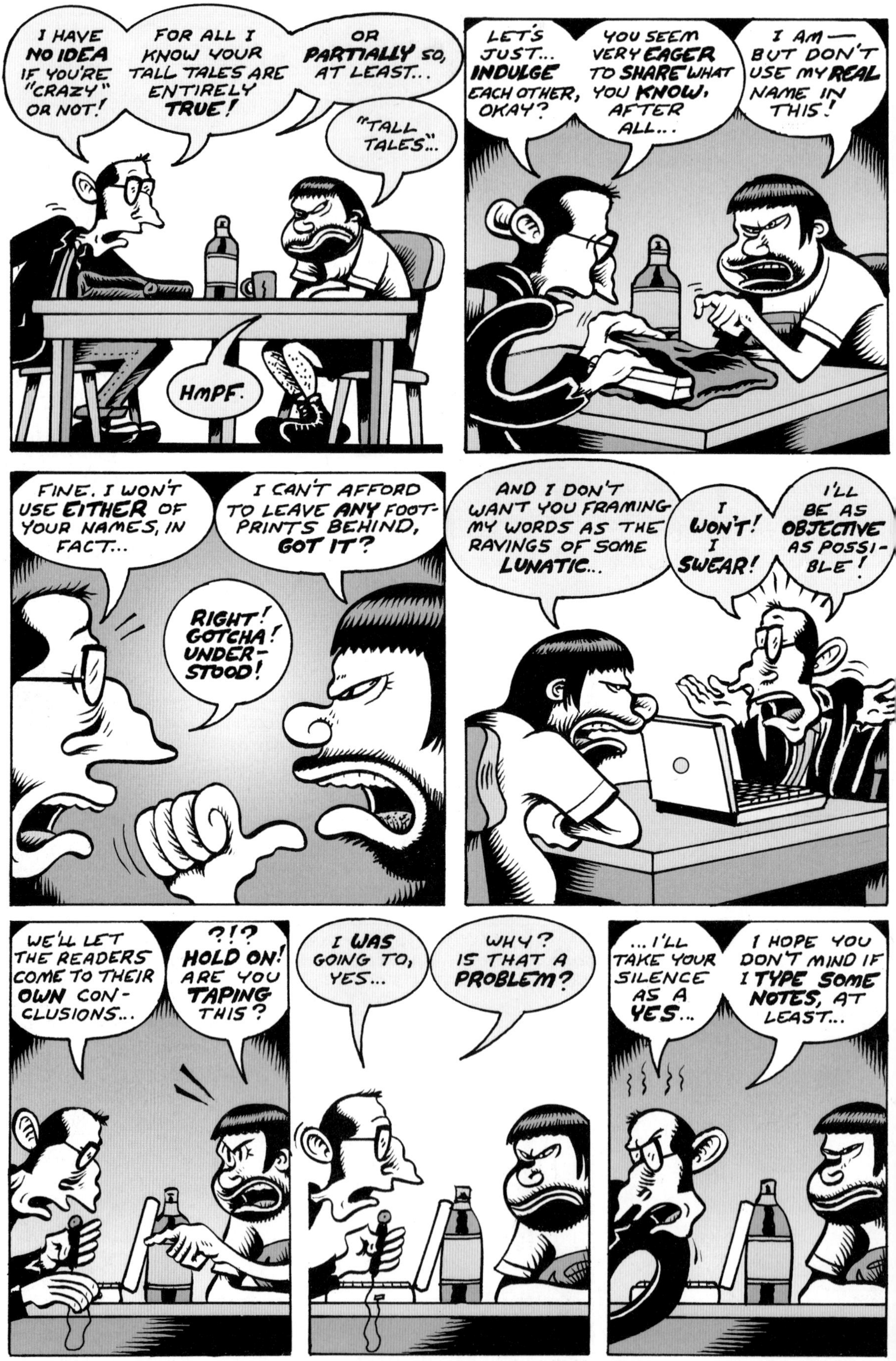
I HAVE NO IDEA IF YOU'RE "CRAZY" OR NOT!
FOR ALL I KNOW YOUR TALL TALES ARE ENTIRELY TRUE!
OR PARTIALLY SO, AT LEAST...
"TALL TALES"...
HMPF.
LET'S JUST... INDULGE EACH OTHER, OKAY?
YOU SEEM VERY EAGER TO SHARE WHAT YOU KNOW, AFTER ALL...
I AM— BUT DON'T USE MY REAL NAME IN THIS!
FINE. I WON'T USE EITHER OF YOUR NAMES, IN FACT...
I CAN'T AFFORD TO LEAVE ANY FOOT-PRINTS BEHIND, GOT IT?
RIGHT! GOTCHA! UNDER-STOOD!
AND I DON'T WANT YOU FRAMING MY WORDS AS THE RAVINGS OF SOME LUNATIC...
I WON'T! I SWEAR!
I'LL BE AS OBJECTIVE AS POSSI-BLE!
WE'LL LET THE READERS COME TO THEIR OWN CON-CLUSIONS...
?!? HOLD ON! ARE YOU TAPING THIS?
I WAS GOING TO, YES...
WHY? IS THAT A PROBLEM?
...I'LL TAKE YOUR SILENCE AS A YES...
I HOPE YOU DON'T MIND IF I TYPE SOME NOTES, AT LEAST...

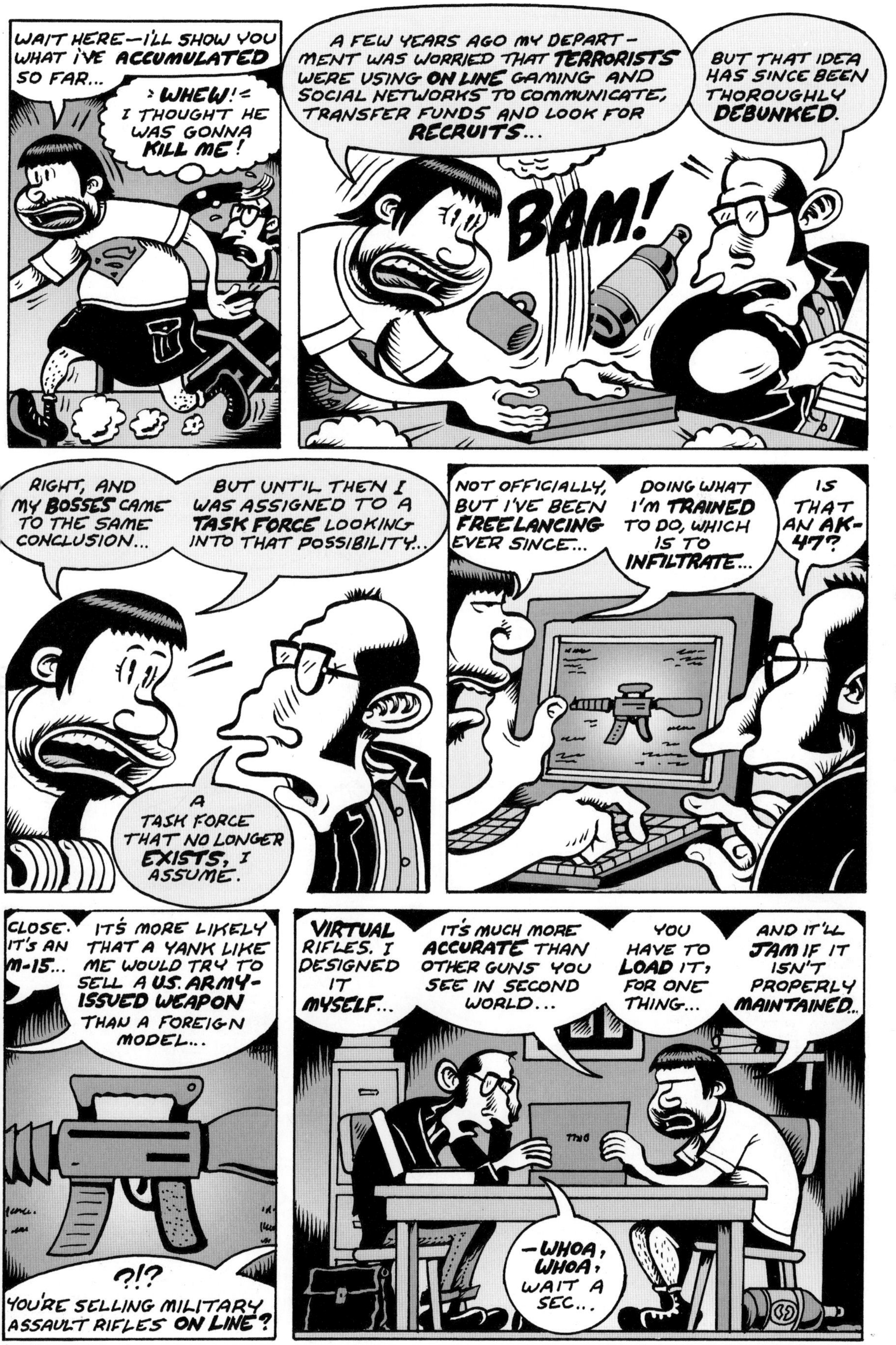
WAIT HERE—I'LL SHOW YOU WHAT I'VE ACCUMULATED SO FAR...
WHEW! I THOUGHT HE WAS GONNA KILL ME!
A FEW YEARS AGO MY DEPARTMENT WAS WORRIED THAT TERRORISTS WERE USING ON LINE GAMING AND SOCIAL NETWORKS TO COMMUNICATE, TRANSFER FUNDS AND LOOK FOR RECRUITS...
BUT THAT IDEA HAS SINCE BEEN THOROUGHLY DEBUNKED.
BAM!
RIGHT, AND MY BOSSES CAME TO THE SAME CONCLUSION...
BUT UNTIL THEN I WAS ASSIGNED TO A TASK FORCE LOOKING INTO THAT POSSIBILITY...
A TASK FORCE THAT NO LONGER EXISTS, I ASSUME.
NOT OFFICIALLY, BUT I'VE BEEN FREE LANCING EVER SINCE...
DOING WHAT I'M TRAINED TO DO, WHICH IS TO INFILTRATE...
IS THAT AN AK-47?
CLOSE. IT'S AN M-15...
IT'S MORE LIKELY THAT A YANK LIKE ME WOULD TRY TO SELL A U.S. ARMY-ISSUED WEAPON THAN A FOREIGN MODEL...
?!?
YOU'RE SELLING MILITARY ASSAULT RIFLES ON LINE?
VIRTUAL RIFLES. I DESIGNED IT MYSELF...
IT'S MUCH MORE ACCURATE THAN OTHER GUNS YOU SEE IN SECOND WORLD...
YOU HAVE TO LOAD IT, FOR ONE THING...
AND IT'LL JAM IF IT ISN'T PROPERLY MAINTAINED...
—WHOA, WHOA, WAIT A SEC...

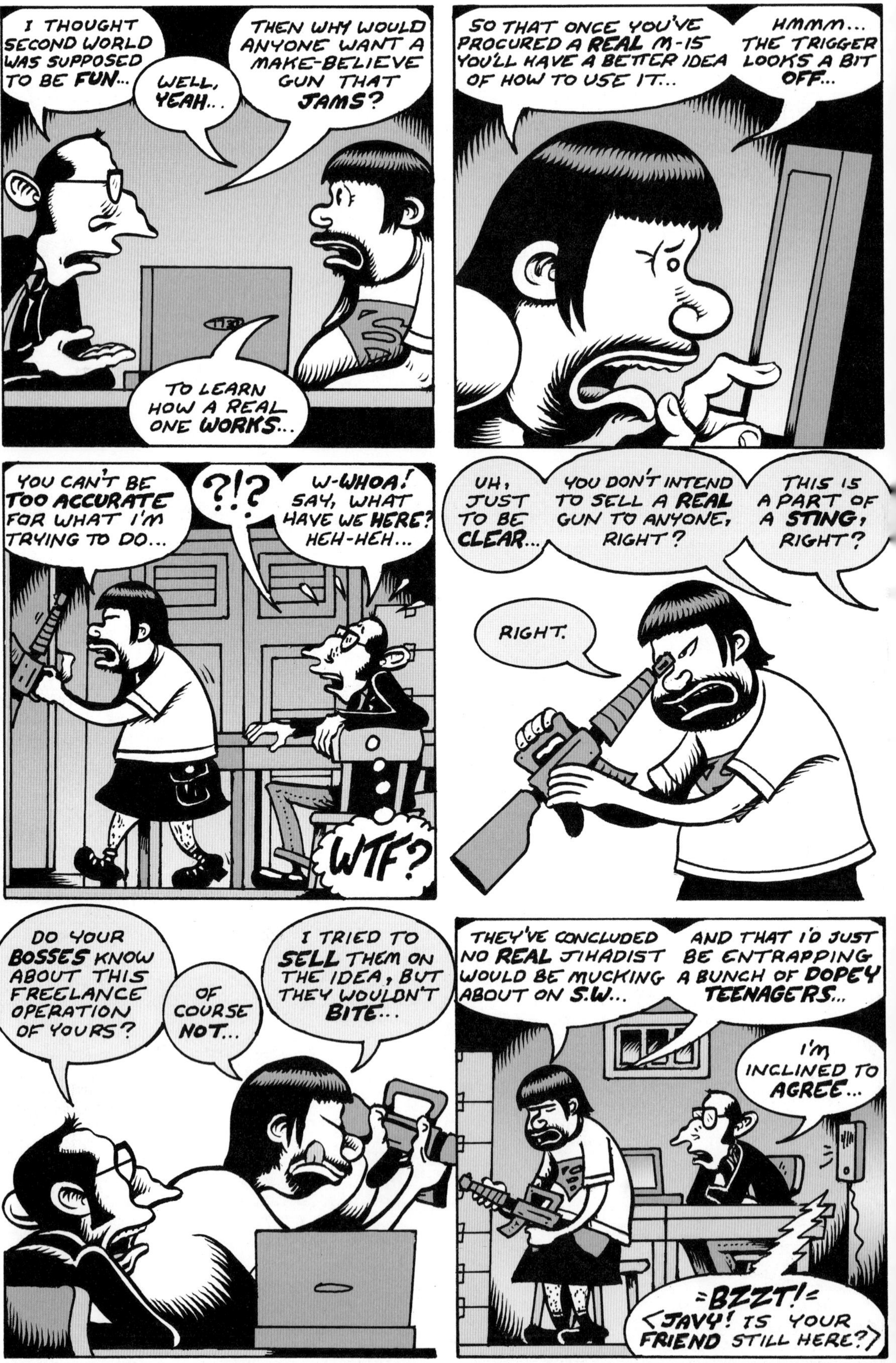
I THOUGHT SECOND WORLD WAS SUPPOSED TO BE FUN...
WELL, YEAH...
THEN WHY WOULD ANYONE WANT A MAKE-BELIEVE GUN THAT JAMS?
TO LEARN HOW A REAL ONE WORKS...
SO THAT ONCE YOU'VE PROCURED A REAL M-15 YOU'LL HAVE A BETTER IDEA OF HOW TO USE IT...
HMMM... THE TRIGGER LOOKS A BIT OFF...
YOU CAN'T BE TOO ACCURATE FOR WHAT I'M TRYING TO DO...
?!?
W-WHOA! SAY, WHAT HAVE WE HERE? HEH-HEH...
WTF?
UH, JUST TO BE CLEAR...
YOU DON'T INTEND TO SELL A REAL GUN TO ANYONE, RIGHT?
THIS IS A PART OF A STING, RIGHT?
RIGHT.
DO YOUR BOSSES KNOW ABOUT THIS FREELANCE OPERATION OF YOURS?
OF COURSE NOT...
I TRIED TO SELL THEM ON THE IDEA, BUT THEY WOULDN'T BITE...
THEY'VE CONCLUDED NO REAL JIHADIST WOULD BE MUCKING ABOUT ON S.W...
AND THAT I'D JUST BE ENTRAPPING A BUNCH OF DOPEY TEENAGERS...
I'M INCLINED TO AGREE...
=BZZT!=
<JAVY! IS YOUR FRIEND STILL HERE?>

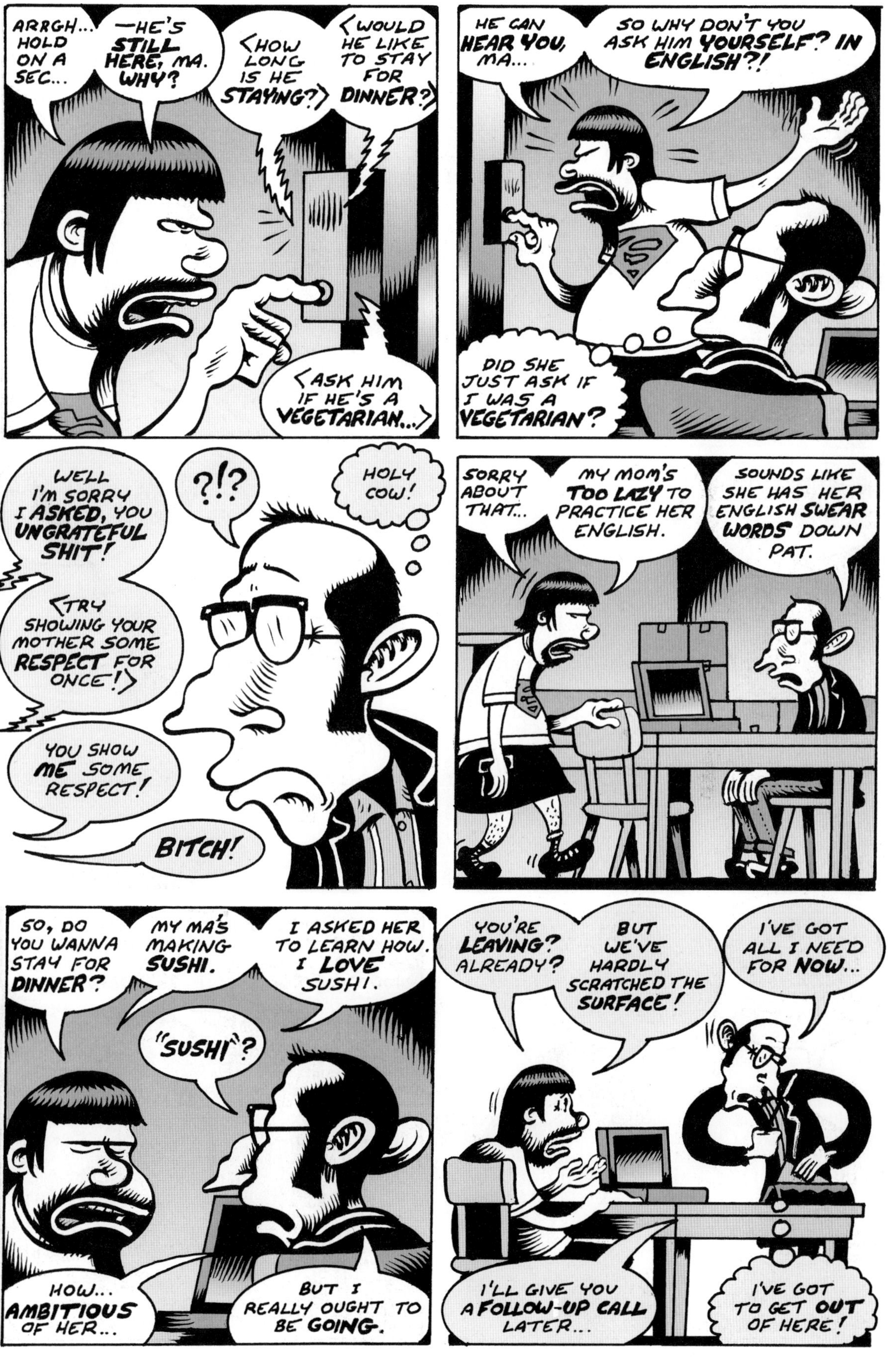
ARRGH... HOLD ON A SEC...
—HE'S STILL HERE, MA. WHY?
<HOW LONG IS HE STAYING?>
<WOULD HE LIKE TO STAY FOR DINNER?>
<ASK HIM IF HE'S A VEGETARIAN...>
HE CAN HEAR YOU, MA...
SO WHY DON'T YOU ASK HIM YOURSELF? IN ENGLISH?!
DID SHE JUST ASK IF I WAS A VEGETARIAN?
WELL I'M SORRY I ASKED, YOU UNGRATEFUL SHIT!
?!?
HOLY COW!
<TRY SHOWING YOUR MOTHER SOME RESPECT FOR ONCE!>
YOU SHOW ME SOME RESPECT!
BITCH!
SORRY ABOUT THAT...
MY MOM'S TOO LAZY TO PRACTICE HER ENGLISH.
SOUNDS LIKE SHE HAS HER ENGLISH SWEAR WORDS DOWN PAT.
SO, DO YOU WANNA STAY FOR DINNER?
MY MA'S MAKING SUSHI.
I ASKED HER TO LEARN HOW. I LOVE SUSHI.
"SUSHI"?
HOW... AMBITIOUS OF HER...
BUT I REALLY OUGHT TO BE GOING.
YOU'RE LEAVING? ALREADY?
BUT WE'VE HARDLY SCRATCHED THE SURFACE!
I'VE GOT ALL I NEED FOR NOW...
I'LL GIVE YOU A FOLLOW-UP CALL LATER...
I'VE GOT TO GET OUT OF HERE!

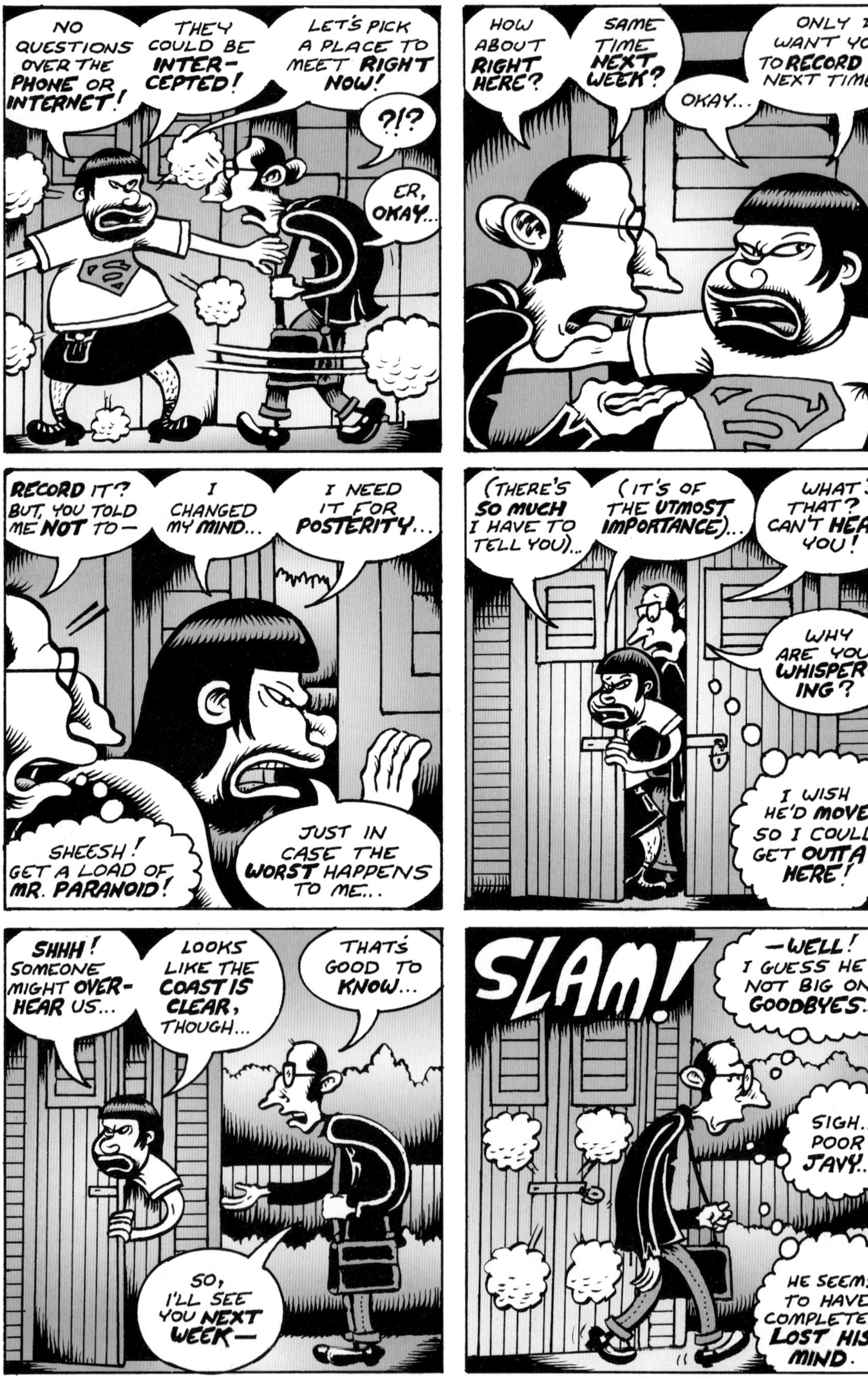
NO QUESTIONS OVER THE PHONE OR INTERNET!
THEY COULD BE INTER-CEPTED!
LET'S PICK A PLACE TO MEET RIGHT NOW!
?!?
ER, OKAY...
HOW ABOUT RIGHT HERE?
SAME TIME NEXT WEEK?
OKAY...
ONLY I WANT YOU TO RECORD US NEXT TIME.
RECORD IT? BUT, YOU TOLD ME NOT TO—
I CHANGED MY MIND...
I NEED IT FOR POSTERITY...
SHEESH! GET A LOAD OF MR. PARANOID!
JUST IN CASE THE WORST HAPPENS TO ME...
(THERE'S SO MUCH I HAVE TO TELL YOU)...
(IT'S OF THE UTMOST IMPORTANCE)...
WHAT'S THAT? I CAN'T HEAR YOU!
WHY ARE YOU WHISPER-ING?
I WISH HE'D MOVE SO I COULD GET OUTTA HERE!
SHHH! SOMEONE MIGHT OVER-HEAR US...
LOOKS LIKE THE COAST IS CLEAR, THOUGH...
THAT'S GOOD TO KNOW...
SO, I'LL SEE YOU NEXT WEEK—
SLAM!
—WELL! I GUESS HE'S NOT BIG ON GOODBYE'S...
SIGH... POOR JAVY...
HE SEEMS TO HAVE COMPLETELY LOST HIS MIND.

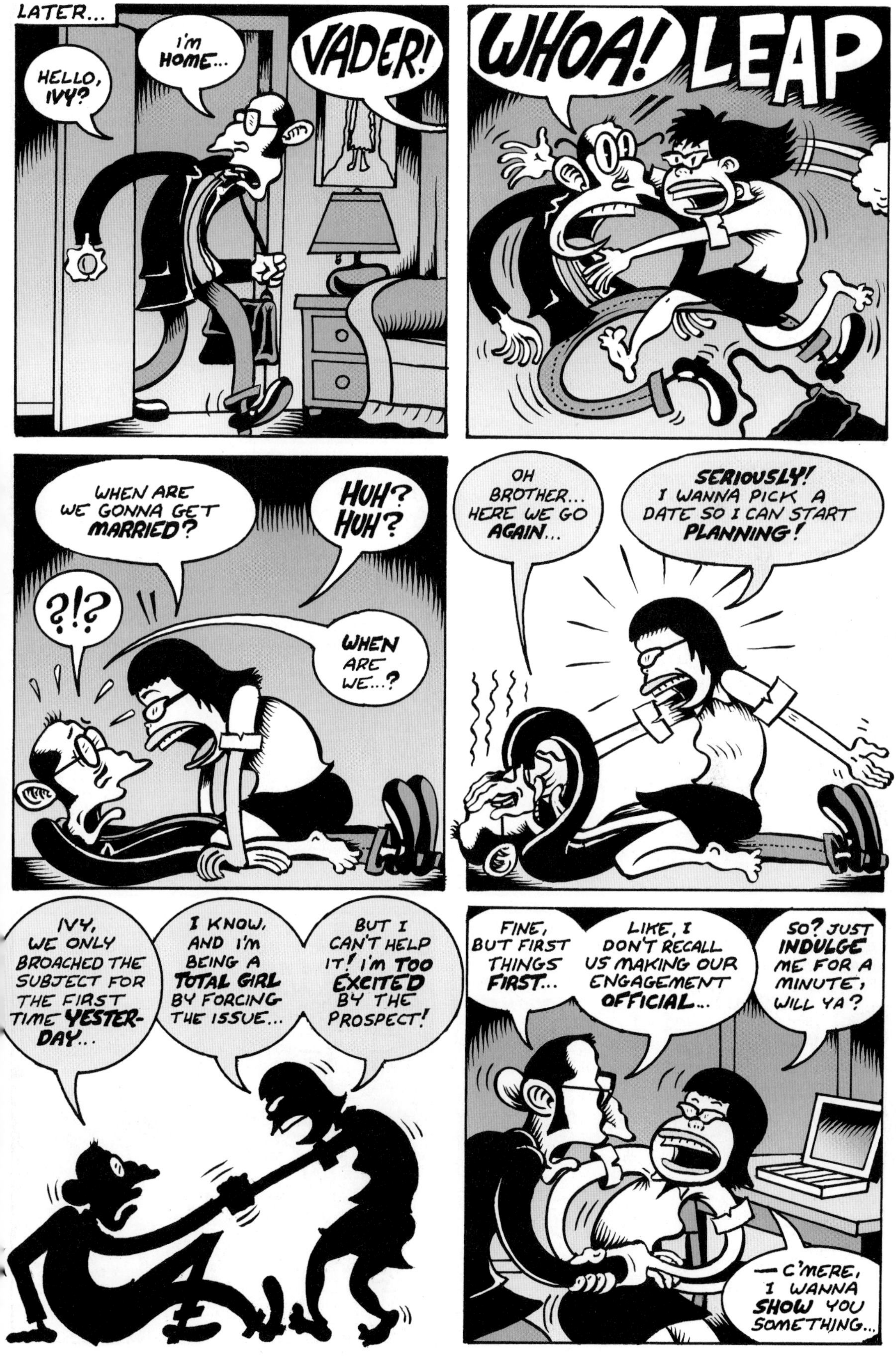
LATER...
HELLO, IVY?
I'M HOME...
VADER!
WHOA!
LEAP
WHEN ARE WE GONNA GET MARRIED?
HUH? HUH?
?!?
WHEN ARE WE...?
OH BROTHER... HERE WE GO AGAIN...
SERIOUSLY! I WANNA PICK A DATE SO I CAN START PLANNING!
IVY, WE ONLY BROACHED THE SUBJECT FOR THE FIRST TIME YESTER-DAY...
I KNOW, AND I'M BEING A TOTAL GIRL BY FORCING THE ISSUE...
BUT I CAN'T HELP IT! I'M TOO EXCITED BY THE PROSPECT!
FINE, BUT FIRST THINGS FIRST...
LIKE, I DON'T RECALL US MAKING OUR ENGAGEMENT OFFICIAL...
SO? JUST INDULGE ME FOR A MINUTE, WILL YA?
—C'MERE, I WANNA SHOW YOU SOMETHING...

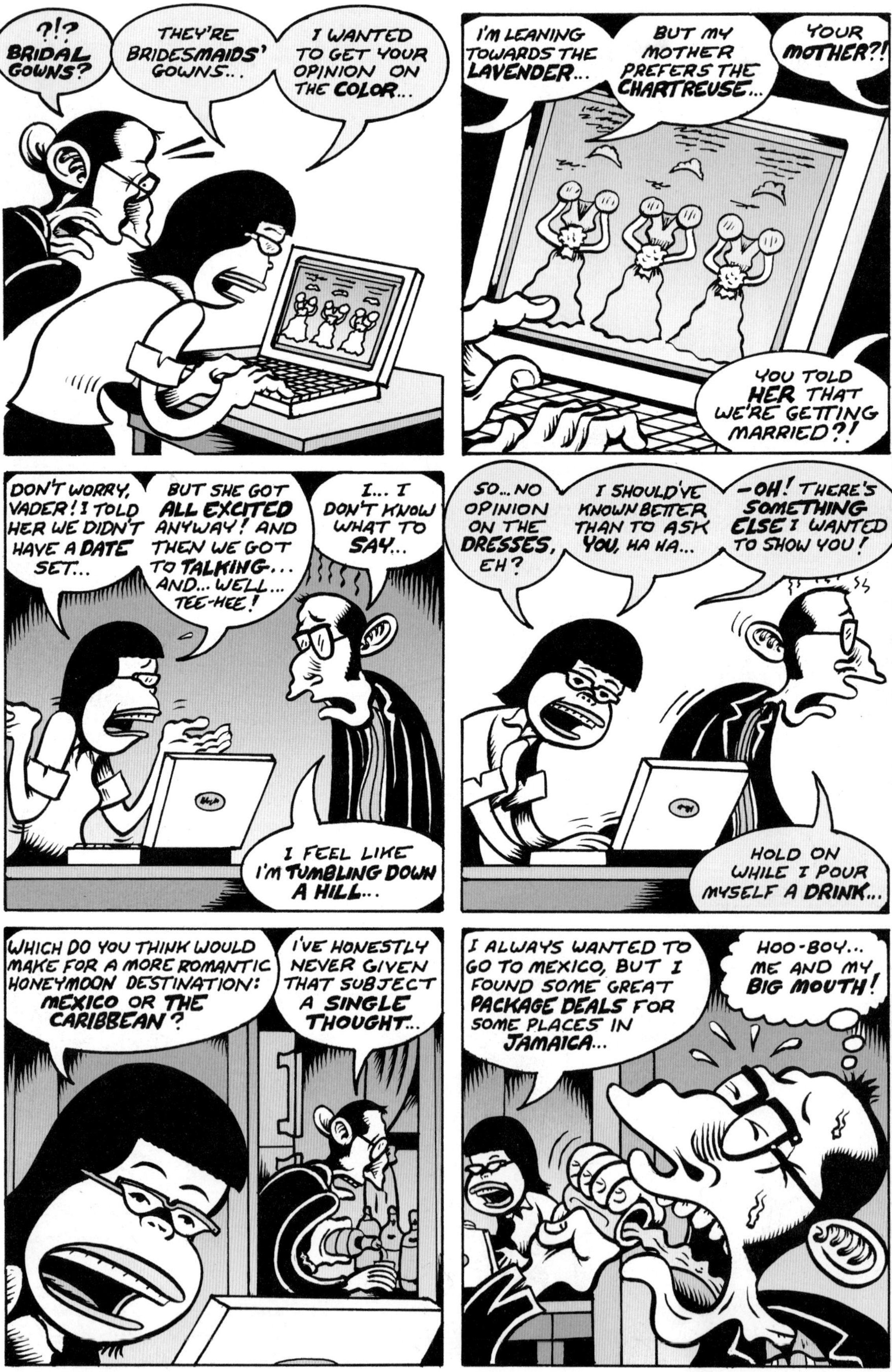
?!? BRIDAL GOWNS?
THEY'RE BRIDESMAIDS' GOWNS...
I WANTED TO GET YOUR OPINION ON THE COLOR...
I'M LEANING TOWARDS THE LAVENDER...
BUT MY MOTHER PREFERS THE CHARTREUSE...
YOUR MOTHER?!
YOU TOLD HER THAT WE'RE GETTING MARRIED?!
DON'T WORRY, VADER! I TOLD HER WE DIDN'T HAVE A DATE SET...
BUT SHE GOT ALL EXCITED ANYWAY! AND THEN WE GOT TO TALKING... AND... WELL... TEE-HEE!
I... I DON'T KNOW WHAT TO SAY...
I FEEL LIKE I'M TUMBLING DOWN A HILL...
SO... NO OPINION ON THE DRESSES, EH?
I SHOULD'VE KNOWN BETTER THAN TO ASK YOU, HA HA...
-OH! THERE'S SOMETHING ELSE I WANTED TO SHOW YOU!
HOLD ON WHILE I POUR MYSELF A DRINK...
WHICH DO YOU THINK WOULD MAKE FOR A MORE ROMANTIC HONEYMOON DESTINATION: MEXICO OR THE CARIBBEAN?
I'VE HONESTLY NEVER GIVEN THAT SUBJECT A SINGLE THOUGHT...
I ALWAYS WANTED TO GO TO MEXICO, BUT I FOUND SOME GREAT PACKAGE DEALS FOR SOME PLACES IN JAMAICA...
HOO-BOY... ME AND MY BIG MOUTH!

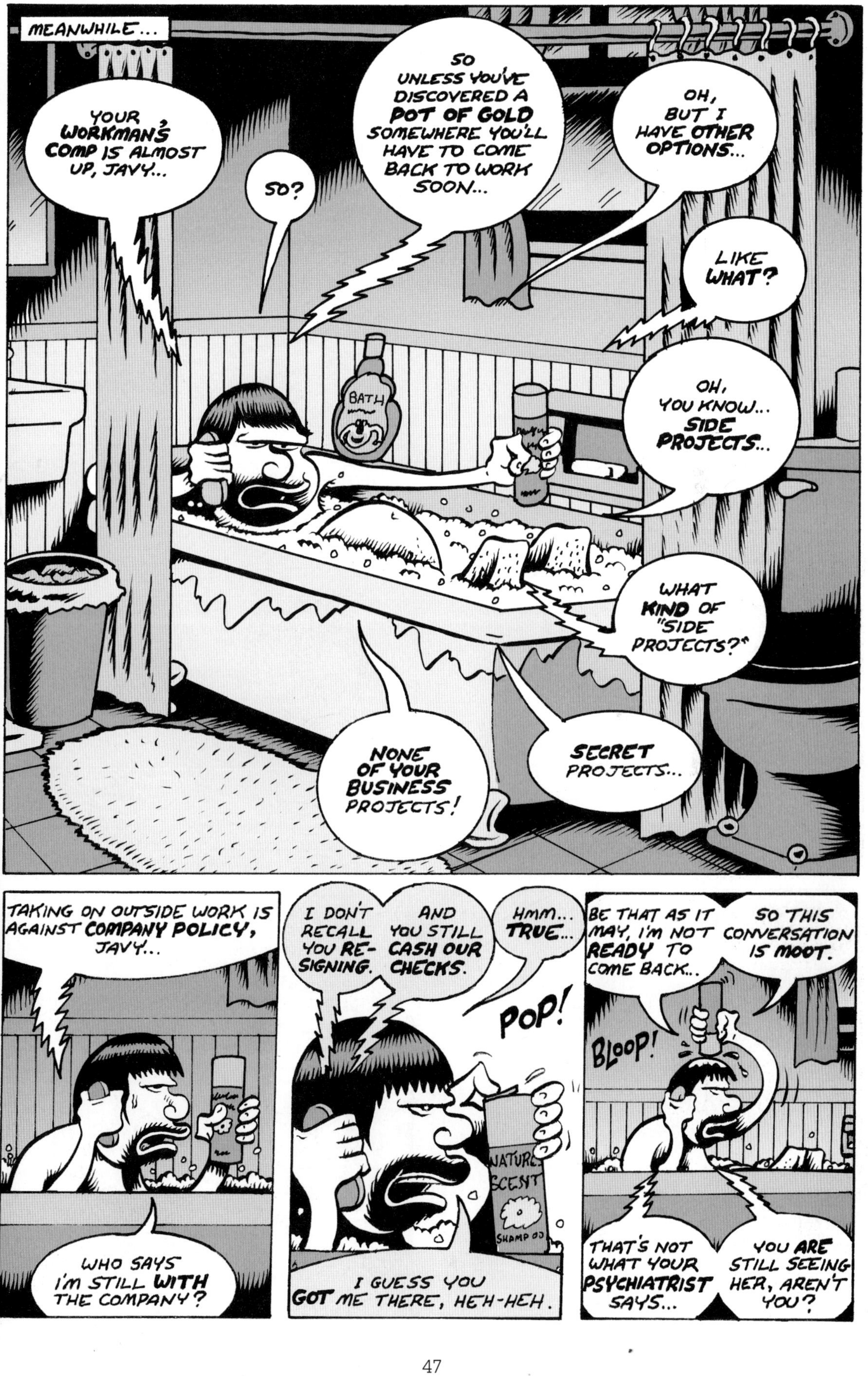
MEANWHILE...
YOUR WORKMAN'S COMP IS ALMOST UP, JAVY...
SO?
SO UNLESS YOU'VE DISCOVERED A POT OF GOLD SOMEWHERE YOU'LL HAVE TO COME BACK TO WORK SOON...
OH, BUT I HAVE OTHER OPTIONS...
LIKE WHAT?
BATH
OH, YOU KNOW... SIDE PROJECTS...
WHAT KIND OF "SIDE PROJECTS?"
NONE OF YOUR BUSINESS PROJECTS!
SECRET PROJECTS...
TAKING ON OUTSIDE WORK IS AGAINST COMPANY POLICY, JAVY...
WHO SAYS I'M STILL WITH THE COMPANY?
I DON'T RECALL YOU RE-SIGNING.
AND YOU STILL CASH OUR CHECKS.
HMM... TRUE...
POP!
NATURE'S SCENT
SHAMPOO
I GUESS YOU GOT ME THERE, HEH-HEH.
BE THAT AS IT MAY, I'M NOT READY TO COME BACK...
SO THIS CONVERSATION IS MOOT.
BLOOP!
THAT'S NOT WHAT YOUR PSYCHIATRIST SAYS...
YOU ARE STILL SEEING HER, AREN'T YOU?

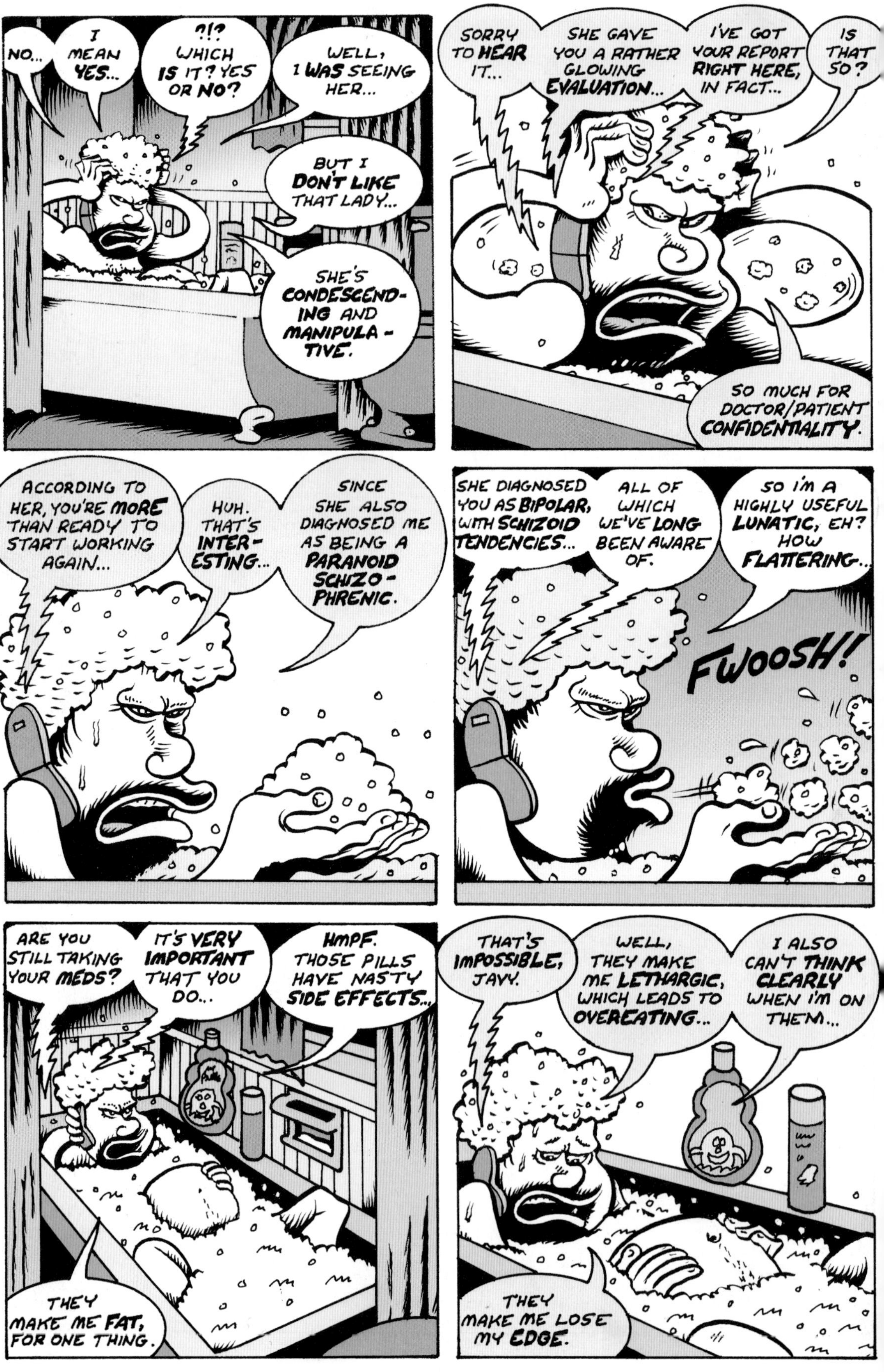
NO...
I MEAN YES...
?!? WHICH IS IT? YES OR NO?
WELL, I WAS SEEING HER...
BUT I DON'T LIKE THAT LADY...
SHE'S CONDESCENDING AND MANIPULATIVE.
SORRY TO HEAR IT...
SHE GAVE YOU A RATHER GLOWING EVALUATION...
I'VE GOT YOUR REPORT RIGHT HERE, IN FACT...
IS THAT SO?
SO MUCH FOR DOCTOR/PATIENT CONFIDENTIALITY.
ACCORDING TO HER, YOU'RE MORE THAN READY TO START WORKING AGAIN...
HUH. THAT'S INTERESTING...
SINCE SHE ALSO DIAGNOSED ME AS BEING A PARANOID SCHIZOPHRENIC.
SHE DIAGNOSED YOU AS BIPOLAR, WITH SCHIZOID TENDENCIES...
ALL OF WHICH WE'VE LONG BEEN AWARE OF.
SO I'M A HIGHLY USEFUL LUNATIC, EH? HOW FLATTERING...
FWOOSH!
ARE YOU STILL TAKING YOUR MEDS?
IT'S VERY IMPORTANT THAT YOU DO...
HMPF. THOSE PILLS HAVE NASTY SIDE EFFECTS...
THEY MAKE ME FAT, FOR ONE THING.
THAT'S IMPOSSIBLE, JAVY.
WELL, THEY MAKE ME LETHARGIC, WHICH LEADS TO OVEREATING...
I ALSO CAN'T THINK CLEARLY WHEN I'M ON THEM...
THEY MAKE ME LOSE MY EDGE.

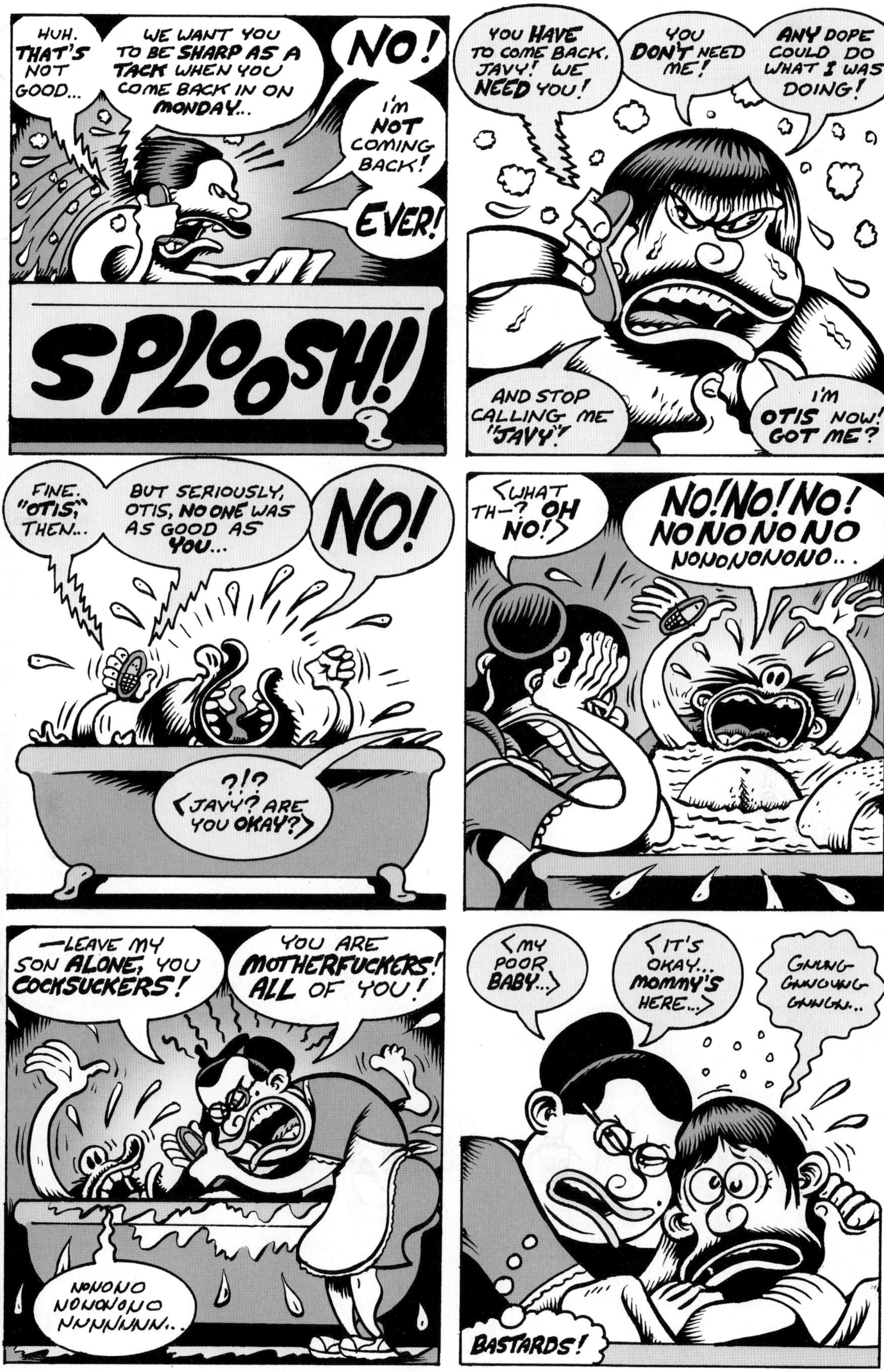

HUH. THAT'S NOT GOOD...
WE WANT YOU TO BE SHARP AS A TACK WHEN YOU COME BACK IN ON MONDAY...
NO!
I'M NOT COMING BACK!
EVER!
SPLOOSH!
YOU HAVE TO COME BACK, JAVY! WE NEED YOU!
YOU DON'T NEED ME!
ANY DOPE COULD DO WHAT I WAS DOING!
AND STOP CALLING ME "JAVY"!
I'M OTIS NOW! GOT ME?
FINE. "OTIS," THEN...
BUT SERIOUSLY, OTIS, NO ONE WAS AS GOOD AS YOU...
NO!
?!? <JAVY? ARE YOU OKAY?>
<WHAT TH—? OH NO!>
NO! NO! NO! NO NO NO NO NONONONONO...
—LEAVE MY SON ALONE, YOU COCKSUCKERS!
YOU ARE MOTHERFUCKERS! ALL OF YOU!
NONONO NONONONO NNNNNNN..
<MY POOR BABY...>
<IT'S OKAY... MOMMY'S HERE...>
GNNNG GNNGNG GNNGN...
BASTARDS!

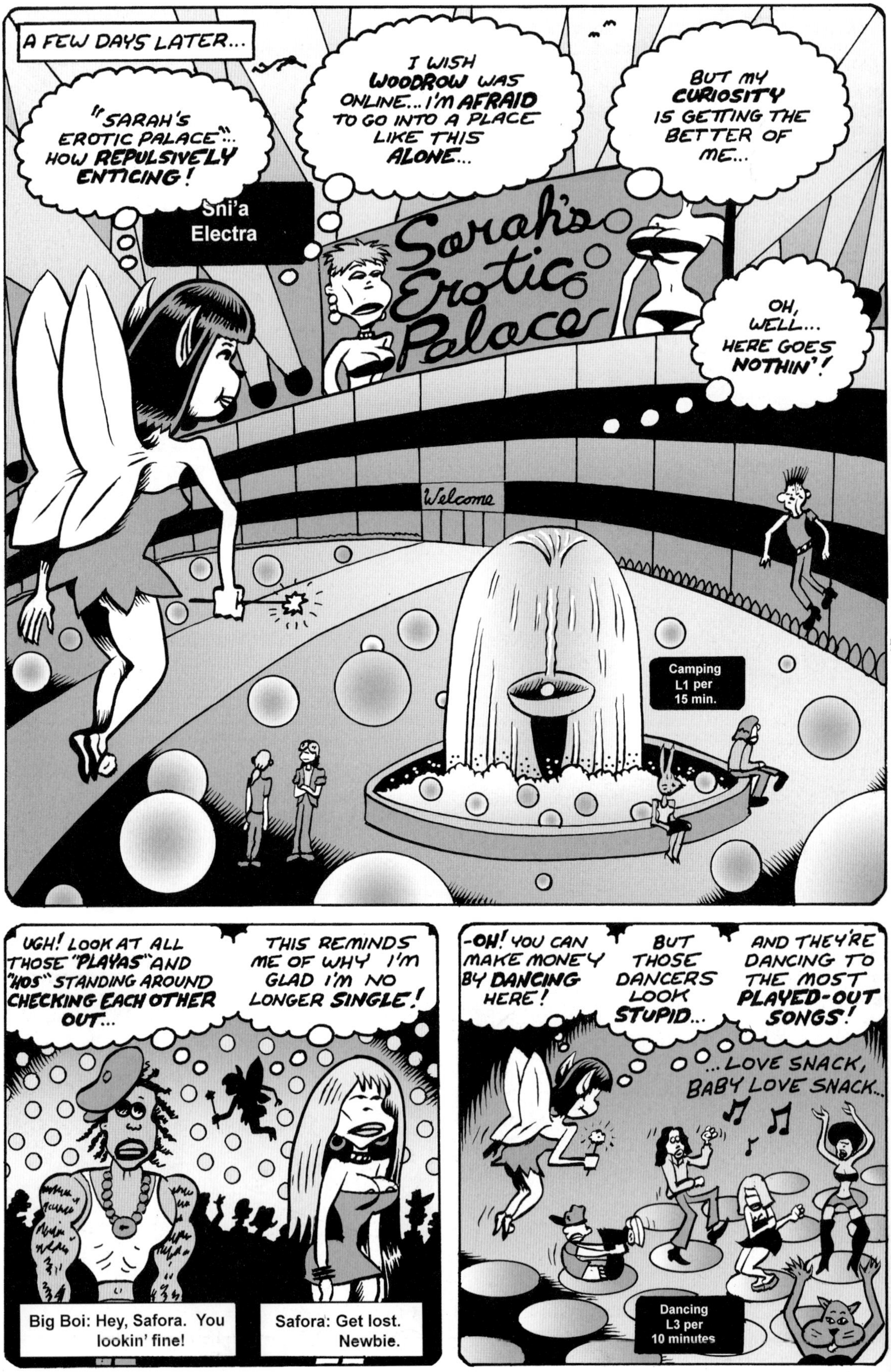
A FEW DAYS LATER...
"SARAH'S EROTIC PALACE"... HOW REPULSIVELY ENTICING!
I WISH WOODROW WAS ONLINE... I'M AFRAID TO GO INTO A PLACE LIKE THIS ALONE...
BUT MY CURIOSITY IS GETTING THE BETTER OF ME...
Sni'a Electra
Sarah's Erotic Palace
OH, WELL... HERE GOES NOTHIN'!
Welcome
Camping L1 per 15 min.
UGH! LOOK AT ALL THOSE "PLAYAS" AND "HOS" STANDING AROUND CHECKING EACH OTHER OUT...
THIS REMINDS ME OF WHY I'M GLAD I'M NO LONGER SINGLE!
Big Boi: Hey, Safora. You lookin' fine!
Safora: Get lost. Newbie.
-OH! YOU CAN MAKE MONEY BY DANCING HERE!
BUT THOSE DANCERS LOOK STUPID...
AND THEY'RE DANCING TO THE MOST PLAYED-OUT SONGS!
...LOVE SNACK, BABY LOVE SNACK...
Dancing L3 per 10 minutes

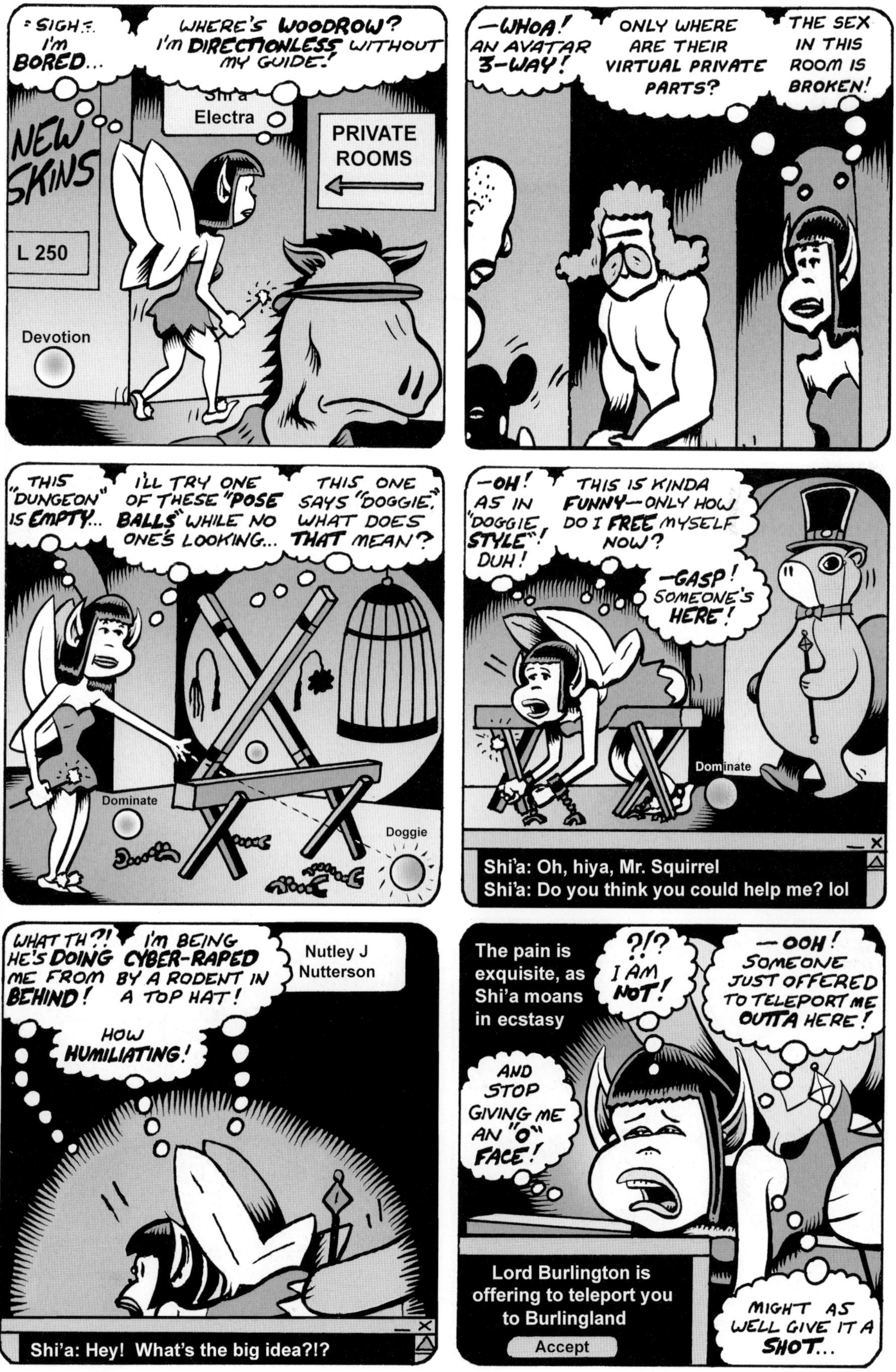
=SIGH= I'm BORED...
WHERE'S WOODROW? I'm DIRECTIONLESS WITHOUT MY GUIDE!
Electra
PRIVATE ROOMS
NEW SKINS
L 250
Devotion
—WHOA! AN AVATAR 3-WAY!
ONLY WHERE ARE THEIR VIRTUAL PRIVATE PARTS?
THE SEX IN THIS ROOM IS BROKEN!
THIS "DUNGEON" IS EMPTY...
I'LL TRY ONE OF THESE "POSE BALLS" WHILE NO ONE'S LOOKING...
THIS ONE SAYS "DOGGIE." WHAT DOES THAT MEAN?
Dominate
Doggie
—OH! AS IN "DOGGIE STYLE"! DUH!
THIS IS KINDA FUNNY—ONLY HOW DO I FREE MYSELF NOW?
—GASP! SOMEONE'S HERE!
Dominate
Shi'a: Oh, hiya, Mr. Squirrel
Shi'a: Do you think you could help me? lol
WHAT TH?! HE'S DOING ME FROM BEHIND!
I'm BEING CYBER-RAPED BY A RODENT IN A TOP HAT!
Nutley J Nutterson
HOW HUMILIATING!
Shi'a: Hey! What's the big idea?!?
The pain is exquisite, as Shi'a moans in ecstasy
?!? I AM NOT!
—OOH! SOMEONE JUST OFFERED TO TELEPORT ME OUTTA HERE!
AND STOP GIVING ME AN "O" FACE!
Lord Burlington is offering to teleport you to Burlingland
Accept
MIGHT AS WELL GIVE IT A SHOT...

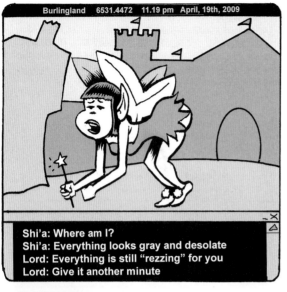

Burlingland 6531.4472 11.19 pm April, 19th, 2009
Shi'a: Where am I?
Shi'a: Everything looks gray and desolate
Lord: Everything is still "rezzing" for you
Lord: Give it another minute
Shi'a: Oh, no! I'm stuck in this stupid pose!
Shi'a: And I'm still making a stupid "O" face!
Shia: How do I get out of this?!?
Lord: Hit the "Stand Up" button at the bottom of the screen
Shi'a: WHEW! Finally!
Shi'a: Uhh... Who are you?
Lord: It's me! Woodrow!
Lord: Welcome to my kingdom, Ivy!
Lord: Er, I mean, "Shi'a"!
Lord: I'll have to get used to your new name -- and your new Avatar!
Shi'a: Oh yeah, and you're using your other avatar. The REGAL one!
Shi'a: Get a load of YOU, Mr. Big Stuff!
Lord: And look at how tiny YOU are
Lord: What are you, an ELF or something?
Shi'a: An elf?!? I'm a FAIRY, ya big dummy!
Shi'a: I gave up trying to design my own avatar, and just went with this pre-made fantasy getup. And I LIKE how tiny it makes me!
Lord: It suits you. You look cute!

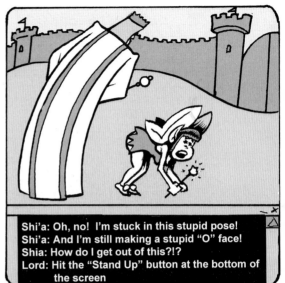

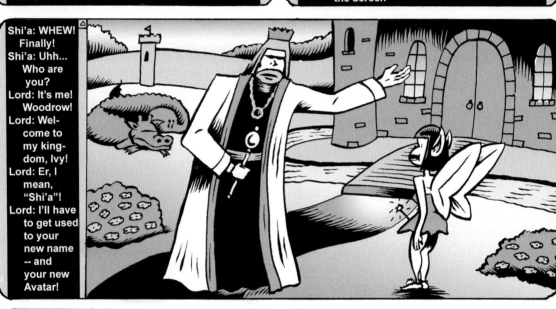

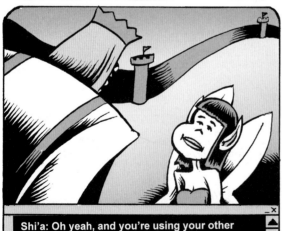

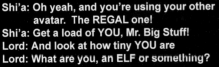

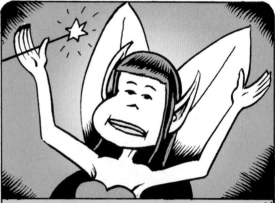

Shi'a: Thanks!
Shi'a: So... NOW where to?
Lord: No exploring for me. I'm in the middle of building something.
Lord: Feel free to explore on your own, though.

Shi'a: WHAT? NO WAY!
Shi'a: I was on my own for 5 minutes before I was sexually assaulted by a SQUIRREL!
Shi'a: I'm sticking with YOU from now on!
Lord: Ha! Suit yourself.

Shi'a: So... Whatcha building?
Lord: A dungeon.
Shi'a: Oh no! Like one of those stupid S&M sex places?
Lord: No. More like a PRISON...

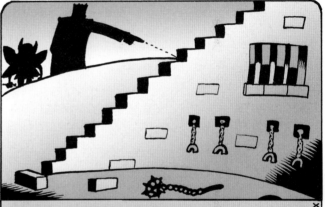

Lord: ...One that an avatar couldn't get out of without my approval.
Shi'a: ?!? Can you DO that?
Lord: Possibly. I intend to find out! Ha ha.
Shi'a: Can we put "Nutty J Nutterson" in there?

Lord: Is that your assailant?
Shi'a: Yeah.
Lord: Very well, then. He'll be our first prisoner.
Shi'a: YES! Awesome!

Lord: Since you're here, I could give you a tour of my "kingdom"
Lord: If you'd like, that is.
Shi'a: Heck, yeah! I wanna see the inside of your castle!
Shi'a: Mind if I "float" instead of walk?
Shi'a: I like to pretend I'm using my wings. LOL!

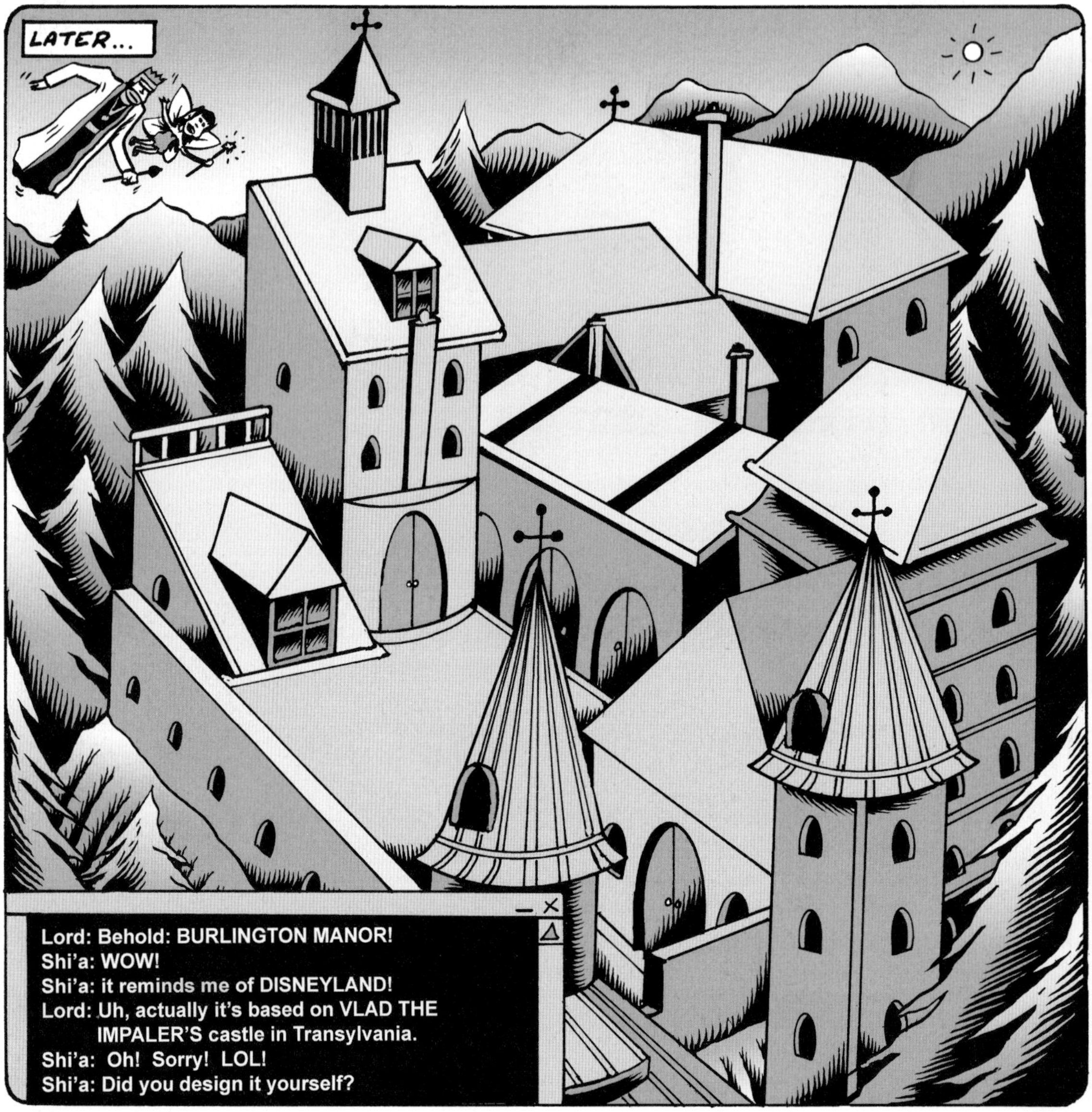
LATER...
Lord: Behold: BURLINGTON MANOR!
Shi'a: WOW!
Shi'a: it reminds me of DISNEYLAND!
Lord: Uh, actually it's based on VLAD THE IMPALER'S castle in Transylvania.
Shi'a: Oh! Sorry! LOL!
Shi'a: Did you design it yourself?

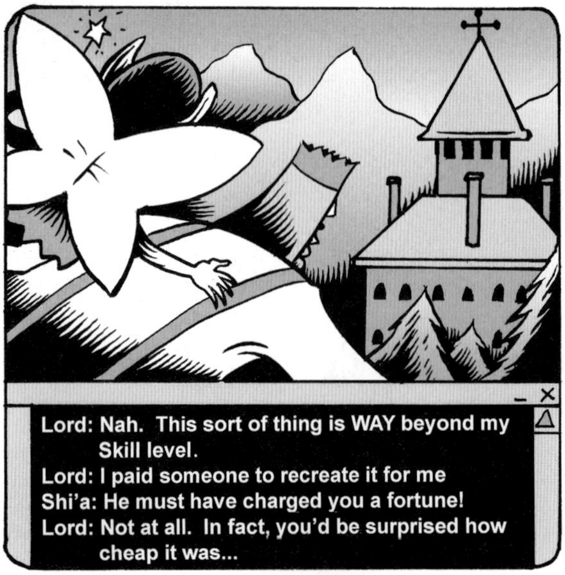
Lord: Nah. This sort of thing is WAY beyond my Skill level.
Lord: I paid someone to recreate it for me
Shi'a: He must have charged you a fortune!
Lord: Not at all. In fact, you'd be surprised how cheap it was...

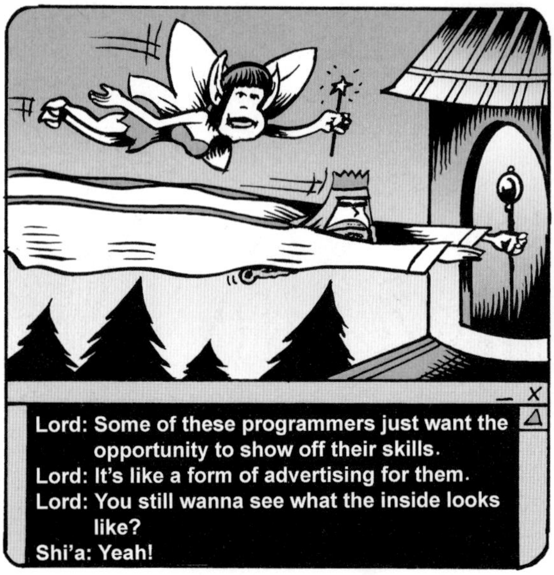
Lord: Some of these programmers just want the opportunity to show off their skills.
Lord: It's like a form of advertising for them.
Lord: You still wanna see what the inside looks like?
Shi'a: Yeah!

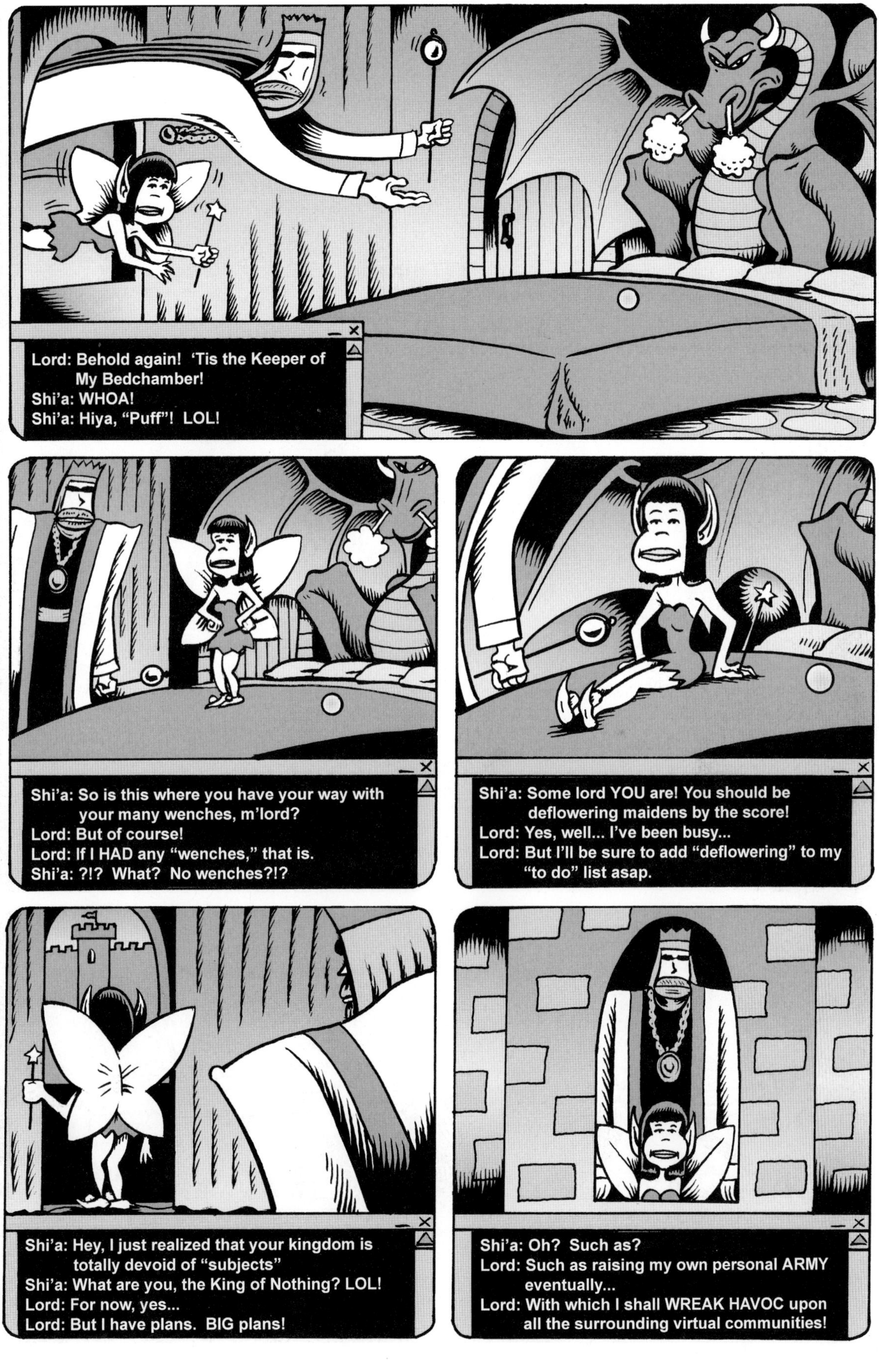
Lord: Behold again! 'Tis the Keeper of My Bedchamber!
Shi'a: WHOA!
Shi'a: Hiya, "Puff"! LOL!
Shi'a: So is this where you have your way with your many wenches, m'lord?
Lord: But of course!
Lord: If I HAD any "wenches," that is.
Shi'a: ?!? What? No wenches?!?
Shi'a: Some lord YOU are! You should be deflowering maidens by the score!
Lord: Yes, well... I've been busy...
Lord: But I'll be sure to add "deflowering" to my "to do" list asap.
Shi'a: Hey, I just realized that your kingdom is totally devoid of "subjects"
Shi'a: What are you, the King of Nothing? LOL!
Lord: For now, yes...
Lord: But I have plans. BIG plans!
Shi'a: Oh? Such as?
Lord: Such as raising my own personal ARMY eventually...
Lord: With which I shall WREAK HAVOC upon all the surrounding virtual communities!

Shi'a: Really? Why?
Lord: I dunno. Something to do, I guess.
Shi'a: That's as good a reason as any!
Shi'a: LOL!

Menu

Shi'a: Can I be in your "army"?
Shi'a: Or is it "boys only"?
Shi'a: I can be your first recruit!
Lord: Okay. Why not?

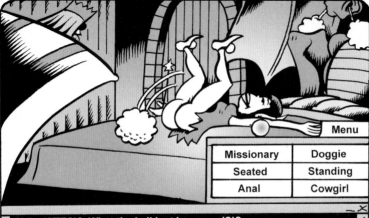

Menu

Missionary	Doggie
Seated	Standing
Anal	Cowgirl

Shi'a: WTF?!? What the hell just happened?!?
Shi'a: I hit that "menu" ball and suddenly I'm in this missionary
      position!
Lord: Oh. Oops! Yeah, this bed comes equipped with various
      sexual "animation" poses.

Shi'a: So I see...
Shi'a: I thought it was gonna
      be a dinner menu! LOL!
Shi'a: I'm gonna try another
      pose... Hold on...

Shi'a: OMG! The "standing"
      position has me leaning
      on "Puff"!
Shi'a: Take advantage of me!
Lord: ?!? Are you serious?

Shi'a: Yeah! I wanna see what it'd be like to have 3-way cartoon sex!
Shi'a: And feel free to boss me around, like I'm your sex slave
Lord: Huh! Very well...
Lord: My first decree is: no more saying "LOL"!
Shi'a: LOL! Oops -- I mean: "Yes, M'Lord." Tee hee!

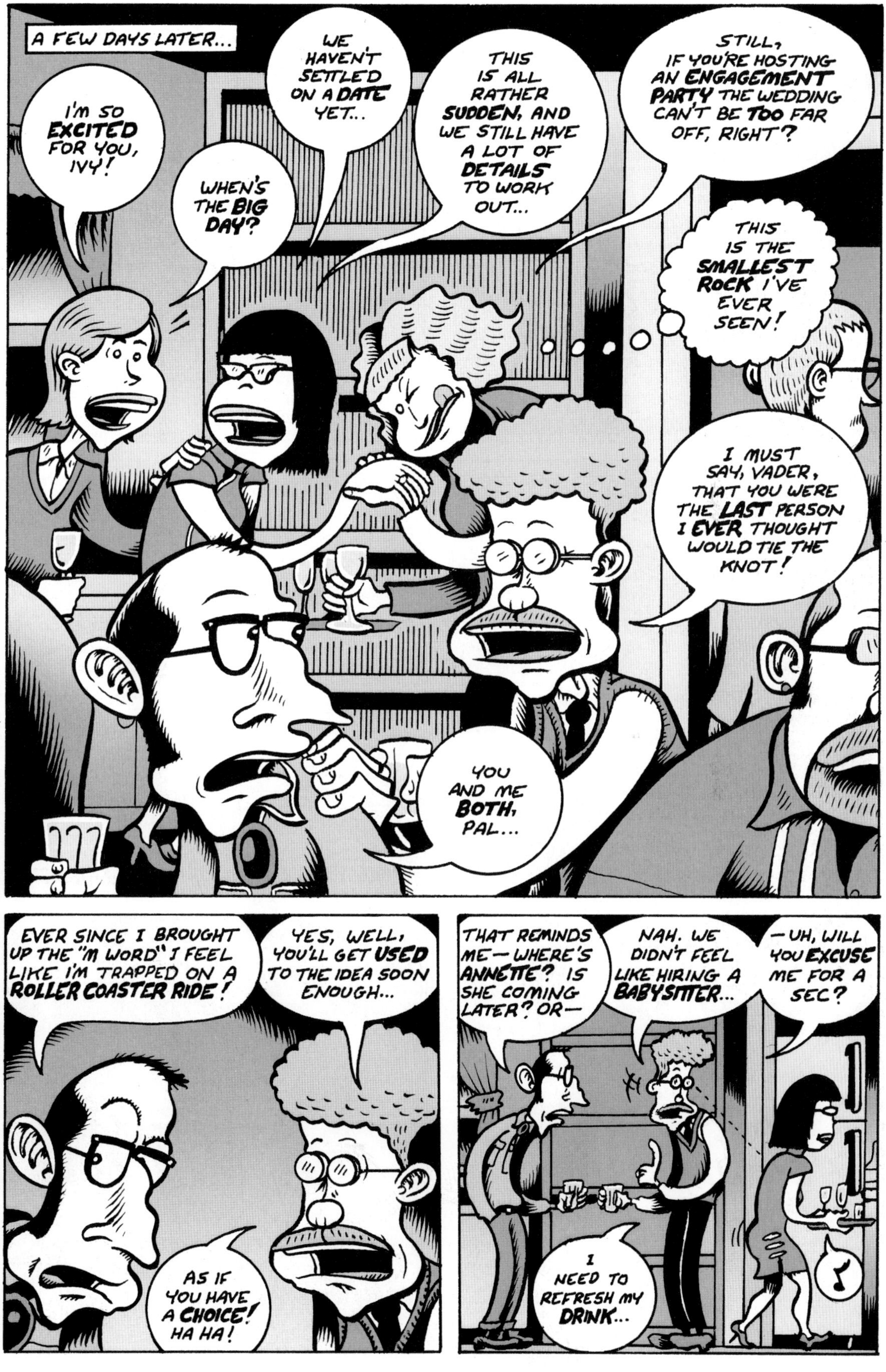
A FEW DAYS LATER...
I'M SO EXCITED FOR YOU, IVY!
WHEN'S THE BIG DAY?
WE HAVEN'T SETTLED ON A DATE YET...
THIS IS ALL RATHER SUDDEN, AND WE STILL HAVE A LOT OF DETAILS TO WORK OUT...
STILL, IF YOU'RE HOSTING AN ENGAGEMENT PARTY THE WEDDING CAN'T BE TOO FAR OFF, RIGHT?
THIS IS THE SMALLEST ROCK I'VE EVER SEEN!
I MUST SAY, VADER, THAT YOU WERE THE LAST PERSON I EVER THOUGHT WOULD TIE THE KNOT!
YOU AND ME BOTH, PAL...
EVER SINCE I BROUGHT UP THE "M WORD" I FEEL LIKE I'M TRAPPED ON A ROLLER COASTER RIDE!
YES, WELL, YOU'LL GET USED TO THE IDEA SOON ENOUGH...
AS IF YOU HAVE A CHOICE! HA HA!
THAT REMINDS ME—WHERE'S ANNETTE? IS SHE COMING LATER? OR—
NAH. WE DIDN'T FEEL LIKE HIRING A BABYSITTER...
—UH, WILL YOU EXCUSE ME FOR A SEC?
I NEED TO REFRESH MY DRINK...

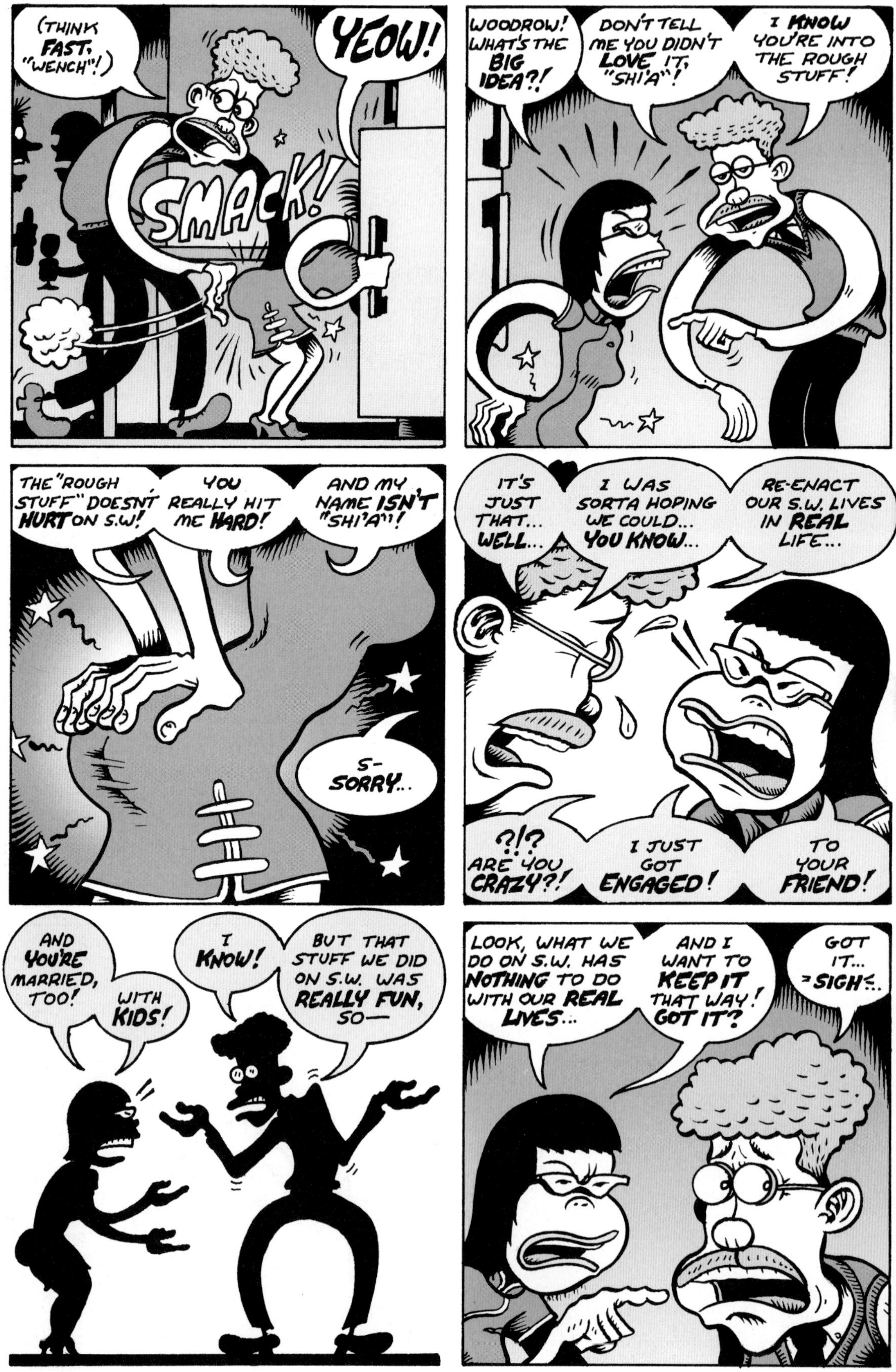
(THINK FAST, "WENCH"!)
YEOW!
SMACK!
WOODROW! WHAT'S THE BIG IDEA?!
DON'T TELL ME YOU DIDN'T LOVE IT, "SHI'A"!
I KNOW YOU'RE INTO THE ROUGH STUFF!
THE "ROUGH STUFF" DOESN'T HURT ON S.W.!
YOU REALLY HIT ME HARD!
AND MY NAME ISN'T "SHI'A"!
S-SORRY...
IT'S JUST THAT... WELL...
I WAS SORTA HOPING WE COULD... YOU KNOW...
RE-ENACT OUR S.W. LIVES IN REAL LIFE...
?!? ARE YOU CRAZY?!
I JUST GOT ENGAGED!
TO YOUR FRIEND!
AND YOU'RE MARRIED, TOO!
WITH KIDS!
I KNOW!
BUT THAT STUFF WE DID ON S.W. WAS REALLY FUN, SO—
LOOK, WHAT WE DO ON S.W. HAS NOTHING TO DO WITH OUR REAL LIVES...
AND I WANT TO KEEP IT THAT WAY! GOT IT?
GOT IT... SIGH...

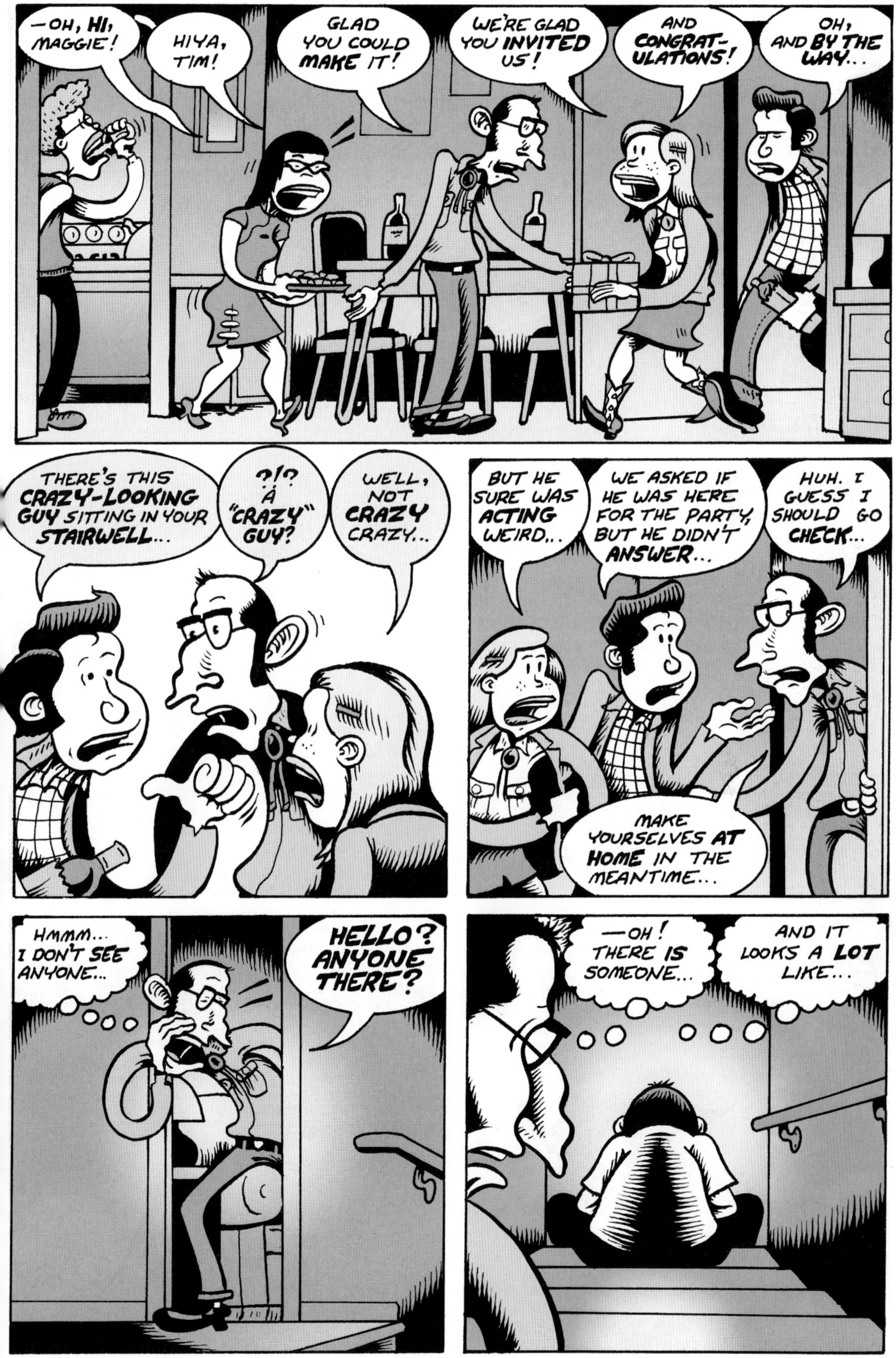
—OH, HI, MAGGIE!
HIYA, TIM!
GLAD YOU COULD MAKE IT!
WE'RE GLAD YOU INVITED US!
AND CONGRAT-ULATIONS!
OH, AND BY THE WAY...
THERE'S THIS CRAZY-LOOKING GUY SITTING IN YOUR STAIRWELL...
?!? A "CRAZY" GUY?
WELL, NOT CRAZY CRAZY...
BUT HE SURE WAS ACTING WEIRD...
WE ASKED IF HE WAS HERE FOR THE PARTY, BUT HE DIDN'T ANSWER...
HUH. I GUESS I SHOULD GO CHECK...
MAKE YOURSELVES AT HOME IN THE MEANTIME...
HMMM... I DON'T SEE ANYONE...
HELLO? ANYONE THERE?
—OH! THERE IS SOMEONE...
AND IT LOOKS A LOT LIKE...

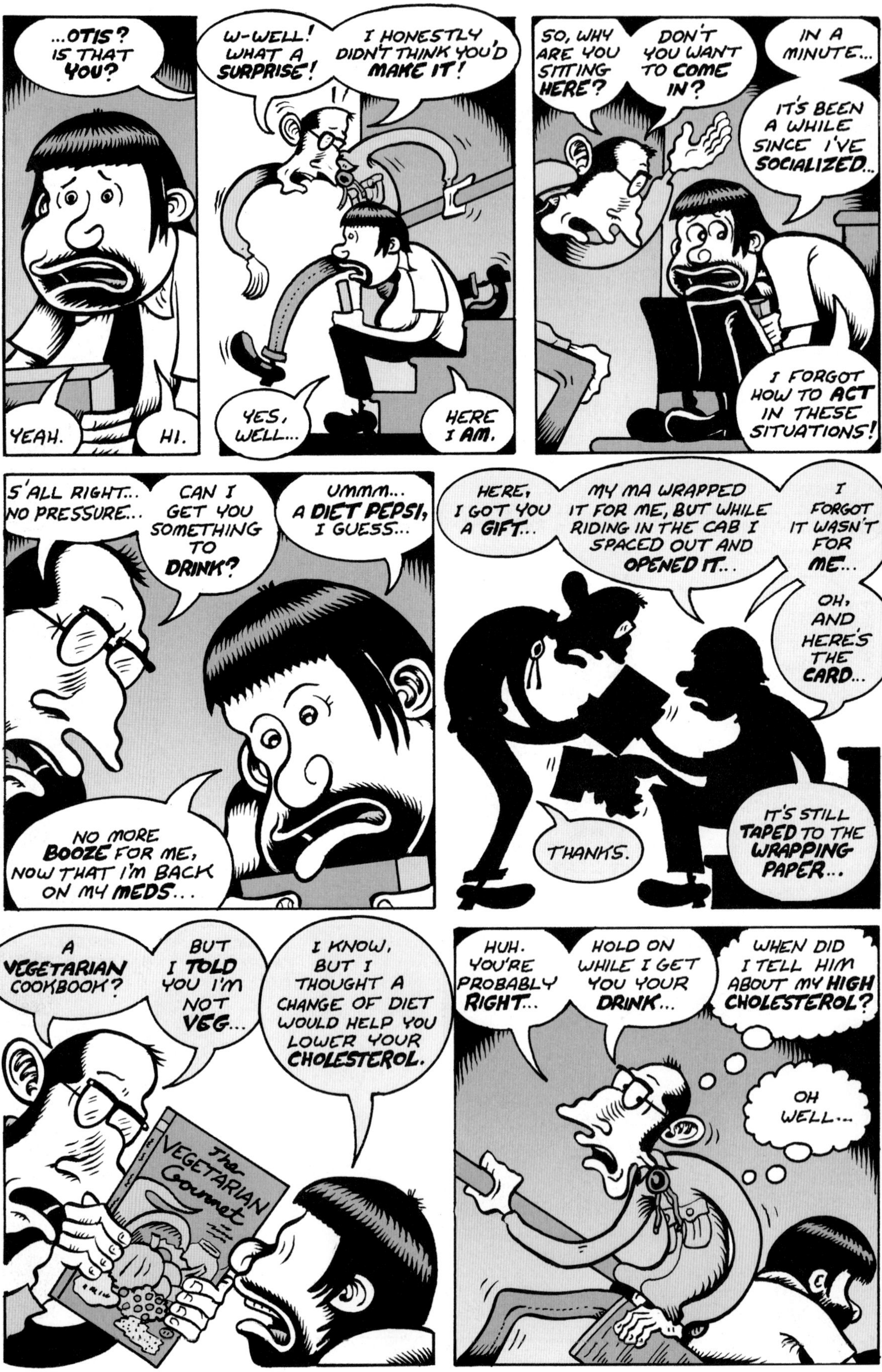
...OTIS? IS THAT YOU?
YEAH.
HI.
W-WELL! WHAT A SURPRISE!
I HONESTLY DIDN'T THINK YOU'D MAKE IT!
YES, WELL...
HERE I AM.
SO, WHY ARE YOU SITTING HERE?
DON'T YOU WANT TO COME IN?
IN A MINUTE...
IT'S BEEN A WHILE SINCE I'VE SOCIALIZED...
I FORGOT HOW TO ACT IN THESE SITUATIONS!
S'ALL RIGHT... NO PRESSURE...
CAN I GET YOU SOMETHING TO DRINK?
UMMM... A DIET PEPSI, I GUESS...
NO MORE BOOZE FOR ME, NOW THAT I'M BACK ON MY MEDS...
HERE, I GOT YOU A GIFT...
MY MA WRAPPED IT FOR ME, BUT WHILE RIDING IN THE CAB I SPACED OUT AND OPENED IT...
I FORGOT IT WASN'T FOR ME...
OH, AND HERE'S THE CARD...
THANKS.
IT'S STILL TAPED TO THE WRAPPING PAPER...
A VEGETARIAN COOKBOOK?
BUT I TOLD YOU I'M NOT VEG...
I KNOW, BUT I THOUGHT A CHANGE OF DIET WOULD HELP YOU LOWER YOUR CHOLESTEROL.
The VEGETARIAN Gourmet
HUH. YOU'RE PROBABLY RIGHT...
HOLD ON WHILE I GET YOU YOUR DRINK...
WHEN DID I TELL HIM ABOUT MY HIGH CHOLESTEROL?
OH WELL...

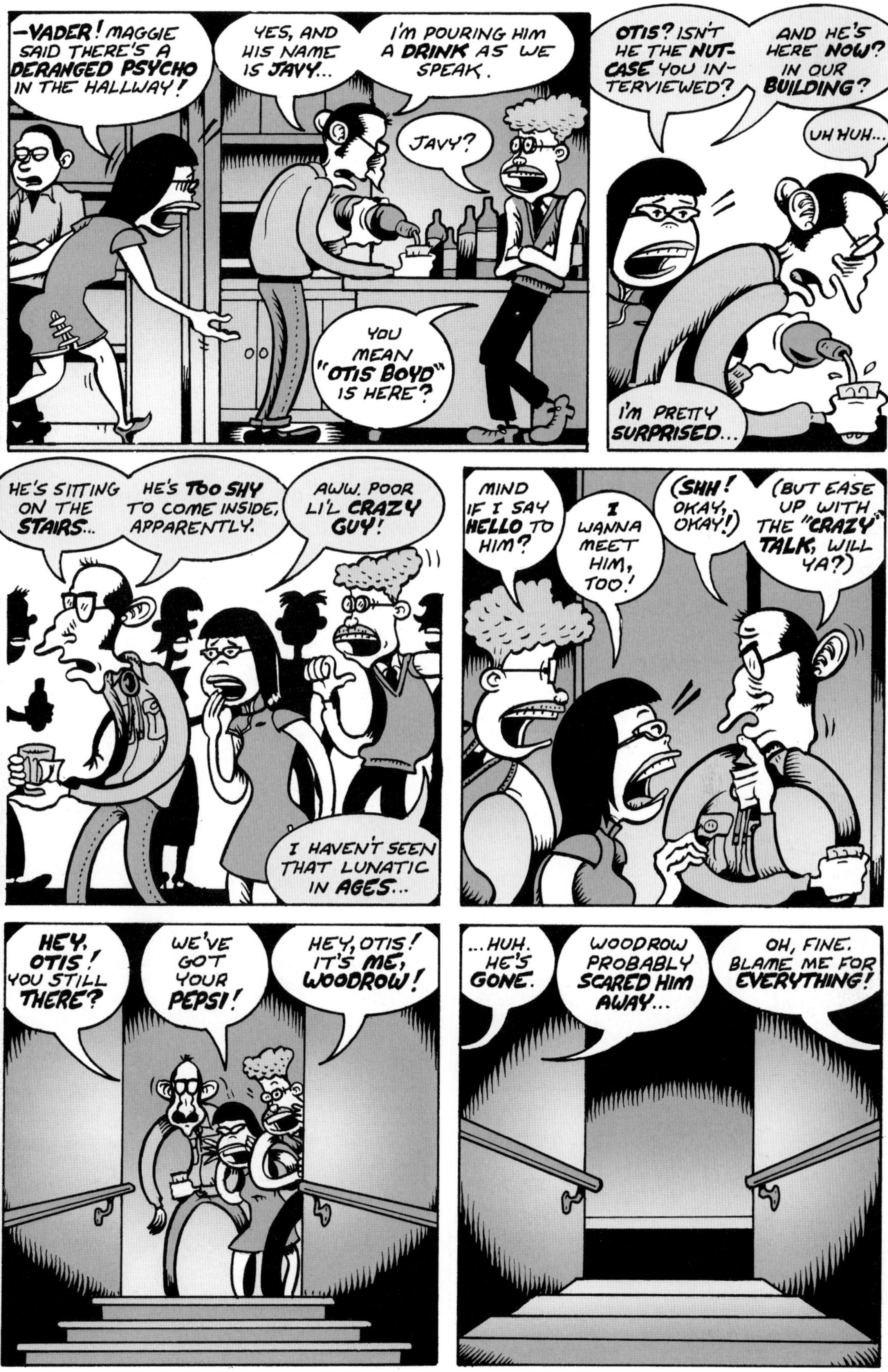
-VADER! MAGGIE SAID THERE'S A DERANGED PSYCHO IN THE HALLWAY!
YES, AND HIS NAME IS JAVY...
I'M POURING HIM A DRINK AS WE SPEAK.
JAVY?
YOU MEAN "OTIS BOYD" IS HERE?
OTIS? ISN'T HE THE NUT-CASE YOU IN-TERVIEWED?
AND HE'S HERE NOW? IN OUR BUILDING?
UH HUH...
I'M PRETTY SURPRISED...
HE'S SITTING ON THE STAIRS...
HE'S TOO SHY TO COME INSIDE, APPARENTLY.
AWW. POOR LI'L CRAZY GUY!
I HAVEN'T SEEN THAT LUNATIC IN AGES...
MIND IF I SAY HELLO TO HIM?
I WANNA MEET HIM, TOO!
(SHH! OKAY, OKAY!)
(BUT EASE UP WITH THE "CRAZY" TALK, WILL YA?)
HEY, OTIS! YOU STILL THERE?
WE'VE GOT YOUR PEPSI!
HEY, OTIS! IT'S ME, WOODROW!
...HUH. HE'S GONE.
WOODROW PROBABLY SCARED HIM AWAY...
OH, FINE. BLAME ME FOR EVERYTHING!

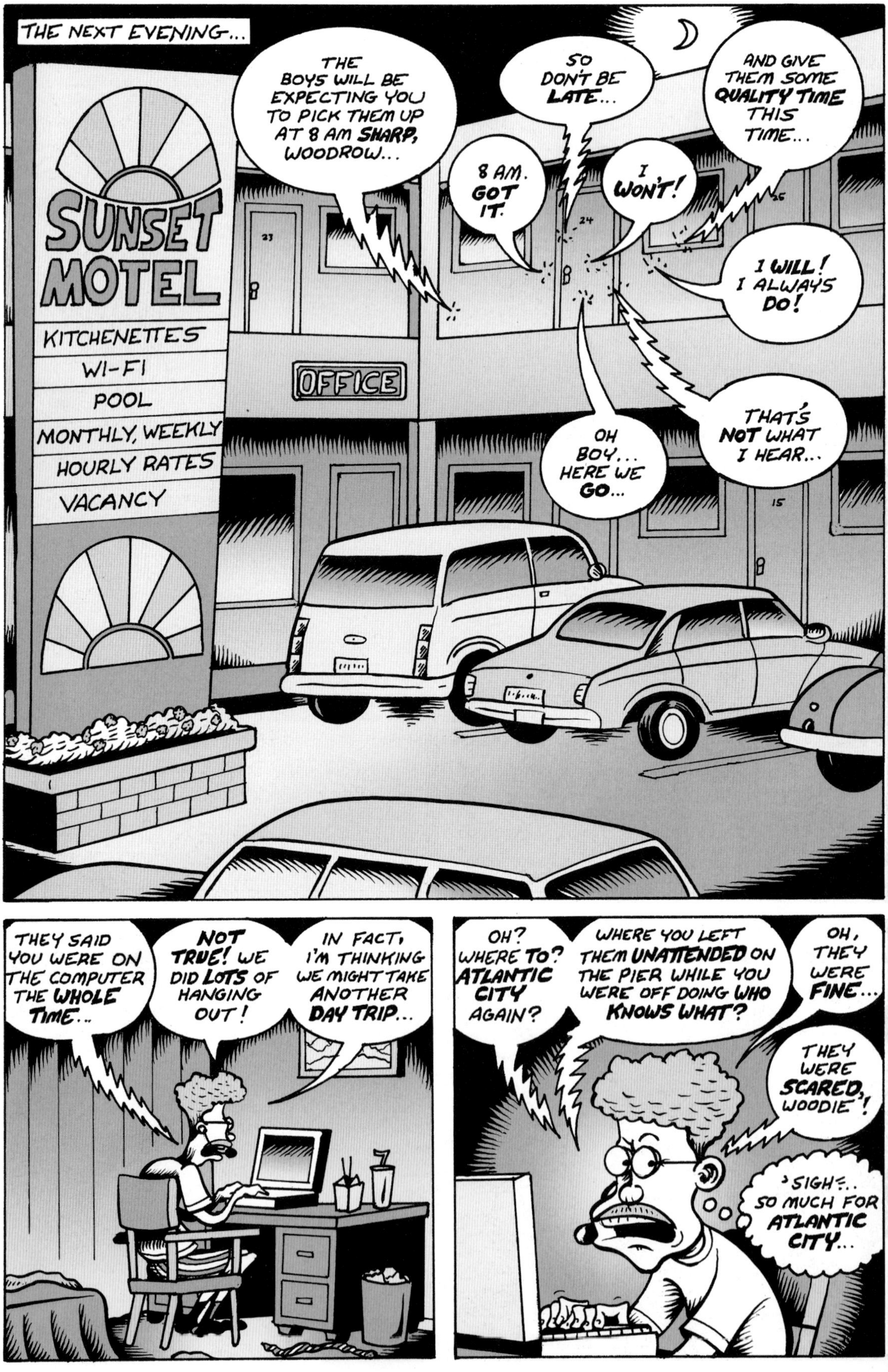
THE NEXT EVENING...
SUNSET MOTEL
KITCHENETTES
WI-FI
POOL
MONTHLY, WEEKLY
HOURLY RATES
VACANCY
OFFICE
THE BOYS WILL BE EXPECTING YOU TO PICK THEM UP AT 8 AM SHARP, WOODROW...
8 AM. GOT IT.
SO DON'T BE LATE...
I WON'T!
AND GIVE THEM SOME QUALITY TIME THIS TIME...
I WILL! I ALWAYS DO!
OH BOY... HERE WE GO...
THAT'S NOT WHAT I HEAR...
THEY SAID YOU WERE ON THE COMPUTER THE WHOLE TIME...
NOT TRUE! WE DID LOTS OF HANGING OUT!
IN FACT, I'M THINKING WE MIGHT TAKE ANOTHER DAY TRIP...
OH? WHERE TO? ATLANTIC CITY AGAIN?
WHERE YOU LEFT THEM UNATTENDED ON THE PIER WHILE YOU WERE OFF DOING WHO KNOWS WHAT?
OH, THEY WERE FINE...
THEY WERE SCARED, WOODIE!
SIGH... SO MUCH FOR ATLANTIC CITY...

SO WHERE ARE YOU TAKING THEM?

I DUNNO! I'LL THINK OF *SOME* PLACE...

OR WE'LL JUST HANG OUT **HERE**. THE BOYS **LOVE** THE SWIMMING POOL.

JAKE GOT AN **EAR** INFECTION FROM THAT POOL...

—HEY, YOU'RE NOT **GAMBLING** ONLINE AGAIN, ARE YOU?

W— **WHAT**? NO!

PokerMania.Com

W-WHAT GAVE YOU **THAT** IDEA?

THE BOYS SAW YOU PLAYING A **CARD GAME** ON THE COMPUTER...

ONLY YOU TOLD THEM YOU WERE PLAYING **SOLITAIRE**...

I **WAS** PLAYING SOLITAIRE!

OOH! NICE **HAND**!

I SUPPOSE IT'S NONE OF MY BUSINESS, NOW THAT WE'RE **DIVORCED**...

STILL, I WORRY YOU'LL SET A **BAD** EXAMPLE...

DON'T WORRY. I LEARNED MY LESSON...

FOLD, YOU **FUCK**!

BUT WHILE WE'RE ON THE SUBJECT...

MIND IF I ASK YOU A **HYPOTHETICAL** QUESTION?

UH-OH. **WHAT**?

LET'S SAY I CAME UP WITH A **NEW** SYSTEM FOR PLAYING POKER...

ONE THAT'S **MATHEMATICALLY PROVEN** TO GET **BETTER** RESULTS...

:SIGH.:

WOODY, **PLEASE.** I—

THE IDEA BEING TO **NEVER FOLD**, BASICALLY...

IT'S MORE OF A **PHILOSOPHY** THAN A "SYSTEM," I GUESS...

MAN! I'm **KICKING ASS** TO-NIGHT!

...rMania.Com

WINNER!

"**NEVER FOLD**," EH?

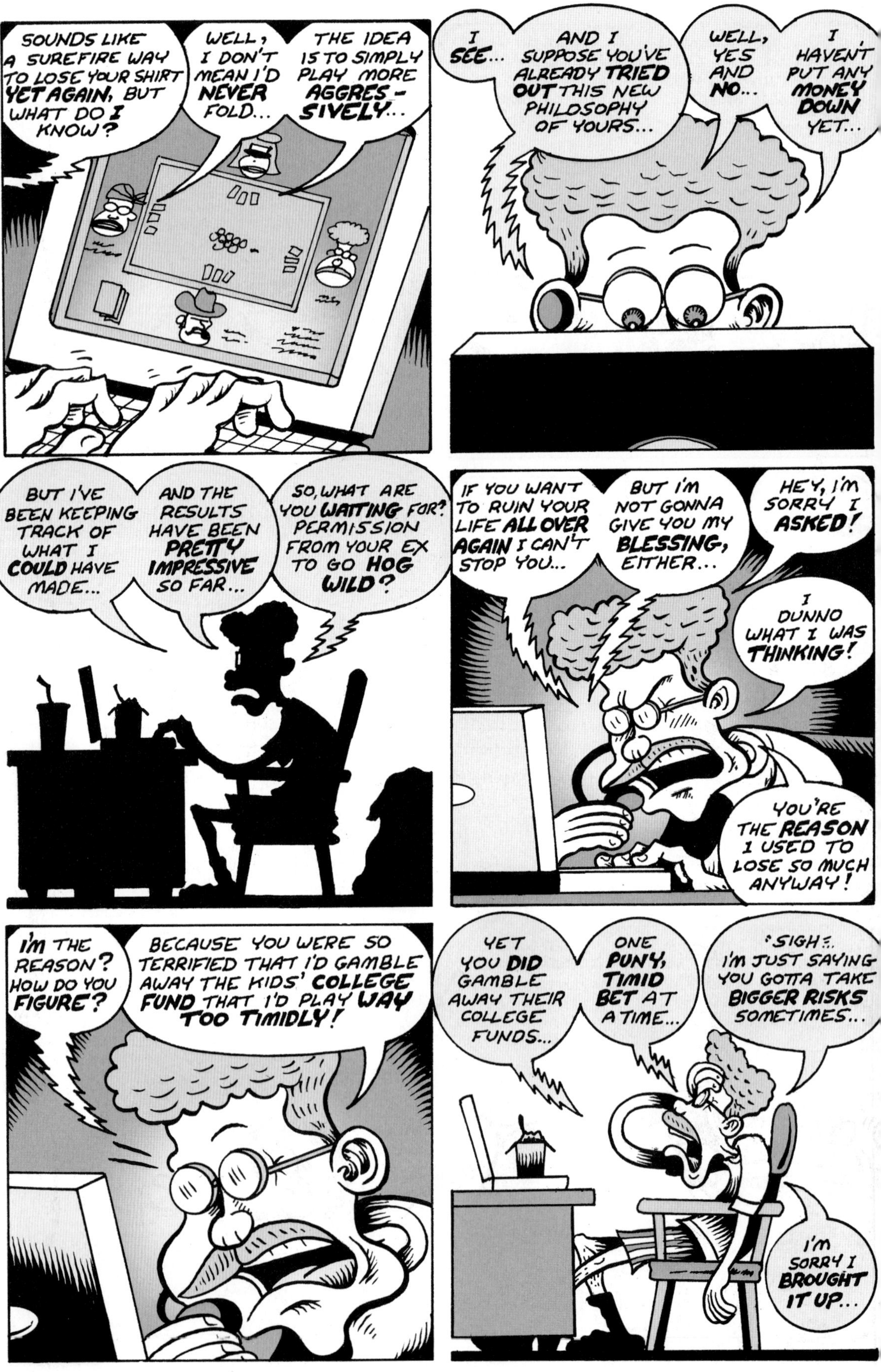
SOUNDS LIKE A SUREFIRE WAY TO LOSE YOUR SHIRT YET AGAIN, BUT WHAT DO I KNOW?
WELL, I DON'T MEAN I'D NEVER FOLD...
THE IDEA IS TO SIMPLY PLAY MORE AGGRES-SIVELY...
I SEE...
AND I SUPPOSE YOU'VE ALREADY TRIED OUT THIS NEW PHILOSOPHY OF YOURS...
WELL, YES AND NO...
I HAVEN'T PUT ANY MONEY DOWN YET...
BUT I'VE BEEN KEEPING TRACK OF WHAT I COULD HAVE MADE...
AND THE RESULTS HAVE BEEN PRETTY IMPRESSIVE SO FAR...
SO, WHAT ARE YOU WAITING FOR? PERMISSION FROM YOUR EX TO GO HOG WILD?
IF YOU WANT TO RUIN YOUR LIFE ALL OVER AGAIN I CAN'T STOP YOU...
BUT I'M NOT GONNA GIVE YOU MY BLESSING, EITHER...
HEY, I'M SORRY I ASKED!
I DUNNO WHAT I WAS THINKING!
YOU'RE THE REASON I USED TO LOSE SO MUCH ANYWAY!
I'M THE REASON? HOW DO YOU FIGURE?
BECAUSE YOU WERE SO TERRIFIED THAT I'D GAMBLE AWAY THE KIDS' COLLEGE FUND THAT I'D PLAY WAY TOO TIMIDLY!
YET YOU DID GAMBLE AWAY THEIR COLLEGE FUNDS...
ONE PUNY, TIMID BET AT A TIME...
SIGH... I'M JUST SAYING YOU GOTTA TAKE BIGGER RISKS SOMETIMES...
I'M SORRY I BROUGHT IT UP...

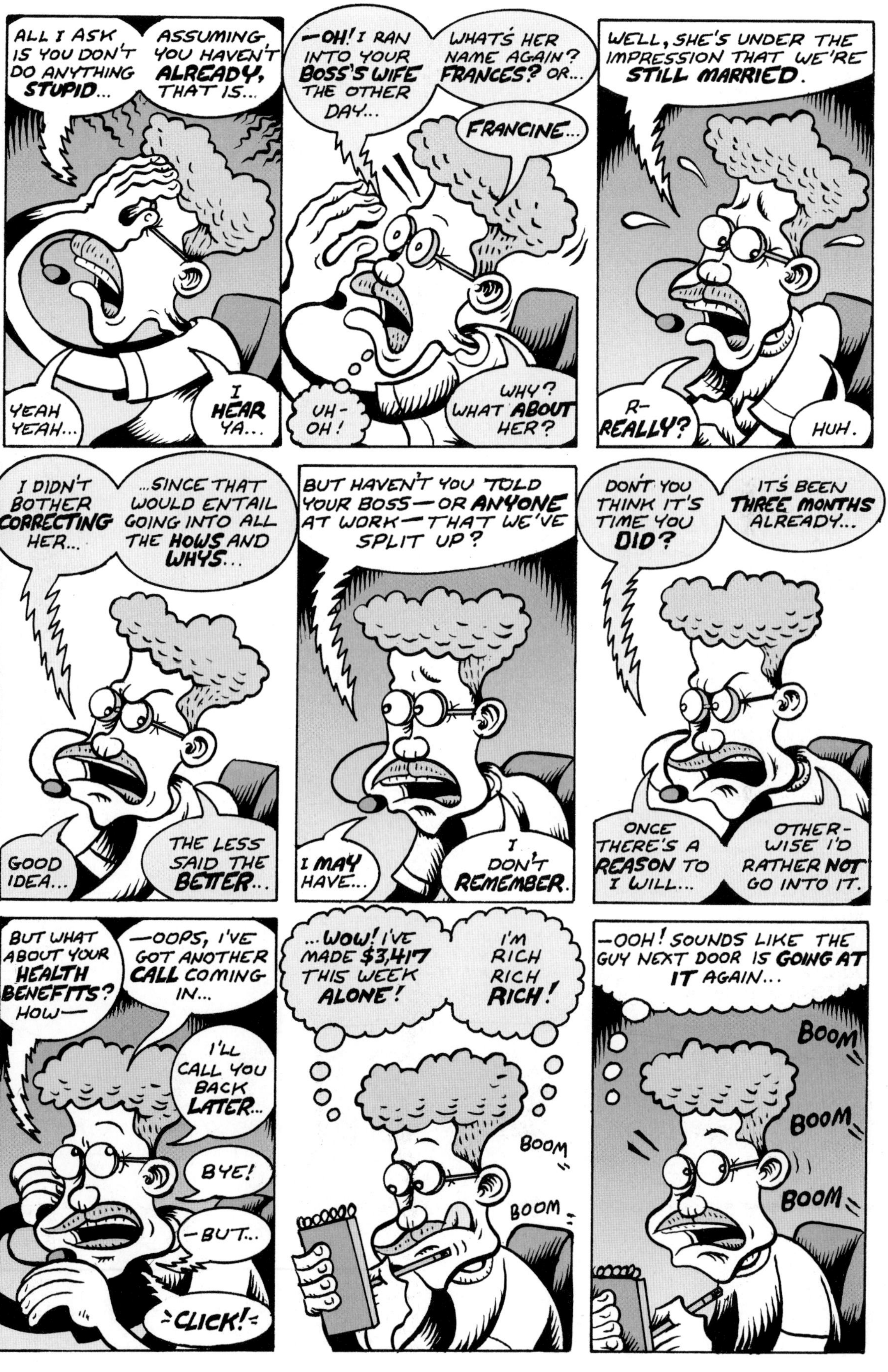

ALL I ASK IS YOU DON'T DO ANYTHING STUPID...
ASSUMING YOU HAVEN'T ALREADY, THAT IS...
YEAH YEAH...
I HEAR YA...
—OH! I RAN INTO YOUR BOSS'S WIFE THE OTHER DAY...
WHAT'S HER NAME AGAIN? FRANCES? OR...
FRANCINE...
UH-OH!
WHY? WHAT ABOUT HER?
WELL, SHE'S UNDER THE IMPRESSION THAT WE'RE STILL MARRIED.
R-REALLY?
HUH.
I DIDN'T BOTHER CORRECTING HER...
...SINCE THAT WOULD ENTAIL GOING INTO ALL THE HOWS AND WHYS...
GOOD IDEA...
THE LESS SAID THE BETTER...
BUT HAVEN'T YOU TOLD YOUR BOSS—OR ANYONE AT WORK—THAT WE'VE SPLIT UP?
I MAY HAVE...
I DON'T REMEMBER.
DON'T YOU THINK IT'S TIME YOU DID?
IT'S BEEN THREE MONTHS ALREADY...
ONCE THERE'S A REASON TO I WILL...
OTHER-WISE I'D RATHER NOT GO INTO IT.
BUT WHAT ABOUT YOUR HEALTH BENEFITS? HOW—
—OOPS, I'VE GOT ANOTHER CALL COMING IN...
I'LL CALL YOU BACK LATER...
BYE!
—BUT...
CLICK!
...WOW! I'VE MADE $3,417 THIS WEEK ALONE!
I'M RICH RICH RICH!
BOOM
BOOM
—OOH! SOUNDS LIKE THE GUY NEXT DOOR IS GOING AT IT AGAIN...
BOOM
BOOM
BOOM

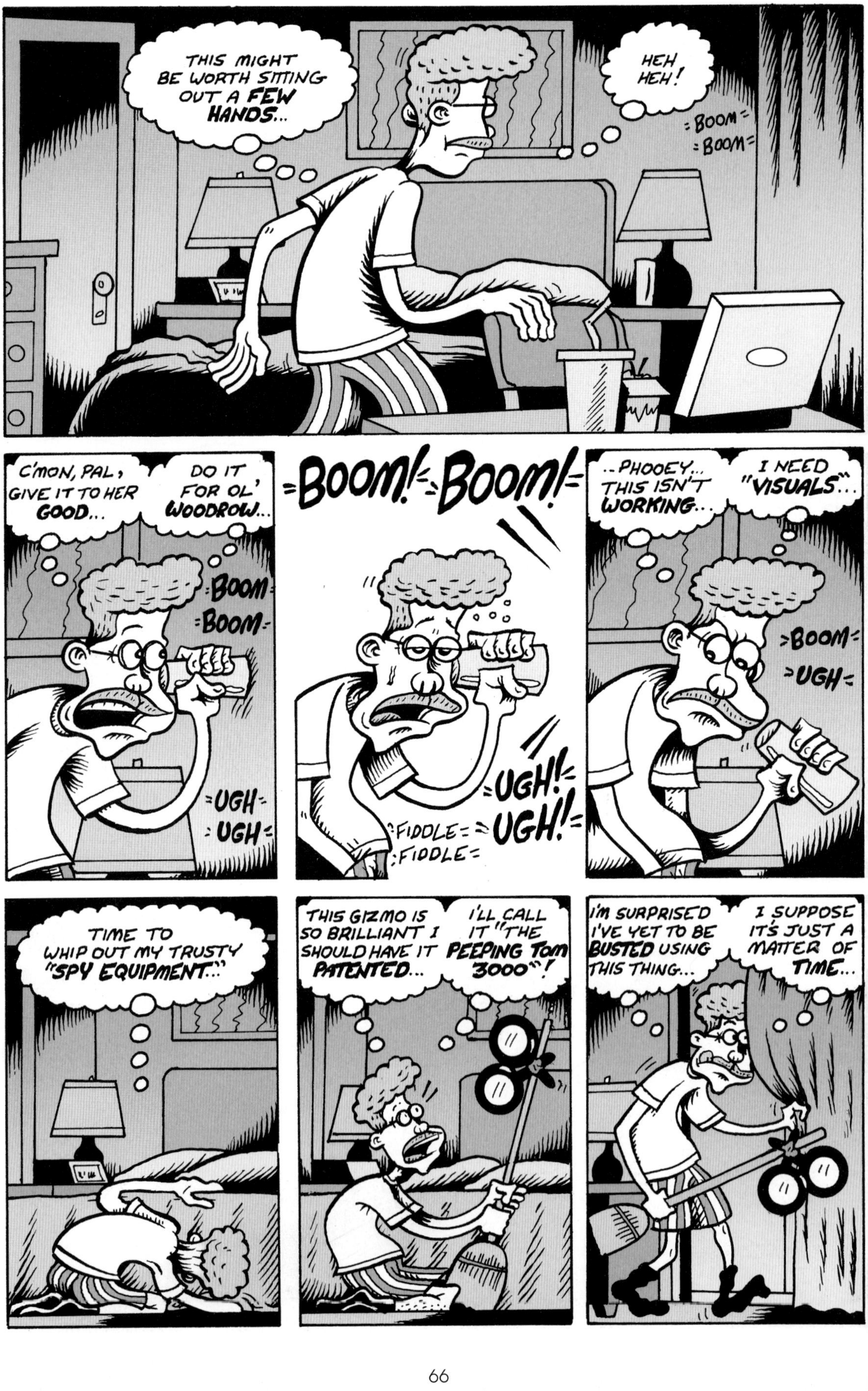
THIS MIGHT BE WORTH SITTING OUT A FEW HANDS...
HEH HEH!
BOOM
BOOM
C'MON, PAL, GIVE IT TO HER GOOD...
DO IT FOR OL' WOODROW...
BOOM
BOOM
UGH
UGH
BOOM! BOOM!
UGH! UGH!
FIDDLE FIDDLE
..PHOOEY... THIS ISN'T WORKING...
I NEED "VISUALS"...
BOOM
UGH
TIME TO WHIP OUT MY TRUSTY "SPY EQUIPMENT."
THIS GIZMO IS SO BRILLIANT I SHOULD HAVE IT PATENTED...
I'LL CALL IT "THE PEEPING TOM 3000"!
I'M SURPRISED I'VE YET TO BE BUSTED USING THIS THING...
I SUPPOSE IT'S JUST A MATTER OF TIME...

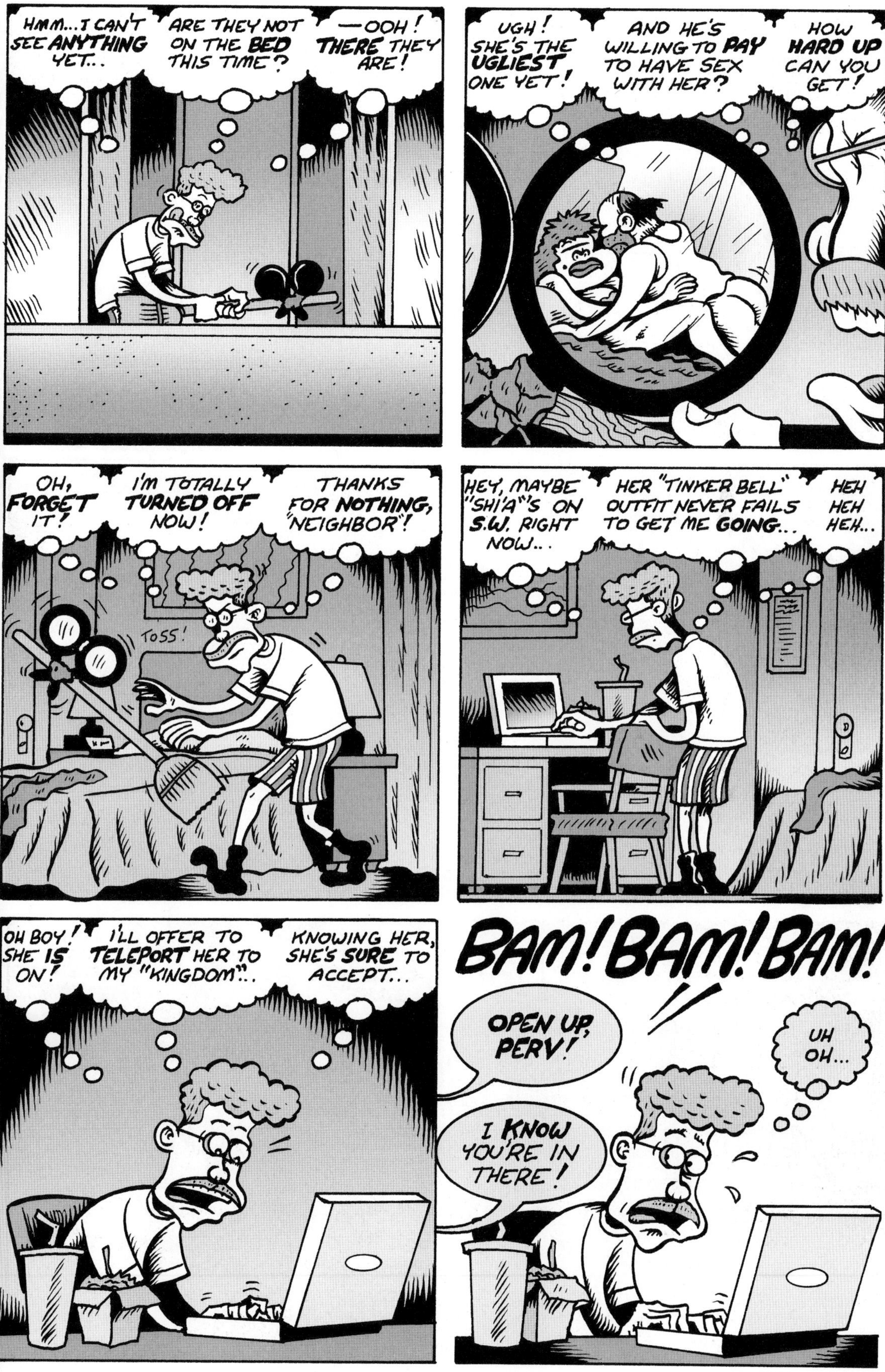
HMM...I CAN'T SEE ANYTHING YET...
ARE THEY NOT ON THE BED THIS TIME?
—OOH! THERE THEY ARE!
UGH! SHE'S THE UGLIEST ONE YET!
AND HE'S WILLING TO PAY TO HAVE SEX WITH HER?
HOW HARD UP CAN YOU GET!
OH, FORGET IT!
I'M TOTALLY TURNED OFF NOW!
THANKS FOR NOTHING, "NEIGHBOR"!
TOSS!
HEY, MAYBE "SHI'A"'S ON S.W. RIGHT NOW...
HER "TINKER BELL" OUTFIT NEVER FAILS TO GET ME GOING...
HEH HEH HEH...
OH BOY! SHE IS ON!
I'LL OFFER TO TELEPORT HER TO MY "KINGDOM"...
KNOWING HER, SHE'S SURE TO ACCEPT...
BAM! BAM! BAM!
OPEN UP, PERV!
I KNOW YOU'RE IN THERE!
UH OH...

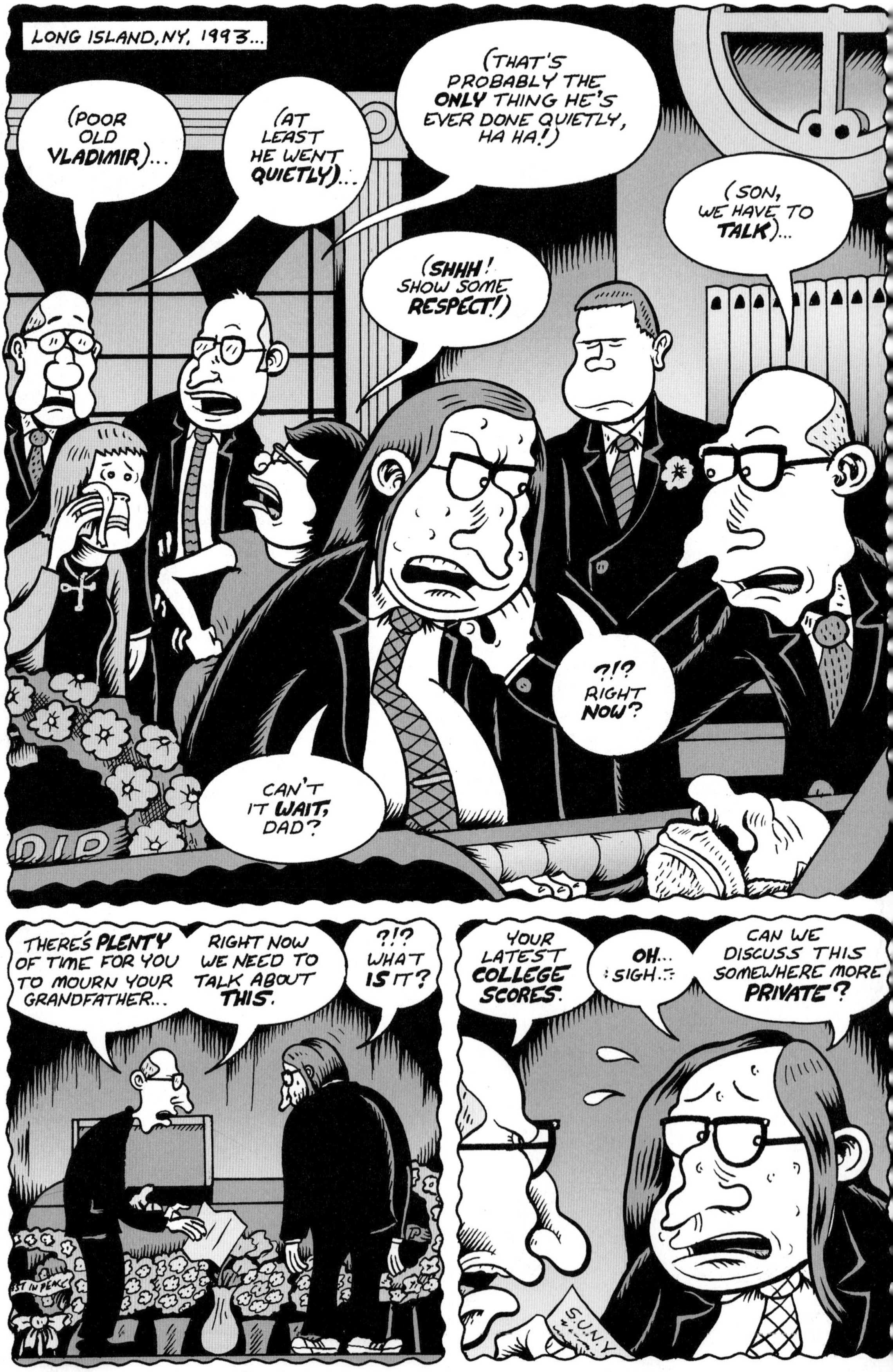
LONG ISLAND, NY, 1993...
(POOR OLD VLADIMIR)...
(AT LEAST HE WENT QUIETLY)...
(THAT'S PROBABLY THE ONLY THING HE'S EVER DONE QUIETLY, HA HA!)
(SHHH! SHOW SOME RESPECT!)
(SON, WE HAVE TO TALK)...
?!? RIGHT NOW?
CAN'T IT WAIT, DAD?
THERE'S PLENTY OF TIME FOR YOU TO MOURN YOUR GRANDFATHER...
RIGHT NOW WE NEED TO TALK ABOUT THIS.
?!? WHAT IS IT?
YOUR LATEST COLLEGE SCORES.
OH... SIGH...
CAN WE DISCUSS THIS SOMEWHERE MORE PRIVATE?
S.U.N.Y

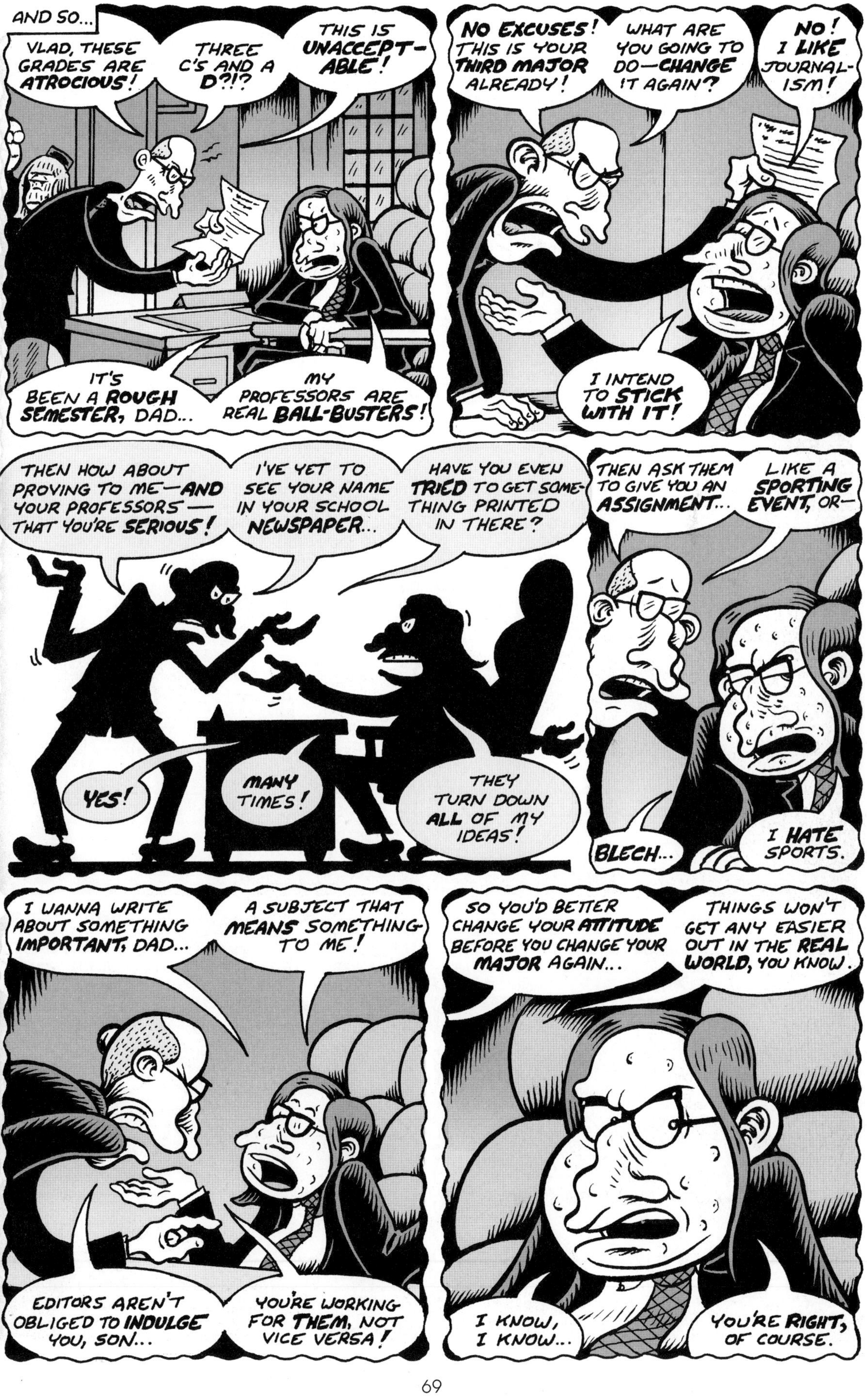
AND SO...
VLAD, THESE GRADES ARE ATROCIOUS!
THREE C'S AND A D?!?
THIS IS UNACCEPTABLE!
IT'S BEEN A ROUGH SEMESTER, DAD...
MY PROFESSORS ARE REAL BALL-BUSTERS!
NO EXCUSES! THIS IS YOUR THIRD MAJOR ALREADY!
WHAT ARE YOU GOING TO DO—CHANGE IT AGAIN?
NO! I LIKE JOURNALISM!
I INTEND TO STICK WITH IT!
THEN HOW ABOUT PROVING TO ME—AND YOUR PROFESSORS—THAT YOU'RE SERIOUS!
I'VE YET TO SEE YOUR NAME IN YOUR SCHOOL NEWSPAPER...
HAVE YOU EVEN TRIED TO GET SOMETHING PRINTED IN THERE?
YES!
MANY TIMES!
THEY TURN DOWN ALL OF MY IDEAS!
THEN ASK THEM TO GIVE YOU AN ASSIGNMENT...
LIKE A SPORTING EVENT, OR—
BLECH...
I HATE SPORTS.
I WANNA WRITE ABOUT SOMETHING IMPORTANT, DAD...
A SUBJECT THAT MEANS SOMETHING TO ME!
EDITORS AREN'T OBLIGED TO INDULGE YOU, SON...
YOU'RE WORKING FOR THEM, NOT VICE VERSA!
SO YOU'D BETTER CHANGE YOUR ATTITUDE BEFORE YOU CHANGE YOUR MAJOR AGAIN...
THINGS WON'T GET ANY EASIER OUT IN THE REAL WORLD, YOU KNOW.
I KNOW, I KNOW...
YOU'RE RIGHT, OF COURSE.

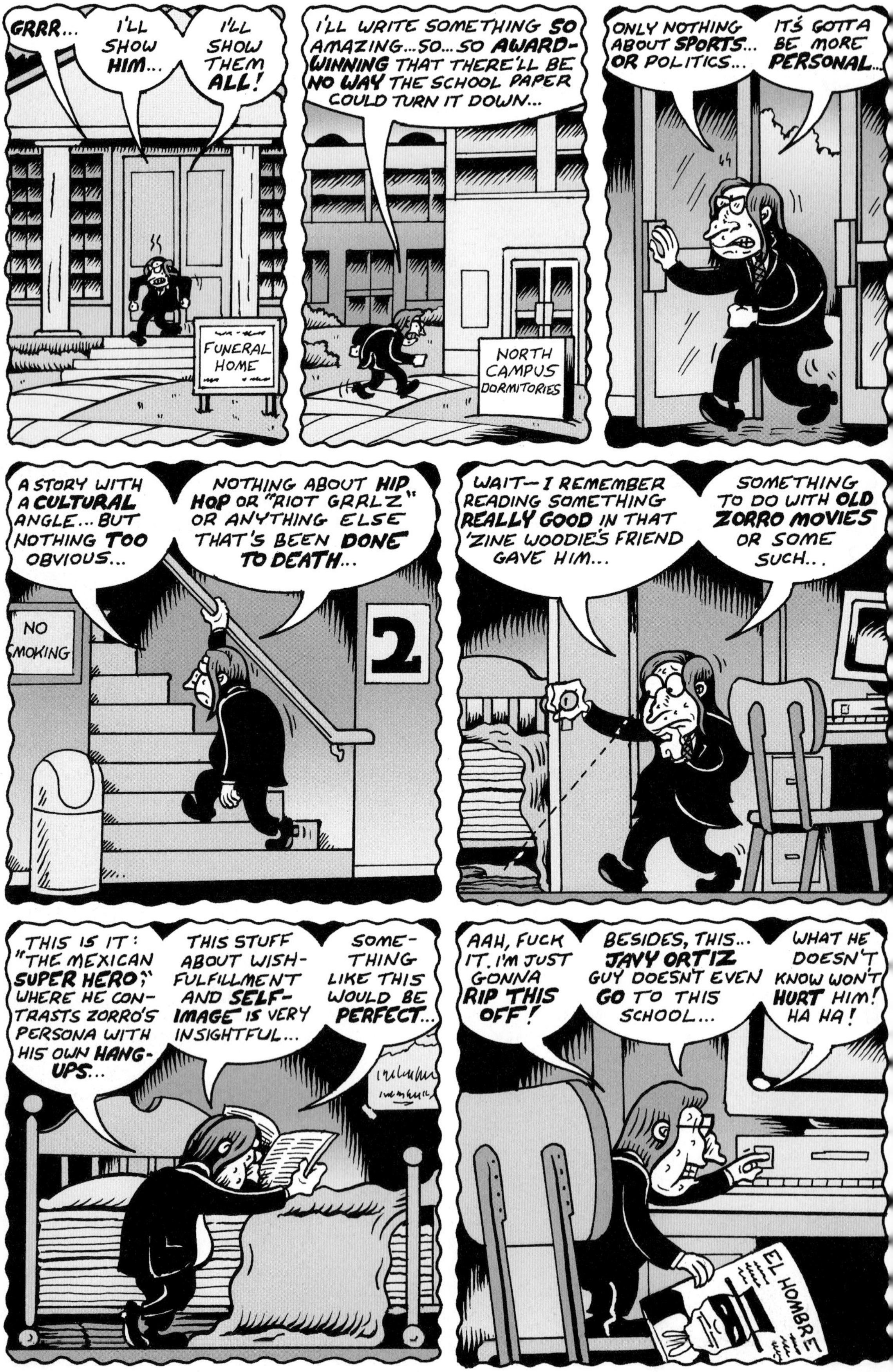
GRRR...
I'LL SHOW HIM...
I'LL SHOW THEM ALL!
FUNERAL HOME
I'LL WRITE SOMETHING SO AMAZING...SO...SO AWARD-WINNING THAT THERE'LL BE NO WAY THE SCHOOL PAPER COULD TURN IT DOWN...
NORTH CAMPUS DORMITORIES
ONLY NOTHING ABOUT SPORTS... OR POLITICS...
IT'S GOTTA BE MORE PERSONAL...
A STORY WITH A CULTURAL ANGLE... BUT NOTHING TOO OBVIOUS...
NOTHING ABOUT HIP HOP OR "RIOT GRRLZ" OR ANYTHING ELSE THAT'S BEEN DONE TO DEATH...
NO SMOKING
2
WAIT— I REMEMBER READING SOMETHING REALLY GOOD IN THAT 'ZINE WOODIE'S FRIEND GAVE HIM...
SOMETHING TO DO WITH OLD ZORRO MOVIES OR SOME SUCH...
THIS IS IT: "THE MEXICAN SUPER HERO," WHERE HE CONTRASTS ZORRO'S PERSONA WITH HIS OWN HANG-UPS...
THIS STUFF ABOUT WISH-FULFILLMENT AND SELF-IMAGE IS VERY INSIGHTFUL...
SOMETHING LIKE THIS WOULD BE PERFECT...
AAH, FUCK IT. I'M JUST GONNA RIP THIS OFF!
BESIDES, THIS... JAVY ORTIZ GUY DOESN'T EVEN GO TO THIS SCHOOL...
WHAT HE DOESN'T KNOW WON'T HURT HIM! HA HA!
EL HOMBRE

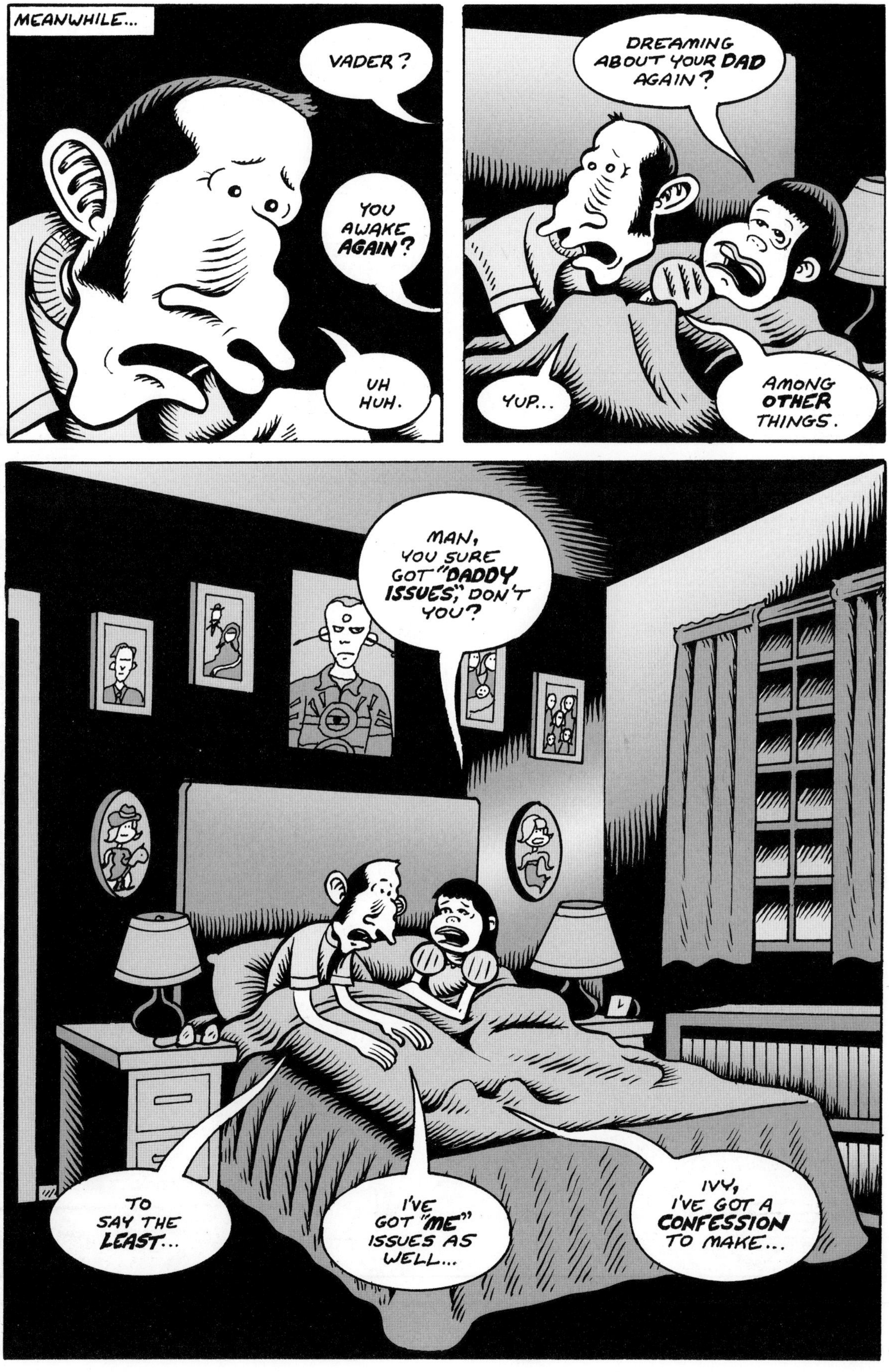
MEANWHILE...
VADER?
YOU AWAKE AGAIN?
UH HUH.
DREAMING ABOUT YOUR DAD AGAIN?
YUP...
AMONG OTHER THINGS.
MAN, YOU SURE GOT "DADDY ISSUES," DON'T YOU?
TO SAY THE LEAST...
I'VE GOT "ME" ISSUES AS WELL...
IVY, I'VE GOT A CONFESSION TO MAKE...

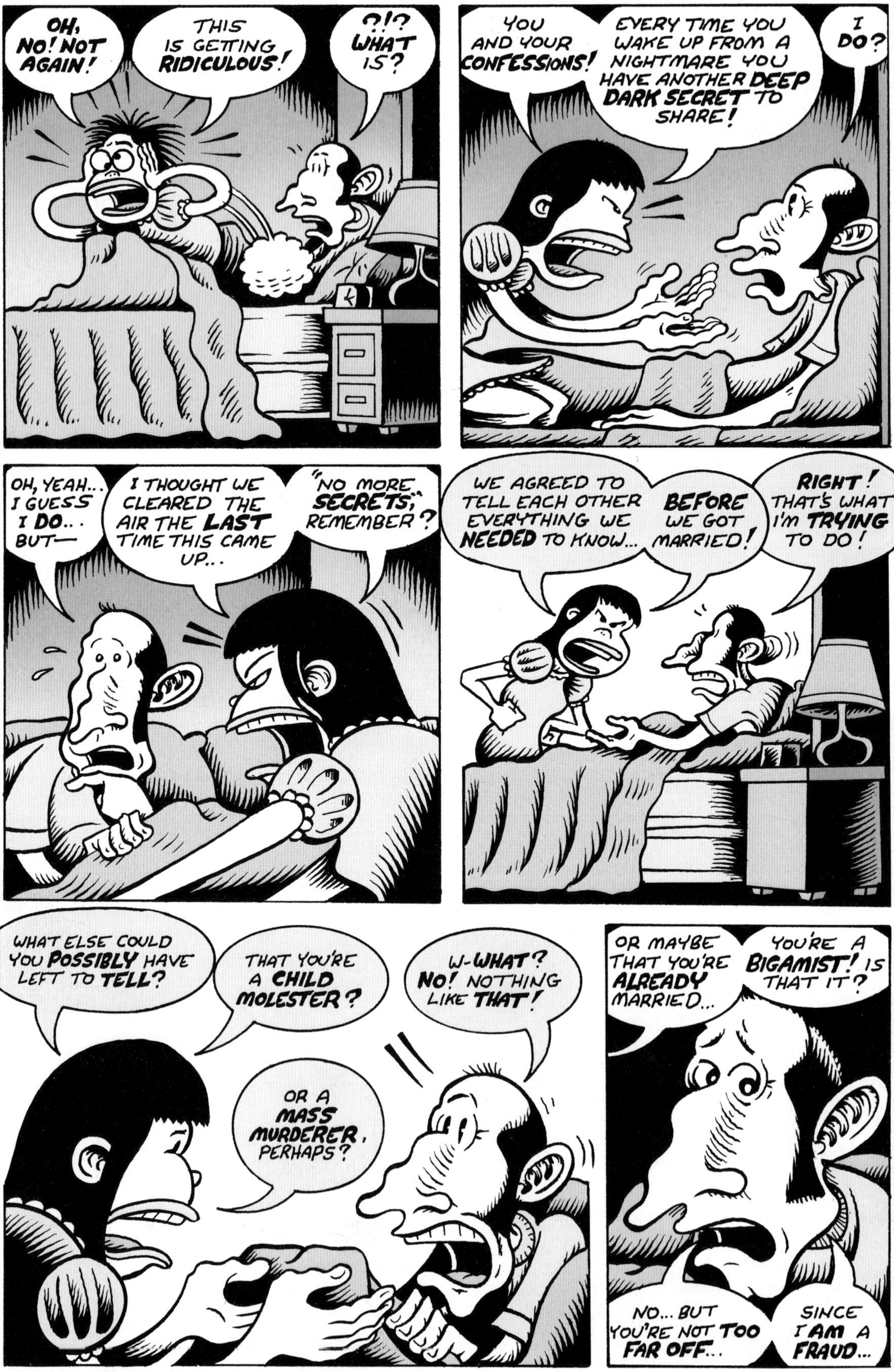
OH, NO! NOT AGAIN!
THIS IS GETTING RIDICULOUS!
?!? WHAT IS?
YOU AND YOUR CONFESSIONS!
EVERY TIME YOU WAKE UP FROM A NIGHTMARE YOU HAVE ANOTHER DEEP DARK SECRET TO SHARE!
I DO?
OH, YEAH... I GUESS I DO... BUT—
I THOUGHT WE CLEARED THE AIR THE LAST TIME THIS CAME UP...
"NO MORE SECRETS," REMEMBER?
WE AGREED TO TELL EACH OTHER EVERYTHING WE NEEDED TO KNOW...
BEFORE WE GOT MARRIED!
RIGHT! THAT'S WHAT I'M TRYING TO DO!
WHAT ELSE COULD YOU POSSIBLY HAVE LEFT TO TELL?
THAT YOU'RE A CHILD MOLESTER?
W-WHAT? NO! NOTHING LIKE THAT!
OR A MASS MURDERER, PERHAPS?
OR MAYBE THAT YOU'RE ALREADY MARRIED...
YOU'RE A BIGAMIST! IS THAT IT?
NO... BUT YOU'RE NOT TOO FAR OFF...
SINCE I AM A FRAUD...

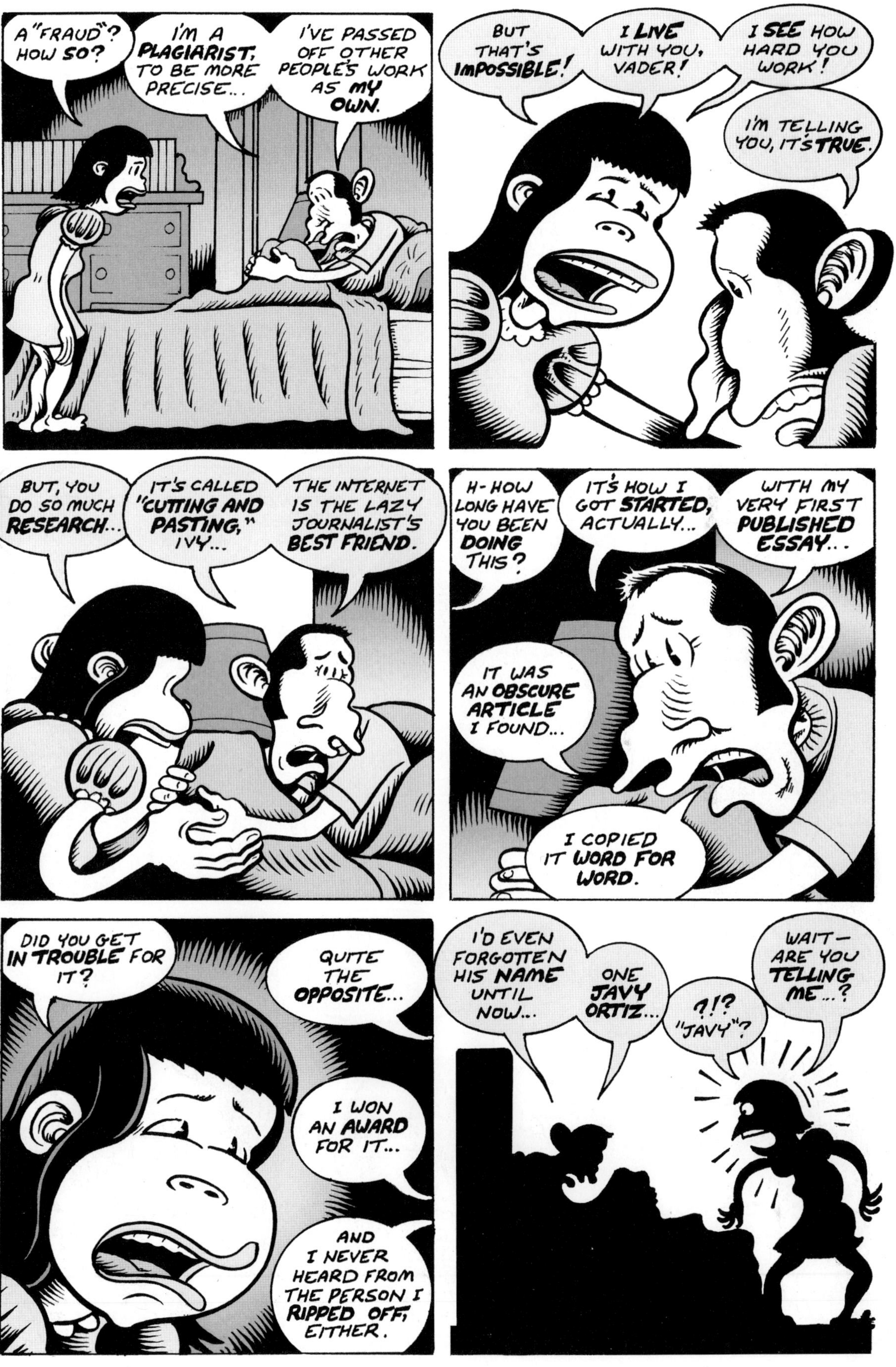
A "FRAUD"? HOW SO?
I'M A PLAGIARIST, TO BE MORE PRECISE...
I'VE PASSED OFF OTHER PEOPLE'S WORK AS MY OWN.
BUT THAT'S IMPOSSIBLE!
I LIVE WITH YOU, VADER!
I SEE HOW HARD YOU WORK!
I'M TELLING YOU, IT'S TRUE.
BUT, YOU DO SO MUCH RESEARCH...
IT'S CALLED "CUTTING AND PASTING," IVY...
THE INTERNET IS THE LAZY JOURNALIST'S BEST FRIEND.
H-HOW LONG HAVE YOU BEEN DOING THIS?
IT'S HOW I GOT STARTED, ACTUALLY...
WITH MY VERY FIRST PUBLISHED ESSAY...
IT WAS AN OBSCURE ARTICLE I FOUND...
I COPIED IT WORD FOR WORD.
DID YOU GET IN TROUBLE FOR IT?
QUITE THE OPPOSITE...
I WON AN AWARD FOR IT...
AND I NEVER HEARD FROM THE PERSON I RIPPED OFF, EITHER.
I'D EVEN FORGOTTEN HIS NAME UNTIL NOW...
ONE JAVY ORTIZ...
?!? "JAVY"?
WAIT— ARE YOU TELLING ME...?

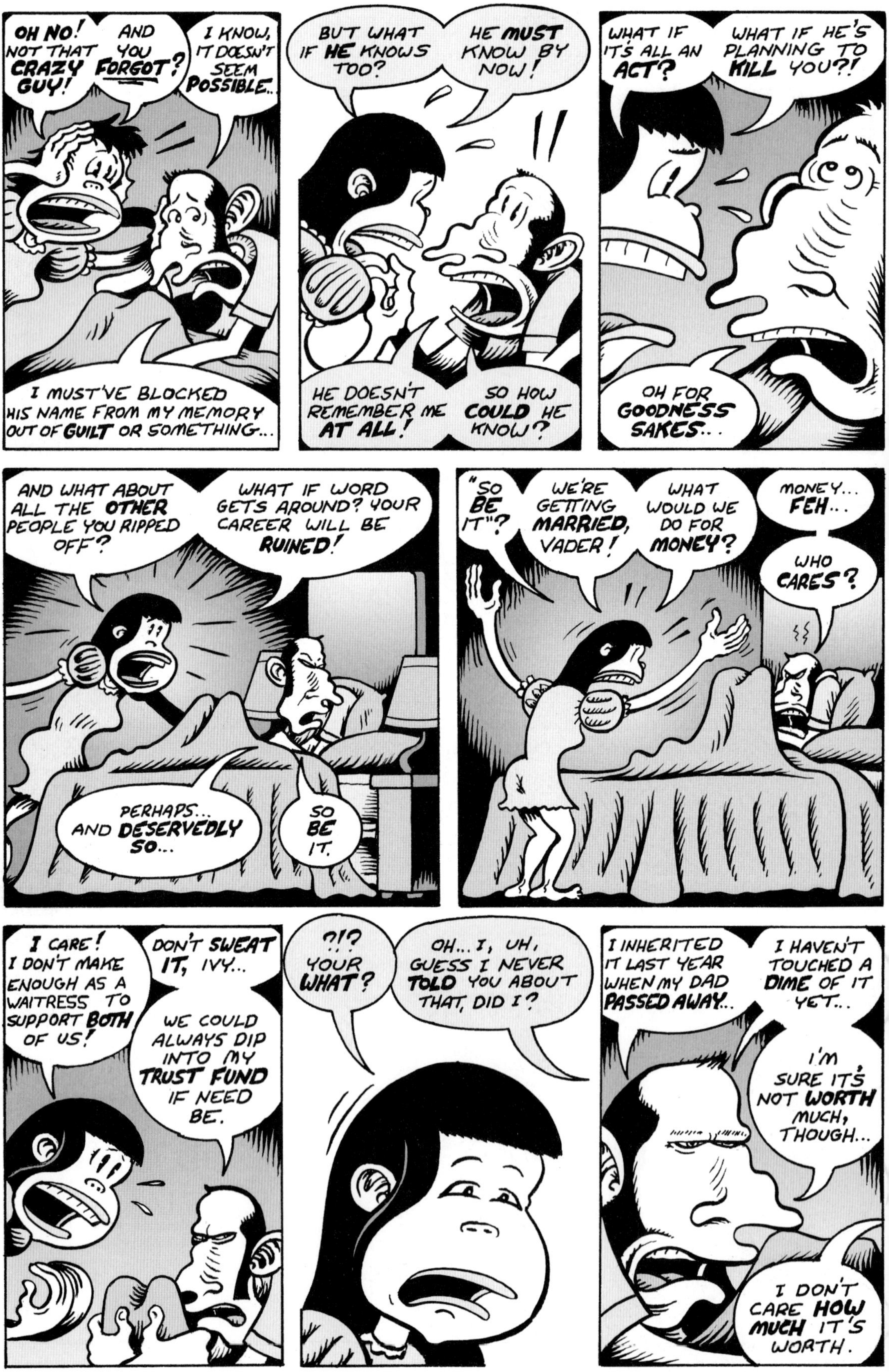
OH NO! NOT THAT CRAZY GUY!
AND YOU FORGOT?
I KNOW, IT DOESN'T SEEM POSSIBLE..
I MUST'VE BLOCKED HIS NAME FROM MY MEMORY OUT OF GUILT OR SOMETHING...
BUT WHAT IF HE KNOWS TOO?
HE MUST KNOW BY NOW!
HE DOESN'T REMEMBER ME AT ALL!
SO HOW COULD HE KNOW?
WHAT IF IT'S ALL AN ACT?
WHAT IF HE'S PLANNING TO KILL YOU?!
OH FOR GOODNESS SAKES...
AND WHAT ABOUT ALL THE OTHER PEOPLE YOU RIPPED OFF?
WHAT IF WORD GETS AROUND? YOUR CAREER WILL BE RUINED!
PERHAPS... AND DESERVEDLY SO...
SO BE IT.
"SO BE IT"?
WE'RE GETTING MARRIED, VADER!
WHAT WOULD WE DO FOR MONEY?
MONEY... FEH...
WHO CARES?
I CARE! I DON'T MAKE ENOUGH AS A WAITRESS TO SUPPORT BOTH OF US!
DON'T SWEAT IT, IVY...
WE COULD ALWAYS DIP INTO MY TRUST FUND IF NEED BE.
?!? YOUR WHAT?
OH... I, UH, GUESS I NEVER TOLD YOU ABOUT THAT, DID I?
I INHERITED IT LAST YEAR WHEN MY DAD PASSED AWAY...
I HAVEN'T TOUCHED A DIME OF IT YET...
I'M SURE IT'S NOT WORTH MUCH, THOUGH...
I DON'T CARE HOW MUCH IT'S WORTH.

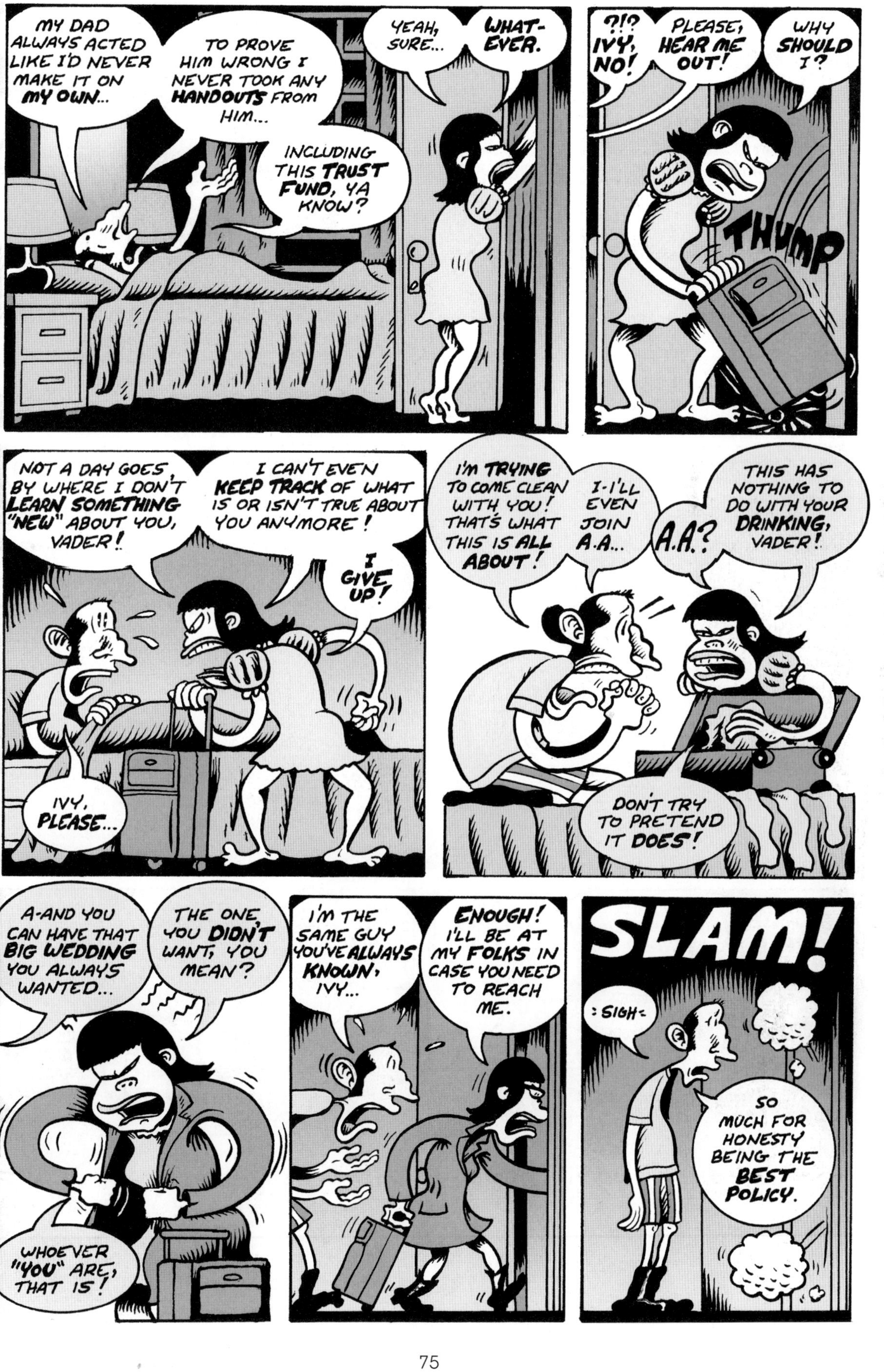

MY DAD ALWAYS ACTED LIKE I'D NEVER MAKE IT ON MY OWN...
TO PROVE HIM WRONG I NEVER TOOK ANY HANDOUTS FROM HIM...
INCLUDING THIS TRUST FUND, YA KNOW?
YEAH, SURE...
WHAT-EVER.
?!? IVY, NO!
PLEASE, HEAR ME OUT!
WHY SHOULD I?
THUMP
NOT A DAY GOES BY WHERE I DON'T LEARN SOMETHING "NEW" ABOUT YOU, VADER!
I CAN'T EVEN KEEP TRACK OF WHAT IS OR ISN'T TRUE ABOUT YOU ANYMORE!
I GIVE UP!
IVY, PLEASE...
I'M TRYING TO COME CLEAN WITH YOU! THAT'S WHAT THIS IS ALL ABOUT!
I-I'LL EVEN JOIN A.A...
A.A.?
THIS HAS NOTHING TO DO WITH YOUR DRINKING, VADER!
DON'T TRY TO PRETEND IT DOES!
A-AND YOU CAN HAVE THAT BIG WEDDING YOU ALWAYS WANTED...
THE ONE YOU DIDN'T WANT, YOU MEAN?
WHOEVER "YOU" ARE, THAT IS!
I'M THE SAME GUY YOU'VE ALWAYS KNOWN, IVY...
ENOUGH! I'LL BE AT MY FOLKS IN CASE YOU NEED TO REACH ME.
SLAM!
:SIGH:
SO MUCH FOR HONESTY BEING THE BEST POLICY.

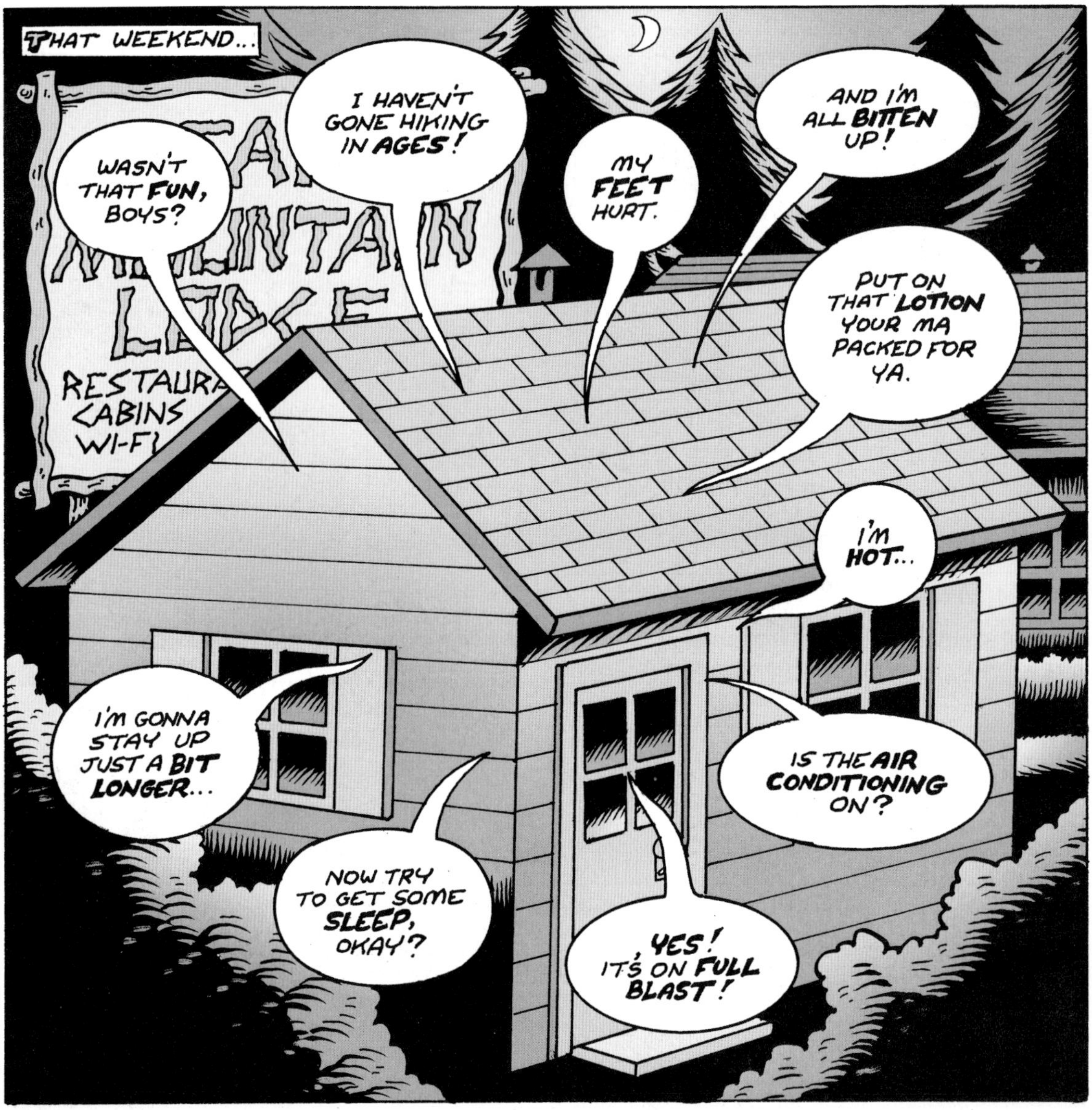
THAT WEEKEND...
WASN'T THAT FUN, BOYS?
I HAVEN'T GONE HIKING IN AGES!
MY FEET HURT.
AND I'M ALL BITTEN UP!
PUT ON THAT LOTION YOUR MA PACKED FOR YA.
I'M HOT...
I'M GONNA STAY UP JUST A BIT LONGER...
IS THE AIR CONDITIONING ON?
NOW TRY TO GET SOME SLEEP, OKAY?
YES! IT'S ON FULL BLAST!

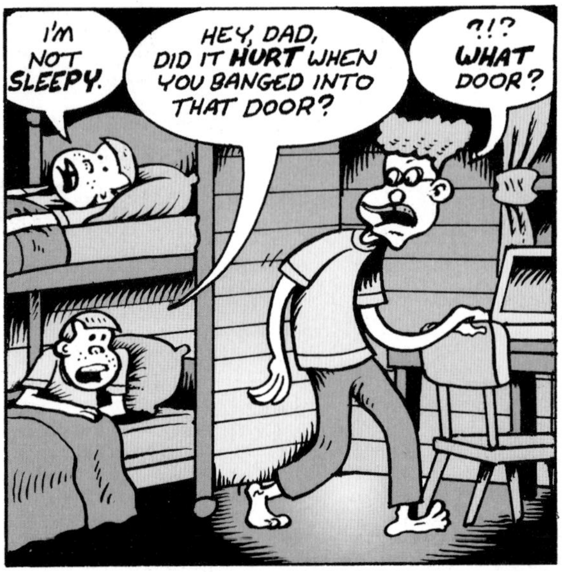
I'M NOT SLEEPY.
HEY, DAD, DID IT HURT WHEN YOU BANGED INTO THAT DOOR?
?!? WHAT DOOR?

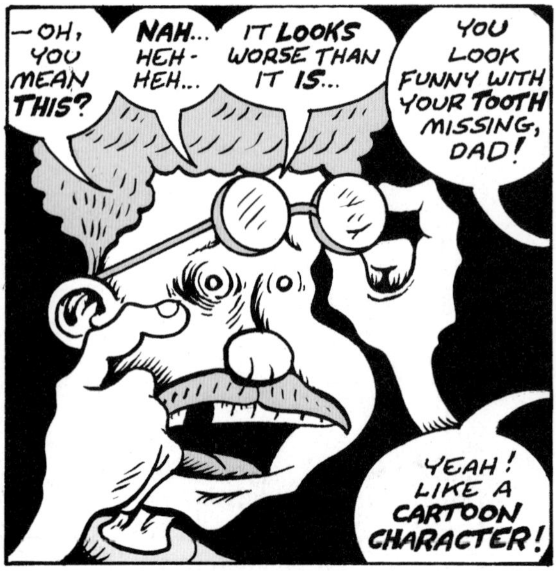
—OH, YOU MEAN THIS?
NAH... HEH-HEH...
IT LOOKS WORSE THAN IT IS...
YOU LOOK FUNNY WITH YOUR TOOTH MISSING, DAD!
YEAH! LIKE A CARTOON CHARACTER!

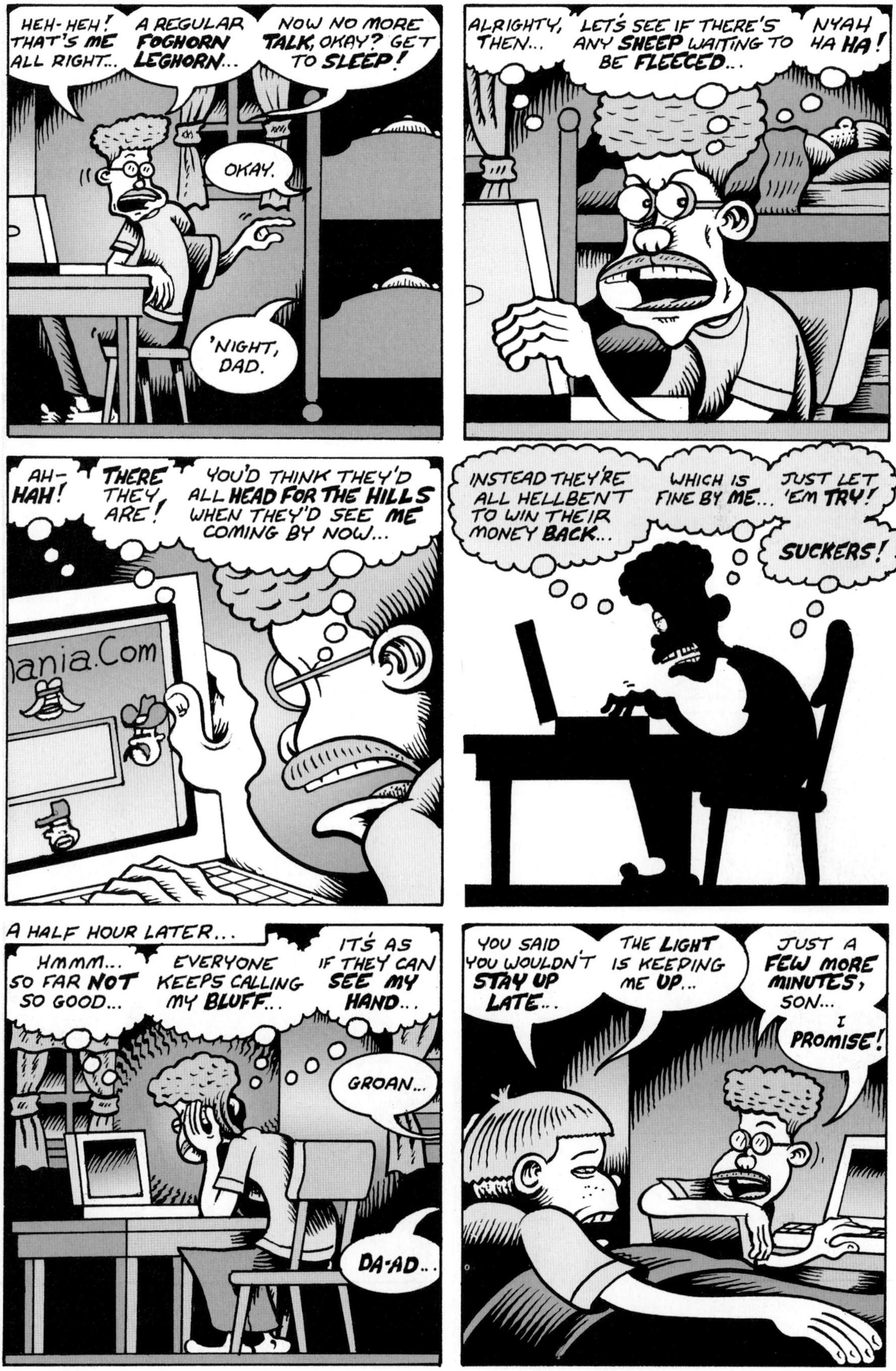
HEH-HEH! THAT'S ME ALL RIGHT...
A REGULAR FOGHORN LEGHORN...
NOW NO MORE TALK, OKAY? GET TO SLEEP!
OKAY.
'NIGHT, DAD.
ALRIGHTY, THEN...
LET'S SEE IF THERE'S ANY SHEEP WAITING TO BE FLEECED...
NYAH HA HA!
AH-HAH!
THERE THEY ARE!
YOU'D THINK THEY'D ALL HEAD FOR THE HILLS WHEN THEY'D SEE ME COMING BY NOW...
INSTEAD THEY'RE ALL HELLBENT TO WIN THEIR MONEY BACK...
WHICH IS FINE BY ME...
JUST LET 'EM TRY!
SUCKERS!
A HALF HOUR LATER...
HMMM... SO FAR NOT SO GOOD...
EVERYONE KEEPS CALLING MY BLUFF...
IT'S AS IF THEY CAN SEE MY HAND...
GROAN...
DA-AD...
YOU SAID YOU WOULDN'T STAY UP LATE...
THE LIGHT IS KEEPING ME UP...
JUST A FEW MORE MINUTES, SON...
I PROMISE!

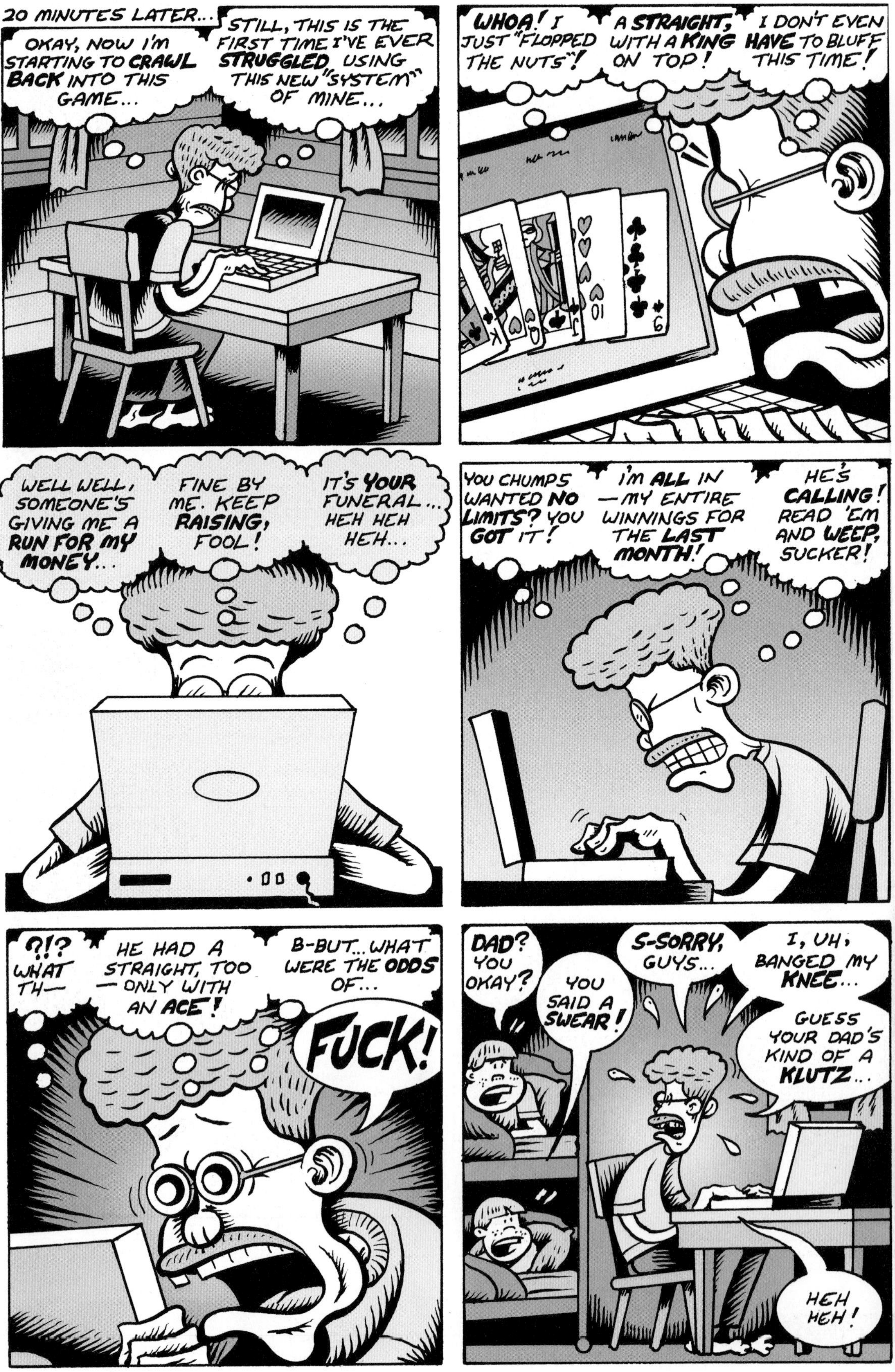
20 MINUTES LATER...
OKAY, NOW I'M STARTING TO CRAWL BACK INTO THIS GAME...
STILL, THIS IS THE FIRST TIME I'VE EVER STRUGGLED USING THIS NEW "SYSTEM" OF MINE...
WHOA! I JUST "FLOPPED THE NUTS"!
A STRAIGHT, WITH A KING ON TOP!
I DON'T EVEN HAVE TO BLUFF THIS TIME!
WELL WELL, SOMEONE'S GIVING ME A RUN FOR MY MONEY...
FINE BY ME. KEEP RAISING, FOOL!
IT'S YOUR FUNERAL... HEH HEH HEH...
YOU CHUMPS WANTED NO LIMITS? YOU GOT IT!
I'M ALL IN —MY ENTIRE WINNINGS FOR THE LAST MONTH!
HE'S CALLING! READ 'EM AND WEEP, SUCKER!
?!? WHAT TH—
HE HAD A STRAIGHT, TOO —ONLY WITH AN ACE!
B-BUT... WHAT WERE THE ODDS OF...
FUCK!
DAD? YOU OKAY?
YOU SAID A SWEAR!
S-SORRY, GUYS...
I, UH, BANGED MY KNEE...
GUESS YOUR DAD'S KIND OF A KLUTZ...
HEH HEH!

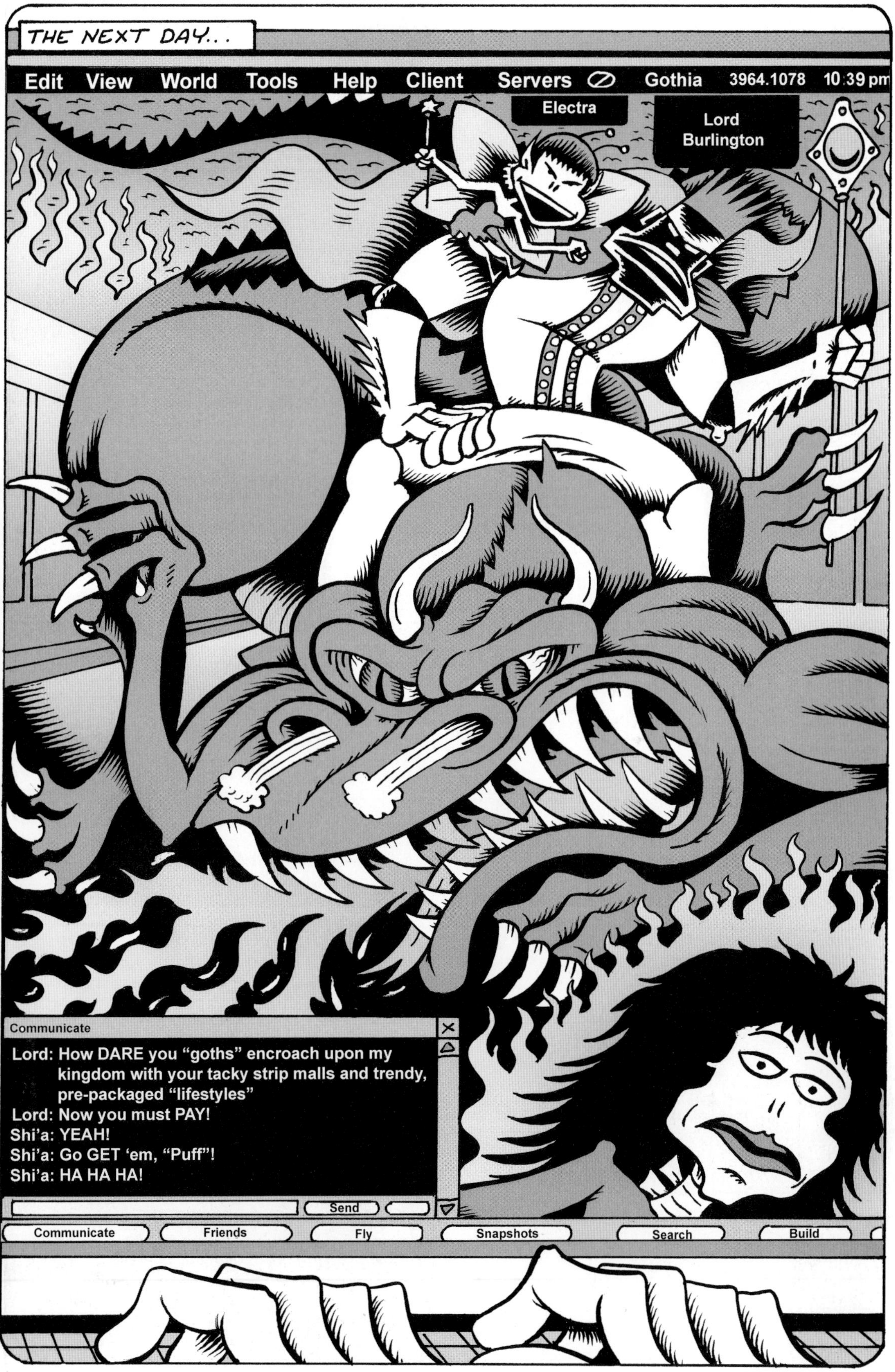
THE NEXT DAY...
Edit View World Tools Help Client Servers Gothia 3964.1078 10:39 pm
Electra
Lord Burlington
Communicate
Lord: How DARE you "goths" encroach upon my kingdom with your tacky strip malls and trendy, pre-packaged "lifestyles"
Lord: Now you must PAY!
Shi'a: YEAH!
Shi'a: Go GET 'em, "Puff"!
Shi'a: HA HA HA!
Send
Communicate
Friends
Fly
Snapshots
Search
Build

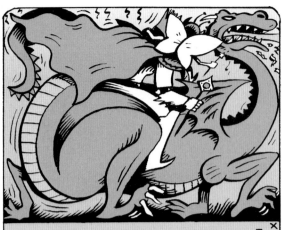

Shi'a: This is the most fun I've had since forever!
Shi'a: Mass destruction is so cathartic!
Lord: Heh heh...
Lord: Ain't THAT the truth...

Shi'a: I only have ONE complaint, though...
Lord: Oh?
Lord: What's that?

Shi'a: That all this damage is only TEMPORARY
Shi'a: It'll all be back to normal within minutes!
Lord: Yes, we only had ourselves a VIRTUAL
     virtual rampage
Lord: Ironic, isn't it?

Shi'a: I wish we could do some real PERMANENT
     damage for a change!
Lord: Actually, I believe we COULD...
Lord: Though it would probably result in us
     being permanently BANNED from SW.

Gothia
Proprietress

Shi'a: Oh...
Shi'a: Though it might be WORTH it!
Lord: Possibly...
Lord: But it'd have to be something MAJOR
     for it to be worth it...
GOTHIA: HEY! I hope you two assholes
       ENJOYED yourselves...

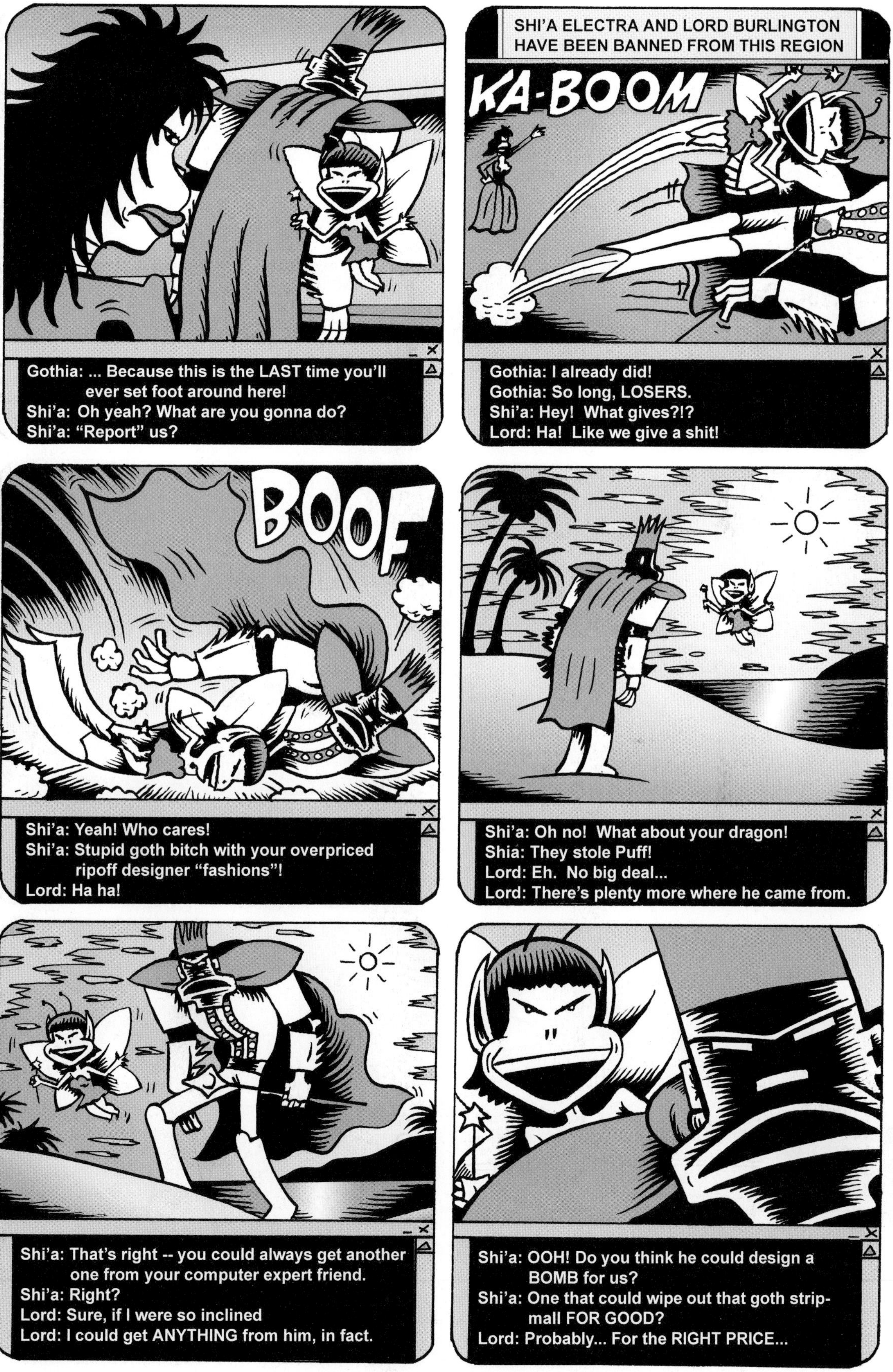
SHI'A ELECTRA AND LORD BURLINGTON HAVE BEEN BANNED FROM THIS REGION
KA-BOOM
Gothia: ... Because this is the LAST time you'll ever set foot around here!
Shi'a: Oh yeah? What are you gonna do?
Shi'a: "Report" us?
Gothia: I already did!
Gothia: So long, LOSERS.
Shi'a: Hey! What gives?!?
Lord: Ha! Like we give a shit!
BOOF
Shi'a: Yeah! Who cares!
Shi'a: Stupid goth bitch with your overpriced ripoff designer "fashions"!
Lord: Ha ha!
Shi'a: Oh no! What about your dragon!
Shia: They stole Puff!
Lord: Eh. No big deal...
Lord: There's plenty more where he came from.
Shi'a: That's right -- you could always get another one from your computer expert friend.
Shi'a: Right?
Lord: Sure, if I were so inclined
Lord: I could get ANYTHING from him, in fact.
Shi'a: OOH! Do you think he could design a BOMB for us?
Shi'a: One that could wipe out that goth strip-mall FOR GOOD?
Lord: Probably... For the RIGHT PRICE...

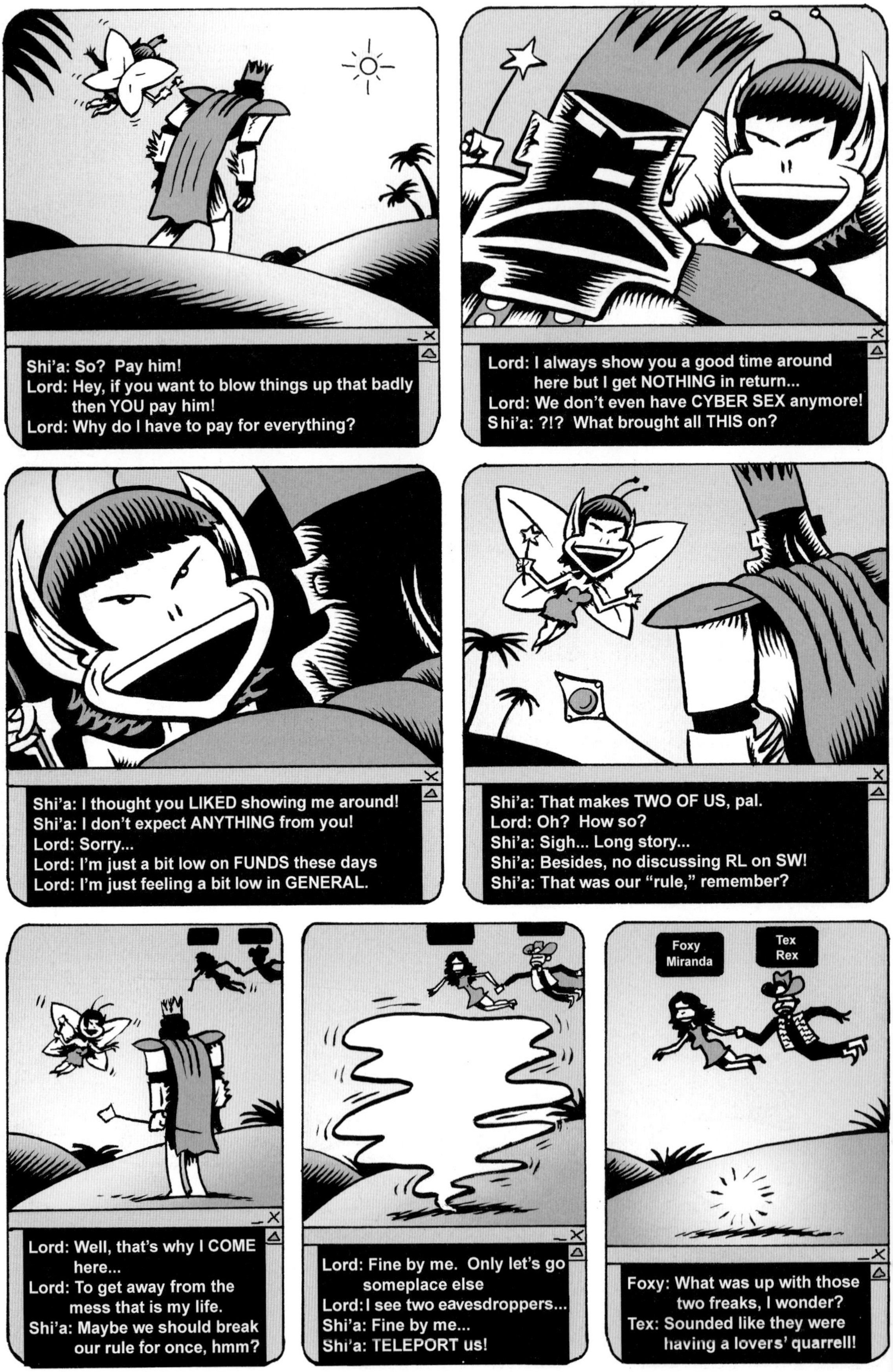
Shi'a: So? Pay him!
Lord: Hey, if you want to blow things up that badly then YOU pay him!
Lord: Why do I have to pay for everything?
Lord: I always show you a good time around here but I get NOTHING in return...
Lord: We don't even have CYBER SEX anymore!
Shi'a: ?!? What brought all THIS on?
Shi'a: I thought you LIKED showing me around!
Shi'a: I don't expect ANYTHING from you!
Lord: Sorry...
Lord: I'm just a bit low on FUNDS these days
Lord: I'm just feeling a bit low in GENERAL.
Shi'a: That makes TWO OF US, pal.
Lord: Oh? How so?
Shi'a: Sigh... Long story...
Shi'a: Besides, no discussing RL on SW!
Shi'a: That was our "rule," remember?
Lord: Well, that's why I COME here...
Lord: To get away from the mess that is my life.
Shi'a: Maybe we should break our rule for once, hmm?
Lord: Fine by me. Only let's go someplace else
Lord: I see two eavesdroppers...
Shi'a: Fine by me...
Shi'a: TELEPORT us!
Foxy Miranda
Tex Rex
Foxy: What was up with those two freaks, I wonder?
Tex: Sounded like they were having a lovers' quarrel!

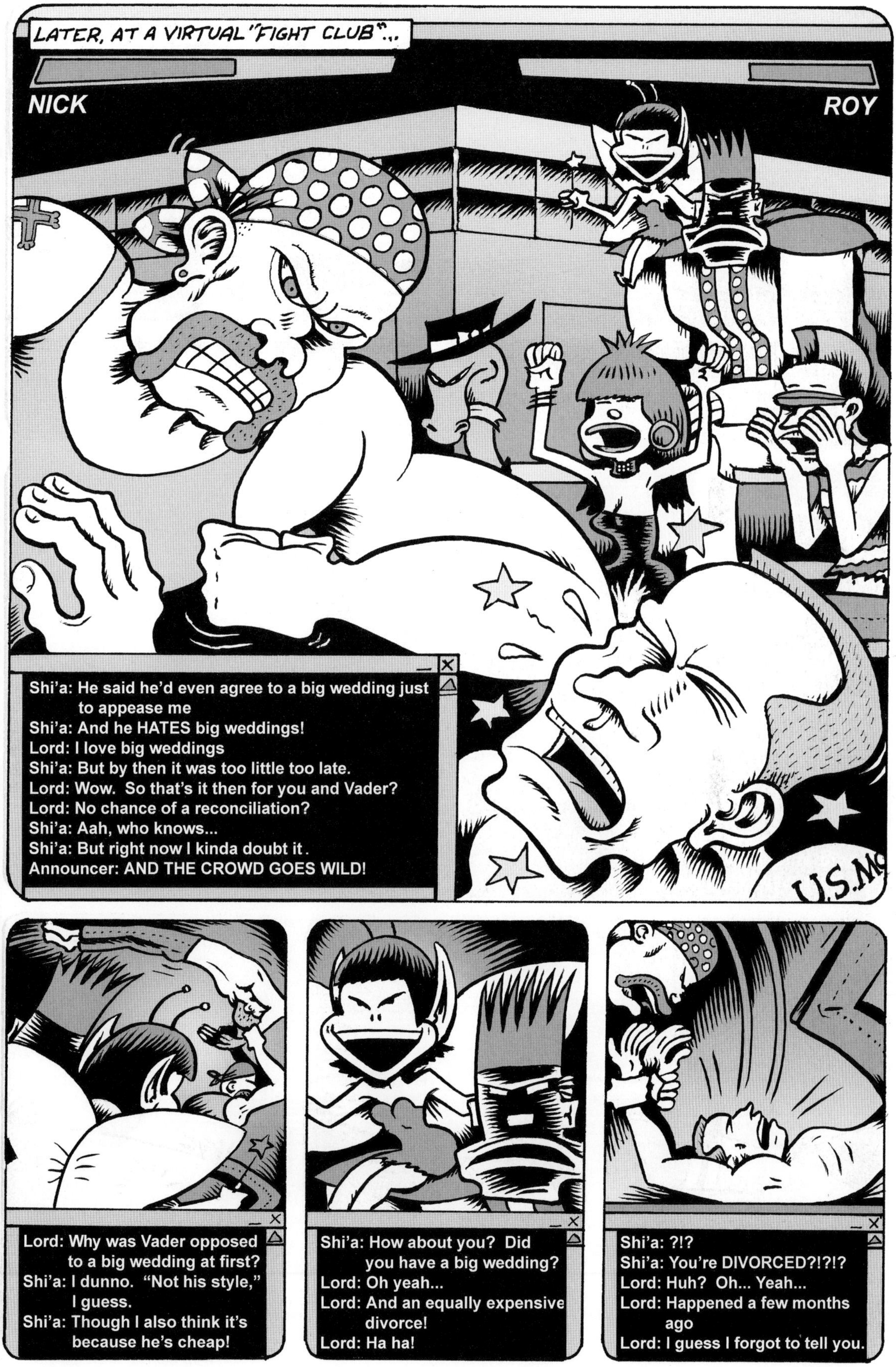
LATER, AT A VIRTUAL "FIGHT CLUB"...
NICK
ROY
Shi'a: He said he'd even agree to a big wedding just to appease me
Shi'a: And he HATES big weddings!
Lord: I love big weddings
Shi'a: But by then it was too little too late.
Lord: Wow. So that's it then for you and Vader?
Lord: No chance of a reconciliation?
Shi'a: Aah, who knows...
Shi'a: But right now I kinda doubt it.
Announcer: AND THE CROWD GOES WILD!
U.S.M
Lord: Why was Vader opposed to a big wedding at first?
Shi'a: I dunno. "Not his style," I guess.
Shi'a: Though I also think it's because he's cheap!
Shi'a: How about you? Did you have a big wedding?
Lord: Oh yeah...
Lord: And an equally expensive divorce!
Lord: Ha ha!
Shi'a: ?!?
Shi'a: You're DIVORCED?!?!?
Lord: Huh? Oh... Yeah...
Lord: Happened a few months ago
Lord: I guess I forgot to tell you.

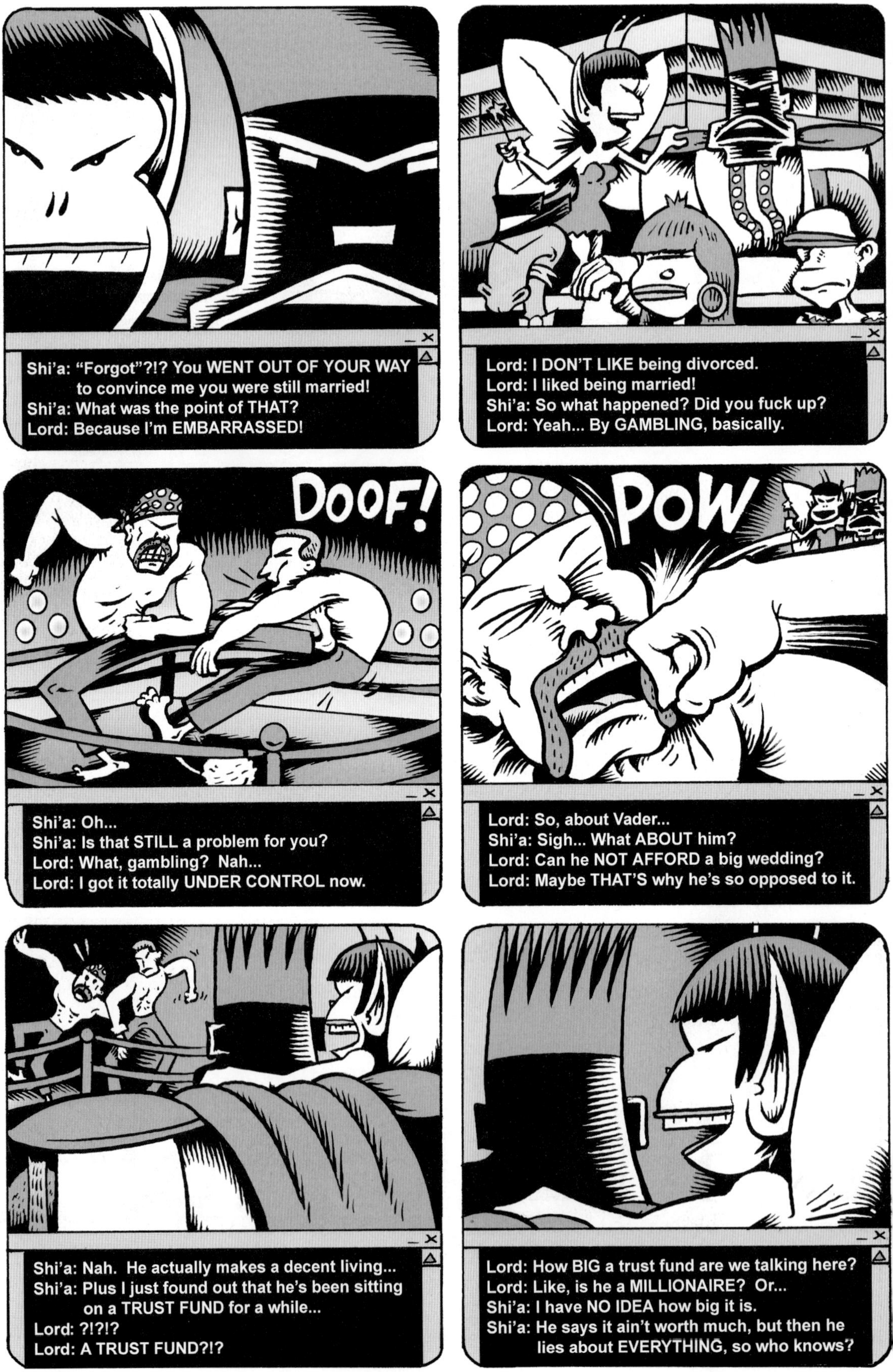
Shi'a: "Forgot"?!? You WENT OUT OF YOUR WAY to convince me you were still married!
Shi'a: What was the point of THAT?
Lord: Because I'm EMBARRASSED!
Lord: I DON'T LIKE being divorced.
Lord: I liked being married!
Shi'a: So what happened? Did you fuck up?
Lord: Yeah... By GAMBLING, basically.
DOOF!
Shi'a: Oh...
Shi'a: Is that STILL a problem for you?
Lord: What, gambling? Nah...
Lord: I got it totally UNDER CONTROL now.
POW
Lord: So, about Vader...
Shi'a: Sigh... What ABOUT him?
Lord: Can he NOT AFFORD a big wedding?
Lord: Maybe THAT'S why he's so opposed to it.
Shi'a: Nah. He actually makes a decent living...
Shi'a: Plus I just found out that he's been sitting on a TRUST FUND for a while...
Lord: ?!?!?
Lord: A TRUST FUND?!?
Lord: How BIG a trust fund are we talking here?
Lord: Like, is he a MILLIONAIRE? Or...
Shi'a: I have NO IDEA how big it is.
Shi'a: He says it ain't worth much, but then he lies about EVERYTHING, so who knows?

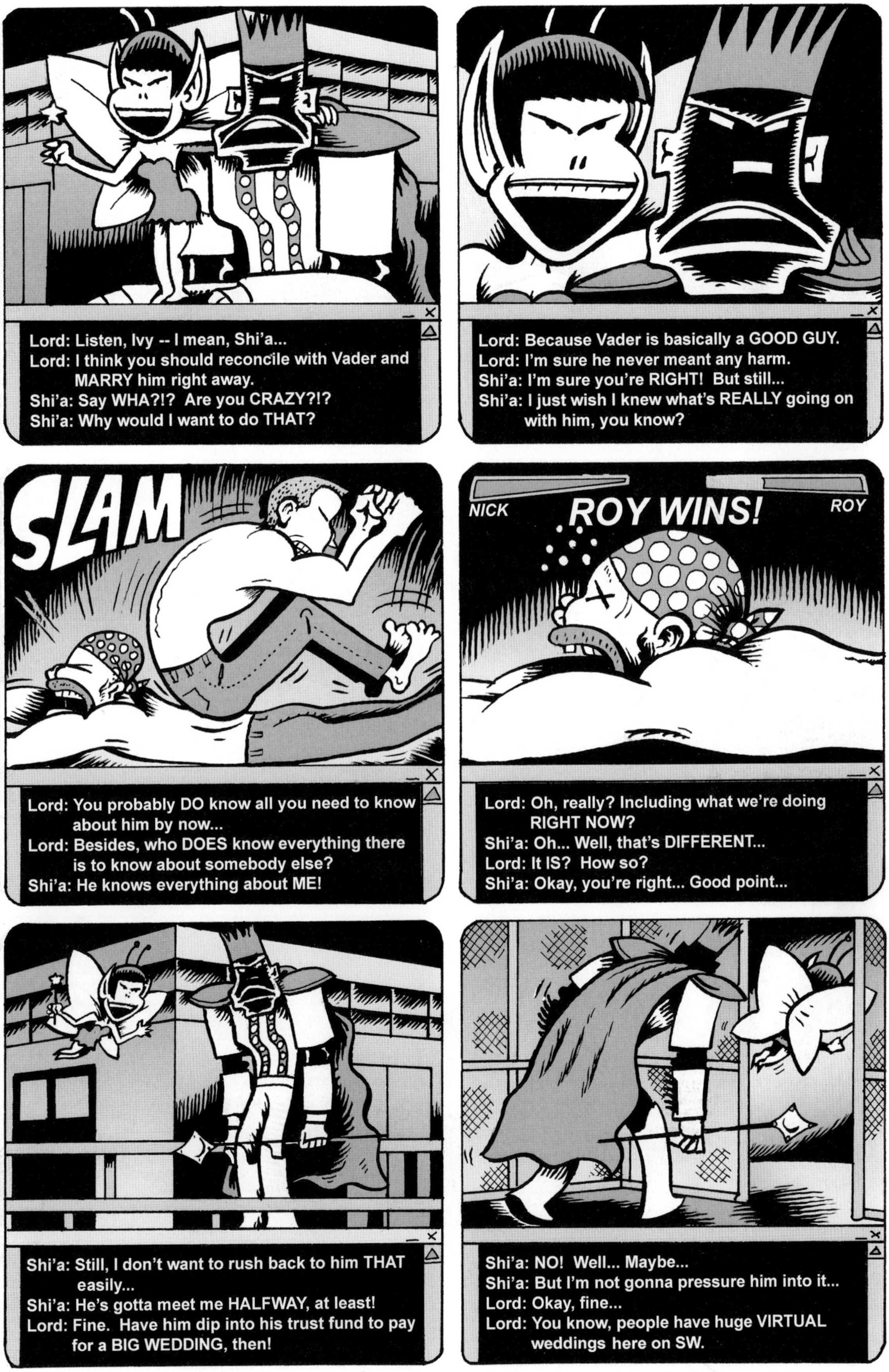
Lord: Listen, Ivy -- I mean, Shi'a...
Lord: I think you should reconcile with Vader and MARRY him right away.
Shi'a: Say WHA?!? Are you CRAZY?!?
Shi'a: Why would I want to do THAT?
Lord: Because Vader is basically a GOOD GUY.
Lord: I'm sure he never meant any harm.
Shi'a: I'm sure you're RIGHT! But still...
Shi'a: I just wish I knew what's REALLY going on with him, you know?
SLAM
Lord: You probably DO know all you need to know about him by now...
Lord: Besides, who DOES know everything there is to know about somebody else?
Shi'a: He knows everything about ME!
NICK
ROY WINS!
ROY
Lord: Oh, really? Including what we're doing RIGHT NOW?
Shi'a: Oh... Well, that's DIFFERENT...
Lord: It IS? How so?
Shi'a: Okay, you're right... Good point...
Shi'a: Still, I don't want to rush back to him THAT easily...
Shi'a: He's gotta meet me HALFWAY, at least!
Lord: Fine. Have him dip into his trust fund to pay for a BIG WEDDING, then!
Shi'a: NO! Well... Maybe...
Shi'a: But I'm not gonna pressure him into it...
Lord: Okay, fine...
Lord: You know, people have huge VIRTUAL weddings here on SW.

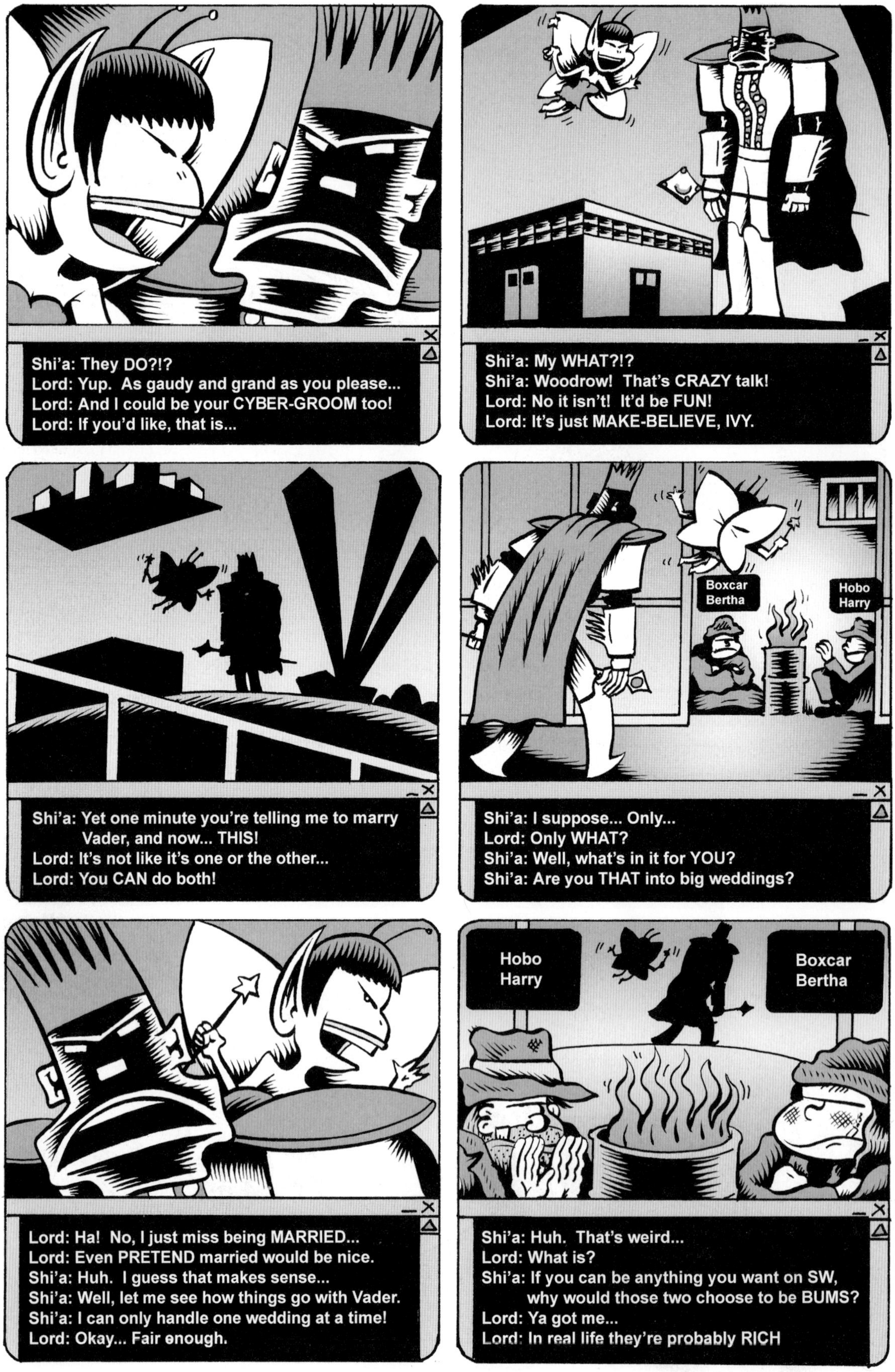
Shi'a: They DO?!?
Lord: Yup. As gaudy and grand as you please...
Lord: And I could be your CYBER-GROOM too!
Lord: If you'd like, that is...
Shi'a: My WHAT?!?
Shi'a: Woodrow! That's CRAZY talk!
Lord: No it isn't! It'd be FUN!
Lord: It's just MAKE-BELIEVE, IVY.
Shi'a: Yet one minute you're telling me to marry Vader, and now... THIS!
Lord: It's not like it's one or the other...
Lord: You CAN do both!
Boxcar Bertha
Hobo Harry
Shi'a: I suppose... Only...
Lord: Only WHAT?
Shi'a: Well, what's in it for YOU?
Shi'a: Are you THAT into big weddings?
Lord: Ha! No, I just miss being MARRIED...
Lord: Even PRETEND married would be nice.
Shi'a: Huh. I guess that makes sense...
Shi'a: Well, let me see how things go with Vader.
Shi'a: I can only handle one wedding at a time!
Lord: Okay... Fair enough.
Hobo Harry
Boxcar Bertha
Shi'a: Huh. That's weird...
Lord: What is?
Shi'a: If you can be anything you want on SW, why would those two choose to be BUMS?
Lord: Ya got me...
Lord: In real life they're probably RICH

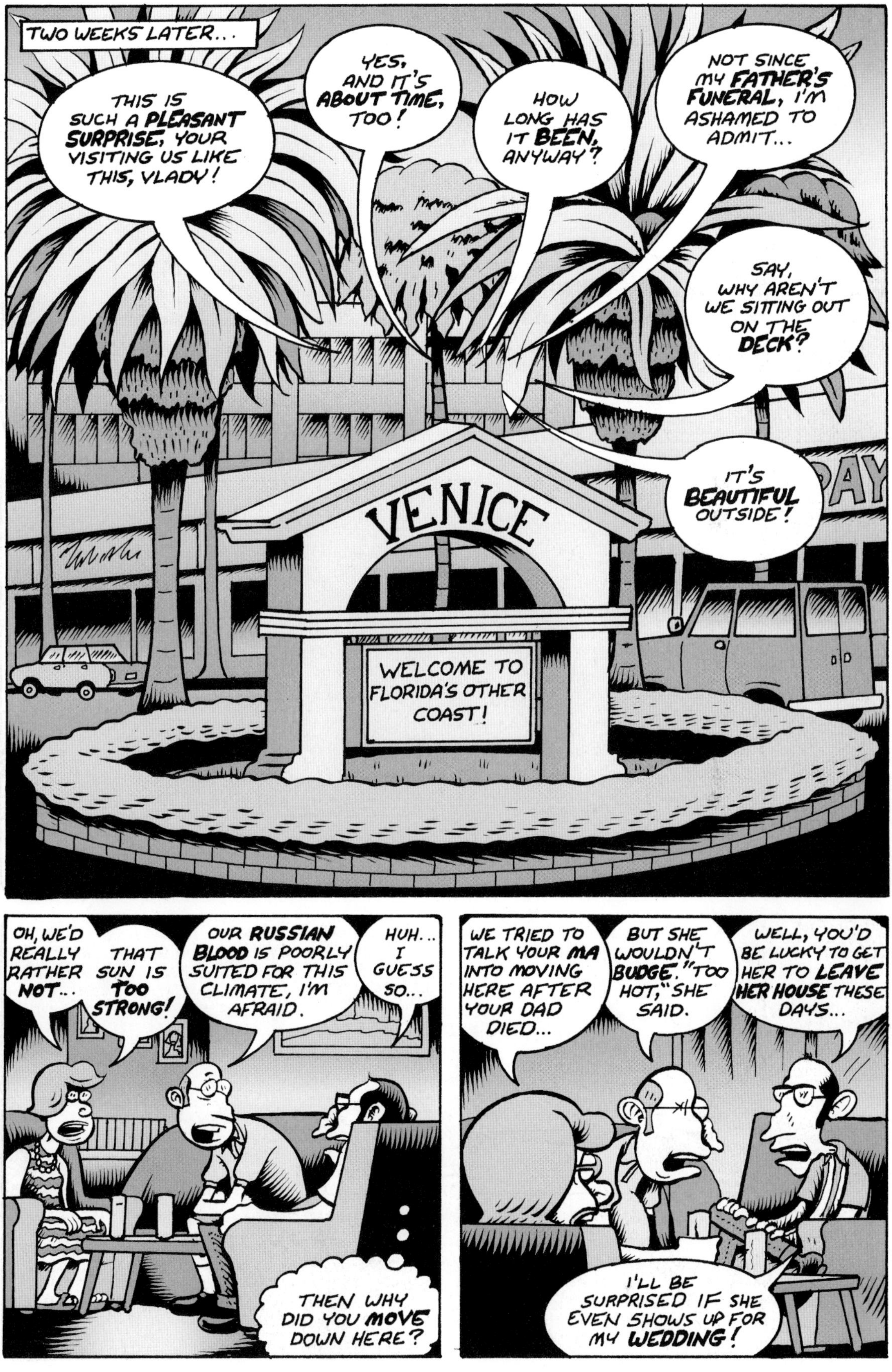
TWO WEEKS LATER...
THIS IS SUCH A PLEASANT SURPRISE, YOUR VISITING US LIKE THIS, VLADY!
YES, AND IT'S ABOUT TIME, TOO!
HOW LONG HAS IT BEEN, ANYWAY?
NOT SINCE MY FATHER'S FUNERAL, I'M ASHAMED TO ADMIT...
SAY, WHY AREN'T WE SITTING OUT ON THE DECK?
IT'S BEAUTIFUL OUTSIDE!
VENICE
WELCOME TO FLORIDA'S OTHER COAST!
OH, WE'D REALLY RATHER NOT...
THAT SUN IS TOO STRONG!
OUR RUSSIAN BLOOD IS POORLY SUITED FOR THIS CLIMATE, I'M AFRAID.
HUH... I GUESS SO...
THEN WHY DID YOU MOVE DOWN HERE?
WE TRIED TO TALK YOUR MA INTO MOVING HERE AFTER YOUR DAD DIED...
BUT SHE WOULDN'T BUDGE. "TOO HOT," SHE SAID.
WELL, YOU'D BE LUCKY TO GET HER TO LEAVE HER HOUSE THESE DAYS...
I'LL BE SURPRISED IF SHE EVEN SHOWS UP FOR MY WEDDING!

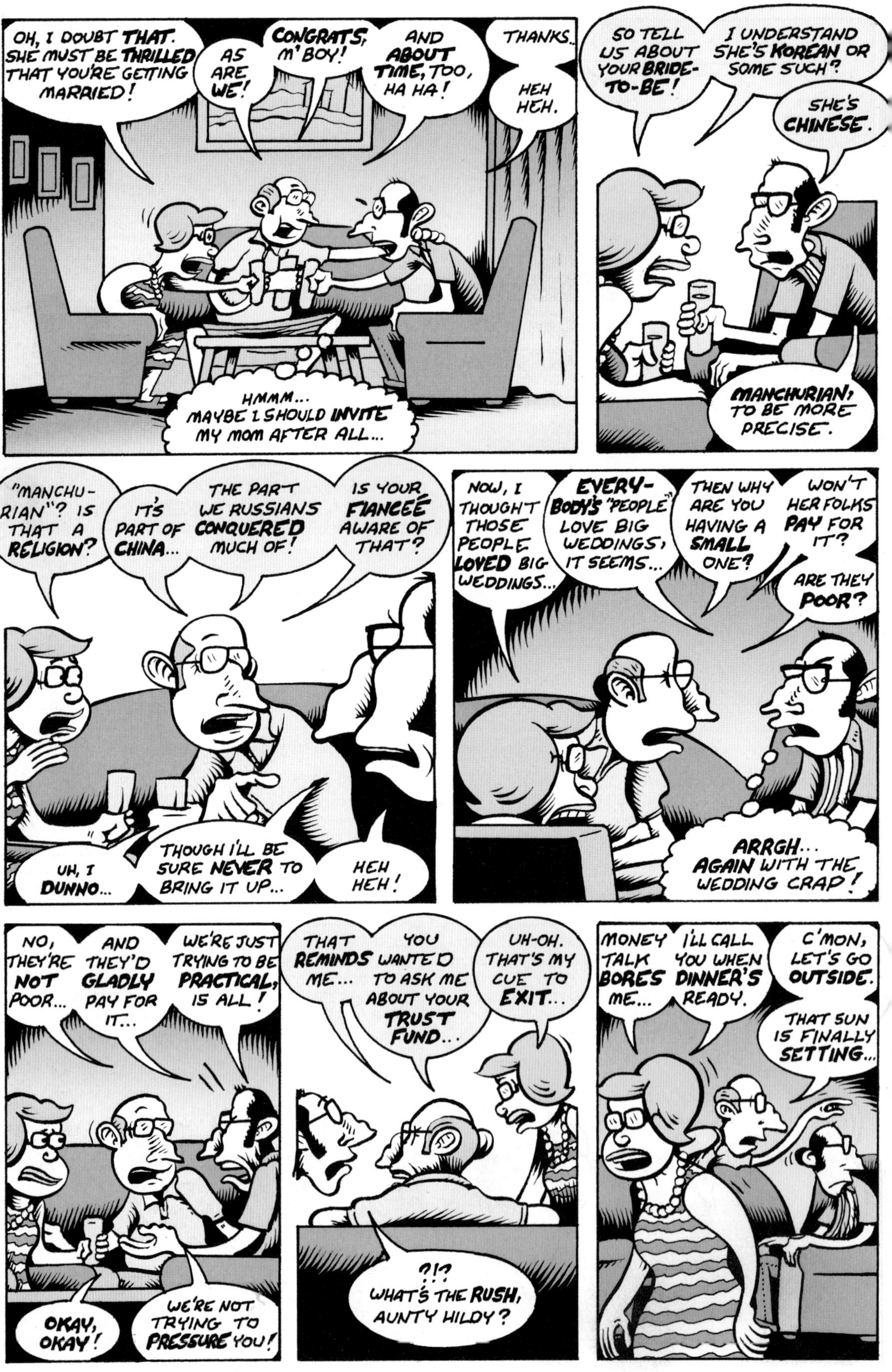

OH, I DOUBT THAT. SHE MUST BE THRILLED THAT YOU'RE GETTING MARRIED!
AS ARE WE!
CONGRATS, M' BOY!
AND ABOUT TIME, TOO, HA HA!
THANKS..
HEH HEH.
HMMM... MAYBE I SHOULD INVITE MY MOM AFTER ALL...
SO TELL US ABOUT YOUR BRIDE-TO-BE!
I UNDERSTAND SHE'S KOREAN OR SOME SUCH?
SHE'S CHINESE.
MANCHURIAN, TO BE MORE PRECISE.
"MANCHU-RIAN"? IS THAT A RELIGION?
IT'S PART OF CHINA...
THE PART WE RUSSIANS CONQUERED MUCH OF!
IS YOUR FIANCEÉ AWARE OF THAT?
UH, I DUNNO...
THOUGH I'LL BE SURE NEVER TO BRING IT UP...
HEH HEH!
NOW, I THOUGHT THOSE PEOPLE LOVED BIG WEDDINGS...
EVERY-BODY'S "PEOPLE" LOVE BIG WEDDINGS, IT SEEMS...
THEN WHY ARE YOU HAVING A SMALL ONE?
WON'T HER FOLKS PAY FOR IT?
ARE THEY POOR?
ARRGH... AGAIN WITH THE WEDDING CRAP!
NO, THEY'RE NOT POOR...
AND THEY'D GLADLY PAY FOR IT...
WE'RE JUST TRYING TO BE PRACTICAL, IS ALL!
OKAY, OKAY!
WE'RE NOT TRYING TO PRESSURE YOU!
THAT REMINDS ME...
YOU WANTED TO ASK ME ABOUT YOUR TRUST FUND...
UH-OH. THAT'S MY CUE TO EXIT...
?!? WHAT'S THE RUSH, AUNTY HILDY?
MONEY TALK BORES ME...
I'LL CALL YOU WHEN DINNER'S READY.
C'MON, LET'S GO OUTSIDE.
THAT SUN IS FINALLY SETTING...

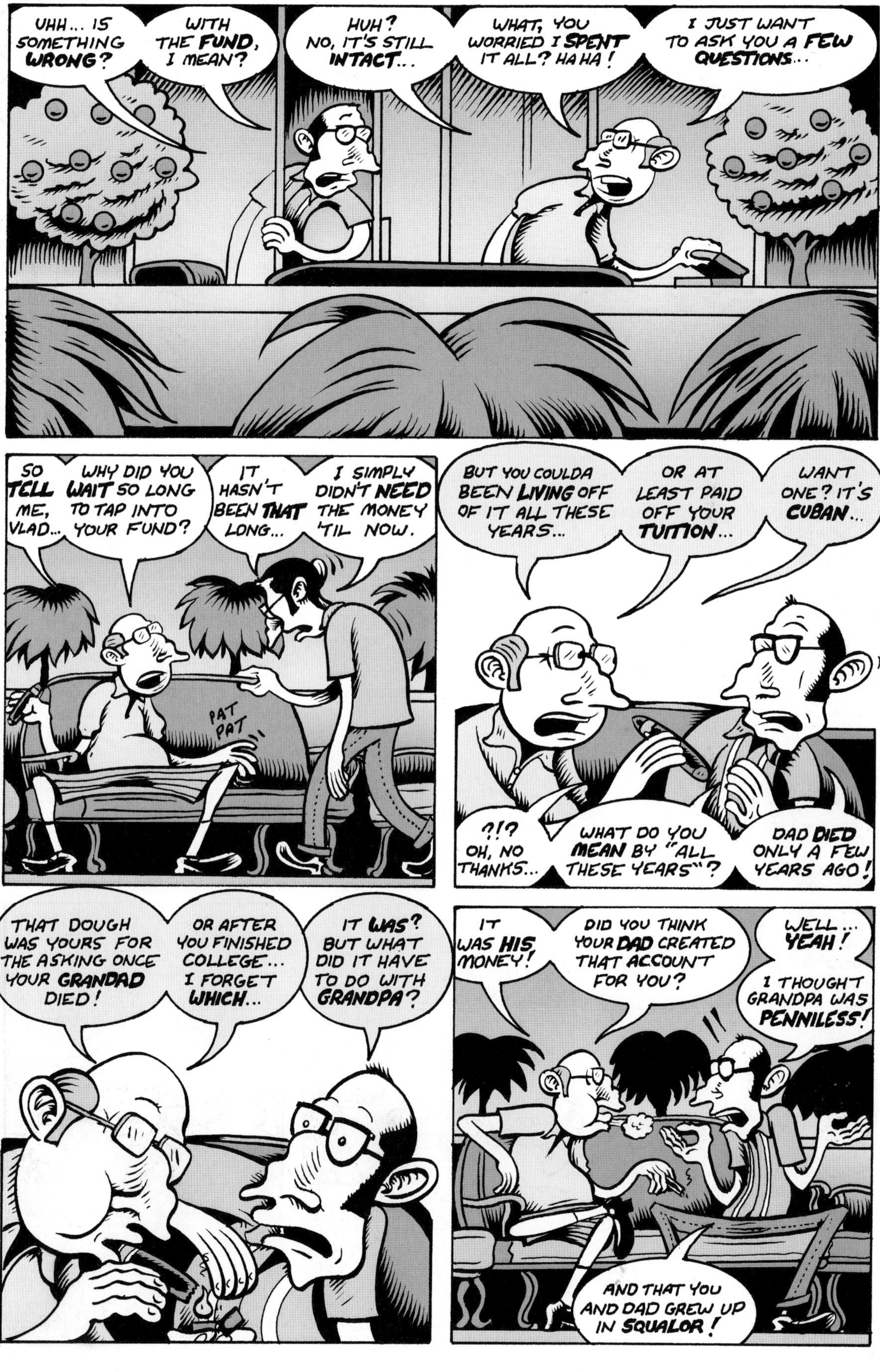
UHH... IS SOMETHING WRONG?
WITH THE FUND, I MEAN?
HUH? NO, IT'S STILL INTACT...
WHAT, YOU WORRIED I SPENT IT ALL? HA HA!
I JUST WANT TO ASK YOU A FEW QUESTIONS...
SO TELL ME, VLAD...
WHY DID YOU WAIT SO LONG TO TAP INTO YOUR FUND?
IT HASN'T BEEN THAT LONG...
I SIMPLY DIDN'T NEED THE MONEY 'TIL NOW.
PAT PAT
BUT YOU COULDA BEEN LIVING OFF OF IT ALL THESE YEARS...
OR AT LEAST PAID OFF YOUR TUITION...
WANT ONE? IT'S CUBAN...
?!? OH, NO THANKS...
WHAT DO YOU MEAN BY "ALL THESE YEARS"?
DAD DIED ONLY A FEW YEARS AGO!
THAT DOUGH WAS YOURS FOR THE ASKING ONCE YOUR GRANDAD DIED!
OR AFTER YOU FINISHED COLLEGE... I FORGET WHICH...
IT WAS? BUT WHAT DID IT HAVE TO DO WITH GRANDPA?
IT WAS HIS MONEY!
DID YOU THINK YOUR DAD CREATED THAT ACCOUNT FOR YOU?
WELL... YEAH!
I THOUGHT GRANDPA WAS PENNILESS!
AND THAT YOU AND DAD GREW UP IN SQUALOR!

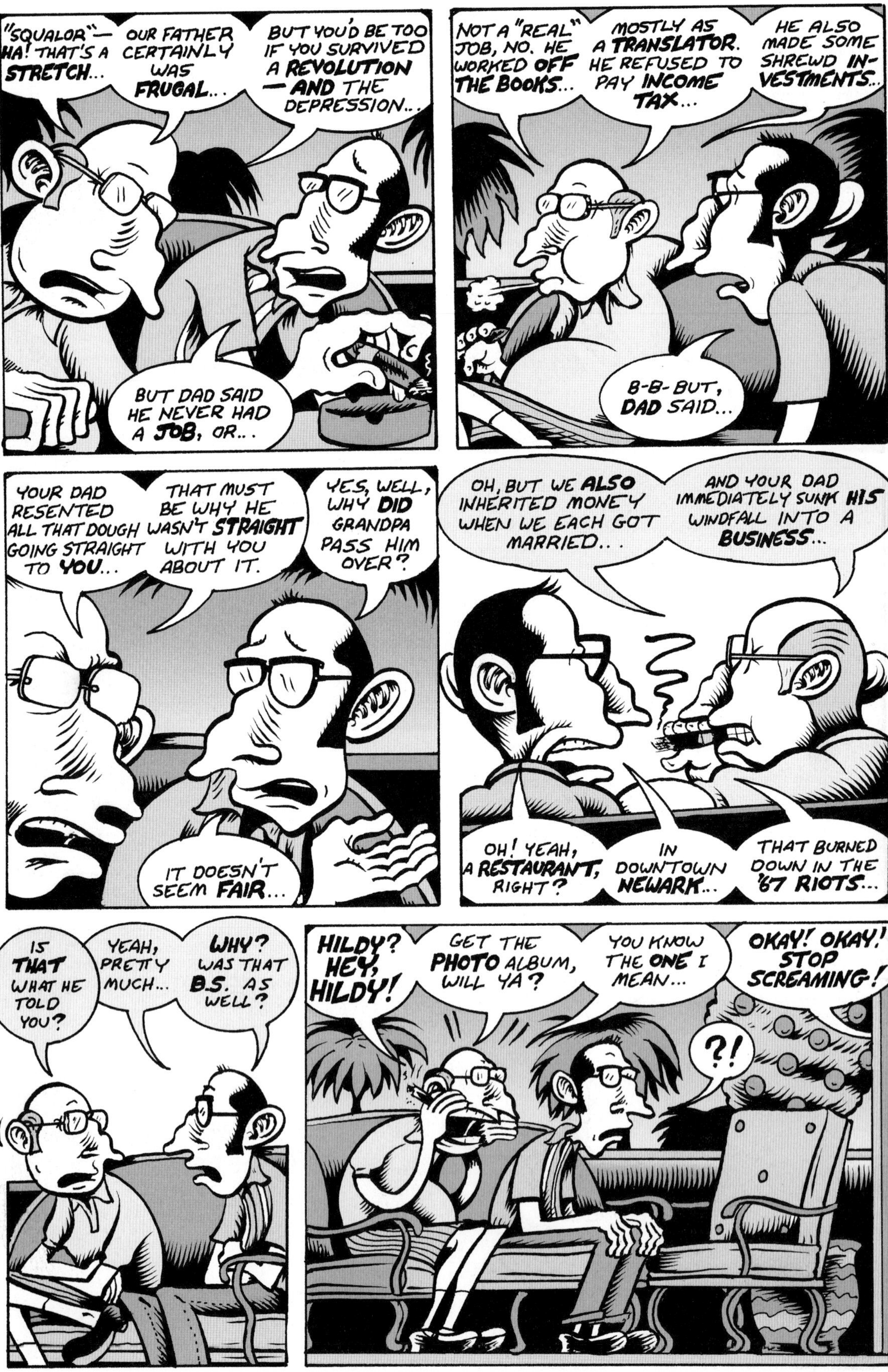
"SQUALOR"— HA! THAT'S A STRETCH...
OUR FATHER CERTAINLY WAS FRUGAL...
BUT YOU'D BE TOO IF YOU SURVIVED A REVOLUTION — AND THE DEPRESSION...
BUT DAD SAID HE NEVER HAD A JOB, OR...
NOT A "REAL" JOB, NO. HE WORKED OFF THE BOOKS...
MOSTLY AS A TRANSLATOR. HE REFUSED TO PAY INCOME TAX...
HE ALSO MADE SOME SHREWD INVESTMENTS...
B-B-BUT, DAD SAID...
YOUR DAD RESENTED ALL THAT DOUGH GOING STRAIGHT TO YOU...
THAT MUST BE WHY HE WASN'T STRAIGHT WITH YOU ABOUT IT.
YES, WELL, WHY DID GRANDPA PASS HIM OVER?
IT DOESN'T SEEM FAIR...
OH, BUT WE ALSO INHERITED MONEY WHEN WE EACH GOT MARRIED...
AND YOUR DAD IMMEDIATELY SUNK HIS WINDFALL INTO A BUSINESS...
OH! YEAH, A RESTAURANT, RIGHT?
IN DOWNTOWN NEWARK...
THAT BURNED DOWN IN THE '67 RIOTS...
IS THAT WHAT HE TOLD YOU?
YEAH, PRETTY MUCH...
WHY? WAS THAT B.S. AS WELL?
HILDY? HEY, HILDY!
GET THE PHOTO ALBUM, WILL YA?
YOU KNOW THE ONE I MEAN...
OKAY! OKAY! STOP SCREAMING!
?!

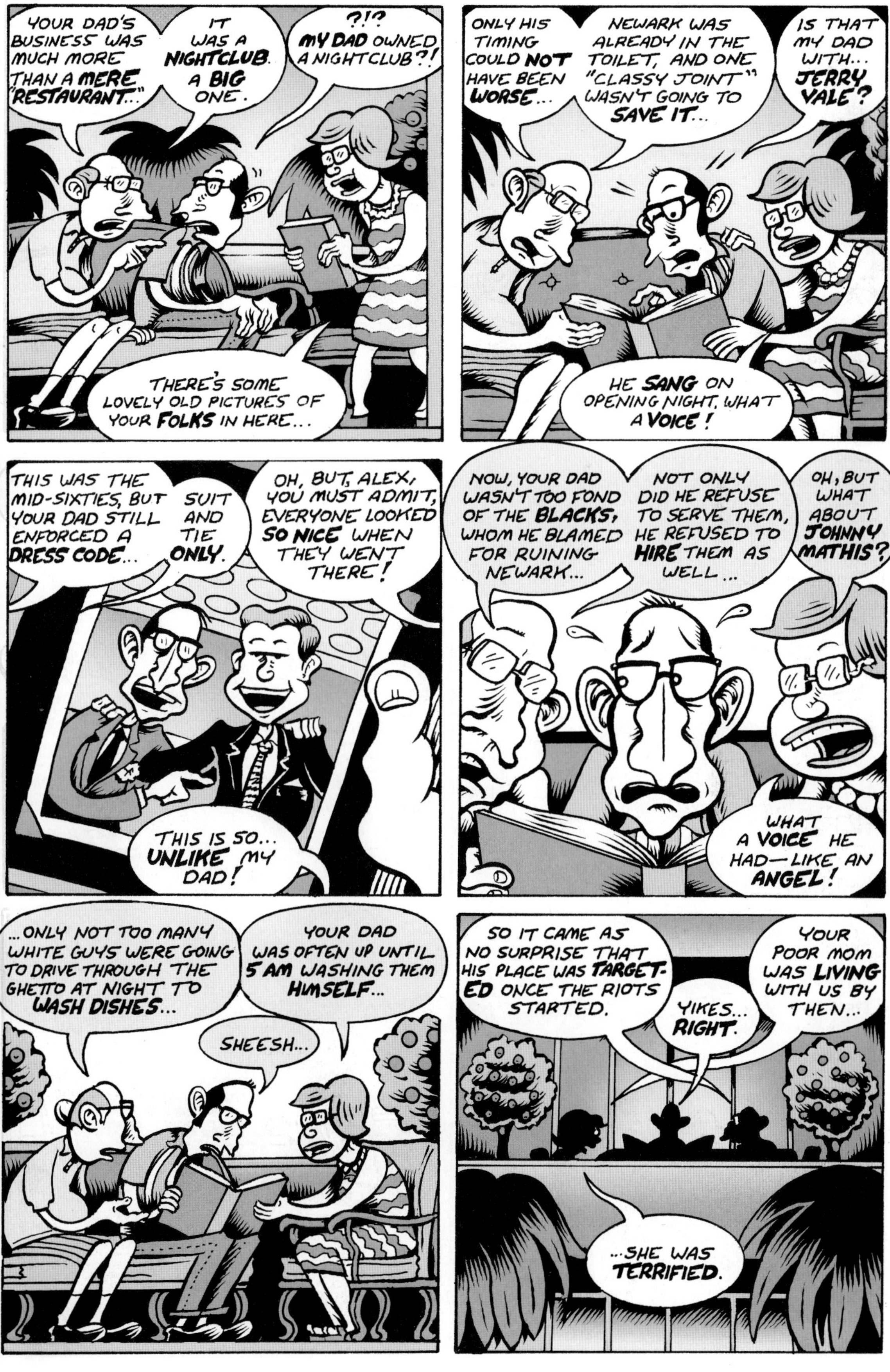
YOUR DAD'S BUSINESS WAS MUCH MORE THAN A MERE "RESTAURANT..."
IT WAS A NIGHTCLUB. A BIG ONE.
?!? MY DAD OWNED A NIGHTCLUB?!
THERE'S SOME LOVELY OLD PICTURES OF YOUR FOLKS IN HERE...
ONLY HIS TIMING COULD NOT HAVE BEEN WORSE...
NEWARK WAS ALREADY IN THE TOILET, AND ONE "CLASSY JOINT" WASN'T GOING TO SAVE IT...
IS THAT MY DAD WITH... JERRY VALE?
HE SANG ON OPENING NIGHT. WHAT A VOICE!
THIS WAS THE MID-SIXTIES, BUT YOUR DAD STILL ENFORCED A DRESS CODE...
SUIT AND TIE ONLY.
OH, BUT, ALEX, YOU MUST ADMIT, EVERYONE LOOKED SO NICE WHEN THEY WENT THERE!
THIS IS SO... UNLIKE MY DAD!
NOW, YOUR DAD WASN'T TOO FOND OF THE BLACKS, WHOM HE BLAMED FOR RUINING NEWARK...
NOT ONLY DID HE REFUSE TO SERVE THEM, HE REFUSED TO HIRE THEM AS WELL...
OH, BUT WHAT ABOUT JOHNNY MATHIS?
WHAT A VOICE HE HAD—LIKE AN ANGEL!
...ONLY NOT TOO MANY WHITE GUYS WERE GOING TO DRIVE THROUGH THE GHETTO AT NIGHT TO WASH DISHES...
YOUR DAD WAS OFTEN UP UNTIL 5 AM WASHING THEM HIMSELF...
SHEESH...
SO IT CAME AS NO SURPRISE THAT HIS PLACE WAS TARGET-ED ONCE THE RIOTS STARTED.
YIKES... RIGHT.
YOUR POOR MOM WAS LIVING WITH US BY THEN...
...SHE WAS TERRIFIED.

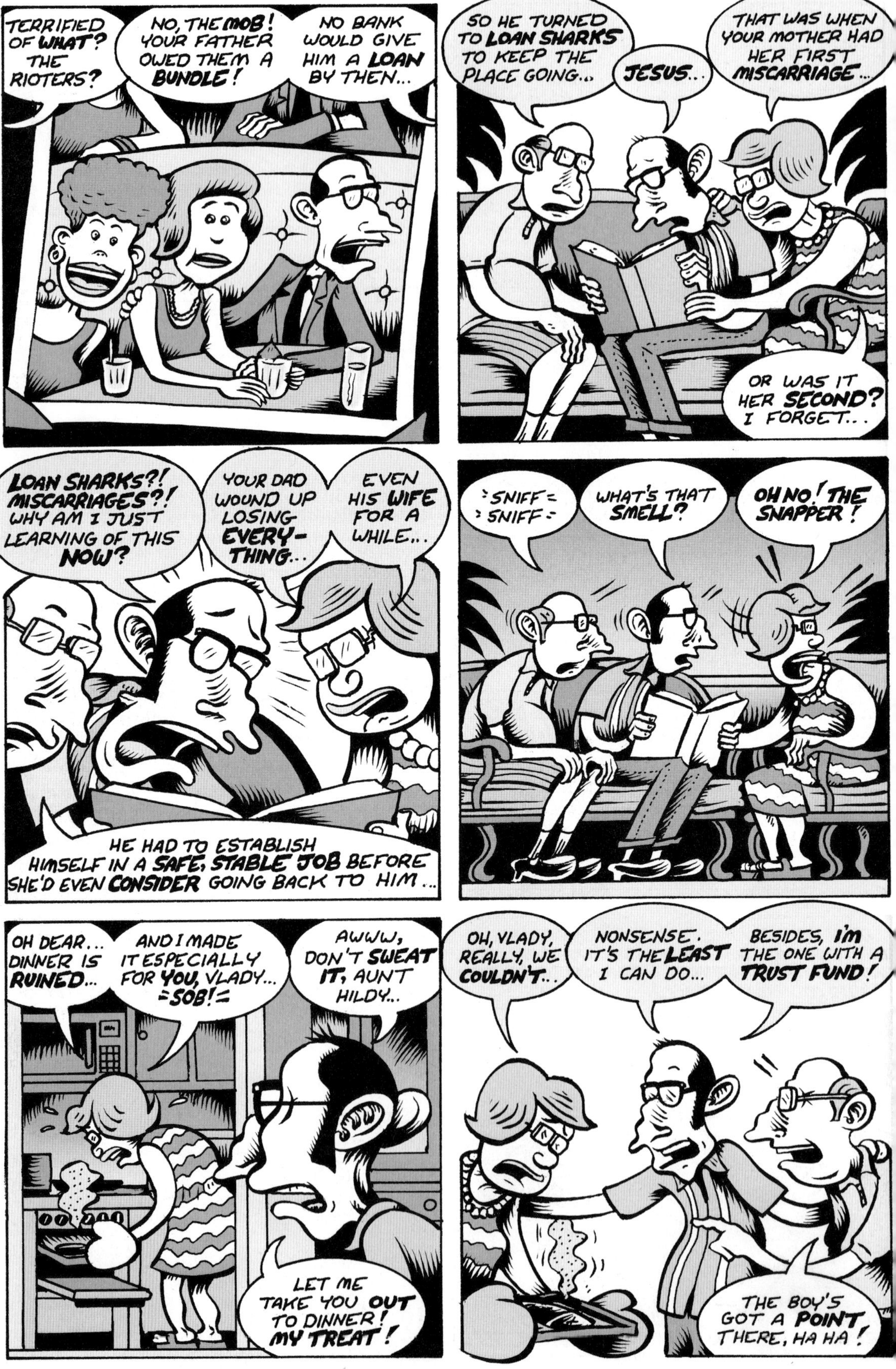
TERRIFIED OF WHAT? THE RIOTERS?
NO, THE MOB! YOUR FATHER OWED THEM A BUNDLE!
NO BANK WOULD GIVE HIM A LOAN BY THEN...
SO HE TURNED TO LOAN SHARKS TO KEEP THE PLACE GOING...
JESUS...
THAT WAS WHEN YOUR MOTHER HAD HER FIRST MISCARRIAGE...
OR WAS IT HER SECOND? I FORGET...
LOAN SHARKS?! MISCARRIAGES?! WHY AM I JUST LEARNING OF THIS NOW?
YOUR DAD WOUND UP LOSING EVERY-THING...
EVEN HIS WIFE FOR A WHILE...
HE HAD TO ESTABLISH HIMSELF IN A SAFE, STABLE JOB BEFORE SHE'D EVEN CONSIDER GOING BACK TO HIM...
=SNIFF= =SNIFF=
WHAT'S THAT SMELL?
OH NO! THE SNAPPER!
OH DEAR... DINNER IS RUINED...
AND I MADE IT ESPECIALLY FOR YOU, VLADY... =SOB!=
AWWW, DON'T SWEAT IT, AUNT HILDY...
LET ME TAKE YOU OUT TO DINNER! MY TREAT!
OH, VLADY, REALLY, WE COULDN'T...
NONSENSE. IT'S THE LEAST I CAN DO...
BESIDES, I'M THE ONE WITH A TRUST FUND!
THE BOY'S GOT A POINT THERE, HA HA!

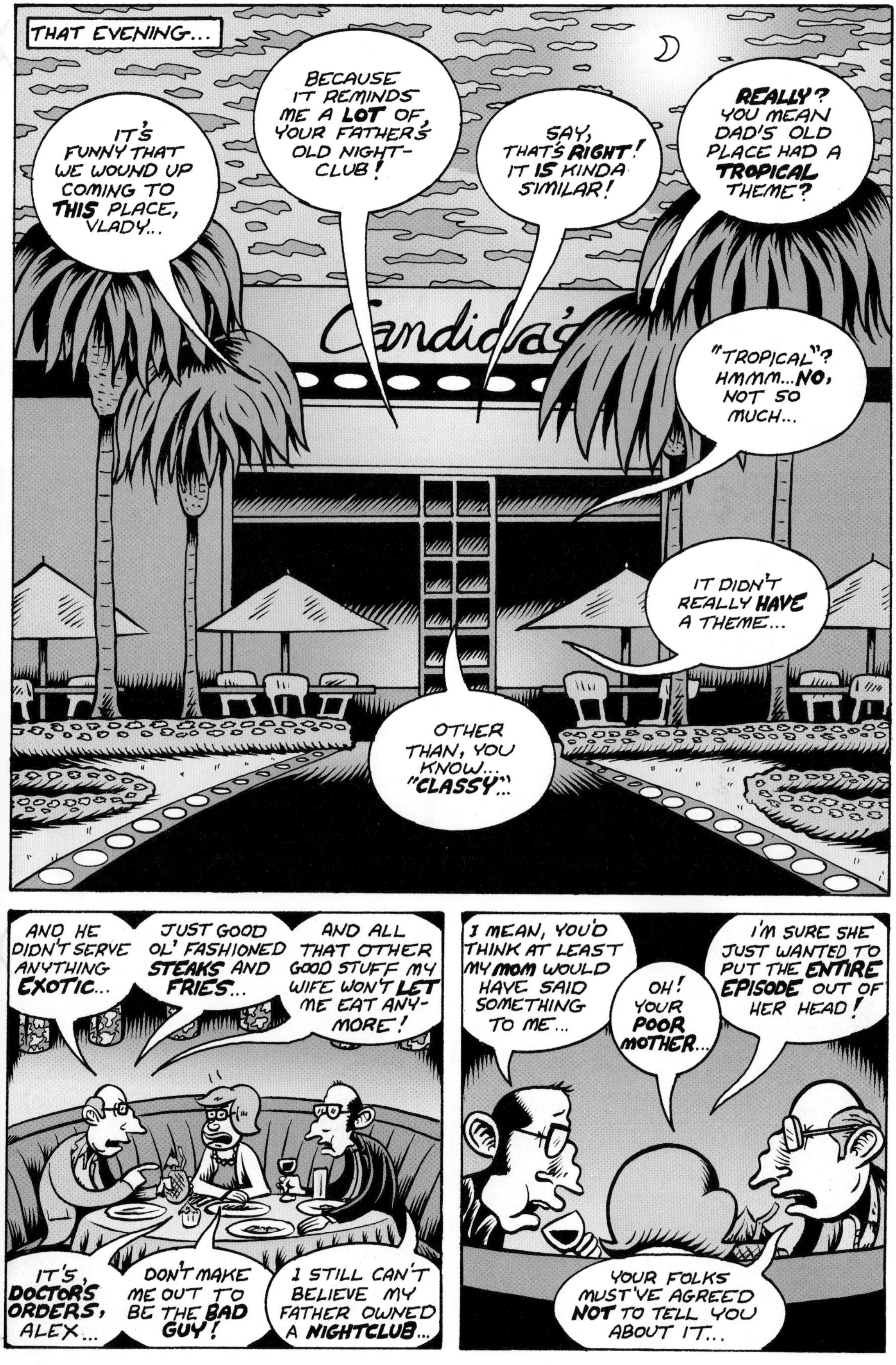
THAT EVENING...
IT'S FUNNY THAT WE WOUND UP COMING TO THIS PLACE, VLADY...
BECAUSE IT REMINDS ME A LOT OF, YOUR FATHER'S OLD NIGHT-CLUB!
SAY, THAT'S RIGHT! IT IS KINDA SIMILAR!
REALLY? YOU MEAN DAD'S OLD PLACE HAD A TROPICAL THEME?
Candida's
"TROPICAL"? HMMM...NO, NOT SO MUCH...
IT DIDN'T REALLY HAVE A THEME...
OTHER THAN, YOU KNOW... "CLASSY"...
AND HE DIDN'T SERVE ANYTHING EXOTIC...
JUST GOOD OL' FASHIONED STEAKS AND FRIES...
AND ALL THAT OTHER GOOD STUFF MY WIFE WON'T LET ME EAT ANY-MORE!
IT'S, DOCTOR'S ORDERS, ALEX...
DON'T MAKE ME OUT TO BE THE BAD GUY!
I STILL CAN'T BELIEVE MY FATHER OWNED A NIGHTCLUB...
I MEAN, YOU'D THINK AT LEAST MY MOM WOULD HAVE SAID SOMETHING TO ME...
OH! YOUR POOR MOTHER...
I'M SURE SHE JUST WANTED TO PUT THE ENTIRE EPISODE OUT OF HER HEAD!
YOUR FOLKS MUST'VE AGREED NOT TO TELL YOU ABOUT IT...

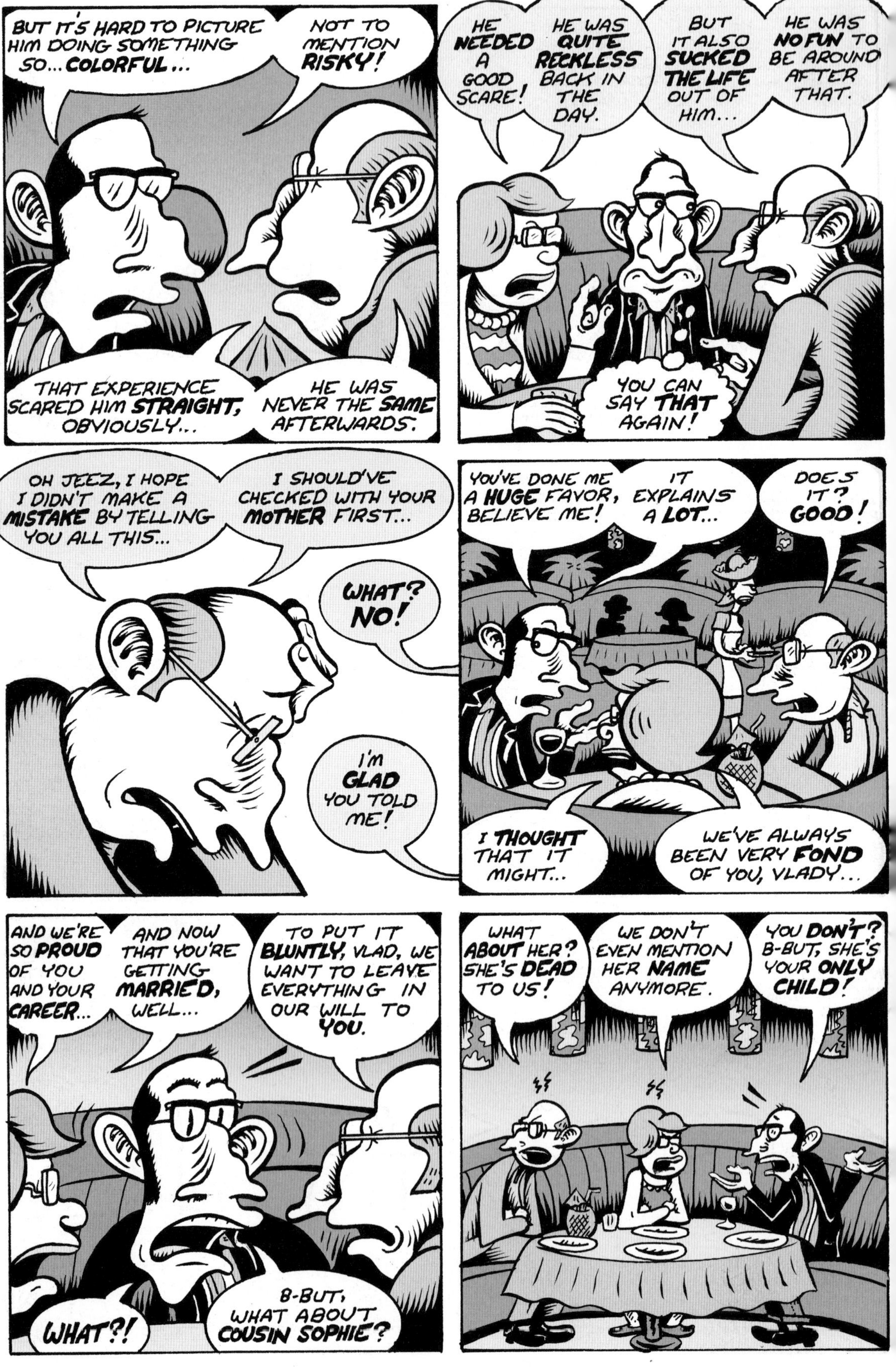
BUT IT'S HARD TO PICTURE HIM DOING SOMETHING SO... COLORFUL...
NOT TO MENTION RISKY!
THAT EXPERIENCE SCARED HIM STRAIGHT, OBVIOUSLY...
HE WAS NEVER THE SAME AFTERWARDS.
HE NEEDED A GOOD SCARE!
HE WAS QUITE RECKLESS BACK IN THE DAY.
BUT IT ALSO SUCKED THE LIFE OUT OF HIM...
HE WAS NO FUN TO BE AROUND AFTER THAT.
YOU CAN SAY THAT AGAIN!
OH JEEZ, I HOPE I DIDN'T MAKE A MISTAKE BY TELLING YOU ALL THIS...
I SHOULD'VE CHECKED WITH YOUR MOTHER FIRST...
WHAT? NO!
I'M GLAD YOU TOLD ME!
YOU'VE DONE ME A HUGE FAVOR, BELIEVE ME!
IT EXPLAINS A LOT...
DOES IT? GOOD!
I THOUGHT THAT IT MIGHT...
WE'VE ALWAYS BEEN VERY FOND OF YOU, VLADY...
AND WE'RE SO PROUD OF YOU AND YOUR CAREER...
AND NOW THAT YOU'RE GETTING MARRIED, WELL...
TO PUT IT BLUNTLY, VLAD, WE WANT TO LEAVE EVERYTHING IN OUR WILL TO YOU.
WHAT?!
B-BUT, WHAT ABOUT COUSIN SOPHIE?
WHAT ABOUT HER? SHE'S DEAD TO US!
WE DON'T EVEN MENTION HER NAME ANYMORE.
YOU DON'T? B-BUT, SHE'S YOUR ONLY CHILD!

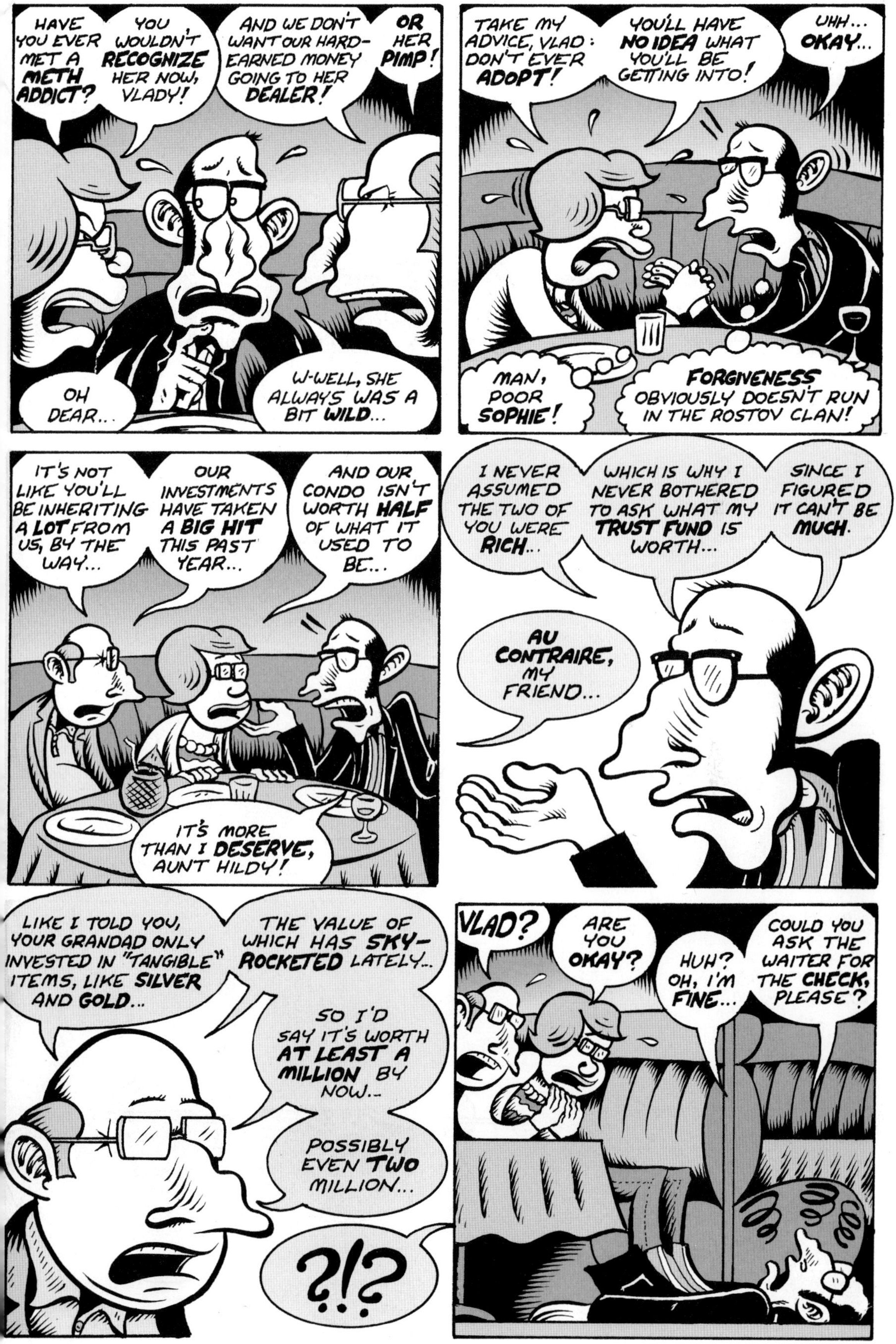

HAVE YOU EVER MET A METH ADDICT?
YOU WOULDN'T RECOGNIZE HER NOW, VLADY!
AND WE DON'T WANT OUR HARD-EARNED MONEY GOING TO HER DEALER!
OR HER PIMP!
OH DEAR...
W-WELL, SHE ALWAYS WAS A BIT WILD...
TAKE MY ADVICE, VLAD: DON'T EVER ADOPT!
YOU'LL HAVE NO IDEA WHAT YOU'LL BE GETTING INTO!
UHH... OKAY...
MAN, POOR SOPHIE!
FORGIVENESS OBVIOUSLY DOESN'T RUN IN THE ROSTOV CLAN!
IT'S NOT LIKE YOU'LL BE INHERITING A LOT FROM US, BY THE WAY...
OUR INVESTMENTS HAVE TAKEN A BIG HIT THIS PAST YEAR...
AND OUR CONDO ISN'T WORTH HALF OF WHAT IT USED TO BE...
IT'S MORE THAN I DESERVE, AUNT HILDY!
I NEVER ASSUMED THE TWO OF YOU WERE RICH...
WHICH IS WHY I NEVER BOTHERED TO ASK WHAT MY TRUST FUND IS WORTH...
SINCE I FIGURED IT CAN'T BE MUCH.
AU CONTRAIRE, MY FRIEND...
LIKE I TOLD YOU, YOUR GRANDAD ONLY INVESTED IN "TANGIBLE" ITEMS, LIKE SILVER AND GOLD...
THE VALUE OF WHICH HAS SKY-ROCKETED LATELY...
SO I'D SAY IT'S WORTH AT LEAST A MILLION BY NOW...
POSSIBLY EVEN TWO MILLION...
?!?
VLAD?
ARE YOU OKAY?
HUH? OH, I'M FINE...
COULD YOU ASK THE WAITER FOR THE CHECK, PLEASE?

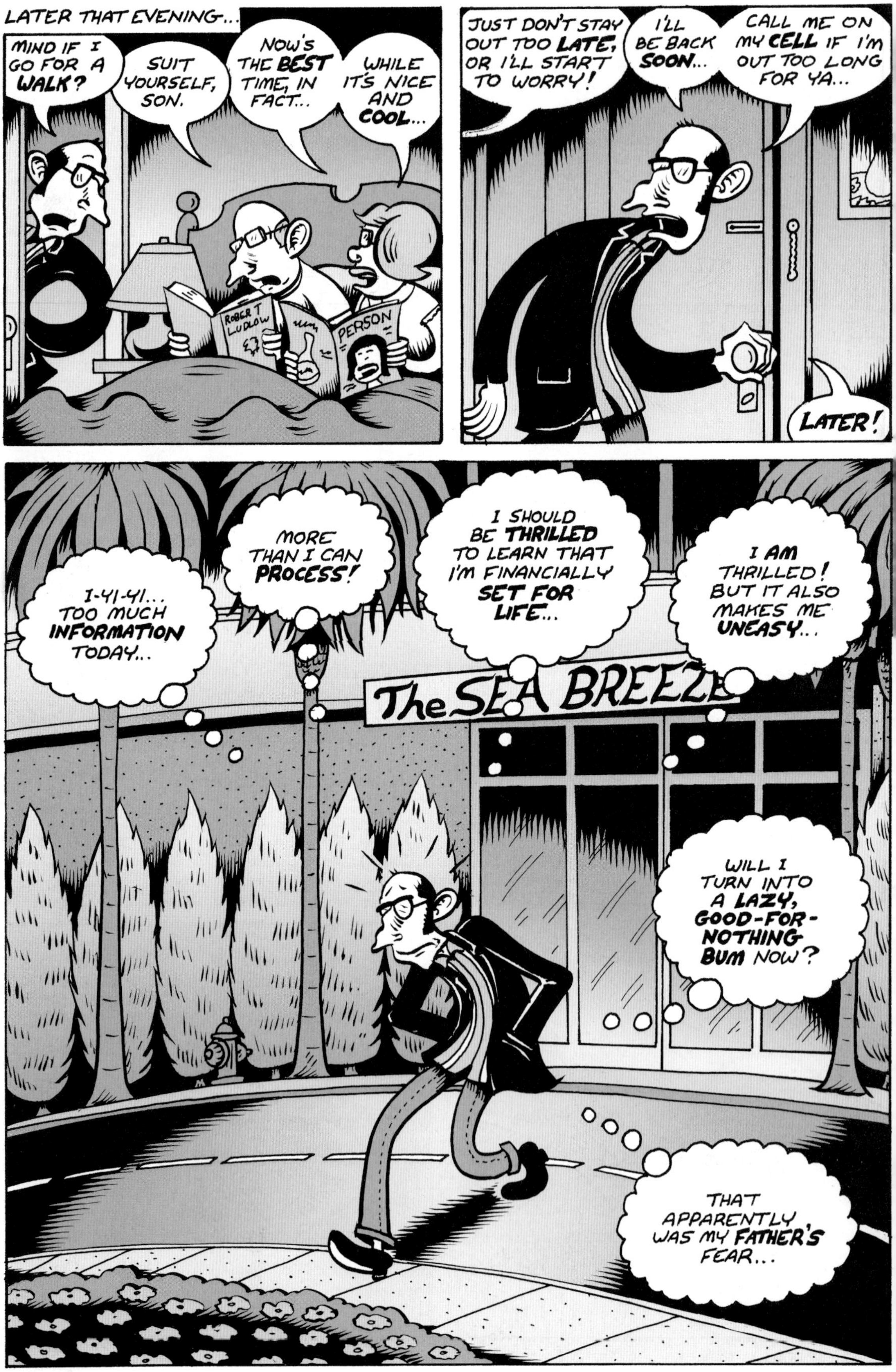
LATER THAT EVENING...
MIND IF I GO FOR A WALK?
SUIT YOURSELF, SON.
NOW'S THE BEST TIME, IN FACT...
WHILE IT'S NICE AND COOL...
ROBERT LUDLOW
PERSON
JUST DON'T STAY OUT TOO LATE, OR I'LL START TO WORRY!
I'LL BE BACK SOON...
CALL ME ON MY CELL IF I'M OUT TOO LONG FOR YA...
LATER!
I-YI-YI... TOO MUCH INFORMATION TODAY...
MORE THAN I CAN PROCESS!
I SHOULD BE THRILLED TO LEARN THAT I'M FINANCIALLY SET FOR LIFE...
I AM THRILLED! BUT IT ALSO MAKES ME UNEASY...
The SEA BREEZE
WILL I TURN INTO A LAZY, GOOD-FOR-NOTHING BUM NOW?
THAT APPARENTLY WAS MY FATHER'S FEAR...

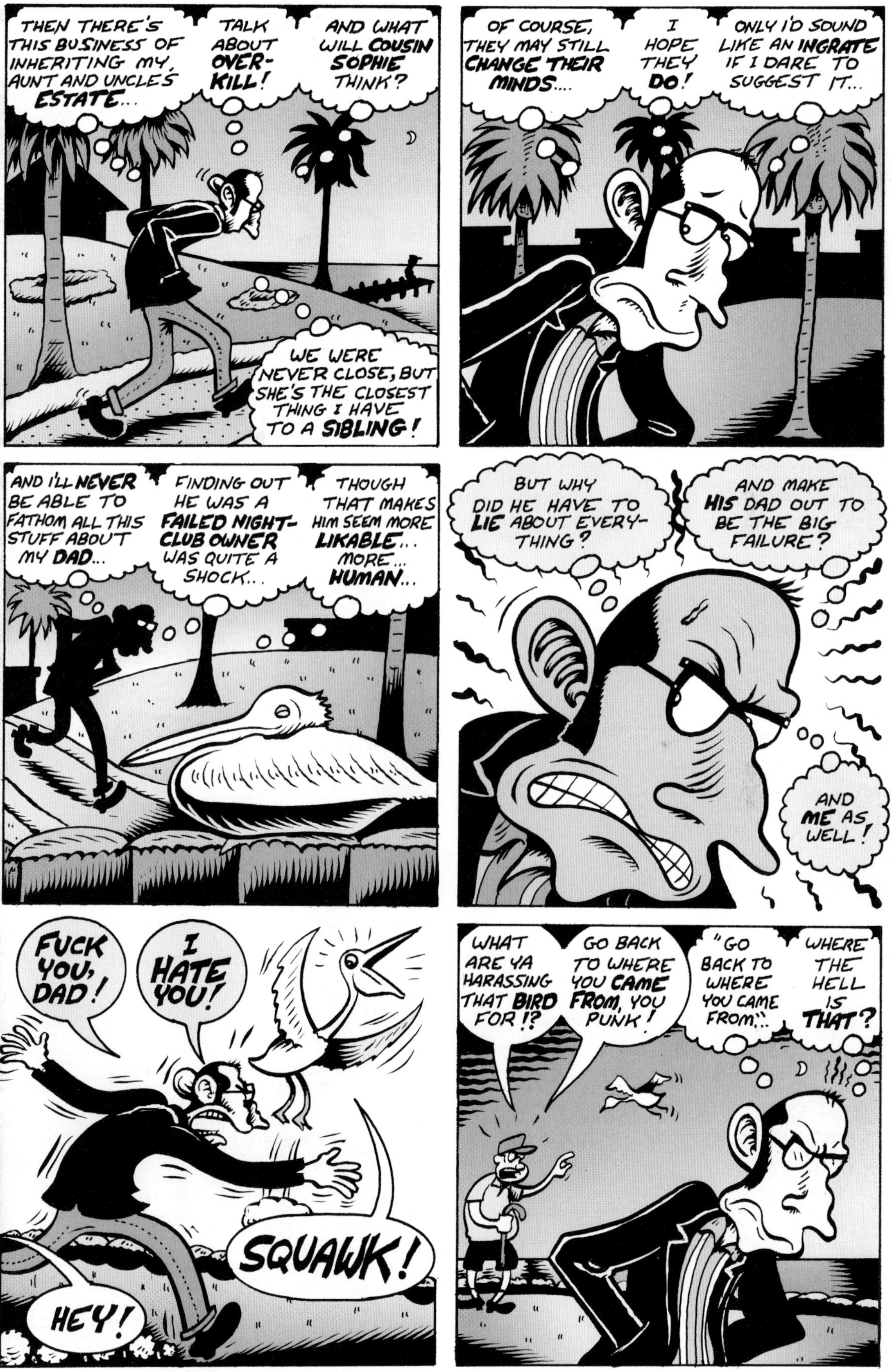
THEN THERE'S THIS BUSINESS OF INHERITING MY AUNT AND UNCLE'S ESTATE...
TALK ABOUT OVER-KILL!
AND WHAT WILL COUSIN SOPHIE THINK?
WE WERE NEVER CLOSE, BUT SHE'S THE CLOSEST THING I HAVE TO A SIBLING!
OF COURSE, THEY MAY STILL CHANGE THEIR MINDS....
I HOPE THEY DO!
ONLY I'D SOUND LIKE AN INGRATE IF I DARE TO SUGGEST IT...
AND I'LL NEVER BE ABLE TO FATHOM ALL THIS STUFF ABOUT MY DAD...
FINDING OUT HE WAS A FAILED NIGHT-CLUB OWNER WAS QUITE A SHOCK...
THOUGH THAT MAKES HIM SEEM MORE LIKABLE... MORE... HUMAN...
BUT WHY DID HE HAVE TO LIE ABOUT EVERY-THING?
AND MAKE HIS DAD OUT TO BE THE BIG FAILURE?
AND ME AS WELL!
FUCK YOU, DAD!
I HATE YOU!
SQUAWK!
HEY!
WHAT ARE YA HARASSING THAT BIRD FOR!?
GO BACK TO WHERE YOU CAME FROM, YOU PUNK!
"GO BACK TO WHERE YOU CAME FROM"...
WHERE THE HELL IS THAT?

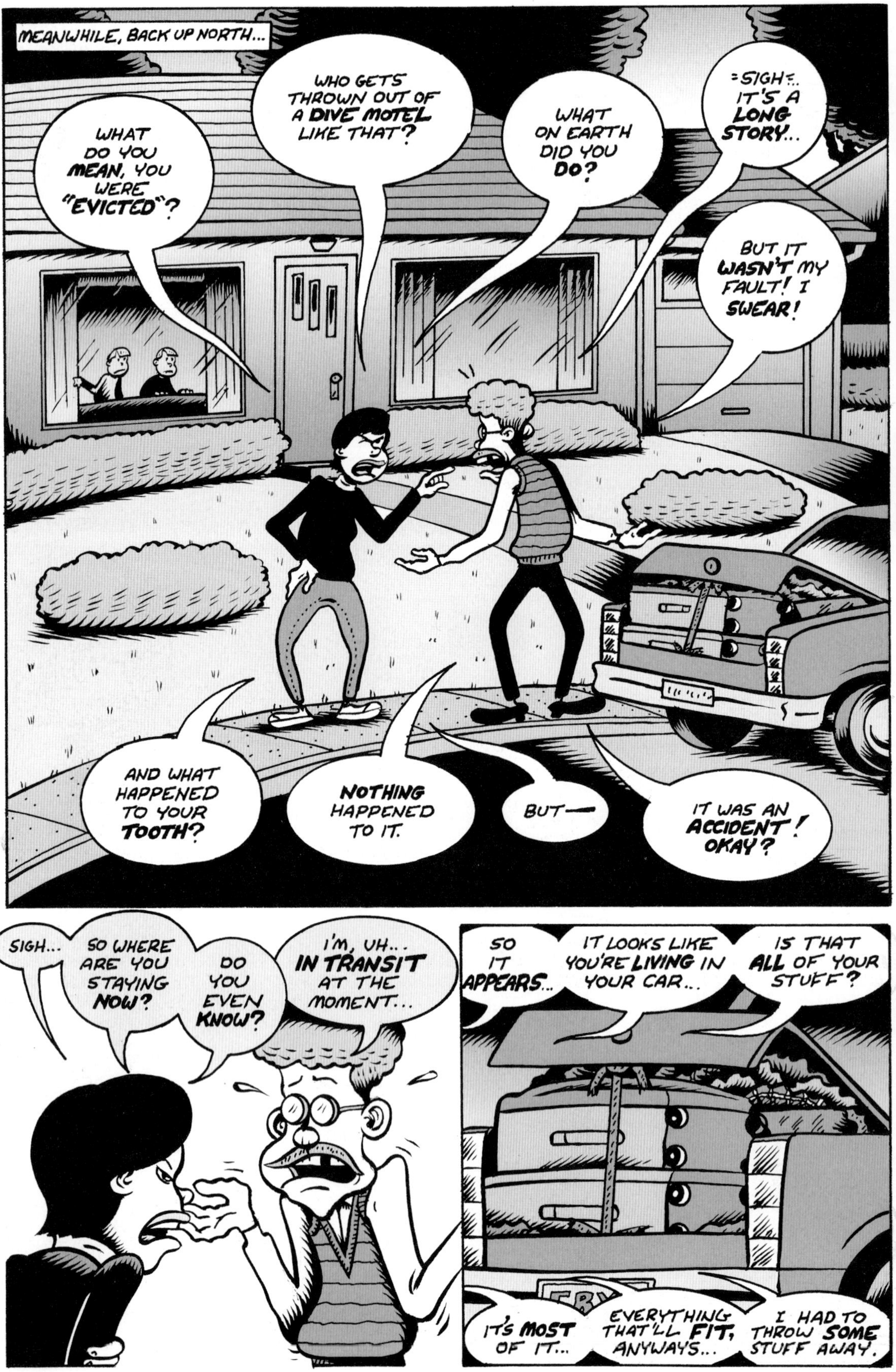
MEANWHILE, BACK UP NORTH...
WHAT DO YOU MEAN, YOU WERE "EVICTED"?
WHO GETS THROWN OUT OF A DIVE MOTEL LIKE THAT?
WHAT ON EARTH DID YOU DO?
=SIGH=.. IT'S A LONG STORY...
BUT IT WASN'T MY FAULT! I SWEAR!
AND WHAT HAPPENED TO YOUR TOOTH?
NOTHING HAPPENED TO IT.
BUT—
IT WAS AN ACCIDENT! OKAY?
SIGH...
SO WHERE ARE YOU STAYING NOW?
DO YOU EVEN KNOW?
I'M, UH... IN TRANSIT AT THE MOMENT...
SO IT APPEARS...
IT LOOKS LIKE YOU'RE LIVING IN YOUR CAR...
IS THAT ALL OF YOUR STUFF?
IT'S MOST OF IT...
EVERYTHING THAT'LL FIT, ANYWAYS...
I HAD TO THROW SOME STUFF AWAY.

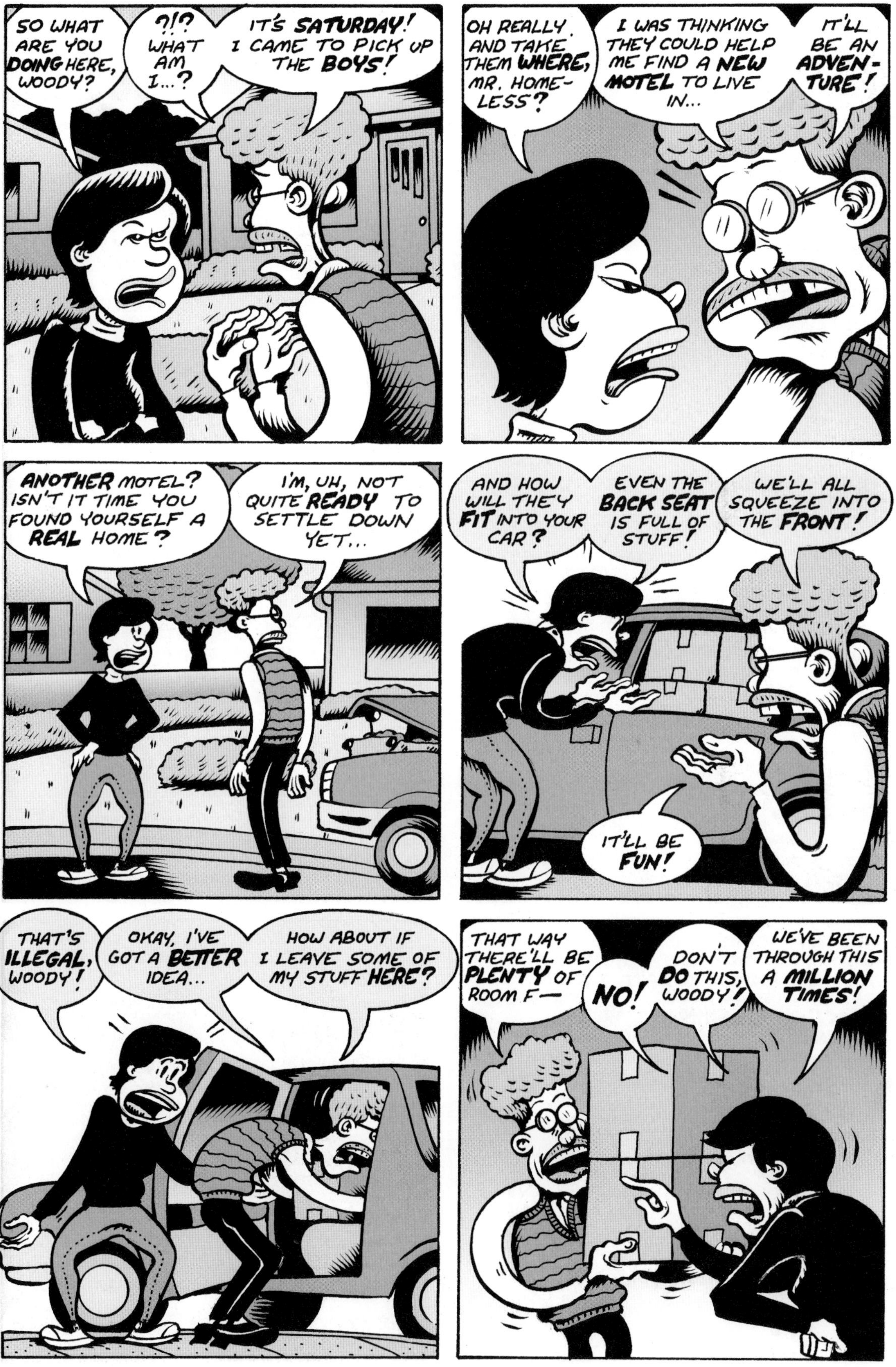
SO WHAT ARE YOU DOING HERE, WOODY?
?!? WHAT AM I...?
IT'S SATURDAY! I CAME TO PICK UP THE BOYS!
OH REALLY. AND TAKE THEM WHERE, MR. HOMELESS?
I WAS THINKING THEY COULD HELP ME FIND A NEW MOTEL TO LIVE IN...
IT'LL BE AN ADVENTURE!
ANOTHER MOTEL? ISN'T IT TIME YOU FOUND YOURSELF A REAL HOME?
I'M, UH, NOT QUITE READY TO SETTLE DOWN YET...
AND HOW WILL THEY FIT INTO YOUR CAR?
EVEN THE BACK SEAT IS FULL OF STUFF!
WE'LL ALL SQUEEZE INTO THE FRONT!
IT'LL BE FUN!
THAT'S ILLEGAL, WOODY!
OKAY, I'VE GOT A BETTER IDEA...
HOW ABOUT IF I LEAVE SOME OF MY STUFF HERE?
THAT WAY THERE'LL BE PLENTY OF ROOM F—
NO!
DON'T DO THIS, WOODY!
WE'VE BEEN THROUGH THIS A MILLION TIMES!

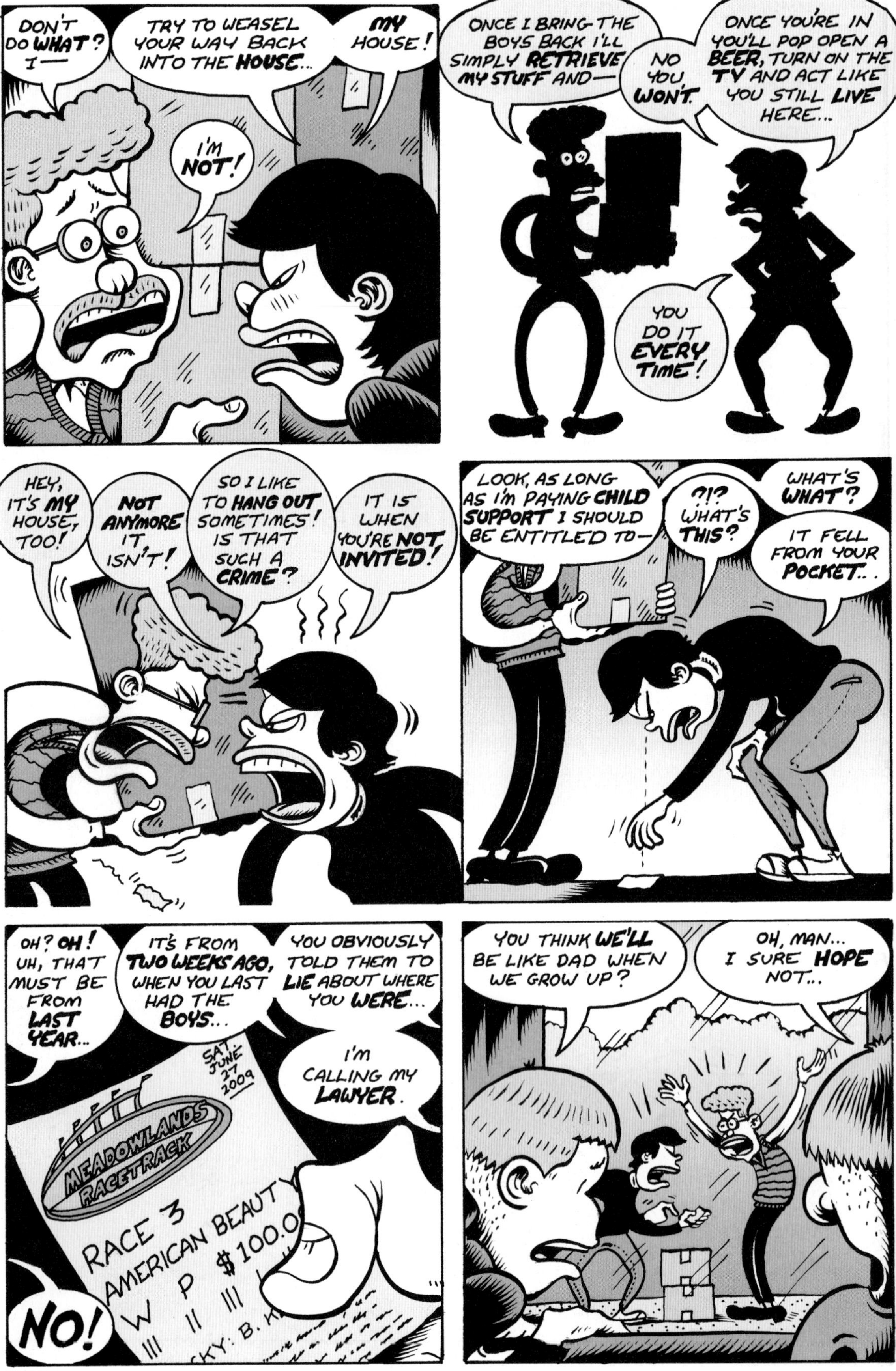
DON'T DO WHAT? I—
TRY TO WEASEL YOUR WAY BACK INTO THE HOUSE...
MY HOUSE!
I'M NOT!
ONCE I BRING THE BOYS BACK I'LL SIMPLY RETRIEVE MY STUFF AND—
NO YOU WON'T.
ONCE YOU'RE IN YOU'LL POP OPEN A BEER, TURN ON THE TV AND ACT LIKE YOU STILL LIVE HERE...
YOU DO IT EVERY TIME!
HEY, IT'S MY HOUSE, TOO!
NOT ANYMORE IT ISN'T!
SO I LIKE TO HANG OUT SOMETIMES! IS THAT SUCH A CRIME?
IT IS WHEN YOU'RE NOT INVITED!
LOOK, AS LONG AS I'M PAYING CHILD SUPPORT I SHOULD BE ENTITLED TO—
?!? WHAT'S THIS?
WHAT'S WHAT?
IT FELL FROM YOUR POCKET...
OH? OH! UH, THAT MUST BE FROM LAST YEAR...
IT'S FROM TWO WEEKS AGO, WHEN YOU LAST HAD THE BOYS...
YOU OBVIOUSLY TOLD THEM TO LIE ABOUT WHERE YOU WERE...
I'M CALLING MY LAWYER.
SAT. JUNE 27 2009
MEADOWLANDS RACETRACK
RACE 3
AMERICAN BEAUTY
$100.0
W P
NO!
YOU THINK WE'LL BE LIKE DAD WHEN WE GROW UP?
OH, MAN... I SURE HOPE NOT...

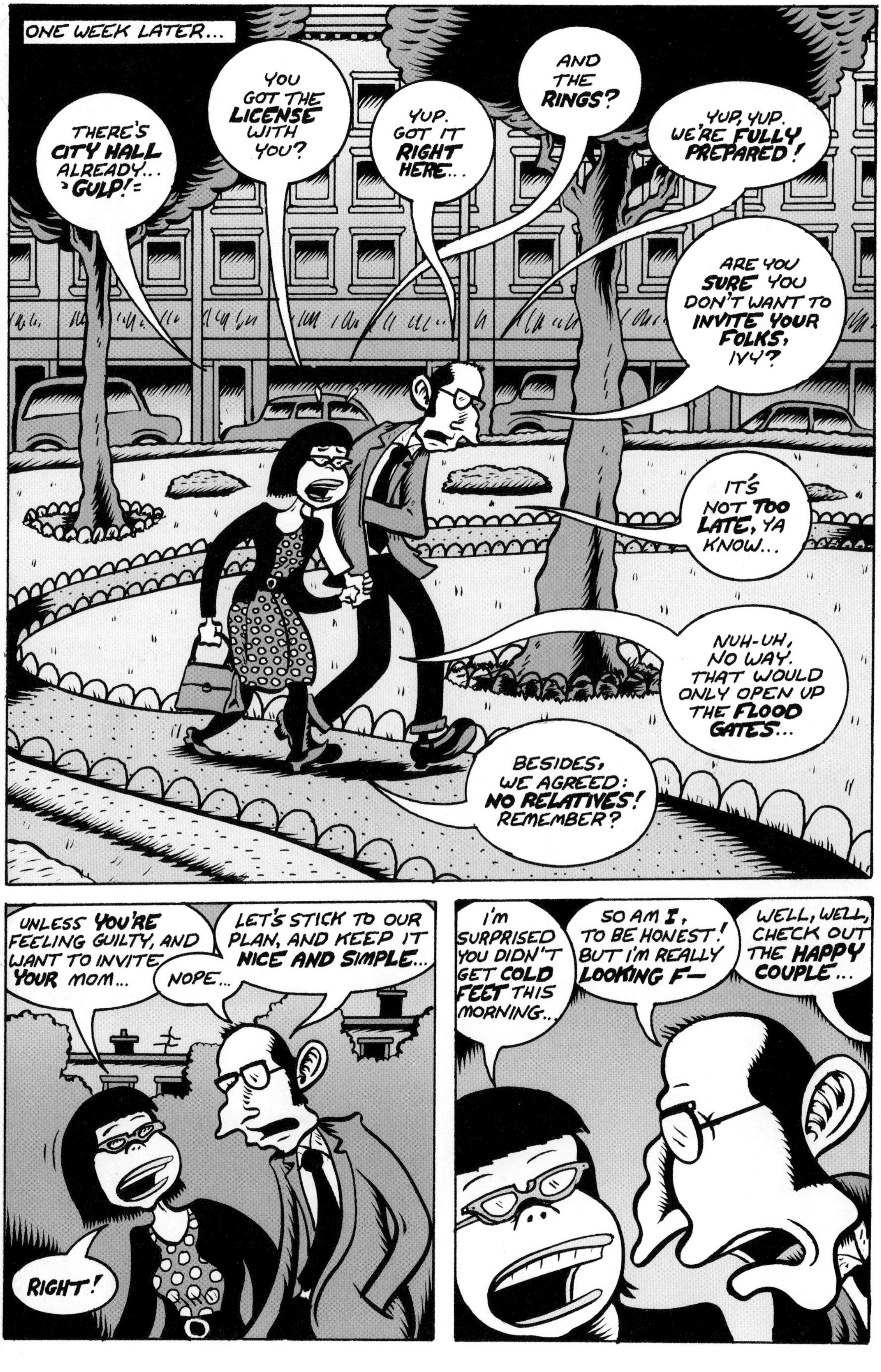
ONE WEEK LATER...
THERE'S CITY HALL ALREADY... GULP!
YOU GOT THE LICENSE WITH YOU?
YUP. GOT IT RIGHT HERE...
AND THE RINGS?
YUP, YUP. WE'RE FULLY PREPARED!
ARE YOU SURE YOU DON'T WANT TO INVITE YOUR FOLKS, IVY?
IT'S NOT TOO LATE, YA KNOW...
NUH-UH, NO WAY. THAT WOULD ONLY OPEN UP THE FLOOD GATES...
BESIDES, WE AGREED: NO RELATIVES! REMEMBER?
UNLESS YOU'RE FEELING GUILTY, AND WANT TO INVITE YOUR MOM...
NOPE...
LET'S STICK TO OUR PLAN, AND KEEP IT NICE AND SIMPLE...
RIGHT!
I'M SURPRISED YOU DIDN'T GET COLD FEET THIS MORNING...
SO AM I, TO BE HONEST! BUT I'M REALLY LOOKING F—
WELL, WELL, CHECK OUT THE HAPPY COUPLE...

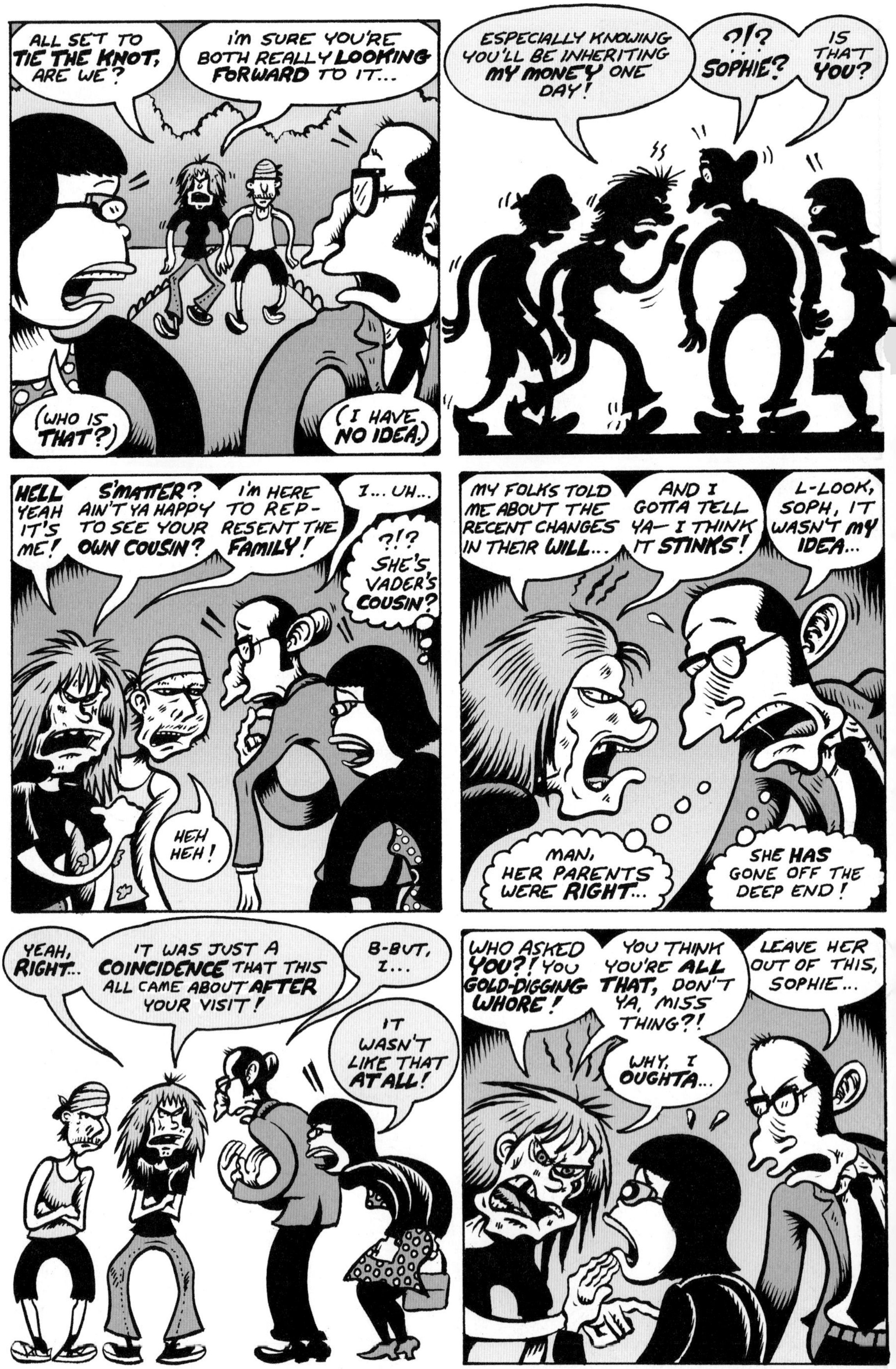
ALL SET TO TIE THE KNOT, ARE WE?
I'M SURE YOU'RE BOTH REALLY LOOKING FORWARD TO IT...
(WHO IS THAT?)
(I HAVE NO IDEA.)
ESPECIALLY KNOWING YOU'LL BE INHERITING MY MONEY ONE DAY!
?!? ... SOPHIE?
IS THAT YOU?
HELL YEAH IT'S ME!
S'MATTER? AIN'T YA HAPPY TO SEE YOUR OWN COUSIN?
I'M HERE TO REP-RESENT THE FAMILY!
I... UH...
?!? SHE'S VADER'S COUSIN?
HEH HEH!
MY FOLKS TOLD ME ABOUT THE RECENT CHANGES IN THEIR WILL...
AND I GOTTA TELL YA— I THINK IT STINKS!
L-LOOK, SOPH, IT WASN'T MY IDEA...
MAN, HER PARENTS WERE RIGHT...
SHE HAS GONE OFF THE DEEP END!
YEAH, RIGHT...
IT WAS JUST A COINCIDENCE THAT THIS ALL CAME ABOUT AFTER YOUR VISIT!
B-BUT, I...
IT WASN'T LIKE THAT AT ALL!
WHO ASKED YOU?! YOU GOLD-DIGGING WHORE!
YOU THINK YOU'RE ALL THAT, DON'T YA, MISS THING?!
LEAVE HER OUT OF THIS, SOPHIE...
WHY, I OUGHTA...

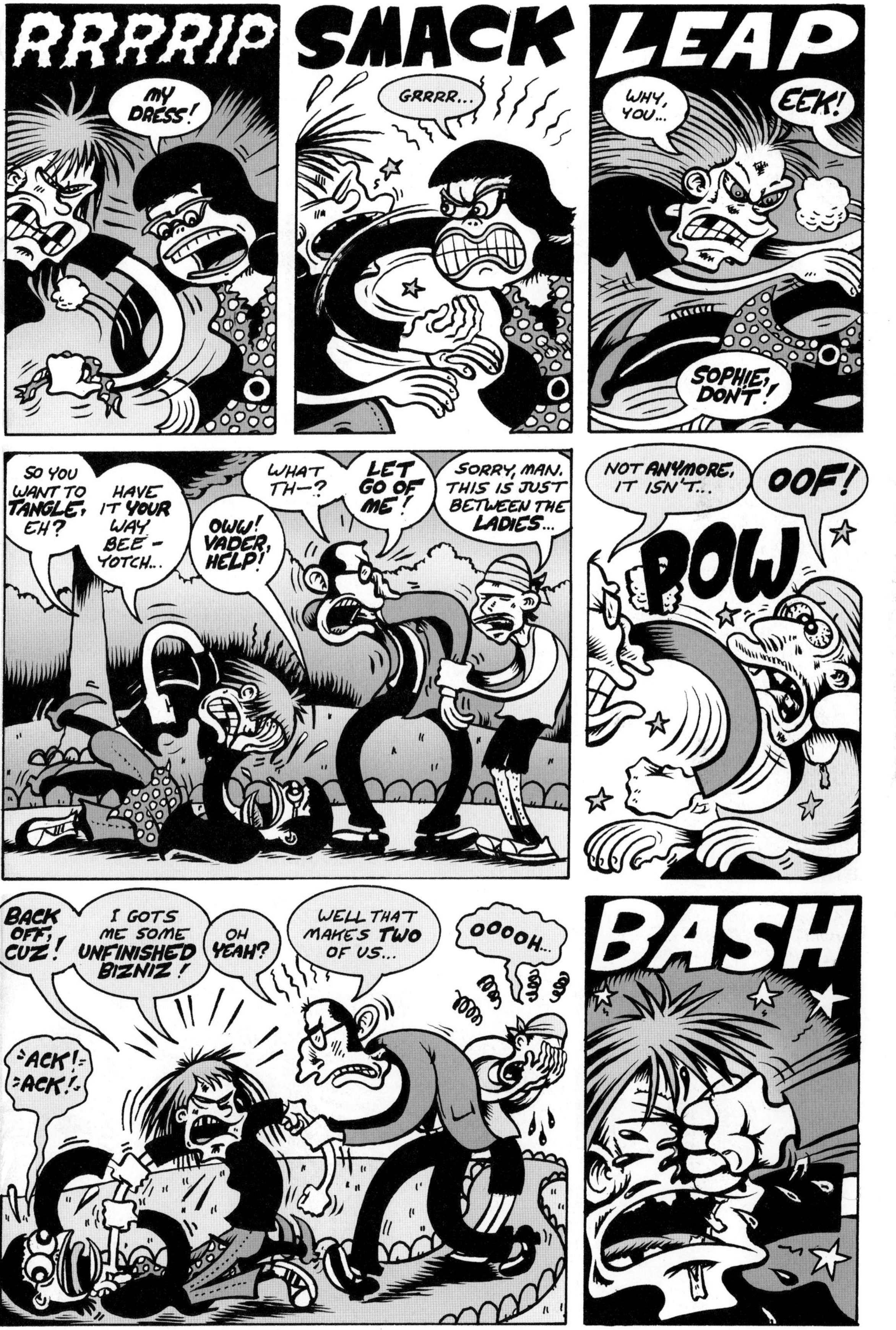
RRRRIP
MY DRESS!
SMACK
GRRRR...
LEAP
WHY, YOU...
EEK!
SOPHIE, DON'T!
SO YOU WANT TO TANGLE, EH?
HAVE IT YOUR WAY BEE-YOTCH...
OWW! VADER, HELP!
WHAT TH--?
LET GO OF ME!
SORRY, MAN. THIS IS JUST BETWEEN THE LADIES...
NOT ANYMORE, IT ISN'T...
OOF!
POW
BACK OFF, CUZ!
I GOTS ME SOME UNFINISHED BIZNIZ!
OH YEAH?
WELL THAT MAKES TWO OF US...
OOOOH...
ACK! ACK!
BASH

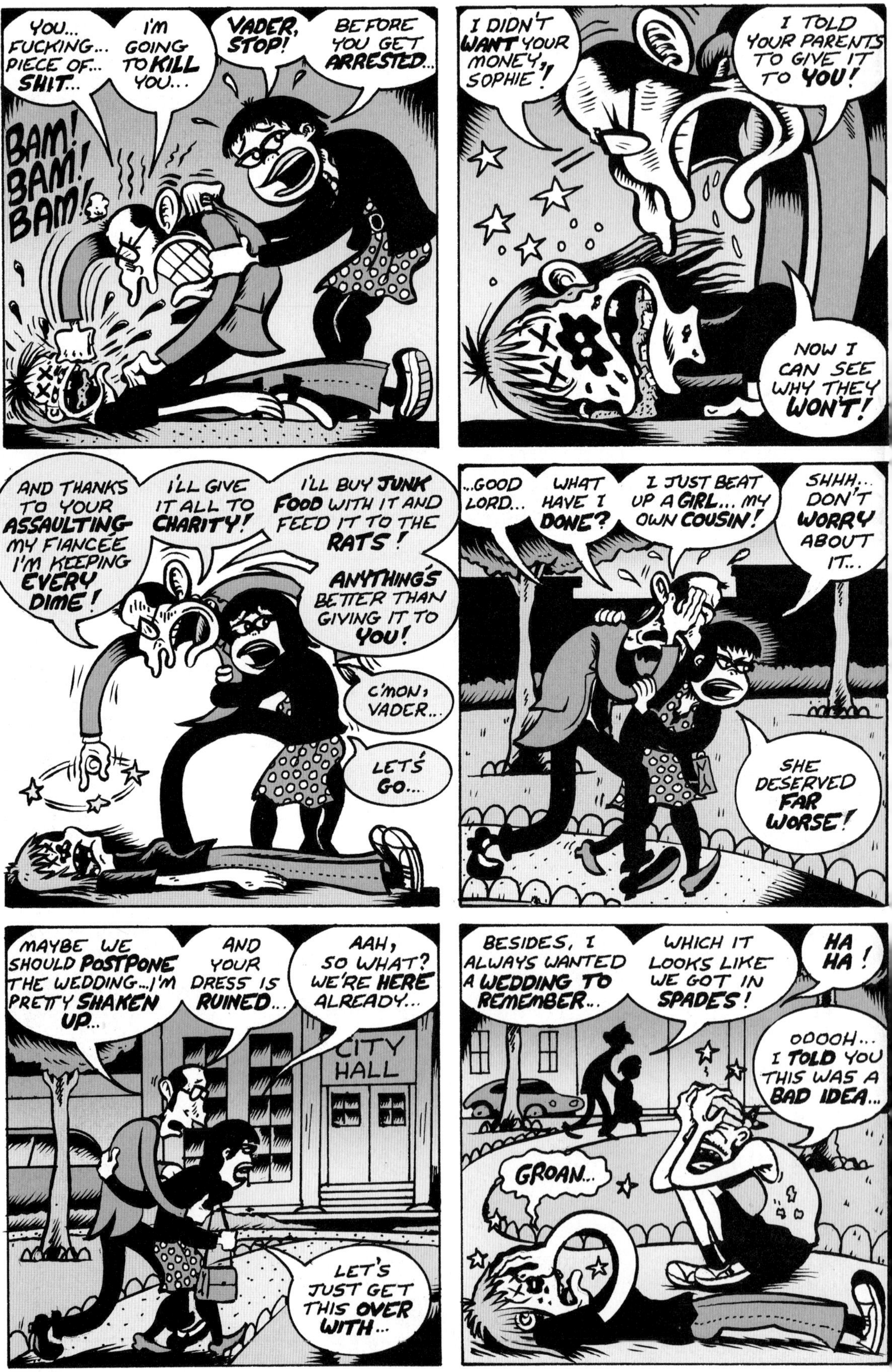
YOU... FUCKING... PIECE OF... SHIT...
I'M GOING TO KILL YOU...
VADER, STOP!
BEFORE YOU GET ARRESTED...
BAM! BAM! BAM!
I DIDN'T WANT YOUR MONEY, SOPHIE!
I TOLD YOUR PARENTS TO GIVE IT TO YOU!
NOW I CAN SEE WHY THEY WON'T!
AND THANKS TO YOUR ASSAULTING MY FIANCÉE I'M KEEPING EVERY DIME!
I'LL GIVE IT ALL TO CHARITY!
I'LL BUY JUNK FOOD WITH IT AND FEED IT TO THE RATS!
ANYTHING'S BETTER THAN GIVING IT TO YOU!
C'MON, VADER...
LET'S GO...
...GOOD LORD...
WHAT HAVE I DONE?
I JUST BEAT UP A GIRL... MY OWN COUSIN!
SHHH... DON'T WORRY ABOUT IT...
SHE DESERVED FAR WORSE!
MAYBE WE SHOULD POSTPONE THE WEDDING...I'M PRETTY SHAKEN UP...
AND YOUR DRESS IS RUINED...
AAH, SO WHAT? WE'RE HERE ALREADY...
CITY HALL
LET'S JUST GET THIS OVER WITH...
BESIDES, I ALWAYS WANTED A WEDDING TO REMEMBER...
WHICH IT LOOKS LIKE WE GOT IN SPADES!
HA HA!
OOOOH... I TOLD YOU THIS WAS A BAD IDEA...
GROAN...

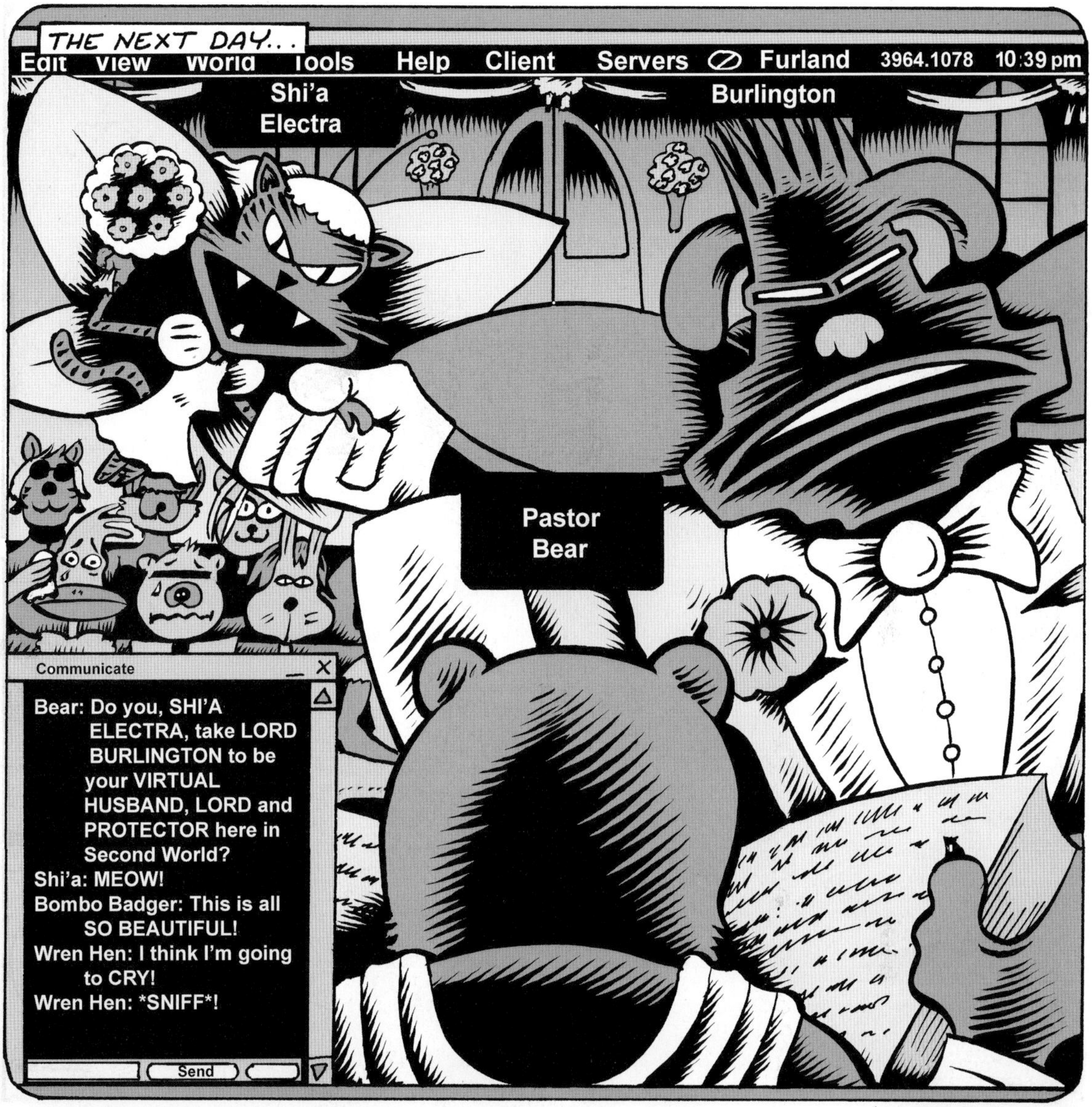
THE NEXT DAY...
Edit View World Tools Help Client Servers Furland 3964.1078 10:39 pm
Shi'a Electra
Burlington
Pastor Bear
Communicate
Bear: Do you, SHI'A ELECTRA, take LORD BURLINGTON to be your VIRTUAL HUSBAND, LORD and PROTECTOR here in Second World?
Shi'a: MEOW!
Bombo Badger: This is all SO BEAUTIFUL!
Wren Hen: I think I'm going to CRY!
Wren Hen: *SNIFF*!
Send

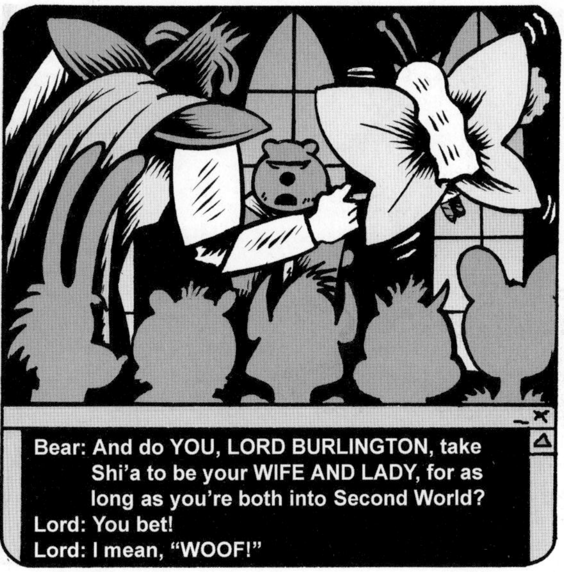
Bear: And do YOU, LORD BURLINGTON, take Shi'a to be your WIFE AND LADY, for as long as you're both into Second World?
Lord: You bet!
Lord: I mean, "WOOF!"

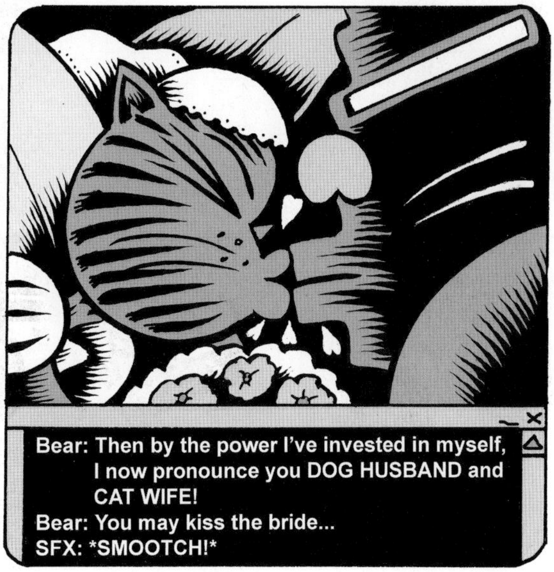
Bear: Then by the power I've invested in myself, I now pronounce you DOG HUSBAND and CAT WIFE!
Bear: You may kiss the bride...
SFX: *SMOOTCH!*

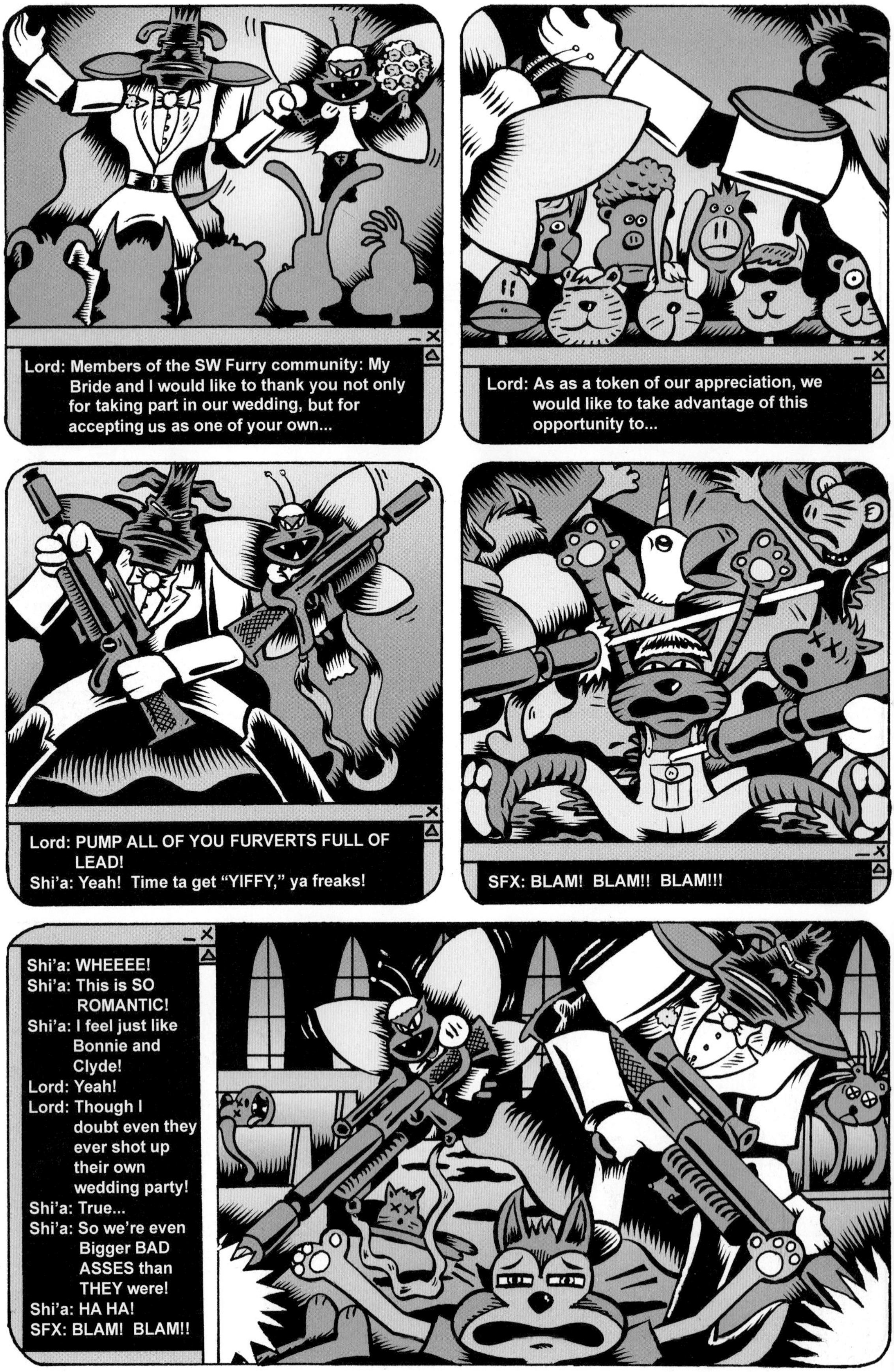

Lord: Members of the SW Furry community: My Bride and I would like to thank you not only for taking part in our wedding, but for accepting us as one of your own...
Lord: As as a token of our appreciation, we would like to take advantage of this opportunity to...
Lord: PUMP ALL OF YOU FURVERTS FULL OF LEAD!
Shi'a: Yeah! Time ta get "YIFFY," ya freaks!
SFX: BLAM! BLAM!! BLAM!!!
Shi'a: WHEEEE!
Shi'a: This is SO ROMANTIC!
Shi'a: I feel just like Bonnie and Clyde!
Lord: Yeah!
Lord: Though I doubt even they ever shot up their own wedding party!
Shi'a: True...
Shi'a: So we're even Bigger BAD ASSES than THEY were!
Shi'a: HA HA!
SFX: BLAM! BLAM!!

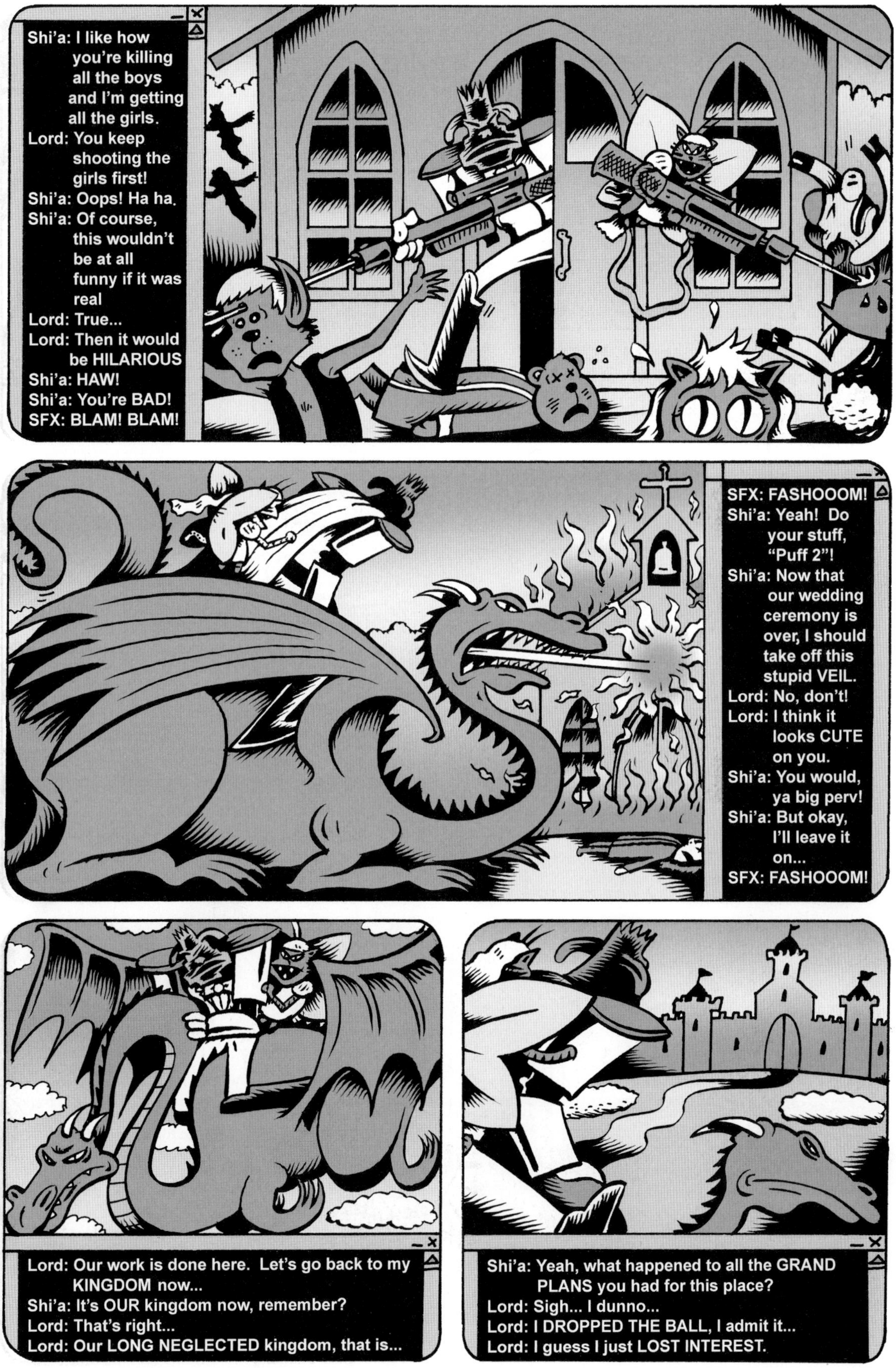
Shi'a: I like how you're killing all the boys and I'm getting all the girls.
Lord: You keep shooting the girls first!
Shi'a: Oops! Ha ha.
Shi'a: Of course, this wouldn't be at all funny if it was real
Lord: True...
Lord: Then it would be HILARIOUS
Shi'a: HAW!
Shi'a: You're BAD!
SFX: BLAM! BLAM!
SFX: FASHOOOM!
Shi'a: Yeah! Do your stuff, "Puff 2"!
Shi'a: Now that our wedding ceremony is over, I should take off this stupid VEIL.
Lord: No, don't!
Lord: I think it looks CUTE on you.
Shi'a: You would, ya big perv!
Shi'a: But okay, I'll leave it on...
SFX: FASHOOOM!
Lord: Our work is done here. Let's go back to my KINGDOM now...
Shi'a: It's OUR kingdom now, remember?
Lord: That's right...
Lord: Our LONG NEGLECTED kingdom, that is...
Shi'a: Yeah, what happened to all the GRAND PLANS you had for this place?
Lord: Sigh... I dunno...
Lord: I DROPPED THE BALL, I admit it...
Lord: I guess I just LOST INTEREST.

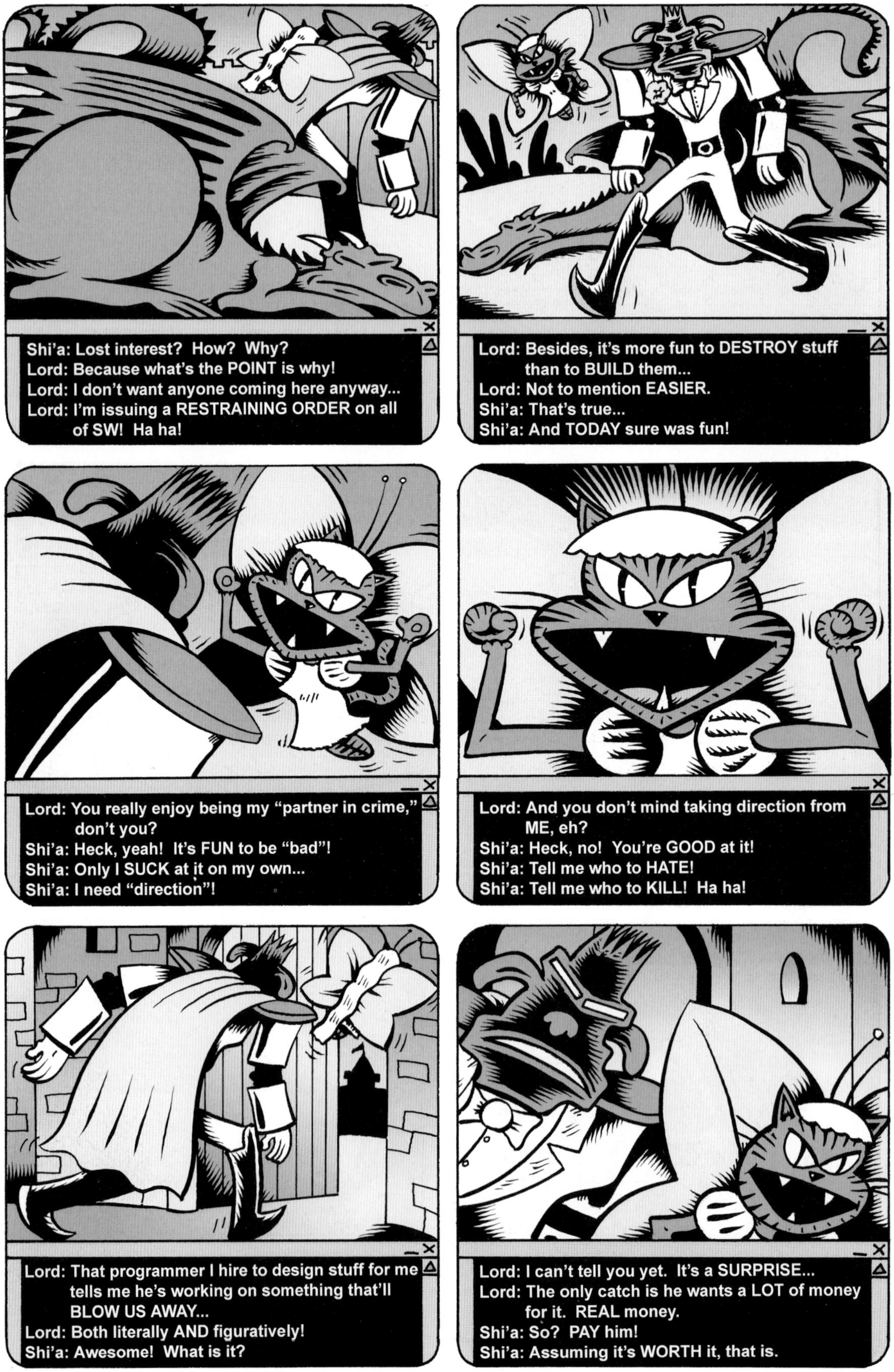
Shi'a: Lost interest? How? Why?
Lord: Because what's the POINT is why!
Lord: I don't want anyone coming here anyway...
Lord: I'm issuing a RESTRAINING ORDER on all of SW! Ha ha!
Lord: Besides, it's more fun to DESTROY stuff than to BUILD them...
Lord: Not to mention EASIER.
Shi'a: That's true...
Shi'a: And TODAY sure was fun!
Lord: You really enjoy being my "partner in crime," don't you?
Shi'a: Heck, yeah! It's FUN to be "bad"!
Shi'a: Only I SUCK at it on my own...
Shi'a: I need "direction"!
Lord: And you don't mind taking direction from ME, eh?
Shi'a: Heck, no! You're GOOD at it!
Shi'a: Tell me who to HATE!
Shi'a: Tell me who to KILL! Ha ha!
Lord: That programmer I hire to design stuff for me tells me he's working on something that'll BLOW US AWAY...
Lord: Both literally AND figuratively!
Shi'a: Awesome! What is it?
Lord: I can't tell you yet. It's a SURPRISE...
Lord: The only catch is he wants a LOT of money for it. REAL money.
Shi'a: So? PAY him!
Shi'a: Assuming it's WORTH it, that is.

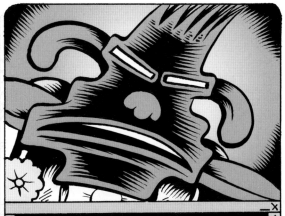

Lord: Oh, I'm SURE it'll be worth it...
Lord: Only I happen to be broke at the moment
Lord: I recently got FIRED from my job.
Shi'a: You DID?!?
Shi'a: How? Why?!?

Lord: Sigh... It's a LONG STORY...
Lord: But meanwhile, YOU recently MARRIED INTO a lot of money, did you not?
Shi'a: Huh? Oh, yeah, I suppose...
Shi'a: Though technically that's VADER'S money

Lord: Actually it's YOUR money as well...
Lord: Unless you signed a PRE-NUP, that is...
Lord: But oh, just forget it!
Lord: I don't need you OR your stupid money!
Shi'a: ?!? What do you mean?!

Lord: Look, if you won't contribute SOMEHOW then I'll just have fun on MY OWN.
Shi'a: Hey! What brought all THIS on?!?
Shi'a: I bet I could scrape up some money some-how, if you need it THAT bad!

Shi'a: Just don't leave me OUT of anything, okay?
Shi'a: Especially if it's something BIG~
Shi'a: I'm your "army," remember?
Lord: That's true. You are vital to the "mission"...
Lord: And I also need an "audience"...

Shi'a: Yeah! We're a TEAM!
Lord: Together we shall be INVINCIBLE!
Lord (lion's roar SFX): RRRRROARRRR!!!
Shi'a (lion's roar SFX): RRRRROARRRR!!!
Shi'a: Ha ha!

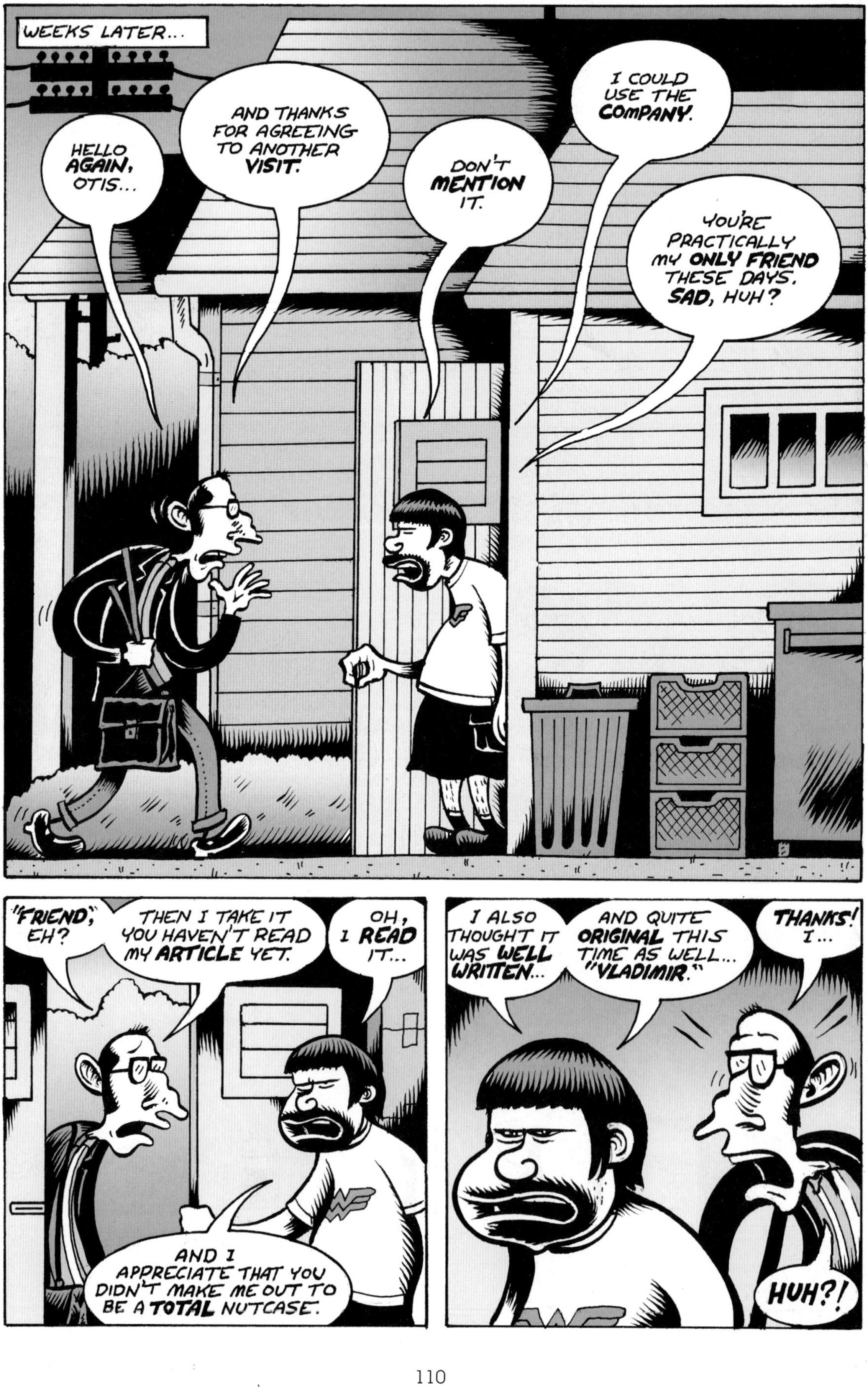
WEEKS LATER...
HELLO AGAIN, OTIS...
AND THANKS FOR AGREEING TO ANOTHER VISIT.
DON'T MENTION IT.
I COULD USE THE COMPANY.
YOU'RE PRACTICALLY MY ONLY FRIEND THESE DAYS. SAD, HUH?
"FRIEND", EH?
THEN I TAKE IT YOU HAVEN'T READ MY ARTICLE YET.
OH, I READ IT...
AND I APPRECIATE THAT YOU DIDN'T MAKE ME OUT TO BE A TOTAL NUTCASE.
I ALSO THOUGHT IT WAS WELL WRITTEN...
AND QUITE ORIGINAL THIS TIME AS WELL... "VLADIMIR."
THANKS! I...
HUH?!

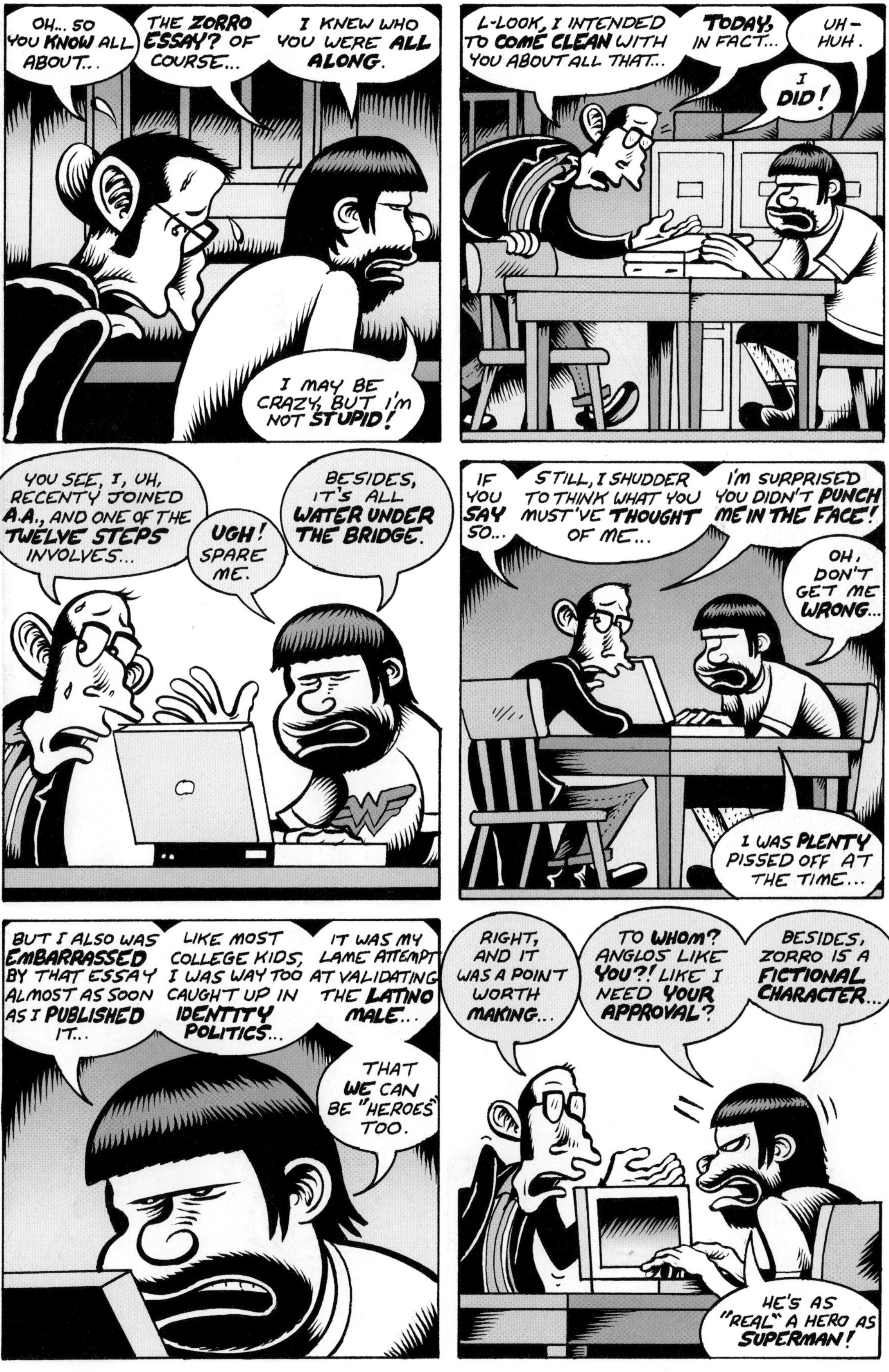

OH... SO YOU KNOW ALL ABOUT...
THE ZORRO ESSAY? OF COURSE...
I KNEW WHO YOU WERE ALL ALONG.
I MAY BE CRAZY, BUT I'M NOT STUPID!
L-LOOK, I INTENDED TO COME CLEAN WITH YOU ABOUT ALL THAT...
TODAY, IN FACT...
UH-HUH.
I DID!
YOU SEE, I, UH, RECENTY JOINED A.A., AND ONE OF THE TWELVE STEPS INVOLVES...
UGH! SPARE ME.
BESIDES, IT'S ALL WATER UNDER THE BRIDGE.
IF YOU SAY SO...
STILL, I SHUDDER TO THINK WHAT YOU MUST'VE THOUGHT OF ME...
I'M SURPRISED YOU DIDN'T PUNCH ME IN THE FACE!
OH, DON'T GET ME WRONG...
I WAS PLENTY PISSED OFF AT THE TIME...
BUT I ALSO WAS EMBARRASSED BY THAT ESSAY ALMOST AS SOON AS I PUBLISHED IT...
LIKE MOST COLLEGE KIDS, I WAS WAY TOO CAUGHT UP IN IDENTITY POLITICS...
IT WAS MY LAME ATTEMPT AT VALIDATING THE LATINO MALE...
THAT WE CAN BE "HEROES" TOO.
RIGHT, AND IT WAS A POINT WORTH MAKING...
TO WHOM? ANGLOS LIKE YOU?! LIKE I NEED YOUR APPROVAL?
BESIDES, ZORRO IS A FICTIONAL CHARACTER...
HE'S AS "REAL" A HERO AS SUPERMAN!

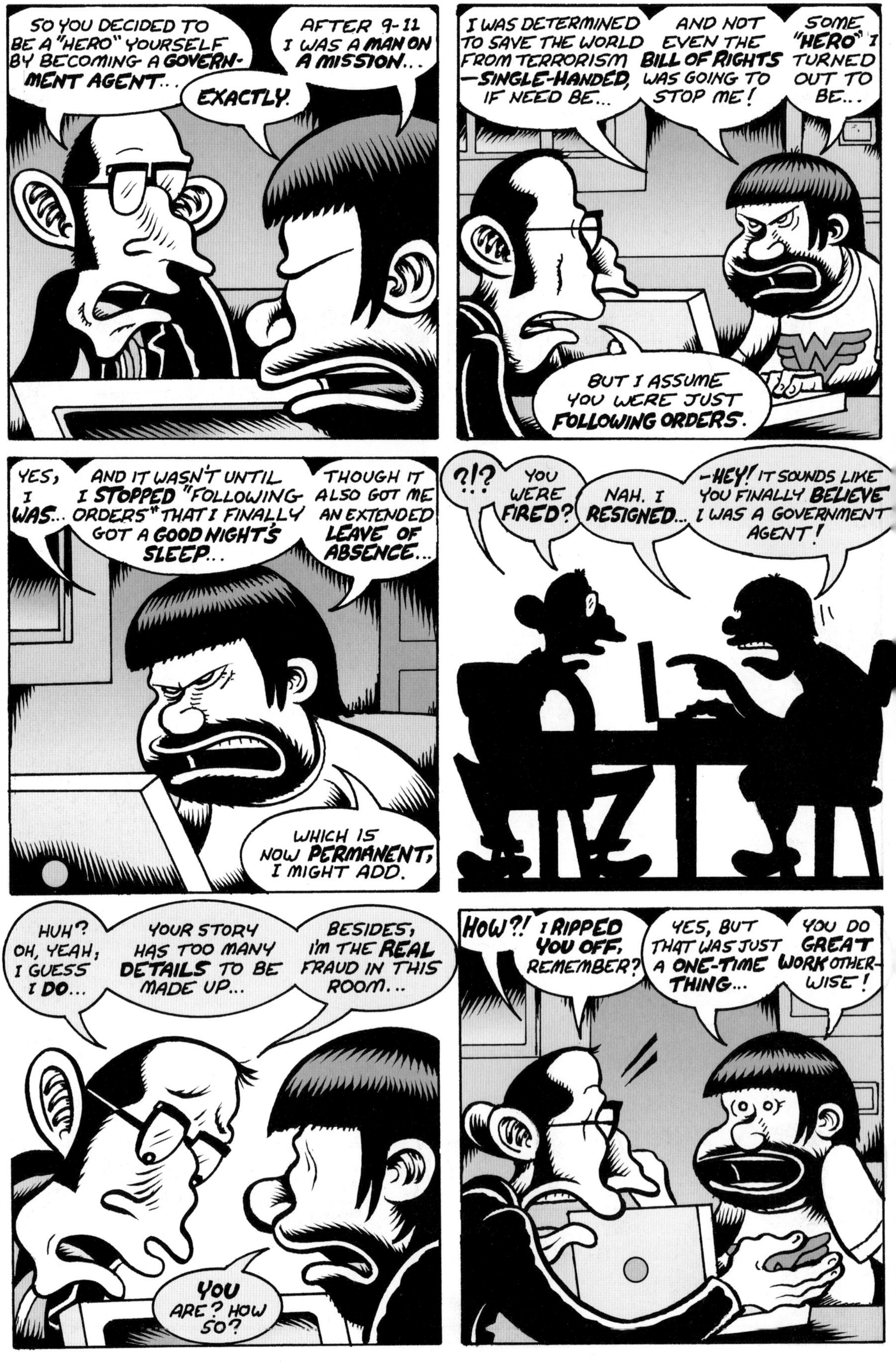
SO YOU DECIDED TO BE A "HERO" YOURSELF BY BECOMING A GOVERNMENT AGENT...
AFTER 9-11 I WAS A MAN ON A MISSION...
EXACTLY.
I WAS DETERMINED TO SAVE THE WORLD FROM TERRORISM —SINGLE-HANDED, IF NEED BE...
AND NOT EVEN THE BILL OF RIGHTS WAS GOING TO STOP ME!
SOME "HERO" I TURNED OUT TO BE...
BUT I ASSUME YOU WERE JUST FOLLOWING ORDERS.
YES, I WAS...
AND IT WASN'T UNTIL I STOPPED "FOLLOWING ORDERS" THAT I FINALLY GOT A GOOD NIGHT'S SLEEP...
THOUGH IT ALSO GOT ME AN EXTENDED LEAVE OF ABSENCE...
WHICH IS NOW PERMANENT, I MIGHT ADD.
?!?
YOU WERE FIRED?
NAH. I RESIGNED...
-HEY! IT SOUNDS LIKE YOU FINALLY BELIEVE I WAS A GOVERNMENT AGENT!
HUH? OH, YEAH, I GUESS I DO...
YOUR STORY HAS TOO MANY DETAILS TO BE MADE UP...
BESIDES, I'M THE REAL FRAUD IN THIS ROOM...
YOU ARE? HOW SO?
HOW?!
I RIPPED YOU OFF, REMEMBER?
YES, BUT THAT WAS JUST A ONE-TIME THING...
YOU DO GREAT WORK OTHERWISE!

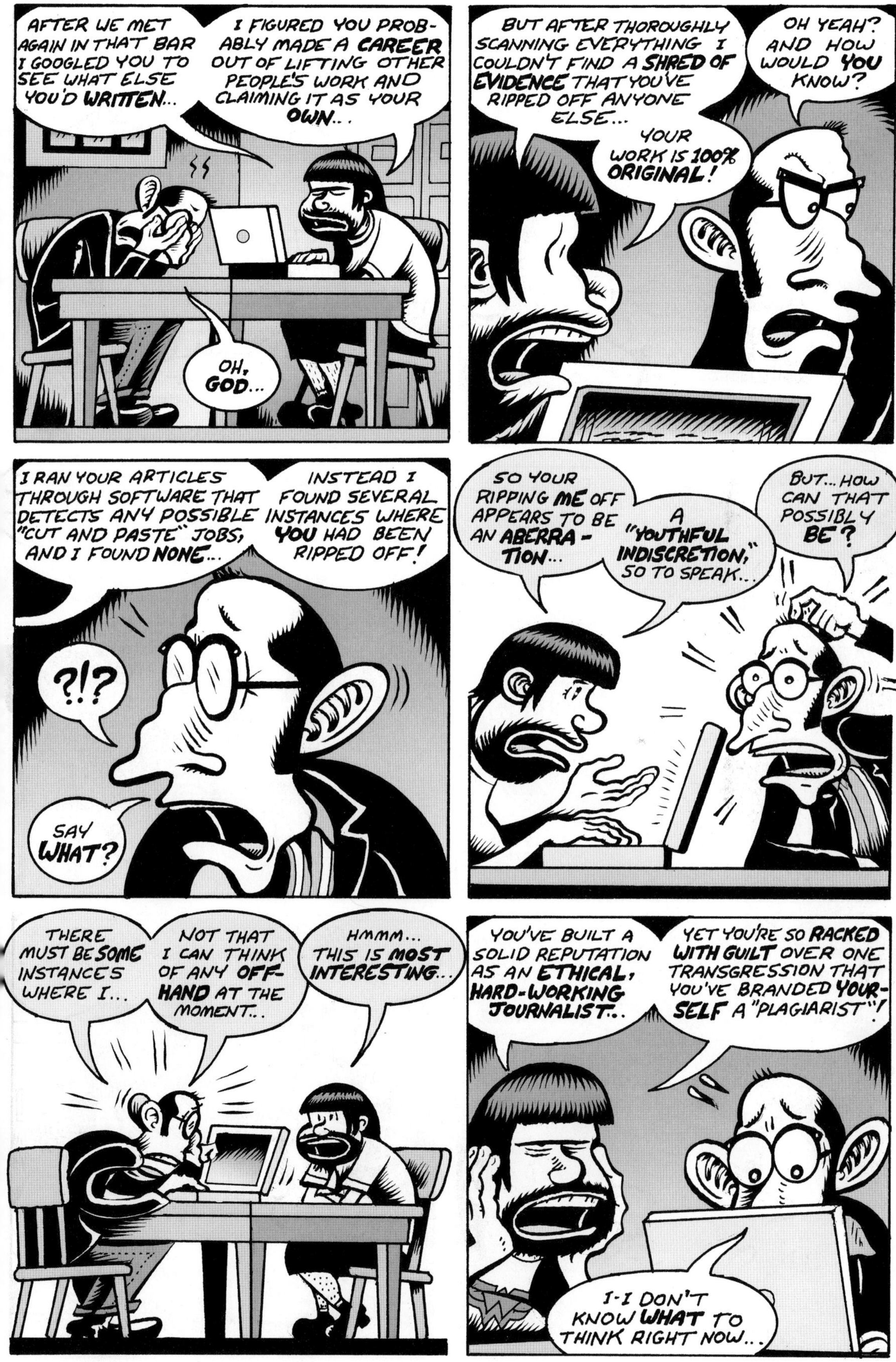
AFTER WE MET AGAIN IN THAT BAR I GOOGLED YOU TO SEE WHAT ELSE YOU'D WRITTEN...
I FIGURED YOU PROBABLY MADE A CAREER OUT OF LIFTING OTHER PEOPLE'S WORK AND CLAIMING IT AS YOUR OWN...
OH, GOD...
BUT AFTER THOROUGHLY SCANNING EVERYTHING I COULDN'T FIND A SHRED OF EVIDENCE THAT YOU'VE RIPPED OFF ANYONE ELSE...
YOUR WORK IS 100% ORIGINAL!
OH YEAH? AND HOW WOULD YOU KNOW?
I RAN YOUR ARTICLES THROUGH SOFTWARE THAT DETECTS ANY POSSIBLE "CUT AND PASTE" JOBS, AND I FOUND NONE...
INSTEAD I FOUND SEVERAL INSTANCES WHERE YOU HAD BEEN RIPPED OFF!
?!?
SAY WHAT?
SO YOUR RIPPING ME OFF APPEARS TO BE AN ABERRATION...
A "YOUTHFUL INDISCRETION," SO TO SPEAK...
BUT... HOW CAN THAT POSSIBLY BE?
THERE MUST BE SOME INSTANCES WHERE I...
NOT THAT I CAN THINK OF ANY OFF-HAND AT THE MOMENT...
HMMM... THIS IS MOST INTERESTING...
YOU'VE BUILT A SOLID REPUTATION AS AN ETHICAL, HARD-WORKING JOURNALIST...
YET YOU'RE SO RACKED WITH GUILT OVER ONE TRANSGRESSION THAT YOU'VE BRANDED YOURSELF A "PLAGIARIST"!
I-I DON'T KNOW WHAT TO THINK RIGHT NOW...

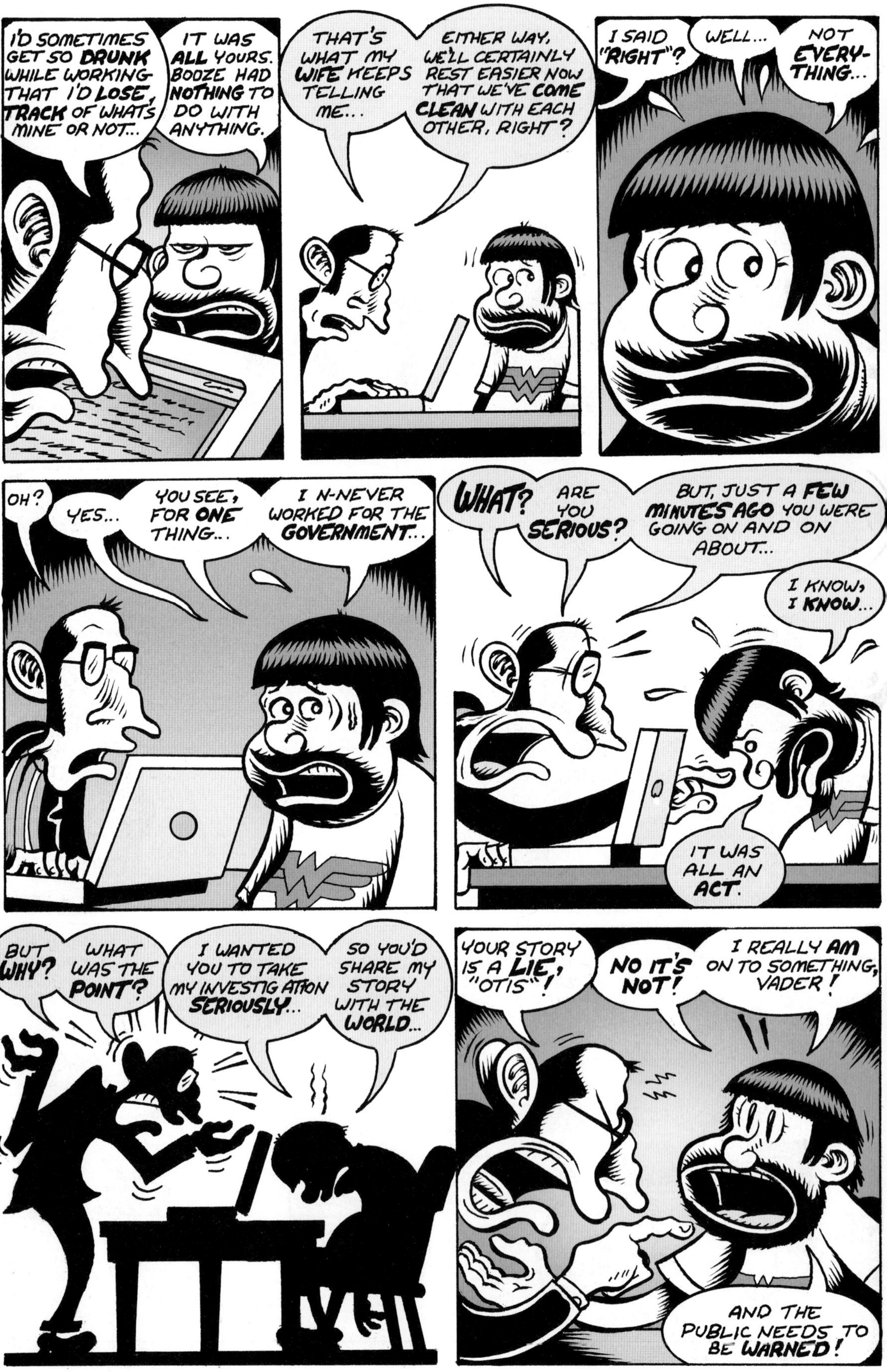
I'D SOMETIMES GET SO DRUNK WHILE WORKING THAT I'D LOSE TRACK OF WHAT'S MINE OR NOT...
IT WAS ALL YOURS. BOOZE HAD NOTHING TO DO WITH ANYTHING.
THAT'S WHAT MY WIFE KEEPS TELLING ME...
EITHER WAY, WE'LL CERTAINLY REST EASIER NOW THAT WE'VE COME CLEAN WITH EACH OTHER, RIGHT?
I SAID "RIGHT"?
WELL...
NOT EVERYTHING...
OH?
YES...
YOU SEE, FOR ONE THING...
I N-NEVER WORKED FOR THE GOVERNMENT...
WHAT?
ARE YOU SERIOUS?
BUT, JUST A FEW MINUTES AGO YOU WERE GOING ON AND ON ABOUT...
I KNOW, I KNOW...
IT WAS ALL AN ACT.
BUT WHY?
WHAT WAS THE POINT?
I WANTED YOU TO TAKE MY INVESTIGATION SERIOUSLY...
SO YOU'D SHARE MY STORY WITH THE WORLD...
YOUR STORY IS A LIE, "OTIS"!
NO IT'S NOT!
I REALLY AM ON TO SOMETHING, VADER!
AND THE PUBLIC NEEDS TO BE WARNED!

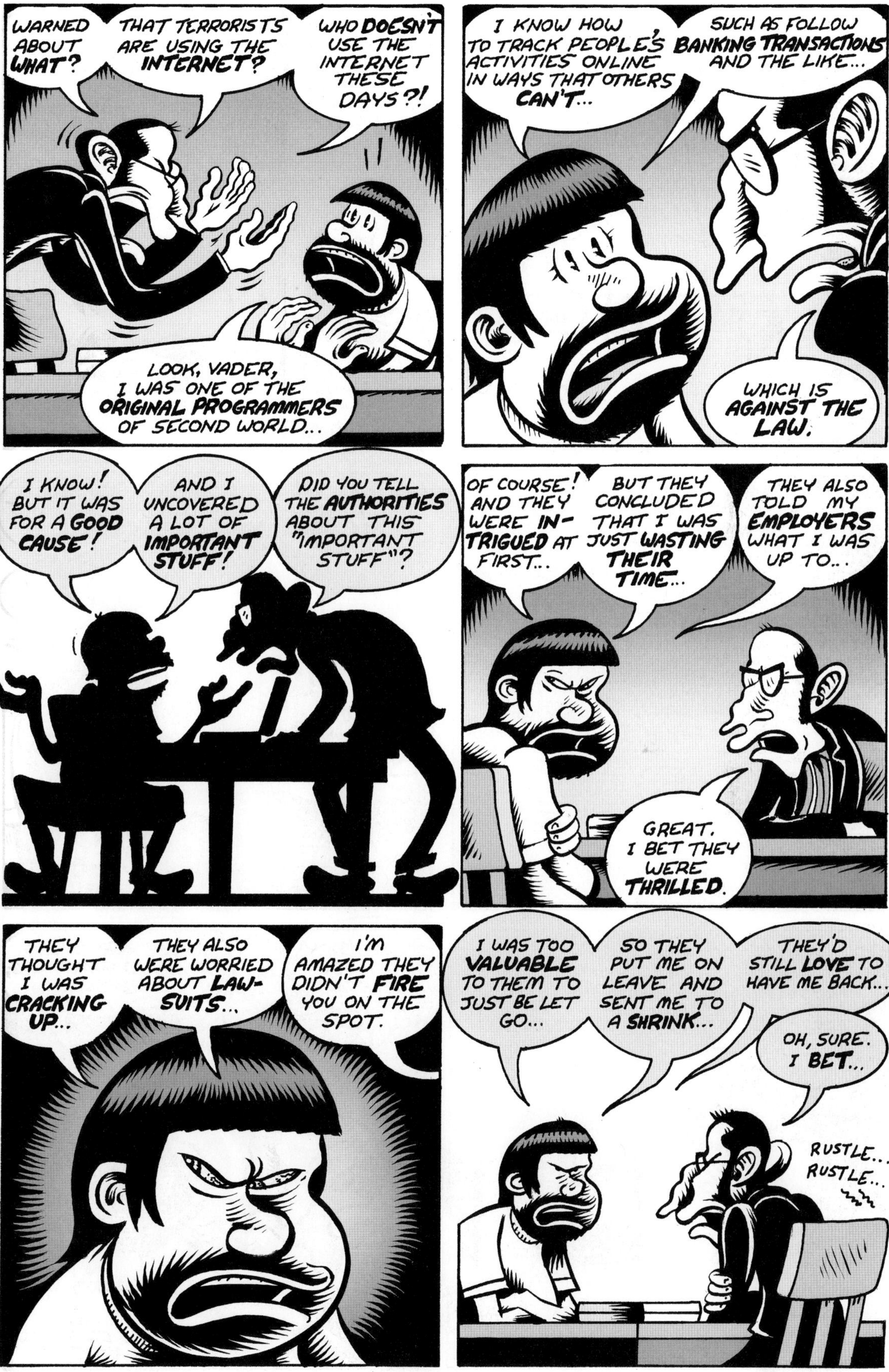
WARNED ABOUT WHAT?
THAT TERRORISTS ARE USING THE INTERNET?
WHO DOESN'T USE THE INTERNET THESE DAYS?!
LOOK, VADER, I WAS ONE OF THE ORIGINAL PROGRAMMERS OF SECOND WORLD...
I KNOW HOW TO TRACK PEOPLE'S ACTIVITIES ONLINE IN WAYS THAT OTHERS CAN'T...
SUCH AS FOLLOW BANKING TRANSACTIONS AND THE LIKE...
WHICH IS AGAINST THE LAW.
I KNOW! BUT IT WAS FOR A GOOD CAUSE!
AND I UNCOVERED A LOT OF IMPORTANT STUFF!
DID YOU TELL THE AUTHORITIES ABOUT THIS "IMPORTANT STUFF"?
OF COURSE! AND THEY WERE INTRIGUED AT FIRST...
BUT THEY CONCLUDED THAT I WAS JUST WASTING THEIR TIME...
THEY ALSO TOLD MY EMPLOYERS WHAT I WAS UP TO...
GREAT. I BET THEY WERE THRILLED.
THEY THOUGHT I WAS CRACKING UP...
THEY ALSO WERE WORRIED ABOUT LAWSUITS...
I'M AMAZED THEY DIDN'T FIRE YOU ON THE SPOT.
I WAS TOO VALUABLE TO THEM TO JUST BE LET GO...
SO THEY PUT ME ON LEAVE AND SENT ME TO A SHRINK...
THEY'D STILL LOVE TO HAVE ME BACK...
OH, SURE. I BET...
RUSTLE... RUSTLE...

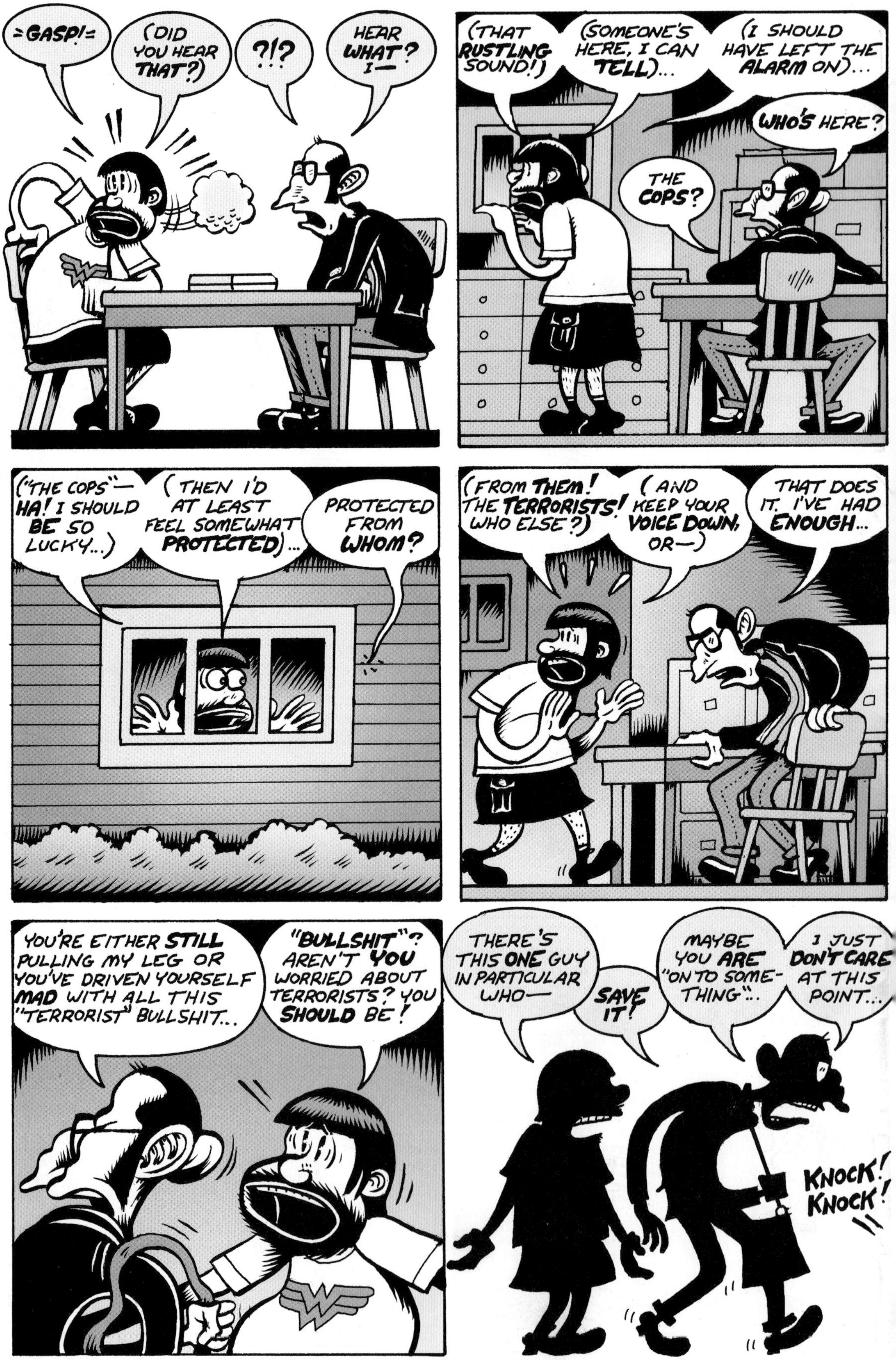
=GASP!=
(DID YOU HEAR THAT?)
?!?
HEAR WHAT? I—
(THAT RUSTLING SOUND!)
(SOMEONE'S HERE, I CAN TELL)...
(I SHOULD HAVE LEFT THE ALARM ON)...
WHO'S HERE?
THE COPS?
("THE COPS"— HA! I SHOULD BE SO LUCKY...)
(THEN I'D AT LEAST FEEL SOMEWHAT PROTECTED)...
PROTECTED FROM WHOM?
(FROM THEM! THE TERRORISTS! WHO ELSE?)
(AND KEEP YOUR VOICE DOWN, OR—)
THAT DOES IT. I'VE HAD ENOUGH...
YOU'RE EITHER STILL PULLING MY LEG OR YOU'VE DRIVEN YOURSELF MAD WITH ALL THIS "TERRORIST" BULLSHIT...
"BULLSHIT"? AREN'T YOU WORRIED ABOUT TERRORISTS? YOU SHOULD BE!
THERE'S THIS ONE GUY IN PARTICULAR WHO—
SAVE IT!
MAYBE YOU ARE "ON TO SOMETHING"...
I JUST DON'T CARE AT THIS POINT...
KNOCK! KNOCK!

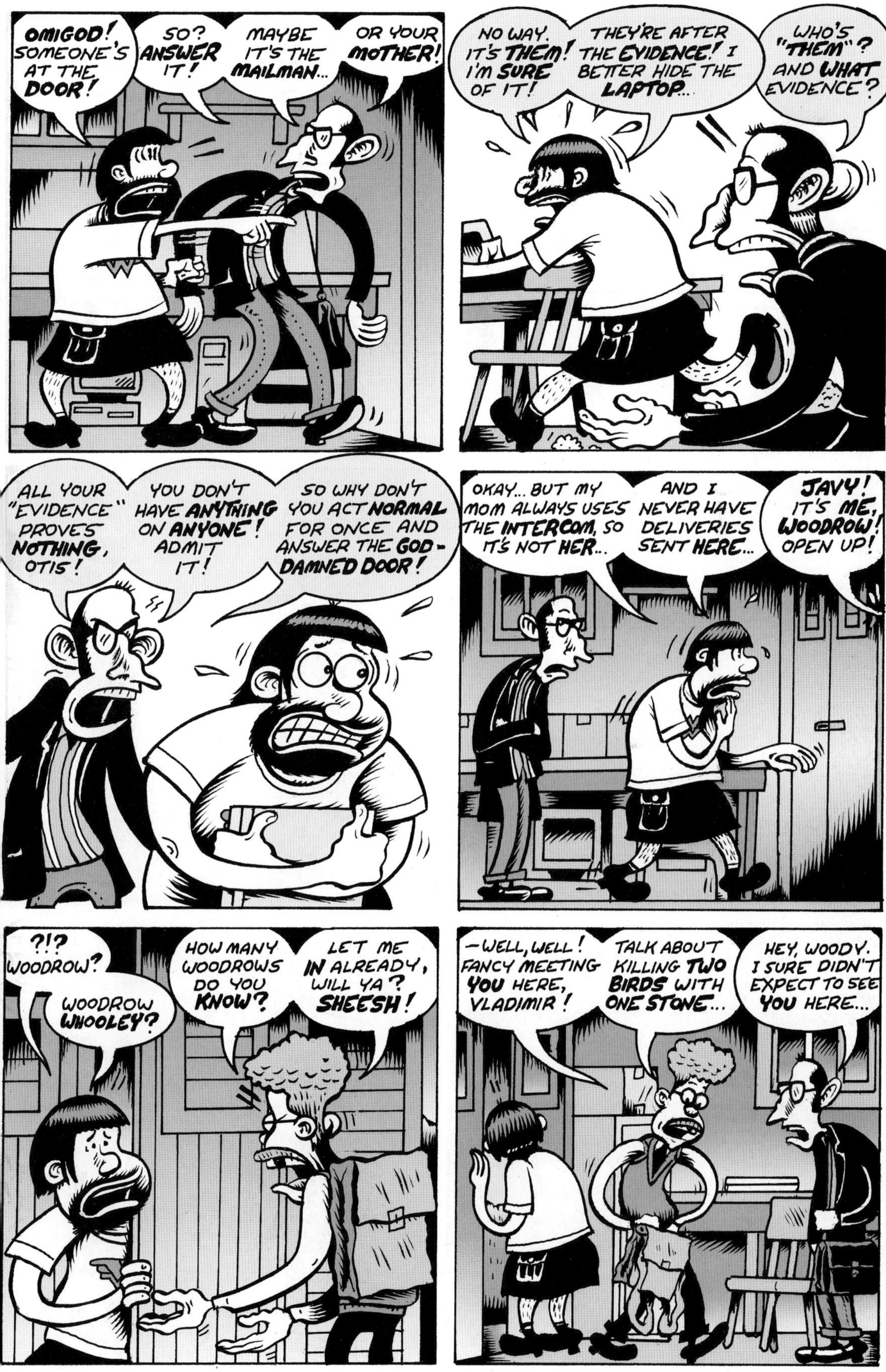
OMIGOD! SOMEONE'S AT THE DOOR!
SO? ANSWER IT!
MAYBE IT'S THE MAILMAN...
OR YOUR MOTHER!
NO WAY. IT'S THEM! I'M SURE OF IT!
THEY'RE AFTER THE EVIDENCE! I BETTER HIDE THE LAPTOP...
WHO'S "THEM"? AND WHAT EVIDENCE?
ALL YOUR "EVIDENCE" PROVES NOTHING, OTIS!
YOU DON'T HAVE ANYTHING ON ANYONE! ADMIT IT!
SO WHY DON'T YOU ACT NORMAL FOR ONCE AND ANSWER THE GOD-DAMNED DOOR!
OKAY... BUT MY MOM ALWAYS USES THE INTERCOM, SO IT'S NOT HER...
AND I NEVER HAVE DELIVERIES SENT HERE...
JAVY! IT'S ME, WOODROW! OPEN UP!
?!? WOODROW?
WOODROW WHOOLEY?
HOW MANY WOODROWS DO YOU KNOW?
LET ME IN ALREADY, WILL YA? SHEESH!
—WELL, WELL! FANCY MEETING YOU HERE, VLADIMIR!
TALK ABOUT KILLING TWO BIRDS WITH ONE STONE...
HEY, WOODY. I SURE DIDN'T EXPECT TO SEE YOU HERE...

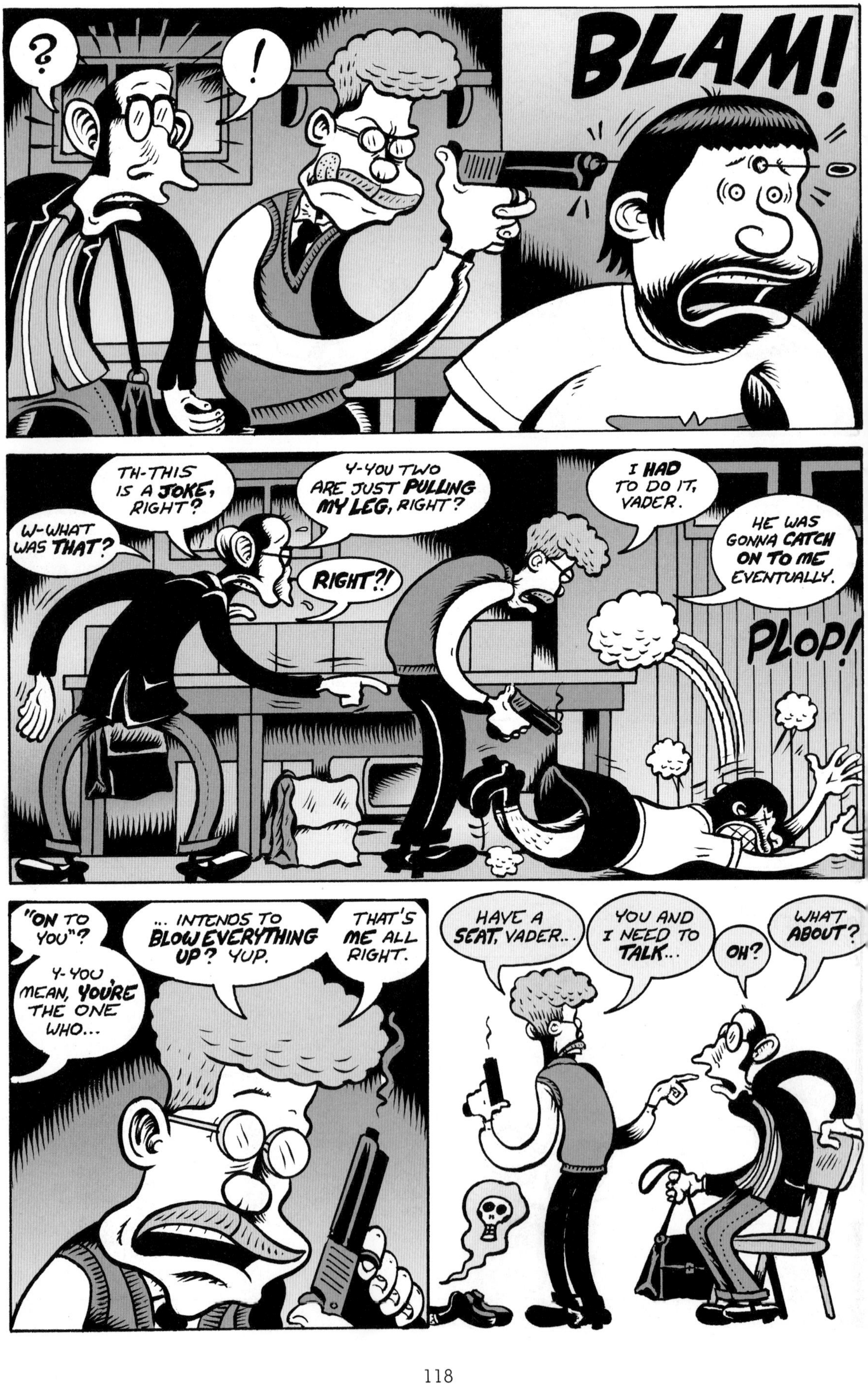
?
!
BLAM!
TH-THIS IS A JOKE, RIGHT?
Y-YOU TWO ARE JUST PULLING MY LEG, RIGHT?
W-WHAT WAS THAT?
RIGHT?!
I HAD TO DO IT, VADER.
HE WAS GONNA CATCH ON TO ME EVENTUALLY.
PLOP!
"ON TO YOU"?
Y-YOU MEAN, YOU'RE THE ONE WHO...
... INTENDS TO BLOW EVERYTHING UP? YUP.
THAT'S ME ALL RIGHT.
HAVE A SEAT, VADER...
YOU AND I NEED TO TALK...
OH?
WHAT ABOUT?

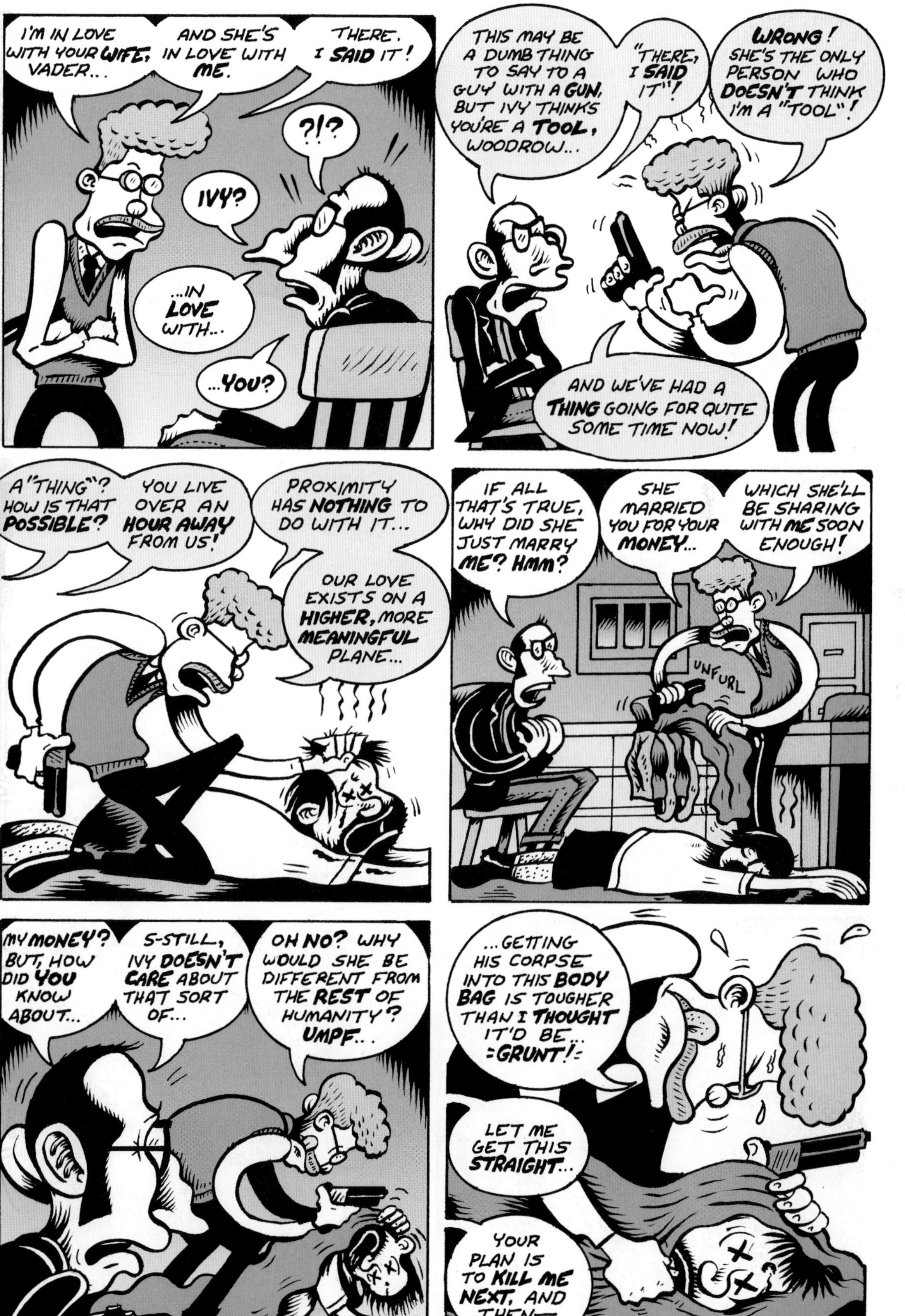
I'M IN LOVE WITH YOUR WIFE, VADER...
AND SHE'S IN LOVE WITH ME.
THERE. I SAID IT!
?!?
IVY?
...IN LOVE WITH...
...YOU?
THIS MAY BE A DUMB THING TO SAY TO A GUY WITH A GUN, BUT IVY THINKS YOU'RE A TOOL, WOODROW...
"THERE, I SAID IT"!
WRONG! SHE'S THE ONLY PERSON WHO DOESN'T THINK I'M A "TOOL"!
AND WE'VE HAD A THING GOING FOR QUITE SOME TIME NOW!
A "THING"? HOW IS THAT POSSIBLE?
YOU LIVE OVER AN HOUR AWAY FROM US!
PROXIMITY HAS NOTHING TO DO WITH IT...
OUR LOVE EXISTS ON A HIGHER, MORE MEANINGFUL PLANE...
IF ALL THAT'S TRUE, WHY DID SHE JUST MARRY ME? HMM?
SHE MARRIED YOU FOR YOUR MONEY...
WHICH SHE'LL BE SHARING WITH ME SOON ENOUGH!
UNFURL
MY MONEY? BUT, HOW DID YOU KNOW ABOUT...
S-STILL, IVY DOESN'T CARE ABOUT THAT SORT OF...
OH NO? WHY WOULD SHE BE DIFFERENT FROM THE REST OF HUMANITY? UMPF...
...GETTING HIS CORPSE INTO THIS BODY BAG IS TOUGHER THAN I THOUGHT IT'D BE... =GRUNT!=
LET ME GET THIS STRAIGHT...
YOUR PLAN IS TO KILL ME NEXT, AND THEN—

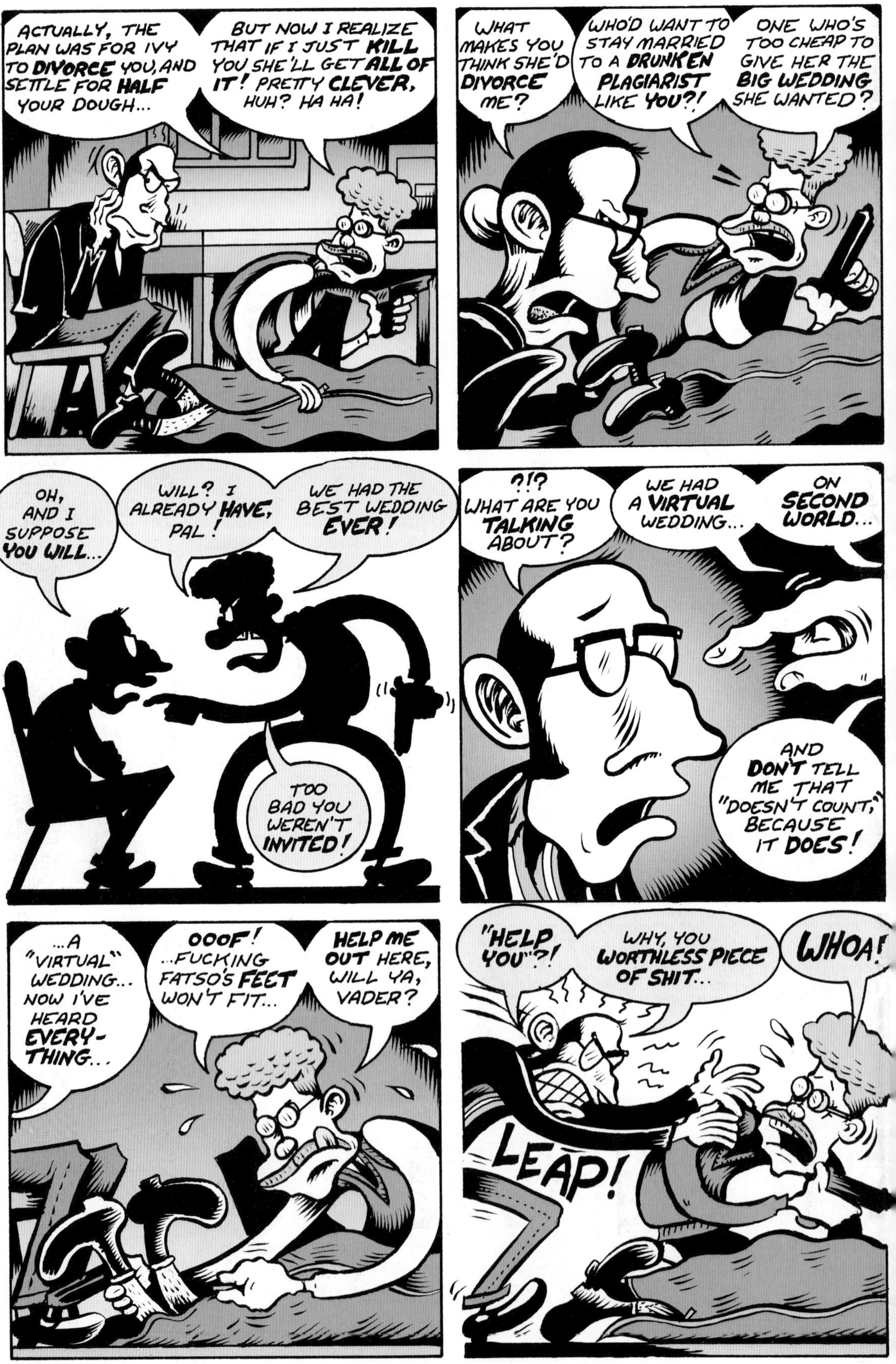

ACTUALLY, THE PLAN WAS FOR IVY TO DIVORCE YOU, AND SETTLE FOR HALF YOUR DOUGH...
BUT NOW I REALIZE THAT IF I JUST KILL YOU SHE'LL GET ALL OF IT! PRETTY CLEVER, HUH? HA HA!
WHAT MAKES YOU THINK SHE'D DIVORCE ME?
WHO'D WANT TO STAY MARRIED TO A DRUNKEN PLAGIARIST LIKE YOU?!
ONE WHO'S TOO CHEAP TO GIVE HER THE BIG WEDDING SHE WANTED?
OH, AND I SUPPOSE YOU WILL...
WILL? I ALREADY HAVE, PAL!
WE HAD THE BEST WEDDING EVER!
TOO BAD YOU WEREN'T INVITED!
?!? WHAT ARE YOU TALKING ABOUT?
WE HAD A VIRTUAL WEDDING...
ON SECOND WORLD...
AND DON'T TELL ME THAT "DOESN'T COUNT," BECAUSE IT DOES!
...A "VIRTUAL" WEDDING... NOW I'VE HEARD EVERY-THING...
OOOF! ...FUCKING FATSO'S FEET WON'T FIT...
HELP ME OUT HERE, WILL YA, VADER?
"HELP YOU"?!
WHY, YOU WORTHLESS PIECE OF SHIT...
WHOA!
LEAP!

BLAM!
THERE! HA! WHO'S WORTHLESS NOW, HUH?
WHO'S THE "PIECE OF SHIT" NOW?
YOU ARE! THAT'S WHO!
HMMM... STILL ALIVE, EH?
NOT FOR LONG, THOUGH...
LOOK, I REALLY DIDN'T WANT TO DO THIS, VADER...
IVY'S SURE TO BE VERY UPSET...
SHE IS FOND OF YOU, AFTER ALL...
BUT CONSIDERING THE CIRCUMSTANCES IT HAD TO BE DONE...
I'M SURE YOU UNDERSTAND.
...WELL WELL! IT'S ALREADY OPENED TO JAVY'S SECOND WORLD ACCOUNT!
HOW CONVENIENT!
LET'S TAKE A LOOK AT HIS INVENTORY...
AH HA! THERE IT IS!
NOW ALL I HAVE TO DO IS TRANSFER IT TO MY ACCOUNT...
AND THEN MAKE A SIMPLE PHONE CALL...

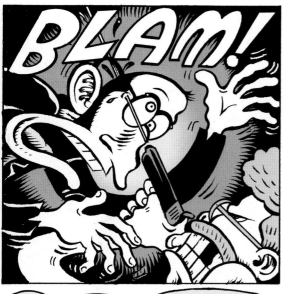

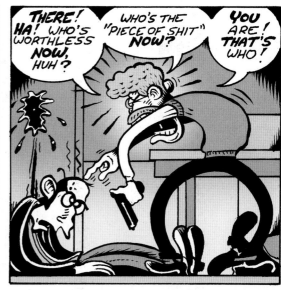

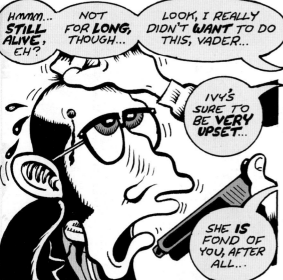

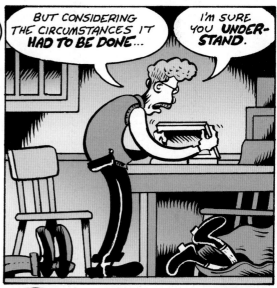

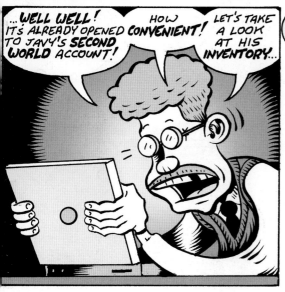

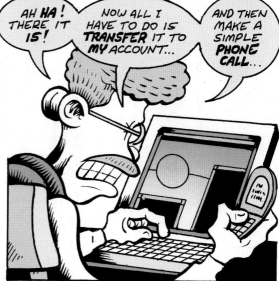

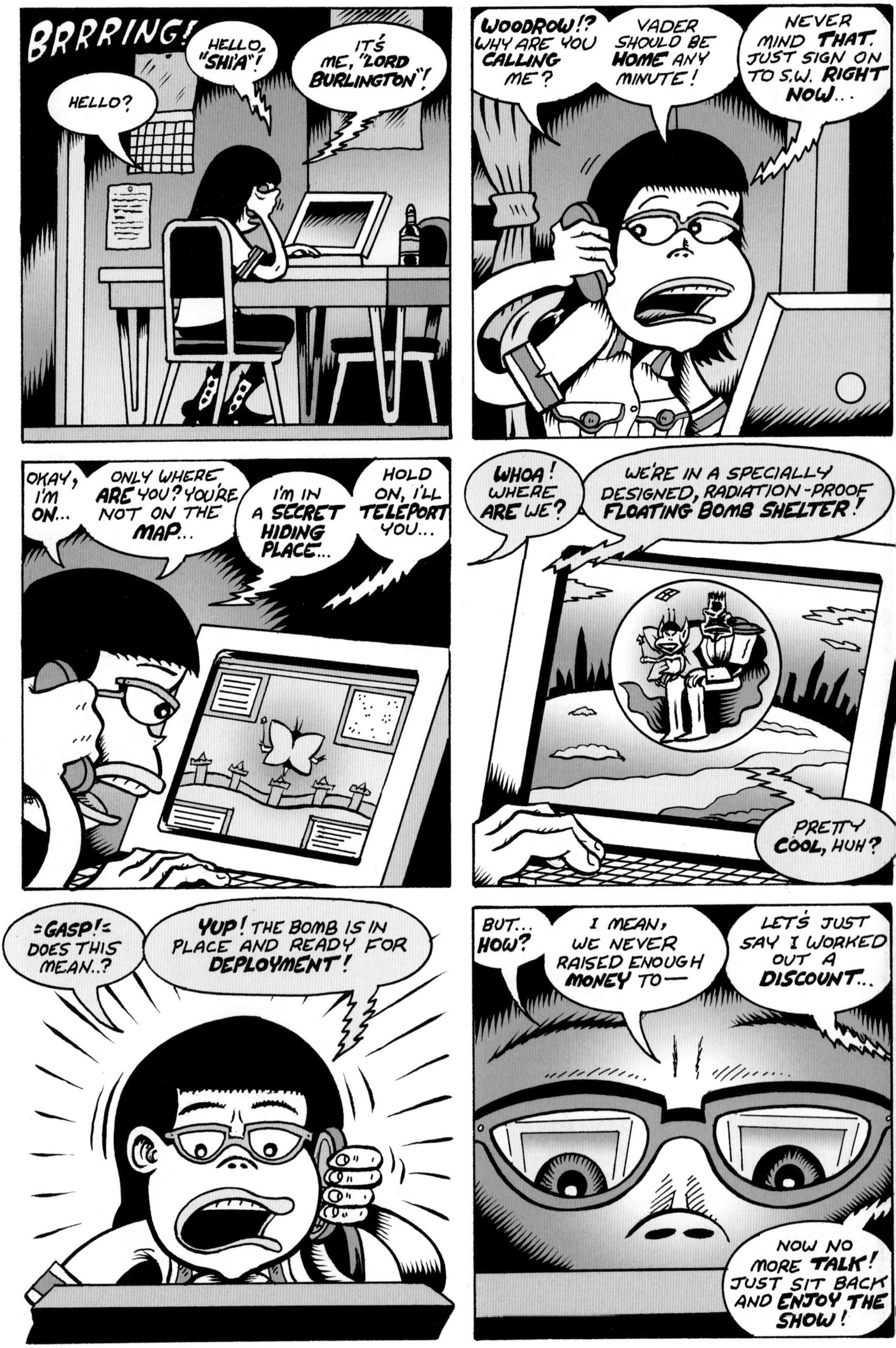
BRRRING!
HELLO?
HELLO, "SHI'A"!
IT'S ME, "LORD BURLINGTON"!
WOODROW!? WHY ARE YOU CALLING ME?
VADER SHOULD BE HOME ANY MINUTE!
NEVER MIND THAT. JUST SIGN ON TO S.W. RIGHT NOW...
OKAY, I'M ON...
ONLY WHERE ARE YOU? YOU'RE NOT ON THE MAP...
I'M IN A SECRET HIDING PLACE...
HOLD ON, I'LL TELEPORT YOU...
WHOA! WHERE ARE WE?
WE'RE IN A SPECIALLY DESIGNED, RADIATION-PROOF FLOATING BOMB SHELTER!
PRETTY COOL, HUH?
=GASP!= DOES THIS MEAN..?
YUP! THE BOMB IS IN PLACE AND READY FOR DEPLOYMENT!
BUT... HOW?
I MEAN, WE NEVER RAISED ENOUGH MONEY TO—
LET'S JUST SAY I WORKED OUT A DISCOUNT...
NOW NO MORE TALK! JUST SIT BACK AND ENJOY THE SHOW!

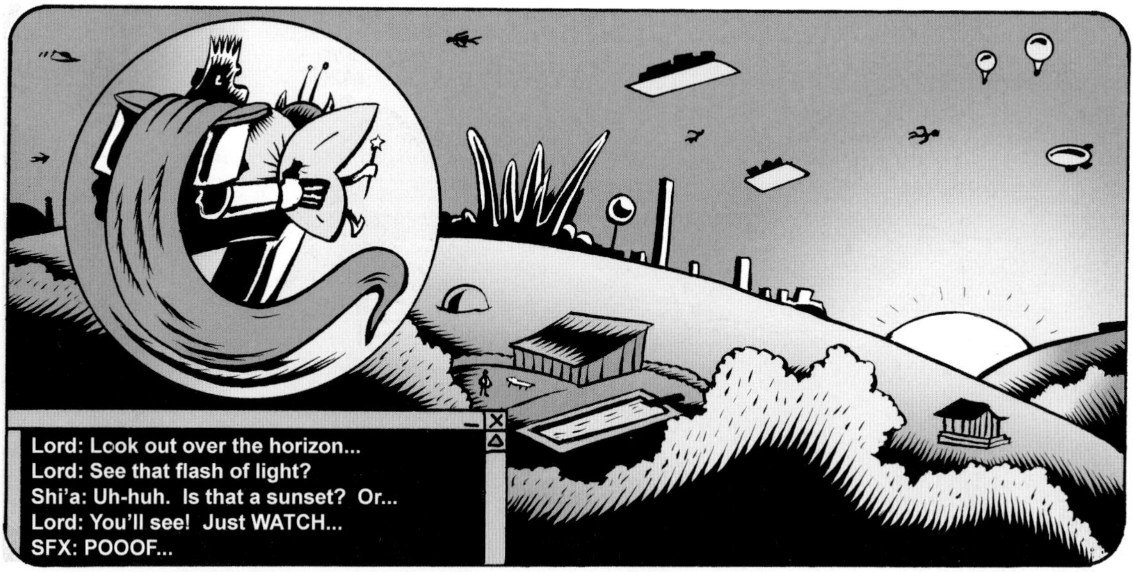
Lord: Look out over the horizon...
Lord: See that flash of light?
Shi'a: Uh-huh. Is that a sunset? Or...
Lord: You'll see! Just WATCH...
SFX: POOOF...

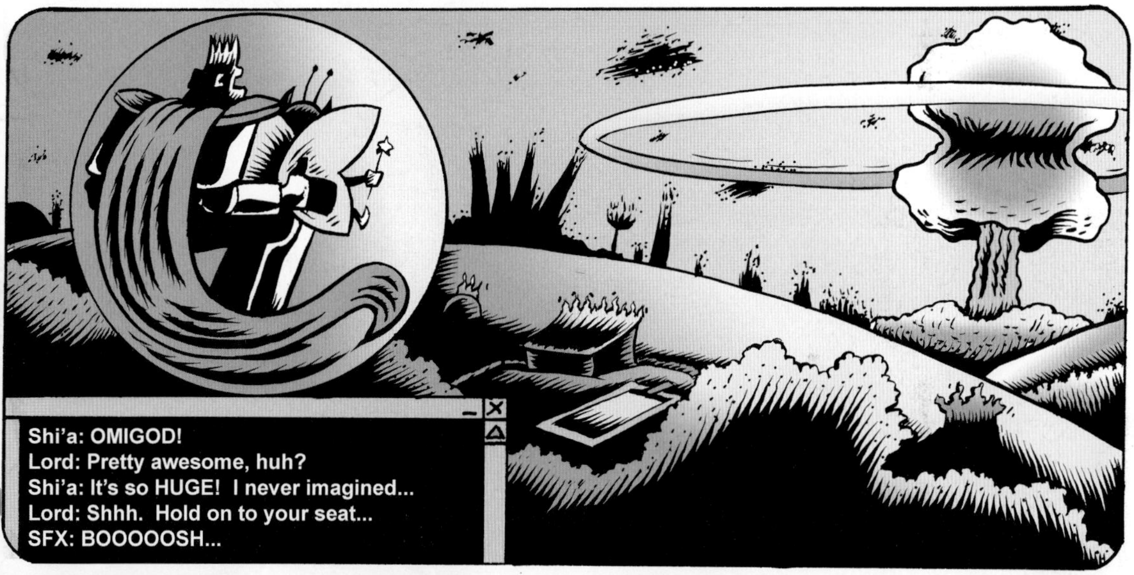
Shi'a: OMIGOD!
Lord: Pretty awesome, huh?
Shi'a: It's so HUGE! I never imagined...
Lord: Shhh. Hold on to your seat...
SFX: BOOOOOSH...

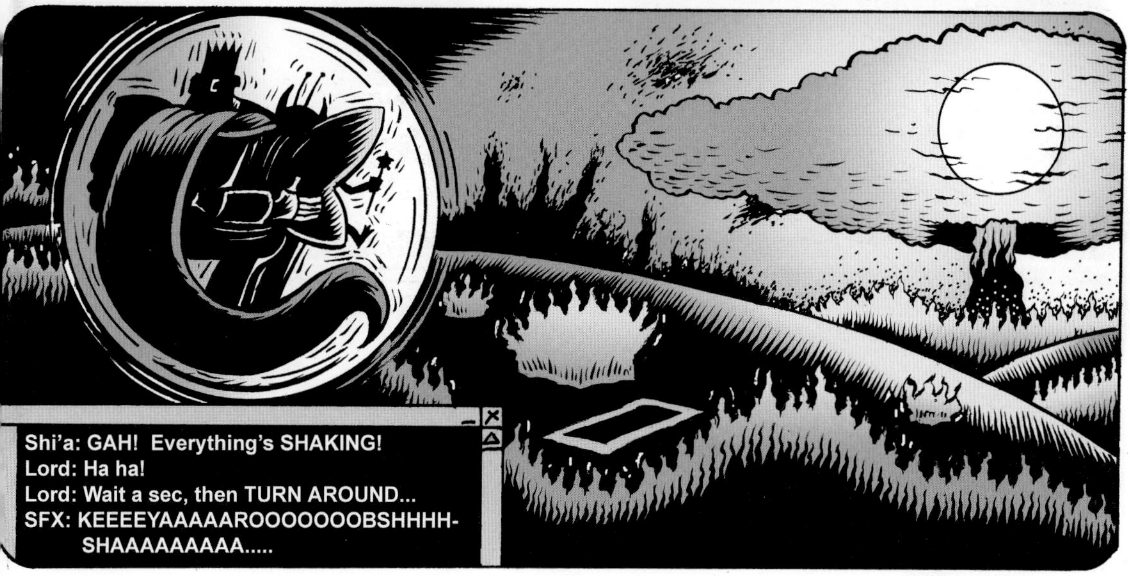
Shi'a: GAH! Everything's SHAKING!
Lord: Ha ha!
Lord: Wait a sec, then TURN AROUND...
SFX: KEEEEYAAAAAROOOOOOOBSHHHH-
SHAAAAAAAAA.....

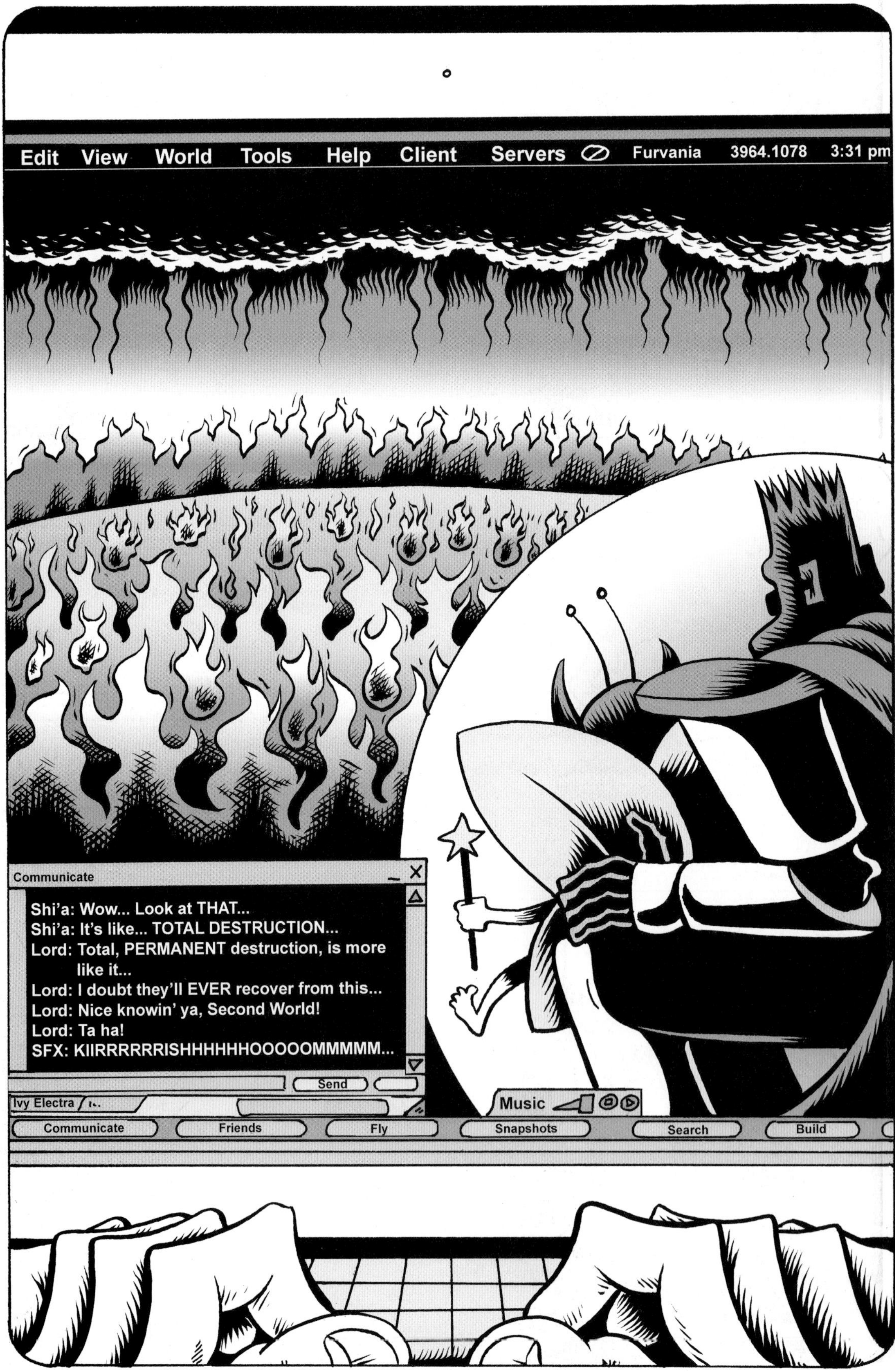
Edit View World Tools Help Client Servers Furvania 3964.1078 3:31 pm
Communicate
Shi'a: Wow... Look at THAT...
Shi'a: It's like... TOTAL DESTRUCTION...
Lord: Total, PERMANENT destruction, is more like it...
Lord: I doubt they'll EVER recover from this...
Lord: Nice knowin' ya, Second World!
Lord: Ta ha!
SFX: KIIRRRRRRISHHHHHHOOOOOMMMMM...
Send
Ivy Electra
Music
Communicate
Friends
Fly
Snapshots
Search
Build

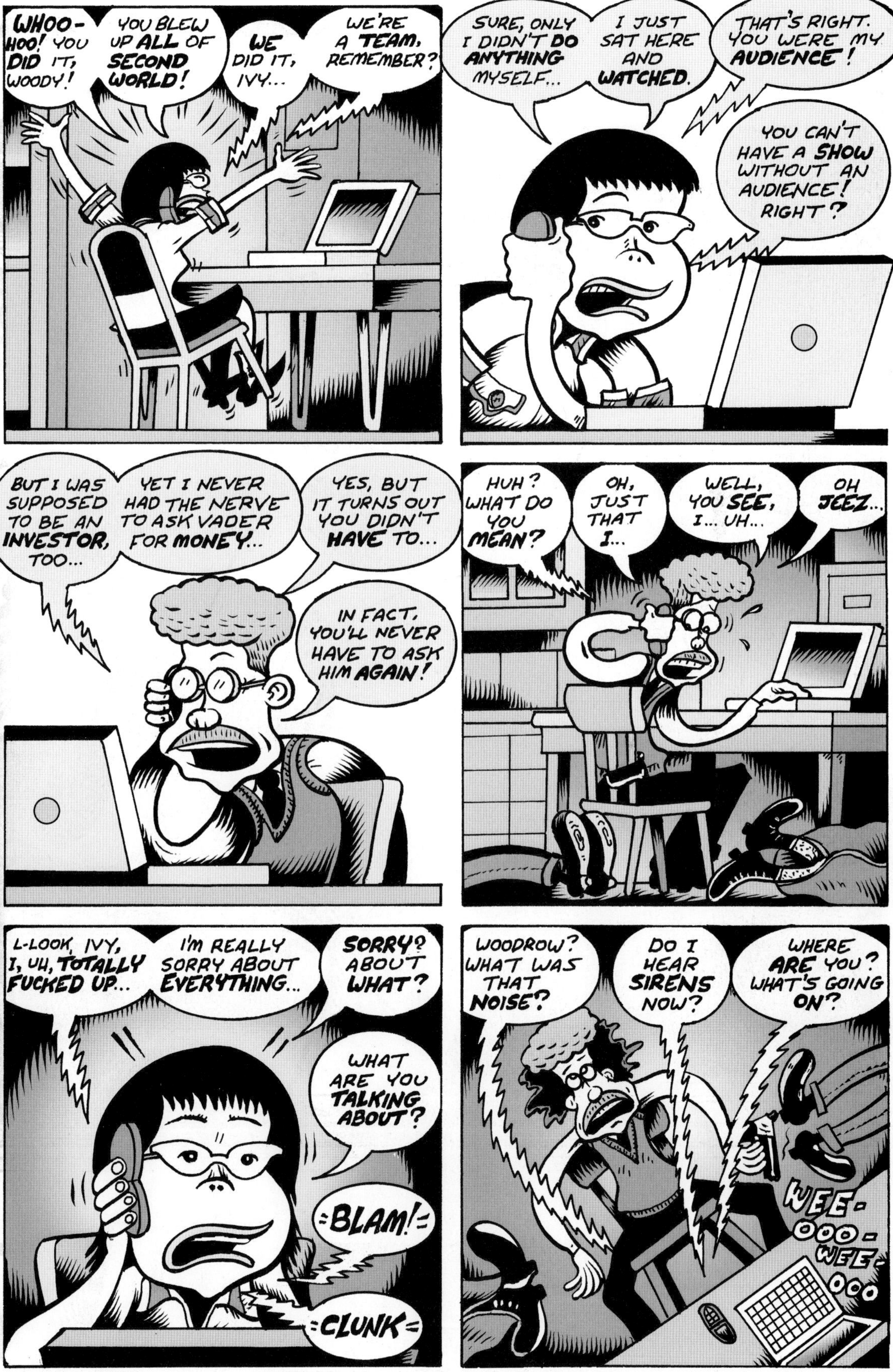
WHOO-HOO! YOU DID IT, WOODY!
YOU BLEW UP ALL OF SECOND WORLD!
WE DID IT, IVY...
WE'RE A TEAM, REMEMBER?
SURE, ONLY I DIDN'T DO ANYTHING MYSELF...
I JUST SAT HERE AND WATCHED.
THAT'S RIGHT. YOU WERE MY AUDIENCE!
YOU CAN'T HAVE A SHOW WITHOUT AN AUDIENCE! RIGHT?
BUT I WAS SUPPOSED TO BE AN INVESTOR, TOO...
YET I NEVER HAD THE NERVE TO ASK VADER FOR MONEY...
YES, BUT IT TURNS OUT YOU DIDN'T HAVE TO...
IN FACT, YOU'LL NEVER HAVE TO ASK HIM AGAIN!
HUH? WHAT DO YOU MEAN?
OH, JUST THAT I...
WELL, YOU SEE, I... UH...
OH JEEZ...
L-LOOK, IVY, I, UH, TOTALLY FUCKED UP...
I'M REALLY SORRY ABOUT EVERYTHING...
SORRY? ABOUT WHAT?
WHAT ARE YOU TALKING ABOUT?
BLAM!
CLUNK
WOODROW? WHAT WAS THAT NOISE?
DO I HEAR SIRENS NOW?
WHERE ARE YOU? WHAT'S GOING ON?
WEE-OOO-WEE-OOO

EPILOGUE

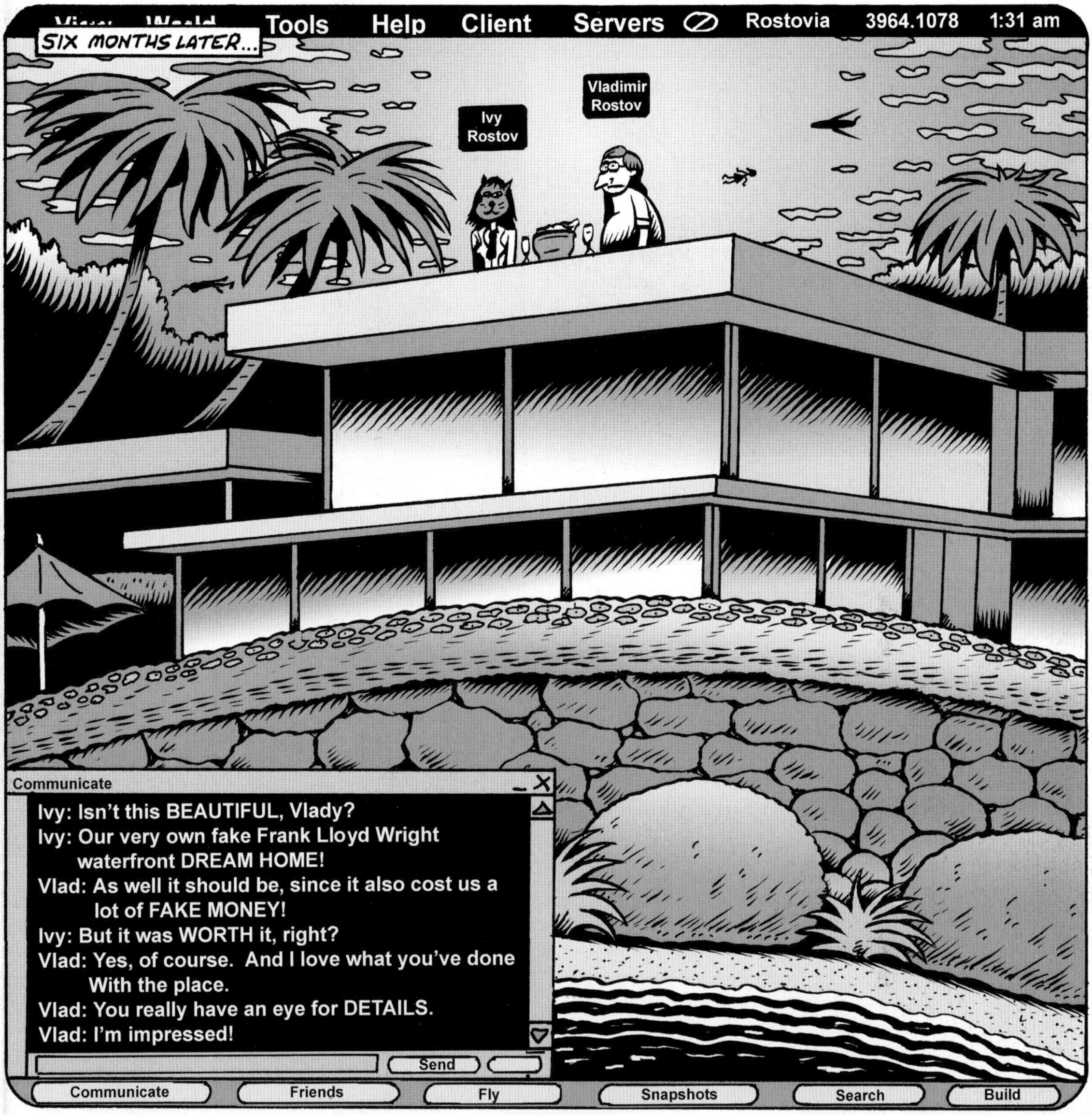
Tools
Help
Client
Servers
Rostovia
3964.1078
1:31 am
SIX MONTHS LATER...
Ivy Rostov
Vladimir Rostov
Communicate
Ivy: Isn't this BEAUTIFUL, Vlady?
Ivy: Our very own fake Frank Lloyd Wright waterfront DREAM HOME!
Vlad: As well it should be, since it also cost us a lot of FAKE MONEY!
Ivy: But it was WORTH it, right?
Vlad: Yes, of course. And I love what you've done With the place.
Vlad: You really have an eye for DETAILS.
Vlad: I'm impressed!
Send
Communicate
Friends
Fly
Snapshots
Search
Build

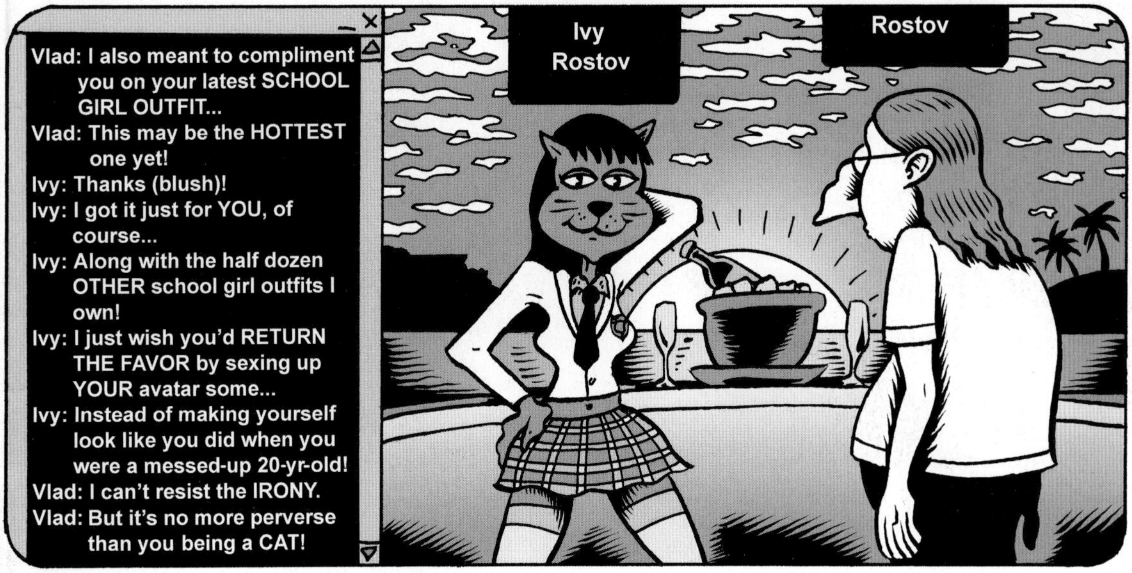
Vlad: I also meant to compliment you on your latest SCHOOL GIRL OUTFIT...
Vlad: This may be the HOTTEST one yet!
Ivy: Thanks (blush)!
Ivy: I got it just for YOU, of course...
Ivy: Along with the half dozen OTHER school girl outfits I own!
Ivy: I just wish you'd RETURN THE FAVOR by sexing up YOUR avatar some...
Ivy: Instead of making yourself look like you did when you were a messed-up 20-yr-old!
Vlad: I can't resist the IRONY.
Vlad: But it's no more perverse than you being a CAT!
Ivy Rostov
Rostov

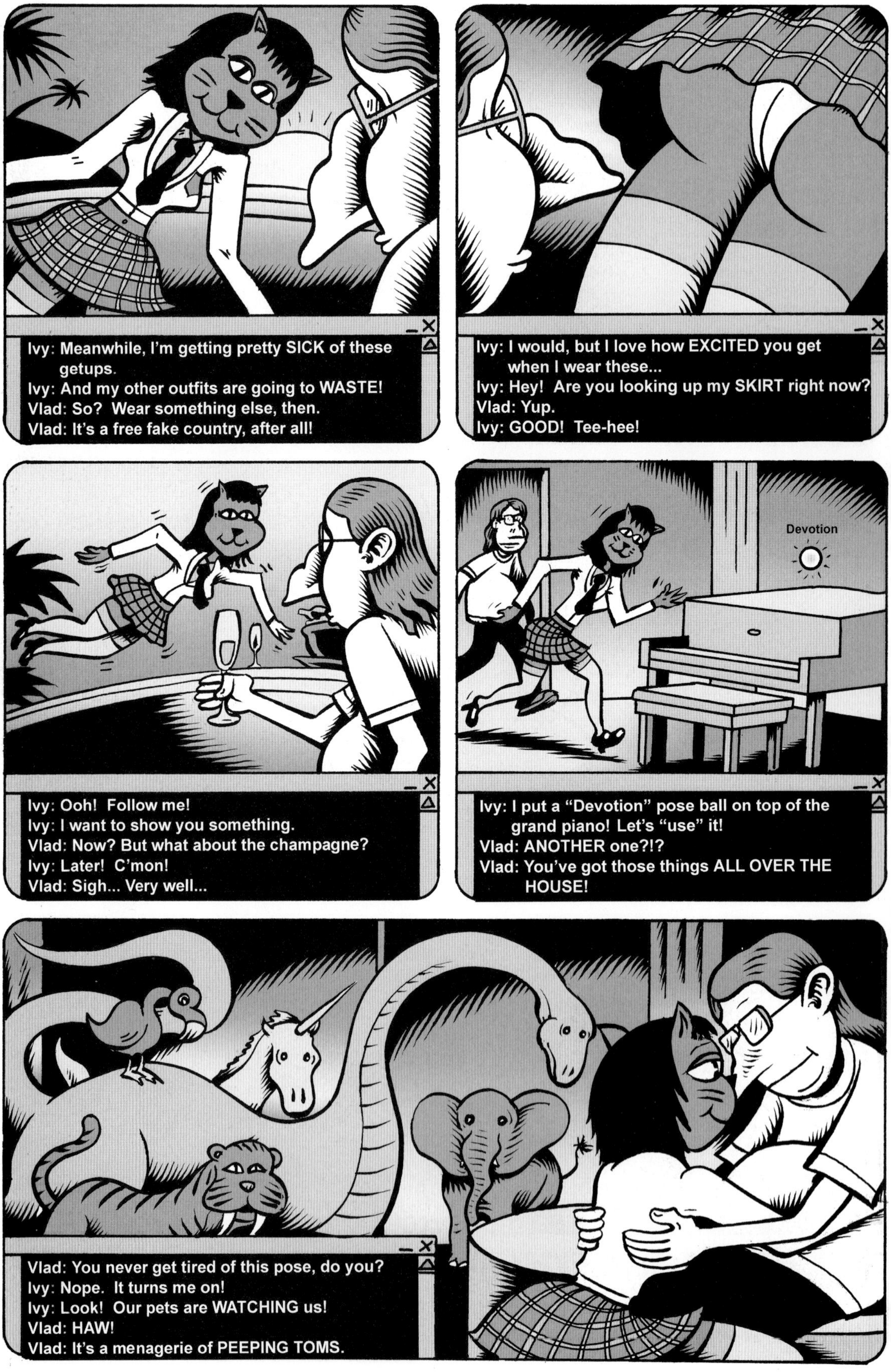
Ivy: Meanwhile, I'm getting pretty SICK of these getups.
Ivy: And my other outfits are going to WASTE!
Vlad: So? Wear something else, then.
Vlad: It's a free fake country, after all!
Ivy: I would, but I love how EXCITED you get when I wear these...
Ivy: Hey! Are you looking up my SKIRT right now?
Vlad: Yup.
Ivy: GOOD! Tee-hee!
Ivy: Ooh! Follow me!
Ivy: I want to show you something.
Vlad: Now? But what about the champagne?
Ivy: Later! C'mon!
Vlad: Sigh... Very well...
Devotion
Ivy: I put a "Devotion" pose ball on top of the grand piano! Let's "use" it!
Vlad: ANOTHER one?!?
Vlad: You've got those things ALL OVER THE HOUSE!
Vlad: You never get tired of this pose, do you?
Ivy: Nope. It turns me on!
Ivy: Look! Our pets are WATCHING us!
Vlad: HAW!
Vlad: It's a menagerie of PEEPING TOMS.

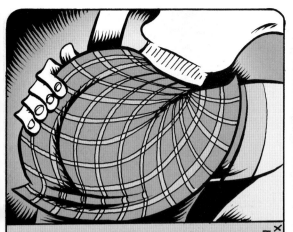

Vlad: I love this bit of business where your leg SLOWLY comes up...
Ivy: And then your hand grabs my ass.
Ivy: Me too!

Vlad: The programmers who animated these poses sure knew their stuff.
Ivy: Um-hmm. Now I wanna DO IT!
Ivy: Let's go upstairs, okay?

Vlad: Hey, what happened to your pregnant belly?
Vlad: You're supposed to be "with child," remember?
Ivy: Oops! I forgot!

Ivy: There. Now I'm a KNOCKED UP schoolgirl.
Ivy: How's THAT for perverse?
Vlad: I love it.
Vlad: It's so... WRONG!

Vlad: So have we settled on what the baby is going to BE yet?
Ivy: You mean if it'll be a boy or a girl?
Ivy: I thought we were going to decide that at the LAST MOMENT. Like it's a SURPRISE.

Vlad: No, I mean what SPECIES will it be.
Vlad: We ARE a "mixed species" couple, after all, so...
Ivy: Oh! Well, I was thinking of making it an entirely DIFFERENT species altogether!

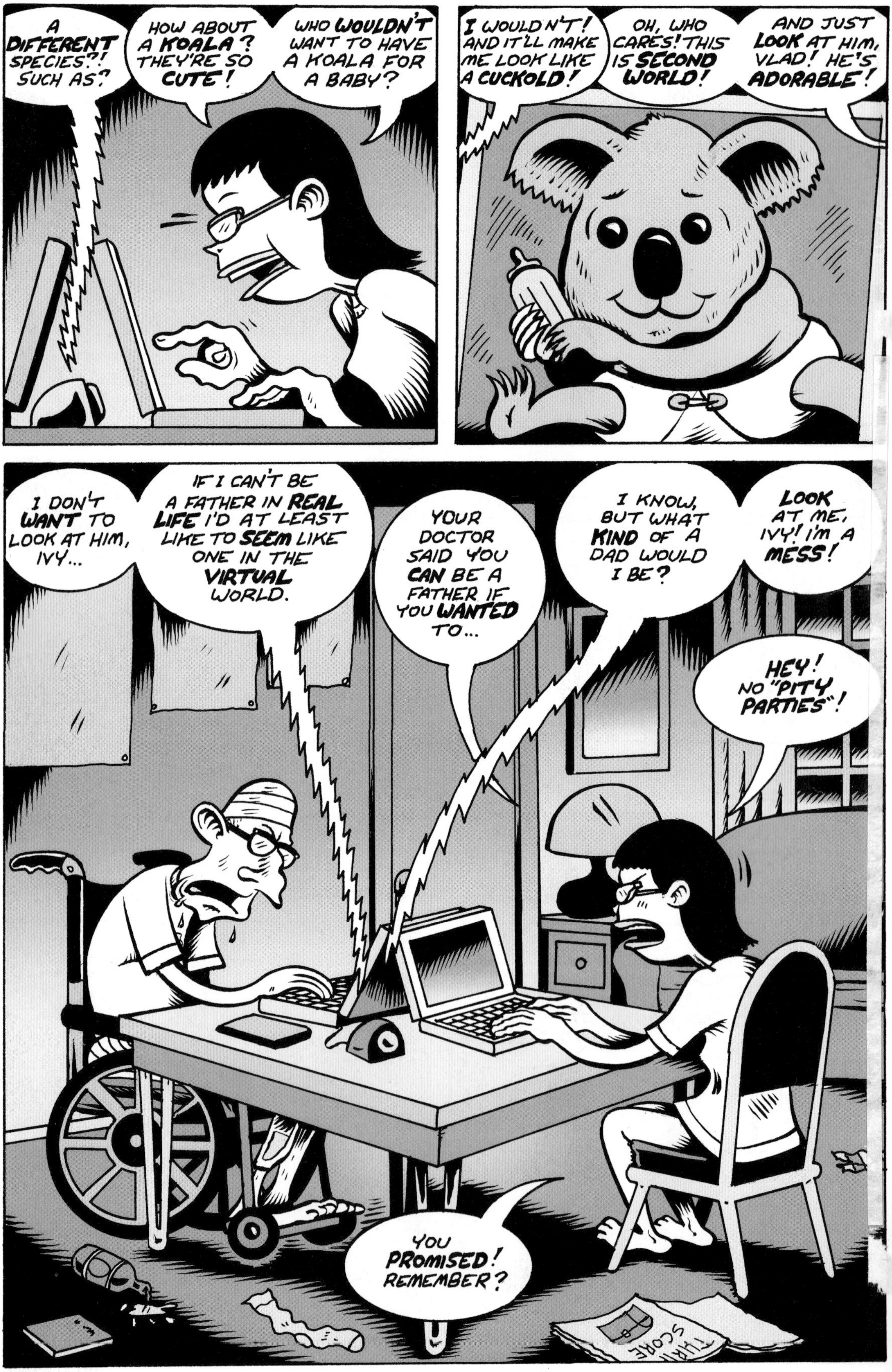
A DIFFERENT SPECIES?! SUCH AS?
HOW ABOUT A KOALA? THEY'RE SO CUTE!
WHO WOULDN'T WANT TO HAVE A KOALA FOR A BABY?
I WOULDN'T! AND IT'LL MAKE ME LOOK LIKE A CUCKOLD!
OH, WHO CARES! THIS IS SECOND WORLD!
AND JUST LOOK AT HIM, VLAD! HE'S ADORABLE!
I DON'T WANT TO LOOK AT HIM, IVY...
IF I CAN'T BE A FATHER IN REAL LIFE I'D AT LEAST LIKE TO SEEM LIKE ONE IN THE VIRTUAL WORLD.
YOUR DOCTOR SAID YOU CAN BE A FATHER IF YOU WANTED TO...
I KNOW, BUT WHAT KIND OF A DAD WOULD I BE?
LOOK AT ME, IVY! I'M A MESS!
HEY! NO "PITY PARTIES"!
YOU PROMISED! REMEMBER?

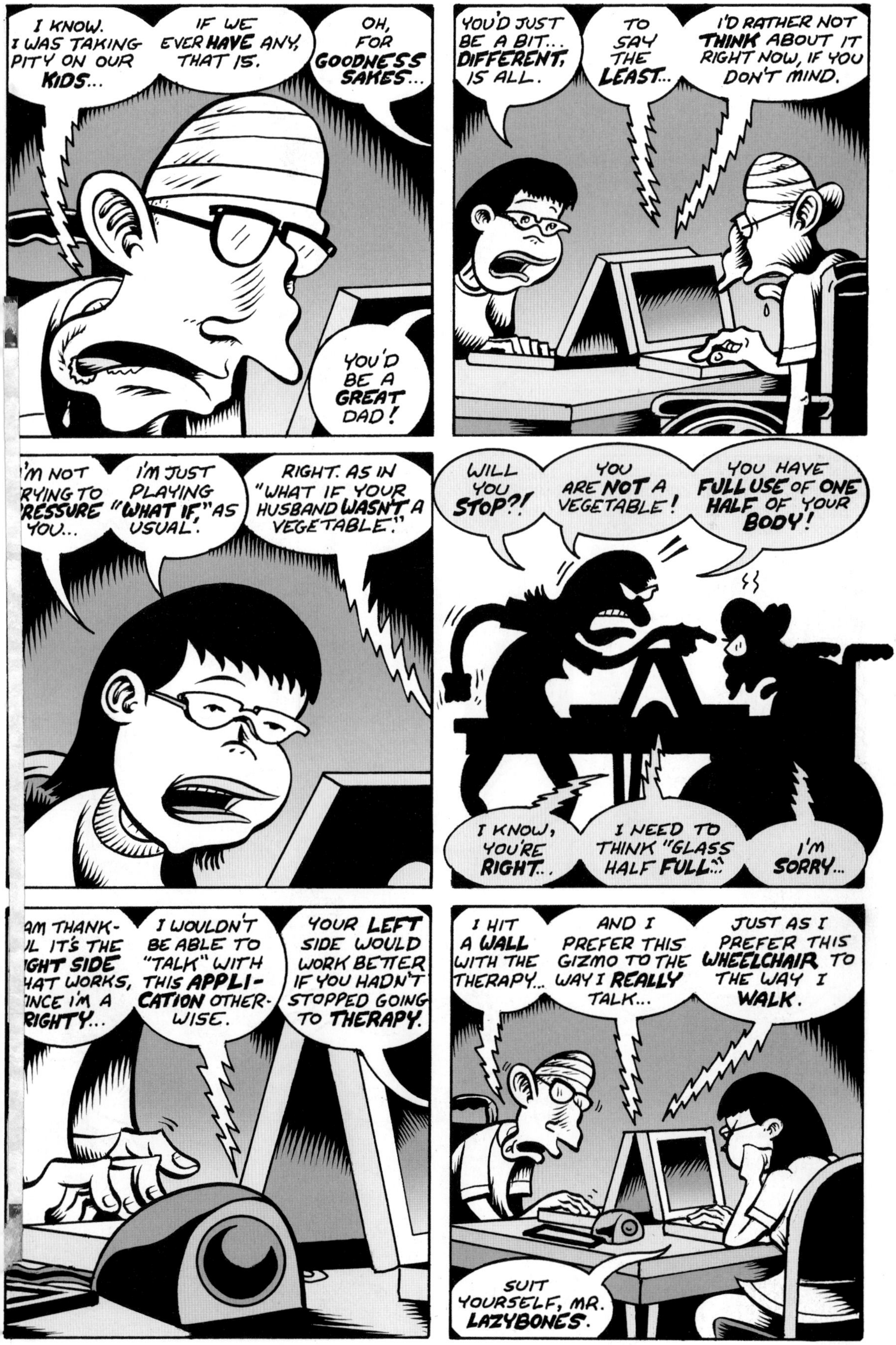

I KNOW. I WAS TAKING PITY ON OUR **KIDS**...
IF WE EVER **HAVE** ANY, THAT IS.
OH, FOR **GOODNESS SAKES**...
YOU'D BE A **GREAT** DAD!
YOU'D JUST BE A BIT... **DIFFERENT,** IS ALL.
TO SAY THE **LEAST**...
I'D RATHER NOT **THINK** ABOUT IT RIGHT NOW, IF YOU DON'T MIND.
'M NOT RYING TO RESSURE YOU...
I'M JUST PLAYING "**WHAT IF**," AS USUAL.
RIGHT. AS IN "WHAT IF YOUR HUSBAND **WASN'T** A VEGETABLE."
WILL YOU **STOP?!**
YOU ARE **NOT** A VEGETABLE!
YOU HAVE **FULL USE** OF **ONE HALF** OF YOUR **BODY**!
I KNOW, YOU'RE **RIGHT**...
I NEED TO THINK "GLASS HALF **FULL**."
I'M **SORRY**...
AM THANK- UL IT'S THE **IGHT SIDE** HAT WORKS, INCE I'M A **RIGHTY**...
I WOULDN'T BE ABLE TO "TALK" WITH THIS **APPLI- CATION** OTHER- WISE.
YOUR **LEFT** SIDE WOULD WORK BETTER IF YOU HADN'T STOPPED GOING TO **THERAPY**.
I HIT A **WALL** WITH THE THERAPY...
AND I PREFER THIS GIZMO TO THE WAY I **REALLY** TALK...
JUST AS I PREFER THIS **WHEELCHAIR** TO THE WAY I **WALK**.
SUIT YOURSELF, MR. **LAZYBONES**.

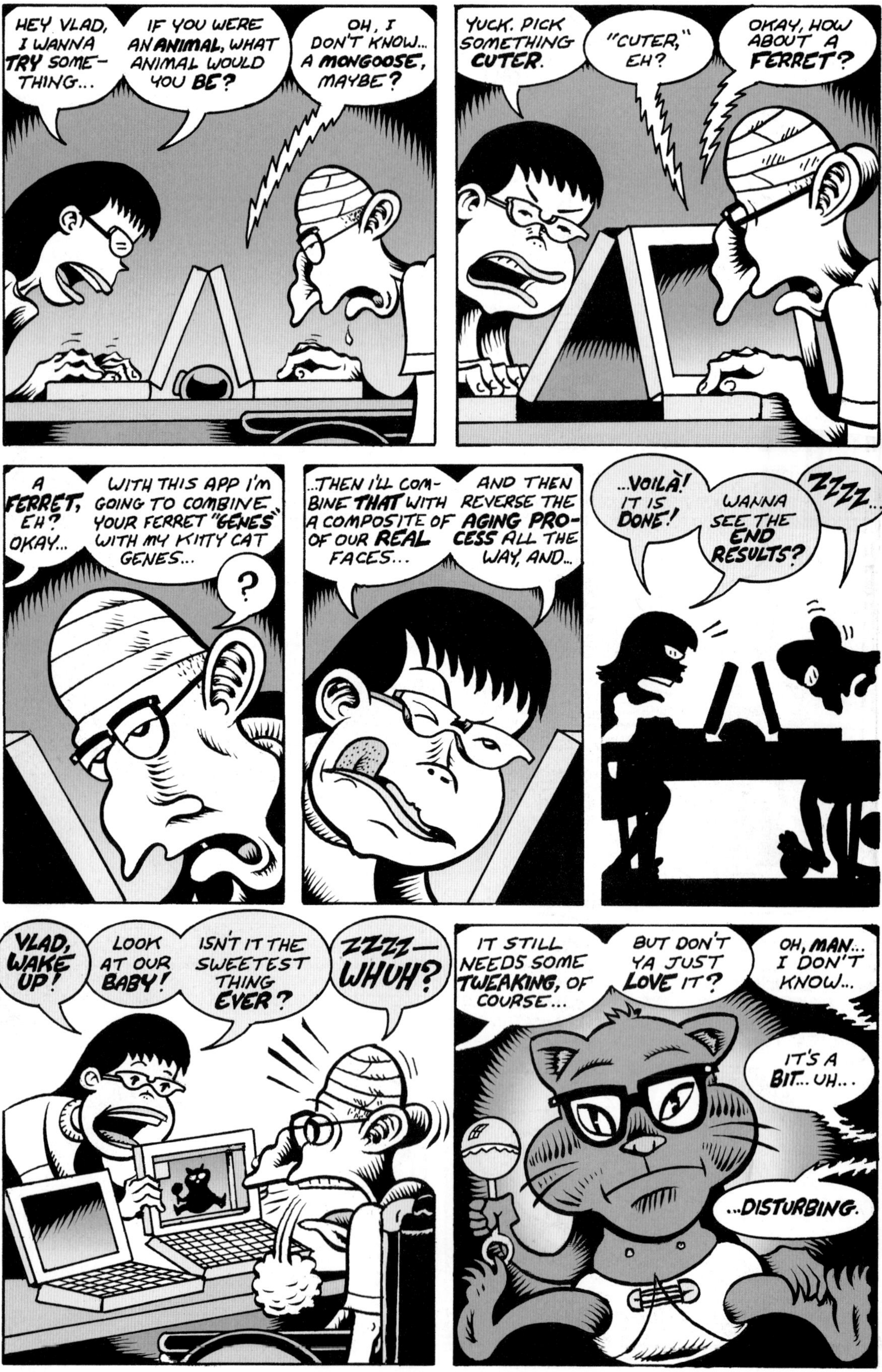
HEY VLAD, I WANNA TRY SOME-THING...
IF YOU WERE AN ANIMAL, WHAT ANIMAL WOULD YOU BE?
OH, I DON'T KNOW... A MONGOOSE, MAYBE?
YUCK. PICK SOMETHING CUTER.
"CUTER," EH?
OKAY, HOW ABOUT A FERRET?
A FERRET, EH? OKAY...
WITH THIS APP I'M GOING TO COMBINE YOUR FERRET "GENES" WITH MY KITTY CAT GENES...
?
...THEN I'LL COM-BINE THAT WITH A COMPOSITE OF OF OUR REAL FACES...
AND THEN REVERSE THE AGING PRO-CESS ALL THE WAY, AND...
...VOILÀ! IT IS DONE!
WANNA SEE THE END RESULTS?
ZZZZ...
VLAD, WAKE UP!
LOOK AT OUR BABY!
ISN'T IT THE SWEETEST THING EVER?
ZZZZ— WHUH?
IT STILL NEEDS SOME TWEAKING, OF COURSE...
BUT DON'T YA JUST LOVE IT?
OH, MAN... I DON'T KNOW...
IT'S A BIT... UH...
...DISTURBING.

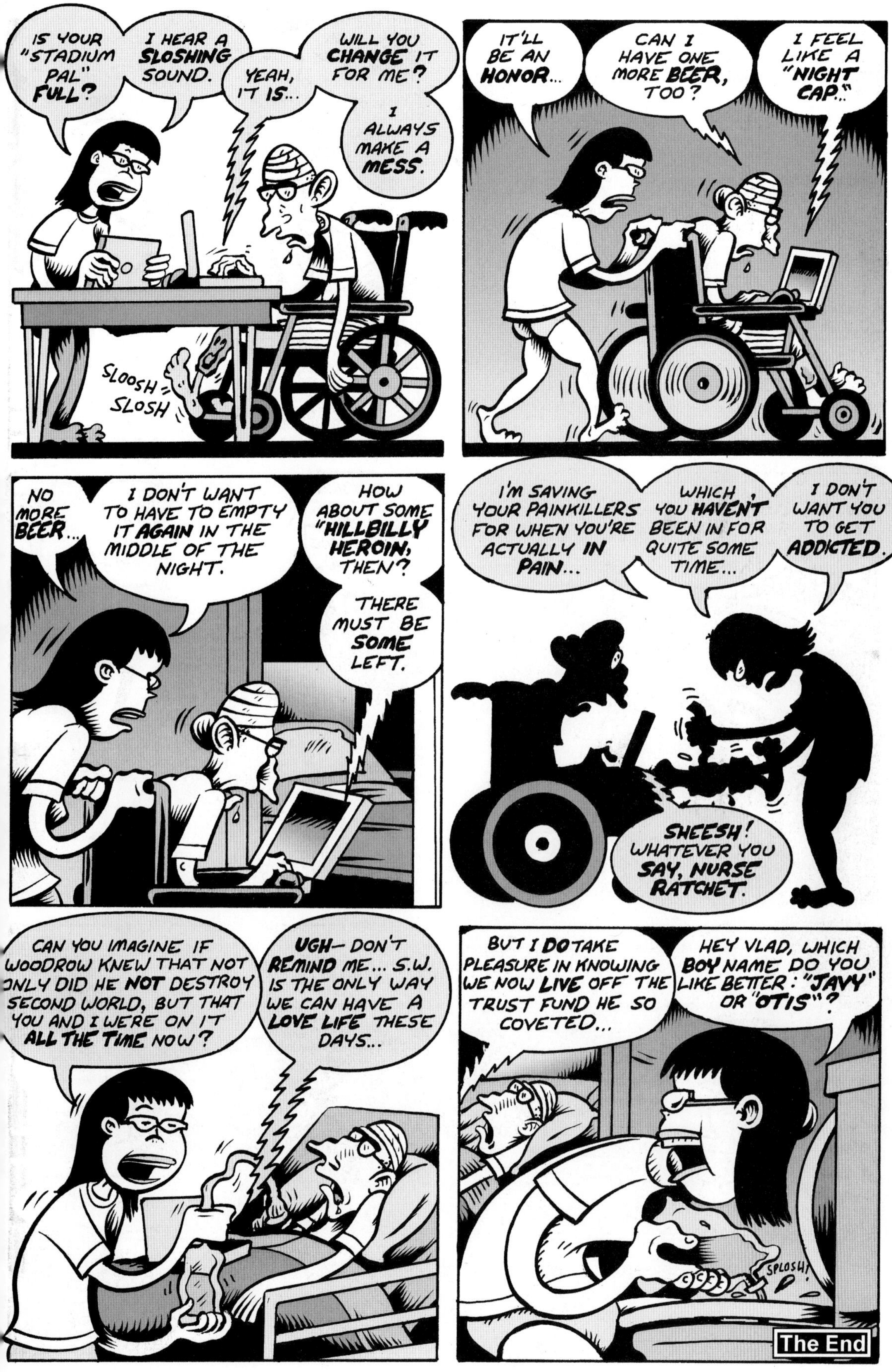
IS YOUR "STADIUM PAL" FULL?
I HEAR A SLOSHING SOUND.
YEAH, IT IS...
WILL YOU CHANGE IT FOR ME?
I ALWAYS MAKE A MESS.
SLOOSH SLOSH
IT'LL BE AN HONOR...
CAN I HAVE ONE MORE BEER, TOO?
I FEEL LIKE A "NIGHT CAP."
NO MORE BEER...
I DON'T WANT TO HAVE TO EMPTY IT AGAIN IN THE MIDDLE OF THE NIGHT.
HOW ABOUT SOME "HILLBILLY HEROIN," THEN?
THERE MUST BE SOME LEFT.
I'M SAVING YOUR PAINKILLERS FOR WHEN YOU'RE ACTUALLY IN PAIN...
WHICH, YOU HAVEN'T BEEN IN FOR QUITE SOME TIME...
I DON'T WANT YOU TO GET ADDICTED.
SHEESH! WHATEVER YOU SAY, NURSE RATCHET.
CAN YOU IMAGINE IF WOODROW KNEW THAT NOT ONLY DID HE NOT DESTROY SECOND WORLD, BUT THAT YOU AND I WERE ON IT ALL THE TIME NOW?
UGH— DON'T REMIND ME... S.W. IS THE ONLY WAY WE CAN HAVE A LOVE LIFE THESE DAYS...
BUT I DO TAKE PLEASURE IN KNOWING WE NOW LIVE OFF THE TRUST FUND HE SO COVETED...
HEY VLAD, WHICH BOY NAME DO YOU LIKE BETTER: "JAVY" OR "OTIS"?
SPLOSH!
The End

/iew World Tools Help Client Servers Furvania 3964.1078 8:11 p

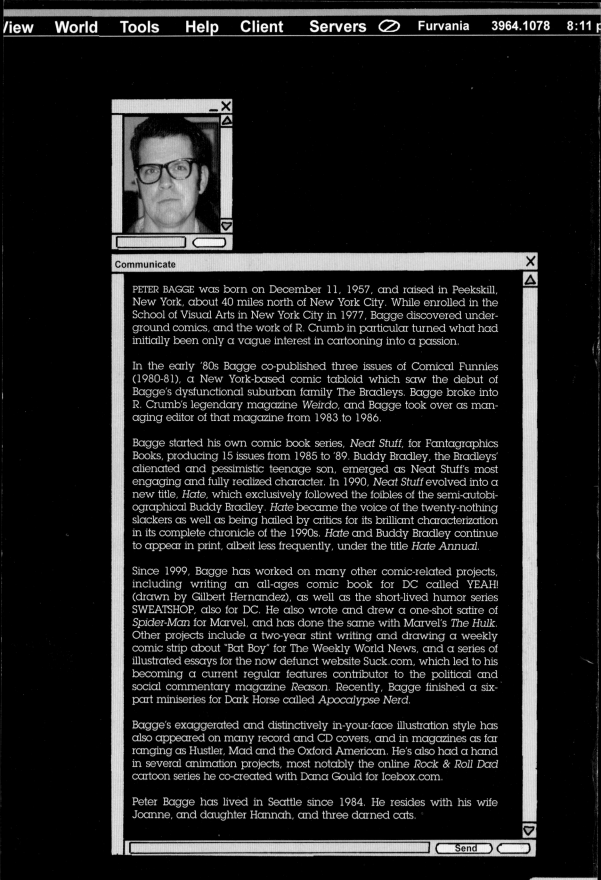

Communicate

PETER BAGGE was born on December 11, 1957, and raised in Peekskill, New York, about 40 miles north of New York City. While enrolled in the School of Visual Arts in New York City in 1977, Bagge discovered underground comics, and the work of R. Crumb in particular turned what had initially been only a vague interest in cartooning into a passion.

In the early '80s Bagge co-published three issues of Comical Funnies (1980-81), a New York-based comic tabloid which saw the debut of Bagge's dysfunctional suburban family The Bradleys. Bagge broke into R. Crumb's legendary magazine *Weirdo*, and Bagge took over as managing editor of that magazine from 1983 to 1986.

Bagge started his own comic book series, *Neat Stuff*, for Fantagraphics Books, producing 15 issues from 1985 to '89. Buddy Bradley, the Bradleys' alienated and pessimistic teenage son, emerged as Neat Stuff's most engaging and fully realized character. In 1990, *Neat Stuff* evolved into a new title, *Hate*, which exclusively followed the foibles of the semi-autobiographical Buddy Bradley. *Hate* became the voice of the twenty-nothing slackers as well as being hailed by critics for its brilliant characterization in its complete chronicle of the 1990s. *Hate* and Buddy Bradley continue to appear in print, albeit less frequently, under the title *Hate Annual*.

Since 1999, Bagge has worked on many other comic-related projects, including writing an all-ages comic book for DC called YEAH! (drawn by Gilbert Hernandez), as well as the short-lived humor series SWEATSHOP, also for DC. He also wrote and drew a one-shot satire of *Spider-Man* for Marvel, and has done the same with Marvel's *The Hulk*. Other projects include a two-year stint writing and drawing a weekly comic strip about "Bat Boy" for The Weekly World News, and a series of illustrated essays for the now defunct website Suck.com, which led to his becoming a current regular features contributor to the political and social commentary magazine *Reason*. Recently, Bagge finished a six-part miniseries for Dark Horse called *Apocalypse Nerd*.

Bagge's exaggerated and distinctively in-your-face illustration style has also appeared on many record and CD covers, and in magazines as far ranging as Hustler, Mad and the Oxford American. He's also had a hand in several animation projects, most notably the online *Rock & Roll Dad* cartoon series he co-created with Dana Gould for Icebox.com.

Peter Bagge has lived in Seattle since 1984. He resides with his wife Joanne, and daughter Hannah, and three darned cats.

Send

Music

nicate Friends Fly Snapshots Search Build

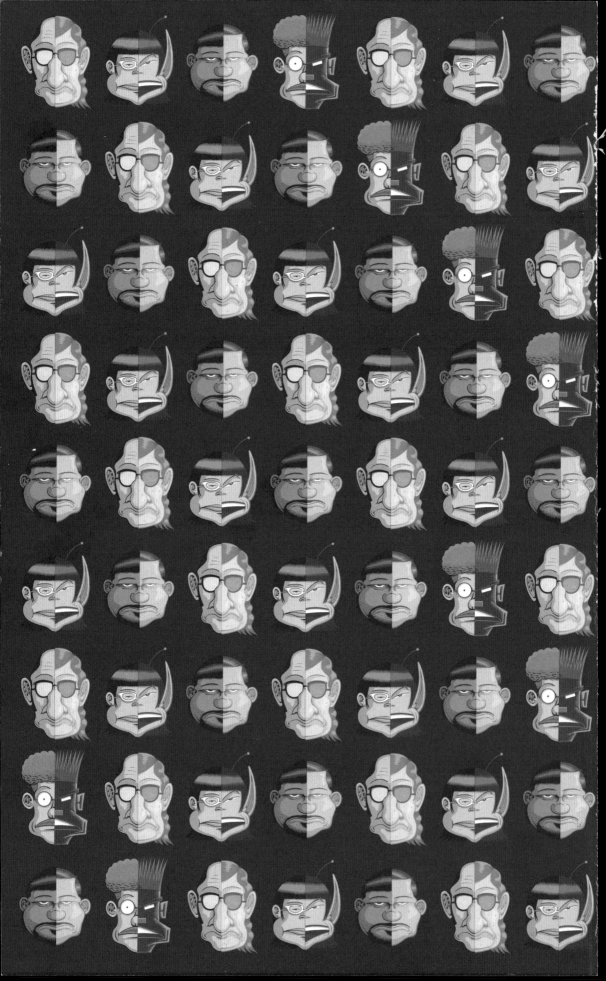